Penguin Education

Introducing Applied Linguistics
S. Pit Corder

Penguin Modern Linguistics Texts
General Editor
David Crystal

Advisory Board
Dwight Bolinger
M. A. K. Halliday
John Lyons
Frank Palmer
James Sledd
C. I. J. M. Stuart

Introducing
Applied Linguistics

S. Pit Corder

Penguin Education

Penguin Education
A Division of Penguin Books Ltd,
Harmondsworth, Middlesex, England
Penguin Books Inc, 7110 Ambassador Road,
Baltimore, Md 21207, USA
Penguin Books Australia Ltd,
Ringwood, Victoria, Australia

First published 1973

Made and printed in Great Britain by
Hazell Watson & Viney Ltd,
Aylesbury, Bucks
Set in Monotype Times

Contents

Preface

My purpose in writing this book has been to show the relevance of those studies which are broadly called linguistic to a number of practical tasks connected with language teaching. There will certainly be some readers who, while not disputing the relevance of linguistic studies to language teaching, will nevertheless criticize my implied restriction of the term 'applied linguistics' to this field of activity, on the grounds that there are practical tasks other than language teaching to which a knowledge of linguistics is relevant. I do not disagree with them in principle, but claim nevertheless that, because of the greater public interest in language teaching and the considerable official support there has been in recent years for research and teaching in the application of linguistics to language teaching, this term has effectively come to be restricted in this way in common usage.

Although this book is intended primarily for practising language teachers and those preparing to become language teachers, it is my hope that it may also be of interest not only to the general reader but also to linguists who wish to know something of the way in which their investigations, methods and discoveries may be put to use by one group of professionals for whom language plays a central part in their activities. I am enough of a purist to believe that 'applied linguistics' presupposes 'linguistics'; that one cannot apply what one does not possess. Consequently, for the reader who already has a knowledge of linguistics the first two sections of the book will contain largely familiar material, although the relative emphasis I have placed upon the different branches of linguistic study reflect the importance they have for language teaching rather than the degree of theoretical adequacy they have attained. For those who have no training in linguistics, these sections are intended to provide an overview or 'shop window' of what linguistics is about, as seen through the eyes of the applied linguist, rather than a formal introduction to the subject. If the presentation I have made stirs their interest, there are now a number of excellent introductions to the subject to which they may turn, some of which figure in the bibliography.

A bibliography is like an anthology; it is a personal reaction to a body of literature. The necessarily broad range of topics which have had to be touched on in this introductory book has posed problems of selection. My guiding principle has been to refer only to those books and articles which in my opinion offer some particular insights into language, its use and how it is learned which are relevant to language teaching. In no sense can the bibliography be regarded as a comprehensive coverage of work either in linguistics or applied linguistics.

This book owes much to discussions over the years not only with my colleagues and students but with many other applied linguists in Britain and overseas. Through these discussions, the model of applied linguistics presented here has developed. More especially I am indebted to those colleagues who have kindly read parts of the book and offered their comments and criticisms: David Crystal, Patrick Allen, Gill and Keith Brown, Clive Criper, Alan Davies, Tony Howatt, Elizabeth Ingram and Henry Widdowson. Whilst they have saved me from a number of inaccuracies and infelicities, they can in no way be held responsible for the opinions which are expressed and the many imperfections and shortcomings which no doubt remain.

Finally, I must express my thanks to my wife for typing the first draft of the book. My admiration for her skill in deciphering my handwriting is equalled only by my gratitude for the patience and understanding she has shown through the whole period during which the book was being written.

Introduction

Language teaching: art and science

People often say that language teaching is an art. If all they mean when they say this is that it is a highly skilled activity which is learned by careful observation and patient practice, then it is a harmless platitude. But what often lies behind the assertion is that science and art are mutually exclusive and that therefore science can play no part in language teaching. We call a particular practical activity an art when it cannot be carried out successfully by following a set of rules of thumb, when our knowledge of all the factors involved is incomplete and when, consequently, many of the decisions on how to proceed must be left to the private knowledge and experience of the practitioner. Language teaching is an activity of this sort. It involves many different considerations or, in technical language, *variables*, the relative importance, or *value* of which, even if we were aware of them all, cannot yet readily be assessed, or *quantified*. For this reason the activity of language teaching cannot be simulated on a computer, i.e. modelled mathematically, or reduced to a systematic set of logically related procedures, or an *algorithm*. But because not all of the variables are known, quanifitable and controllable, it does not mean that none of them are. There are, for example, all those factors which must be taken into account in any teaching task: the aptitude and personality of the pupils, their intellectual capacities, their attitude or motivation towards learning. These are all matters which have been investigated by educational psychologists and some aspects of them at least are now describable, measurable and controllable.

But there is a considerable body of knowledge available about the nature of human language, about how it is learned and what part it plays in the life of the individual and the community. These are matters of scientific investigation by those who study human language, the linguists, and must have a bearing on some of the questions which arise in the planning and execution of a language-teaching programme. Linguistics provides a growing body of scientific knowledge about language which can guide the activity of the language teacher. How this knowledge can be turned to good effect is the topic of this book.

Applied linguistics and language teaching

This is not another book on language teaching, still less an instructional manual on how to teach languages. There are plenty of books on this subject, reliable, unreliable and positively misleading. This one is about the contribution that the discoveries and methods of those who study language scientifically, that is, the linguist, the psycholinguist and the sociolinguist (to mention only the most important groups), can make to the solution of some of the problems which arise in the course of planning, organizing and carrying out a language-teaching programme. It is a book about applied linguistics.

Theories about the nature of human language are, of course, of use to other people besides the language teacher. It would be a mistake to associate applied linguistics exclusively with language teaching. There are other people who are engaged in practical activities which involve language in a central role for whom a knowledge of its nature could be of use in dealing with problems which arise in their work: the speech therapist, the literary critic, the communications engineer, for example. We do not uniquely associate applied linguistics with any single one of these activities. Whilst applied linguistics and language teaching may be closely associated, they are not one and the same activity.

The application of linguistic knowledge to some object – or applied linguistics, as its name implies – is an activity. It is not a theoretical study. It makes use of the findings of theoretical studies. The applied linguist is a consumer, or user, not a producer, of theories. If we use the term 'theory' as it is used in science, then there is no such thing as a 'theory of language teaching' or a 'theory of speech therapy' or a 'theory of literary criticism'. Language teaching is also an activity, but teaching languages is not the same activity as applied linguistics. However, if we interpret language teaching in the very broadest sense, to include all the planning and decision-making which takes place outside the classroom, then there may be an element of applied linguistics in all language teaching. Just as there may be an element of applied linguistics in all speech therapy or all literary criticism.

This, then, is a book about applied linguistics in language teaching; about those parts of the total language teaching operation in which decisions are made in the light of a knowledge of the nature of human language, how it is learned and its role in society. It deals with those parts of the operation which are potentially susceptible to some sort of systematization based upon scientifically acquired knowledge.

In spite of the many hundreds of years through which language has been studied in our civilization, we still know little about many of its aspects. The pace of investigation has quickened in recent years and the methods of investigation have increasingly been made more rigorous, to the point that we can now, with some justification and within certain defined boundaries, claim that linguistic studies are scientific. That is why I said that applied linguistics deals with that part of the language teaching operation which is potentially susceptible of some sort of rigorous systematization. We are still a long way from achieving such a systematization, as will become apparent in later chapters. For this reason linguistics can, as yet, scarcely claim to give firm answers to any but a few problems in language teaching. Applied linguistics as a field of study is scarcely twenty years old. The reader must judge for himself how much has been achieved in that time.

The language-teaching operation

I referred in the last section to the 'total language-teaching operation'. I did so because the simple term, *teaching*, is too vague in its meaning. In its popular use it refers most often to the activity of the teacher in the classroom in his interaction with his pupils. But teachers know that this represents only the end point of a time-consuming activity, planning, detailed preparation, correcting, assessing progress, all of which are an important, indeed, indispensable part of their work. What teachers do not always so readily recognize is that they, too, are dependent upon the work of others who also have a hand in, and, in some measure, determine, what goes on in the classroom. Teachers use textbooks, equipment, visual and other aids, they work to a syllabus and to a timetable, and often submit their pupils to examinations or tests prepared by others. These materials and plans are frequently things that they have little or no part in, but which contribute to, or even control, to some extent, what goes on in the classroom. In the total teaching operation, then, I include all planning and decision-making at whatever level which bears directly or indirectly on what goes on in the classroom. If we take the task of the teacher to be that of creating the conditions in which learning can most advantageously take place, then all decisions which bear on that objective are part of the total teaching operation. Some of these decisions at least will be made in the light of our current understanding of the nature of language.

Decisions and plans are made at various levels. At the highest level the decisions are political and made by governments and ministries. Decisions at this level are of a very general nature: whether languages are to be taught; which languages are to be taught; and how much money is to be available for training and paying teachers. One might think that linguistics had no contribution to make at this level. This is certainly the case in most European countries, but in many multi-lingual states in Africa and Asia the decisions about which languages to teach and at what level in the educational system to teach them are difficult ones and are made, at least in part, on the basis of studies made by sociolinguists into the distribution and various functions of different languages in the community, and the role that these languages have in the political and commercial life of the community and in its contacts with the world outside. This is an area of linguistic studies sometimes known as *language planning*.

When such fundamentally political decisions have been made there is another aspect of planning and decision-making which is based on economic, administrative and social considerations within the country. For how long, for what purposes and to whom shall certain languages be taught? Decisions of this sort may be taken at a lower point in the administrative hierarchy, often regionally, and sometimes, depending upon the administrative structure of the educational system, in the school itself. And here again the sociolinguist has a part to play.

We can group together all these fundamental decisions concerned with determining the aims and providing the means of language learning as the apex of the hierarchical structure of the total language-teaching operation. The second level is concerned with the implementation of these decisions, in general with the problems of what to teach and how to organize it. This is what this book is about, since it is at this level that the contribution of linguistics to language teaching is principally effective. Applied linguistics has to do with the devising of syllabuses and materials for carrying out the intentions of education authorities whether local or national. Syllabuses relate to specific languages to be taught to more or less specific groups of learners for more or less specific purposes within more or less specific limitations of time and money. Textbooks and teaching materials of all sorts are the concrete realizations of the syllabus plan.

The third level at which decisions are made about language teaching is that of the classroom. The linguistic contribution at this level is clearly psychological, and is concerned with how people learn second languages. But many other considerations play a part: general pedagogic principles concerned with motivation, attitudes, intelligence and personality. These are largely non-linguistic, and are just as important in the teaching of other subjects as in the teaching of languages. Those who plan at the second level do not have the detailed information available to the classroom teacher, and can only take account of these variables in the most general way. One does not meet syllabuses or teaching materials specifically devised for intelligent but uninterested twelve year olds!

The devising of syllabuses and the preparation of materials and textbooks for language teaching has traditionally been carried out by experienced teachers and this is still largely so. But increasingly nowadays, as in other fields of curriculum development, this is being done as a cooperative effort, in which experienced teachers work together with specialists in the subject matter (often themselves trained teachers). The specialists in this case are what I am calling applied linguists.

We can summarize the contents of the last two sections in the following Table:

Table 1 **Hierarchy of planning functions in the total language-teaching operation**

Level 1	Political	Government	Whether, what language, whom to teach
Level 2	Linguistic, Sociolinguistic	Applied linguist	What to teach, when to teach, how much to teach
Level 3	Psycholinguistic, Pedagogic	Classroom teacher	How to teach

Success in language teaching

The applied linguist is a contributor to the whole language-teaching operation. He does not control it, nor does the classroom teacher, nor, for that matter, does the headmaster or the Minister of Education. It is a cooperative venture. The better each contributor's understanding of the principles upon which decisions are made at all levels, the better chances the whole operation has of being successful. But we must expect that all along the line compromises will have to be made. For example, psycholinguistic knowledge might suggest that there is some optimum age for beginning the study of foreign languages. Political and economic considerations might indicate that it was undesirable on a cost–benefit analysis to devote the necessary funds to providing qualified teachers at that level. The two principles would be in conflict. The final plan would represent a compromise. All the contributors to a total teaching operation are involved in its success: society, as represented by the education authorities, the applied linguist and the classroom teacher. But, as in all educational operations, the difficulty is to define what is meant by success. Society might define it in terms of social integration, commercial pay-off, or some concept of the 'educated man'; the teacher might define it in terms of academic achievement, or the 'fulfilment of the individual'; the applied linguist in terms of the attainment of some measurable performance skills in the language. But it is individuals who learn language and they do so for many different reasons: because they enjoy it, because it is useful in their academic advancement or in their future careers, or because it opens for them opportunities for social and cultural contact and enrichment. They do not all necessarily seek, or need, the same level of performance ability or even the same set of linguistic skills. What is success for one may be failure for another. The individual learner is very much concerned with success in his own terms.

For any measurement of success one needs a yardstick or a measuring instrument. No one has proposed as yet a means of measuring success in language learning in society's terms – cultural, social or commercial. But to the extent that the teacher's, the learner's and the applied linguist's aims can be specified in linguistic terms as the attainment of specific skills and knowledge, a way of measuring these can be devised. What we can describe we can, in general, measure. Linguistics gives us a framework for describing what we mean by skill in, and knowledge of, a language and consequently makes it possible in principle to show that one way of teaching or one set of teaching materials is more effective than another for achieving a particular aim with a particular group of learners. There can be no systematic improvement in language teaching without reference to the knowledge about language which linguistics gives us.

Part One
Language and Language Learning

Chapter 1
Views of Language

What is language?

The decisions we make when we are carrying out some sort of practical task are consciously or unconsciously influenced by the views we hold about the nature of the thing we are dealing with. Everyone has what we can call an 'informal theory' about language and, if they are teachers of language, about how it is learned. The theory is informal, because it is not explicit – that is, expressed in a strictly logical form – and consequently may well contain hidden inconsistencies and contradictions. In this sense, it is unscientific. Perhaps it would be more accurate to say that everybody holds several informal theories about language, part of one theory being inconsistent with parts of another. Language is a very complex thing, and it cannot yet be fully accounted for by anyone within one wholly consistent and comprehensive theory. Certainly linguists have found it so. For this reason, when asked the question *What is language?*, the linguist is likely to reply by asking another question *Why do you want to know?* If we teach language, the way we approach our task will be influenced, or even determined, by what we believe language to be, by the particular informal theory or theories we have about it which seem to be relevant to the particular problem we are faced with.

There is generally a close connection between the way we talk about something and the way we regard it. The language we use about it betrays our views on what it is. If we want to know what someone believes language is, we must listen to the language he uses to talk about it. If we do this we soon notice that people seem to hold at one and the same time incompatible views about its nature. For example, we regularly hear people talking about 'using language': *He used some awful language*; *He used a word I didn't understand; What use is French?* This suggests that language is an object like a tool, which we can pick up, use for some purpose and put down again. People sometimes even actually call language a tool. We also talk about people 'possessing' a language. Shakespeare was reported by Jonson as *having* 'small Latin and less Greek'. Children are said to 'acquire' language. Apparently we sometimes 'lose' it: *I can't find the right word*. Now, if language was solely regarded as behaviour of a particular sort this would be a strange way of talking about it. Can we talk about 'walking' in the same way? Can we say that we 'use' walking to get somewhere? or 'acquire', 'possess' or 'lose' walking?

Linguists, especially, often talk about how language 'works', as if it were an object like an alarm clock, whose functioning could be understood from a study of its internal structure of springs and cogwheels. It is significant that while a study of the internal structure of a clock will tell you *how* it works, it won't tell you what clocks are *for*. This notion of internal structure evidently lies behind such statements as: *This sentence has a complex structure* or, in teaching, the phrase: *Learning a new construction*. Although we typically think of mechanisms as being lifeless objects, we frequently refer to language as if it were a living organism. We speak about the 'birth' of a language, of its 'growth', 'development' and 'decline'. Languages have periods of 'blossoming' and 'flowering' (always in the past); they are 'related' to each other in 'families', or 'descended' from each other. They are 'living' or 'dead'. They also have physical and moral qualities; they are 'beautiful', 'ugly', 'vulgar', 'debased' or 'decadent'.

I am not seriously suggesting that people actually believe that language is a concrete object which can be handled physically like a tool. These ways of talking about language are metaphorical. But it is interesting that we have to resort to metaphor to talk about language at all. The metaphors all have this in common though, they all treat language as an *object*. They 'reify' language.

We also find people talking about language as an 'event'. A conversation 'takes place', words 'crop up' in a discussion. We even speak about someone's speech as 'the event of the evening'.

Language is something we 'know'. We ask someone if he 'knows' French or German, or if he 'knows' some word or other. It is also something we 'do'. We write, read, speak well or badly. In this case we are treating it as skilled behaviour which we have to learn, and which improves through practice.

Our language about language reveals a variety of different ways of regarding it which, even if we admit that they are often metaphorical, nevertheless imply a certain logical inconsistency. The question is not so much which of these views is 'right'; they are all in their way valid, but none of them is complete or comprehensive. We just have to admit that language is such a complex phenomenon that no one viewpoint can see it as a whole. The question we really need to ask is not which view is 'right', but which view is useful, which view is relevant to language teaching. Can we say that any of the approaches to language as knowledge, as behaviour, as skill, as habit, as an event or an object can safely be disregarded by the language teacher?

The problem of 'psychic distance'

As has often been pointed out, the study of a language, as also the study of any other characteristic of man and society, is beset by the difficulty that it deals with something utterly familiar. Everybody 'knows' about language, because they use it all the time, everybody 'knows' about society and social behaviour, because they are members of society. It is all, somehow, 'natural'. The contrast with what we know about our physical environment, its constitution and operation, is striking. Even quite simple physical facts such as the laws governing the swing of a pendulum or the acceleration of falling bodies are unexpected, even counter-intuitive. But equally 'elementary' facts about society, or about language, once they are pointed out, appear obvious. The difficulty, then, of studying man's social behaviour, including his language, is not so much that of access to the data – we have, in a sense, all too much of it – but to exteriorize it, to separate it from ourselves, to achieve an objective point of view or, to follow Chomsky's terminology (1968a), to achieve a 'psychic distance' from what we are studying. Scientific knowledge is public knowledge; it is objective in the sense that it is open to scrutiny and disproof by anyone who knows how to set about it. The linguist, in studying language, attempts to achieve this psychic distance, and in so doing necessarily 'objectivizes' or 'reifies' language. He has been helped in this because much of the traditional study of language was concerned with 'dead' languages and his data were 'texts'. In that case it was much easier to achieve a 'psychic distance' since the observer was not studying directly his own behaviour or that of his own or any still-existing society. He could more readily divorce the study of the language from the study of the people who spoke it and from their culture. Indeed the reason for studying a language was often that it *had* become something strange and incomprehensible, and it arose from the need to explain ancient or traditional religious or literary texts. The linguist is, however, aware of what he is doing when he adopts this point of view and it does not mean that he believes that language is 'a thing', or that it has objective reality in the way that a pendulum or a falling solid object has.

Nevertheless, the achievement of this 'psychic distance' is by no means easy, not even for linguists. All too frequently, they, like language teachers, make statements or assumptions based, not on objective study, but on intuitive 'private' knowledge. How often does a teacher say that such and such a word is *never* used in a particular context? Has he based this statement on his or another's objective research? Such private intuitions, for the unwary, may be easily expressed in a prescriptive form or as value judgements. When someone asserts: 'People don't say that', is this a statement of fact whose truth can be demonstrated, or is it really a value judgement? Does it really mean that it is socially unacceptable to say that? Here again we can ask: is this statement based upon objective investigation of what native speakers do and do not find acceptable in a particular situation, or does it merely represent the private judgement of the teacher or linguist? Or the prejudices of his social group or class? Social attitudes to language can also be studied scientifically. They are what Bloomfield (1944) called 'tertiary responses' to language. They have been a subject of a recent study by Mittins (1970).

But if someone says, 'That [bit of language] is not correct', we are not always sure whether he is making a value judgement – asserting that the form in question was not in accordance with some socially prescribed 'norm' of language use (as in *Double negatives are incorrect*), which may be more often honoured in the breach; or a statement of an observed fact, that no speaker of the language would ever utter such a sequence of words (as in *This is my story one man*). There will be some discussion of this problem in chapter 2.

Language and the individual

The first way we can approach language is as a phenomenon of the individual person. It is concerned with describing and explaining language as a matter of human behaviour. People speak and write, they also evidently read and understand what they hear. They are not born doing so; they have to acquire these skills. Not everybody seems to develop them to the same degree. People may suffer accidents or disease which impair their performance. Language is thus seen as part of human psychology, a particular sort of behaviour, the behaviour which has as its principal function that of communication.

The trouble with the term 'behaviour' is that it is often taken to refer only to more or less overt, and describable, physical movements and acts. Yet part of language behaviour – that of understanding spoken or written language, for example – has little or no physically observable signs. It is true we can sometimes *infer* that understanding has taken place by the changes that take place in the other person's behaviour. When someone has been prohibited from doing something, we may infer that he has understood the prohibition by observing that thereafter he never behaves in that way. We cannot, of course, be absolutely sure that his subsequent behaviour is a result of his understanding; it might be due to a loss of interest or inclination. So behaviour must be taken to include unobservable activity, often only to be inferred from other observable behaviour.

Once we admit that the study of language behaviour involves describing and explaining the unobservable, the situation becomes much more complicated, because we have to postulate some set of processes, some internal mechanism which operates when we speak and understand. We have to postulate something we can call a mind. The study of language from this point of view can then be seen as a study of the specific properties, processes and states of the mind whose outward manifestations are observable behaviour; what we have to 'know' in order to perform linguistically. As Chomsky (1968a) has said, what the linguist who adopts this approach is trying to do is 'establish certain general properties of human intelligence. Linguistics is simply the subfield of psychology that deals with these aspects of the mind' (p. 24).

But we are not born speaking and understanding language. We have to acquire it, so this approach to language is not only concerned with what goes on when we speak and understand, what has been called *linguistic performance*, but how we come to be able to do these things. Language behaviour is evidently such a complex skill that it seems almost incredible that it can be acquired by an infant in such a short time. This has led people to propose that the disposition to acquire it must be innate, and the fact that only human beings possess language must mean that there is something peculiar to the human species that predisposes it to acquire language. Some linguists and psychologists go so far as to suggest that the human infant is born with a specific, genetically determined, language learning capacity. Others, more cautious in their views, propose only that the ability and predisposition to acquire language is a function of the general cognitive capacities of the human being which enable him to learn at all.

This approach to language, as a phenomenon of the individual, is thus principally concerned with explaining how we acquire language, and its relation to general human cognitive systems, and with the psychological mechanisms underlying the comprehension and production of speech; much less with the problem of what language is for, that is, its function as communication, since this necessarily involves more than a single individual.

Language as a social phenomenon

People do talk to themselves subvocally, sometimes audibly, and any account of language must take this into consideration. We often speak of this as *thinking aloud*. Clearly there is some close connection between thought and language. The difficulty is to investigate it, as can be seen in Adams (1972). In language teaching, however, it is the use of language as an act of communication between people that is central; that is, its social function. There would be no point in acquiring what is admittedly a very complex sort of behaviour unless it was useful, to the individual and to the society to which he belongs. Language is, of course, not the only form of human behaviour which communicates. Perhaps all overt behaviour communicates, in the sense that we draw conclusions about someone from anything he does, the clothes he wears, the way he walks or does his hair. But it is an *incidental* function of non-linguistic behaviour, not its principal or sole function. On the other hand language is not the only sort of behaviour whose principal function is communication. We point, wave, raise our eyebrows, 'clear our throat' and 'avert our eyes'. Nor is all vocal behaviour linguistic: screams and cries are not part of language. Perhaps even the predictable 'good-byes', 'hullos' and 'how do you dos' are only language-like behaviour. Language, or verbal behaviour, is a special sort of communicative behaviour. It is the job of the linguist to distinguish what is language from other sorts of vocal and nonvocal communication.

A speaker behaves as he does because his audience is as it is. We cannot hope to explain what happens in a conversation without taking into account the characteristics and behaviour of the hearer as well as the speaker. After all, both are 'performing' linguistically. Language in this second approach is a social event. It can be fully described only if we know all about the people who are involved in it, their personalities, their beliefs, attitudes, knowledge of the world, their relationship to each other, their social status, what activity they are engaged in, why they are talking at all, what has gone before, linguistically and nonlinguistically, what happens after, where they are and a host of other facts about them and the situation.

If people want to play a game together they have to agree on the rules. If communication is to take place, the participants must share the same conventions. My idiosyncratic cries and gestures are largely uninterpretable by an observer; just as utterances in a foreign language are largely uninterpretable. We can communicate with people only because they share with us a set of 'agreed' ways of behaving. Language in this sense is the possession of a social group, an indispensable set of rules which permits its members to relate to each other, to interact with each other, to cooperate with each other: it is a social institution. Animals, too, share a set of conventional communicative signals, and, of course, humans and animals who live together develop a common set of signals by which they communicate. My dog can tell me when he wants to go for a walk, and I can tell him to come to me without recourse to human language. It has, however, always been taken for granted that there is a fundamental difference in kind, not just degree of complexity, between human language and animal communication systems. Only very recently has this age-old assumption been questioned. It may turn out, as a result of continuing studies by ethologists, that the distinction is, after all, not as sharp as has always been assumed (Gardner and Gardner, 1969).

The linguistic approach to language

It may seem curious to characterize the third approach to language as 'linguistic', thereby suggesting either that the other approaches are not concerned with language, or that the term *linguistic* is being used in a rather special way. And, indeed, that is precisely the case. It is used here to refer to the approach to language which has been that adopted by the study known as linguistics. But even here there is some possibility of confusion. Whilst Professor Allen entitled his inaugural lecture *The Linguistic Study of Languages* (1966) thereby adopting the same meaning of linguistic as I am doing, we also find in Hjelmslev's book *Language* (1963) the expression 'linguistic linguistics', suggesting that linguistics may include, not just the particular approach that I am now going to outline, but also the two I have already spoken about. In this, Hjelmslev was already foretelling the direction in which linguistics is increasingly appearing to move, that is, as an all-embracing study of language. This has sometimes been referred to as *macro-linguistics*. I shall, in fact, throughout this book use the term linguistics and linguist in this general, all-embracing sense, unless it is necessary in a particular context to specify more exactly which approach is being considered, as it is in this section.

The linguistic study of language has sometimes been called the study of language 'for its own sake' (de Saussure, 1961). If we discount the implication that language can be studied for some 'useful' end such as language teaching, then this definition distinguishes this approach to language from the others already outlined, by establishing linguistics as an *independent* study, whereas the other approaches could be regarded as falling respectively within general psychology and general sociology. The descriptive framework and methods of study of language in the individual must have some compatibility with the study of other aspects of human behaviour and cognitive capacities. Similarly, the study of language as a social phenomenon must be consonant with theories of social structure, social behaviour and human culture. But the linguistic study of language sets up its own theoretical apparatus, has its own methods of working and ways of regarding and selecting its data. The linguistic approach is the most 'objectivizing' approach: it is concerned with language as a system; it aims to elucidate the structure of language. It classifies linguistic entities and establishes the relations between them. In the most general sense it is concerned with the relation between meanings and sounds. To explain this relation it has traditionally set up various 'levels of description' which account for the different sorts of entities it deals with and the different sorts of relations it finds between them. These levels bear such familiar names as syntax and morphology, phonology and phonetics, lexis and semantics; or, more popularly, grammar, vocabulary and pronunciation.

The linguistic approach to language is probably the most familiar approach as it is certainly the one with the longest history inside and outside Europe. It is also for that reason probably the theoretically most advanced and complex. Its data are not people and their behaviour, but texts and recorded utterances. It is not concerned with distinctions between hearers and speakers, nor is it concerned with how people come to acquire languages or what part language plays in society.

The sheer success and sophistication of the linguistic approach to language has, however, been bought dearly. As I have said, this way of looking at language is necessarily the most objectivizing. But language is not, after all, a thing with real existence. Objectivizing means abstraction. By abstracting in this way, the linguistic study of language has tended to lose its connections with man and society. The more sophisticated the theories and descriptions of language structure have become, the less reason there has seemed to be to prefer one way of describing it over another. We have come to a point where the only grounds for deciding which is a better description or theory must be sociological or psychological, that is, on its compatibility with one of the other approaches.

Implications for language teaching

The object in teaching a language, unless it is simply that of getting pupils over an important educational hurdle, is to enable the learner to behave in such a way that he can participate to some degree and for certain purposes as a member of a community other than his own. The degree to which any particular learner may wish to participate will vary. He may seek only to read technical literature, or he may wish to preach the gospel in a foreign country. These varying degrees of participation require different levels of skill in language performance. They also imply some division of linguistic behaviour into different sorts of skill – these different types have conventionally different names: writing, speaking, taking dictation, reading aloud and so on. Just how different these various sorts of language performance are as far as the mechanisms underlying them are concerned may be questioned (see chapter

6). What is clear is that teaching languages is, and always has been, thought of as developing a set of performance skills in the learner, and syllabuses and timetables are often expressed in terms of the skills being taught. *Today we'll have a reading lesson. Tomorrow is the conversation class.* If in any discussion of language teaching we talk about developing skills, such as speaking or understanding speech, we are adopting a psychological view of language; we are considering it as a matter of individual behaviour. Whether we consider that behaviour to be a set of habits or possible responses, a body of knowledge, or a set of rules depends upon the particular psychological account that we adopt of the language behaviour of the individual and how it is acquired. It will, for example, determine our attitude to the function and use of drills, the giving of grammatical explanations, the value of repetition and learning by heart, the utility of dictation and the importance of just listening. Whatever decision we make in the field of methods implies the adopting of a view of language as a phenomenon of individual psychology. What characterized so-called 'traditional' language teaching was not so much that it lacked an awareness of the psychological dimension of language, as that it limited the range of behaviour or skill aimed at. But this is not a reason for being critical of it. The skills it attempted to develop were, after all, presumably those which society thought appropriate at the time. Its methods were, in part, determined by this. What one can nowadays justifiably say about 'traditional' language teaching is that its methods are no longer appropriate to a new set of demands and expectations.

However, when we talk about acceptable and unacceptable behaviour or appropriate and inappropriate language, we are taking a view of language as a social institution, a body of socially conditioned or culturally determined ways of behaving. What is incorrect or inappropriate is simply that which is not in conformity with the shared norms of a particular group. In language teaching we are preparing the learner to participate in some other social group, some language community other than his own, to play a part or fulfil a role in that community. Unacceptable or inappropriate language prevents him from interacting or communicating satisfactorily with other members of that community; he may fail to achieve his ends, he may fail to communicate or be misunderstood, he may give offence or make himself ridiculous.

Learners do not all have the same social objectives in learning languages. The range of roles they wish to achieve will vary. Few will wish to be poets in the new language community; some may wish to be wives or husbands; most will have to be content to be 'foreigners'. In planning language-teaching operations we must know what social roles are to be aimed at, what personal objectives the learner may wish to achieve. In other words, we have to decide what 'sort' of language to teach him. The concept of 'a language' or 'a dialect' is a sociological not a 'linguistic' linguistic one. We teach *a* language, not just *language*.

Perhaps the most cogent criticism of traditional language teaching with its insistence on correctness, the rules of the grammar, and its limited objectives, is that it lacked this sociological dimension. It assumed that a language was a 'linguistic' linguistic concept. Little thought seems to have been given to the notion of appropriateness, to the way that language behaviour is responsive to differing social situations. It is one of the great virtues of modern language teaching that it adopts a more social approach to language, and is concerned with the problems of its communicative function in different social situations. We see this in the modern insistence on presenting language in situation, in dialogue form rather than isolated exemplificatory sentences; in the use of audio-visual materials and in the emphasis on 'natural' linguistic examples. No more of *la plume de ma tante* or 'the postillion has been struck by lightning'.

The relevance of the 'linguistic' linguistic approach to language is too obvious to need much discussion at this point. The division of what is taught into pronunciation, vocabulary and grammar is clearly derived from the linguistic 'levels' of language description. But we still meet a confusion between this approach and the psychological approach when we listen to the interminable discussions over 'the teaching of grammar'. The trouble is that the term 'grammar' is, like the term 'language' itself, as Quirk, Greenbaum, Leech and Svartvik, (1972, pp. 8–12) have pointed out, ambiguous. It is used both in a psychological and a linguistic sense. Teachers sometimes try to resolve this ambiguity by saying that what we ought to be doing is to teach people the language, not teach people *about* the language. What they mean is that we are trying to turn out *performers* in the language rather than *linguists*, people who can 'talk the language' rather than 'talk *about* the language'. It is, of course, perfectly true that linguists can often talk at length about a language they cannot speak. One of the criticisms raised against traditional methods was that they succeeded sometimes better in the latter task than the former. The 'teaching of grammar', then, may be understood *psychologically* as enabling the learner to produce utterances which would be called grammatical by the linguist, and *linguistically*, as telling the learner about the grammatical rules of the language. Whether doing the latter is a useful way of doing the former is indeed a matter of debate in the psychology of language teaching. The answer to the question 'ought we to teach grammar?' is, therefore, *psychologically*, 'yes', and *linguistically*, 'perhaps'. No such ambiguity seems to attach to the teaching of pronunciation. Although both the linguist and teacher are capable of saying a lot *about* the pronunciation of a language, there does not seem to have been the same debate on the 'teaching of pronunciation'. It is generally understood only in the psychological sense: getting the learner to behave in a certain way. Nor does the 'teaching of vocabulary' seem to be ambiguous. The reason for this is interesting. Unlike 'talking about grammar or pronunciation', talking about vocabulary is something we do a good deal of in our everyday conversation. When we give a definition of any sort we are 'talking about' vocabulary. It is almost the only sort of 'talking about' vocabulary that the ordinary teacher can do. The linguist can do a little, but not much, better. 'Talking about vocabulary' is one accepted way of 'teaching vocabulary' and it has never provoked the same criticism that the 'teaching of grammar' has in its 'linguistic' sense. There are, of course, additional ways of teaching vocabulary, for example, by ostensive methods, which have their justification more in psychology than linguistics.

The relevance of the linguistic approach to language in language teaching is that it provides by far the most detailed and comprehensive descriptions of language. One has only to imagine what it would be like to have to draw up a syllabus for a language-teaching operation in psychological terms, i.e. in terms of the skills and types of verbal behaviour to be taught, to realize that this is the case. Plans of this kind are sometimes met with, though they scarcely merit the name syllabus; they are more in the nature of general aims, e.g.: 'at the end of the course the learner must be able to write without too many grammatical mistakes, converse fluently with a native speaker and be able to read easily and freely in non-technical literature.' To attempt to draw up a syllabus in sociological terms might appear to be easier: 'The learner must be able to find his way around as a tourist in the foreign country, buy tickets, book hotel rooms, ask the way, etc., in the language.' The difficulty in both these cases is that however long the list of accomplishments may be, they are bound to be vague, unspecific, and unsystematic.

The fact is that if we wish to specify a really detailed plan for a language-teaching operation this must be expressed in 'linguistic' linguistic terms – lists of grammatical structures and vocabulary, and lists of sounds and other features of pronunciation to be 'mastered'. The linguistic approach is responsible for determining how we *describe* what we are to teach. This is not the same as saying that it *determines* what we teach. It contributes nothing to specifying how we teach.

Chapter 2
Functions of Language

Language as a means of communication

After the general discussion about ways of regarding language in the preceding chapter, it might be thought surprising that anyone has been brave enough to attempt a definition of anything so complex. In spite of this there have been innumerable such attempts, none of them wholly satisfactory or comprehensive. But most of them in one way or another try to work into the definition some statement about the *function* of language, usually in the form of such phrases as: *by which man communicates*; *a system of communication*; *for the purposes of communication*. In the last chapter the notion of language as a means of communication was regarded as a sociological way of looking at language, since it involved taking into account speaker and hearer as well as many other features of the speech situation. I shall here go a little further into this matter of the communicative function of language. First of all, we have to make a distinction between intentional and unintentional communication. If we see a friend walking along the road, unobserved by him, we may be able within fairly broad limits to draw certain conclusions about him, his state of mind or health, where he is going and why, just from the way he is walking. In this sense his walk 'tells' us something, but no one would suggest that he is walking in that way *in order to* communicate with us, though this may sometimes be done, as when we say of someone: *She flounced out of the room and slammed the door*. All our behaviour is in some measure communicative, in the sense that the 'receiver' learns something he didn't know before, even though the 'sender' has no specific intention of informing him of anything. It is useful, following Marshall (1970, p. 235) to refer to this aspect of behaviour as *informative*, keeping the term *communicative* for behaviour which is used with the intention of informing. Walking, then, or any other activity may, incidentally, convey information to an outside observer. This may also include our vocal activity. Just as we can tell something about a person by his walk, so we can infer certain things about a person by his voice. To begin with, everyone has something individual about his voice or way of speaking. It is true that a quality of voice or an accent can, to some extent, be deliberately disguised, or a person can deliberately adopt the characteristics of someone else's voice. This is the skill mimics have. In such cases these 'indexical' characteristics, as they have been called by Abercrombie (1967) are being used for intentional communication, i.e. to mislead. Similarly we can tell when a person is angry, excited or tired by the 'tone' of his voice, as we can by the manner of his walking or many other aspects of his behaviour. All our behaviour is, then, potentially informative and may also be used for communication.

This does not however mean that the 'receiver' can always 'read the signs'. To be informed or communicated to we obviously need a certain amount of general or particular knowledge, amongst which may be a knowledge of certain conventions. The distinction between intentional and non-intentional communication lies in the 'sender's' head. The distinction between being informed or not being informed, or communicated to or not being communicated to, lies in the 'receiver's' head.

The second distinction we have to make is between linguistic and non-linguistic communication. When I wave to someone in order to attract his attention, I am communicating intentionally with him; I do this as part of some deliberate plan of action, as a prelude, for example, to telling him something or borrowing something from him. My gesture must be of such a sort that he interprets it as a *call* and not just as a *greeting* or a *farewell* or a *warning*. In other words he must understand it for communication to be successful. In any society, how a wave or other gesture is interpreted is a matter of a shared convention of behaviour between sender and receiver.

Communicative behaviour is essentially a matter of convention. A wave is, however, not a bit of linguistic communication. If I called out to him, *Hey, Bill, come here a moment*, my intentions would be exactly the same, only this time my communication would be generally regarded as linguistic. If on the other hand I simply shouted some ill-articulated noise, it might be difficult to decide whether this was a truly linguistic or non-linguistic communication. The line is difficult to draw. Where it is drawn ultimately depends on the linguist; what phenomena his theories are meant to explain. What is quite clear is that it is not just a question of whether or not we use our organs of speech to communicate. After all we can use coughs, shouts, yawns, sighs and a large range of 'vocal signals' as intentional communicative acts, which few would regard as 'linguistic'. And of course, we can communicate linguistically through the visual channel, through writing, and this does not involve the use of the vocal organs at all.

The line between linguistic and non-linguistic communication is not a hard and fast one. It ultimately depends upon the theoretical decisions of the linguist as to what falls within his field of study. Different linguists will draw the line in different places. But most linguists would agree that the central characteristic of linguistic behaviour is that it is made up of a large but finite number of arbitrary but conventional signs which may combine in various complex ways to signal differences in meaning; linguistic behaviour is typically *verbal*. The distinction between vocal and non-vocal behaviour on the other hand, whether communicative or informative, is merely a matter of whether the vocal organs are involved. The fact that linguistic communication is typically associated in people's minds with vocal behaviour is, in a sense, an 'historical accident' often called 'the primacy of speech'. By this we mean that linguistic communicative behaviour normally develops first in a vocal form both in the development of the individual and in human societies.

We must make a distinction then, between behaviour, whether vocal or not, which is potentially informative and that which is intentionally communicative. We can also make various distinctions within communicative behaviour (whether linguistic or not) according to the nature of what is being communicated. I shall take up this theme again later in much greater detail in connection with specifically linguistic behaviour, but at this point it is useful to make a preliminary distinction between the *attitudinal* and *cognitive* functions of linguistic behaviour (Lyons, 1972). The attitudinal function of linguistic behaviour is the use of this behaviour to express our state of mind and emotions, to establish *rapport* with our hearers and to promote feelings of solidarity, confidence and goodwill; the cognitive function of communication is to express our perceptions, imaginings and beliefs about 'states of affairs'. Analysed in this way it appears that animal signalling behaviour has exclusively the first function. Animals appear to react to situations in such a way that the human scientific observer can in principle predict from his knowledge of the total situation what signals, vocal or otherwise, will occur and what effect they will have on other animals of the same or different species. In other words, we categorize certain animal behaviour as the expression of fear, friendliness, aggression and so on, because other animals react to this behaviour by flight, approach, preparation to fight and so on. We pair fear-behaviour with a flight response and then go on to say that the animal is 'warning' other animals of danger. If we choose to call this process 'communication', as is frequently done, we are not thereby entitled to assume that it is 'intentional' in the sense that I have been using it in connection with human behaviour. Intention necessarily presupposes choice. The account of animal signalling excludes the notion of choice. To be justified in ascribing intentional communication to an animal we should have to show that it 'recognized' that its behaviour would have certain effects and that it used such signals to produce that effect. The clearest proof of such intentional behaviour would be if an animal could be shown to signal fear or pleasure inappropriately, i.e. to misinform. There is no clear evidence yet that this happens (Marshall, 1970, pp. 235–6).

Returning now to the cognitive function of linguistic behaviour, it appears that animal signalling systems, whether intentional or not, do not have a cognitive function. Similarly, human communicative behaviour, both linguistic and non-linguistic, may have an attitudinal function, but only linguistic behaviour has a cognitive function. We may communicate fear, goodwill or pleasure linguistically or non-linguistically, but we cannot assert that something is dangerous or pleasant except linguistically.

Communication and meaning

I have said that we can communicate intentionally by other than linguistic means. Our choice of posture, gesture, 'tone of voice', facial expression, our manner of walking, dressing or eating, can all be manipulated to tell people something. But for us to be successful the 'receivers' must know the system of conventions which we follow. A 'tired' walk is, to a large extent, physiologically determined but it can be simulated. There is an 'accepted' way of walking which means 'tired'. A great deal of perhaps not very good acting is based upon conventions of this sort: *running one's hand through one's hair*; *stifling a yawn*; *clapping one's hand to one's mouth*. Probably all our behaviour has a conventional element in it, because it is learned in society and, for that very reason, the form it takes will be specific to the social group in which it is learned. For plentiful illustration of this see La Barre (1972). This is part of what we mean by culture. It is by the deliberate manipulation of our behaviour within a permitted range and according to a conventional system that we communicate purposefully. Let me here emphasize that we do not need to know *consciously* what the rules are to use them to communicate. This is obviously true of language. It is also true of other communicative behaviour.

Any deliberate manipulation of bodily behaviour for communicative purposes within the conventions, other than what I have called linguistic, is generally called *paralinguistic*: gesture, posture, facial expression, and the tempo, pitch and quality of speech. There is a strong tendency for paralinguistic behaviour to accompany linguistic behaviour like a counterpoint, and again like melodies in counterpoint they intermingle, as, for instance, when we gesture towards something in the place of some verbal expression: *Just pass me that . . .* [gesture]*!* Or, as frequently happens in shops or offices: *And your name is. . . .?*, accompanied by a raising of the eyebrows or a tilt of the head.

Very little of man's behaviour, linguistic or otherwise, is wholly predictable. If it were, it would not tell the observer anything he did not already know. Hence it would not be informative. If everybody had the same voice quality or dressed in the same way, these aspects of behaviour would not carry information. Probably we should not even have words for them in our language. They would simply be immutable aspects of the world to be taken for granted, like having a nose, a matter in which we exercise no choice. But when we have a choice, we have the possibility of using it for communication. Choice implies some range of perceptibly distinct alternatives – some sort of a conventional system; it implies meaning.

What is communicated?

Traditional accounts of language typically tend to state its function as being the communication of 'thought'. But even if we interpret the word 'thought' in the most liberal fashion, to include beliefs, opinions, judgements, perceptions, this clearly is too limited an account. We can test this by prefixing a few utterances with the words 'I think' and see if they make sense, or better, if the addition makes no important change in the meaning. If we do this we shall find a whole class of utterances which are little affected by the addition, but another large class which suffer a significant change of meaning:

The Government has made another mistake
You should see a doctor
Rebecca will get back tomorrow
That's a lovely blouse!

These sentences seem to be relatively little changed in their meaning by adding 'I think' before them, but what about:

Bet you can't answer this one
Good old Bill!
Can you tell me the way to the Odeon?
Ouch, that hurts!
I'd be glad to, of course
You shall have my answer tomorrow

The overestimation of the function of language as a vehicle for the expression of thoughts comes from the fact that those historically most interested in language were philosophers and logicians, preoccupied with the propositional aspect of language, with its truth value. They tended to concentrate their attention on just those sorts of sentences which could be analysed as expressing true or false propositions. But it is difficult to see how expressions of desires, pleasure, pain, satisfaction, or questions or orders could be true or false except inasmuch as they presupposed something true or false. We can't say that the sentence *Pass the salt!* is true or false in itself. We can only say that the perceptions or presuppositions about the situation in which it is uttered may be factually false, i.e. there may be no salt about. Similarly, a question such as: *How many legs has the boa constrictor?* is neither true nor false. What is false is the implied assumption that it has any legs at all!

Whilst language may be used to express our thoughts, this is certainly not its only function. It may be true that most sentences contain some element or elements which presuppose or assert certain beliefs, opinions or perceptions about our immediate situation or the world in general, but this is by no means the same as saying that the function of language is to express our thoughts.

The first thing, then, that we have to face is that we cannot say what the function of a bit of language may be if we take it in isolation from its context and the situation in which it is made. The same string of words may be uttered on different occasions with quite different intentions and effects. It is not sufficient simply to record what words are uttered, we have to ask why they are uttered. We can only do this successfully, as we have seen, if we have a lot of information about the speaker, the hearer and the situation. When, recently, an official was reported in a newspaper as saying that the local river 'should be treated as an open sewer', the journalist who reported the speech noted that he presumed that this was to be understood as a *warning* and not an *invitation*. I still cannot make up my mind whether the notice, 'Pedestrians Cross Here', is an *instruction* to pedestrians or a *warning* to motorists. Behind any apparently neutral or innocent 'statement of fact' there may lurk some other intention. This is the problem of talking about the communicative functions of language. We cannot just neatly classify utterances according to their grammatical forms, e.g. imperative, interrogative, declarative and so on, and then say that each form has one and only one function. On the contrary, we have to say that any utterance may have simultaneously several functions and there is no simple one-to-one relation between the form of an utterance and its function, although there may be a statistical relation (of probability), for example, between an interrogative sentence and the function of asking a question.

In the preceding section I made a distinction between the attitudinal function and cognitive function of speech in connection with the distinction between linguistic and non-linguistic behaviour. The cognitive function is clearly related to what I have here been calling that element of an utterance which expresses our beliefs, our perceptions or imaginings of a situation or the world in general. This part of an utterance (if it has such a component at all and refers to a particular time and place) can be judged as factually true or false. It is sometimes called, for this reason, the *propositional* or *content* element in the utterance (cf. Searle, 1969). Of course, it may be part of our intention to mislead, that is, to present as our opinion or perception something which is contrary to the way we in fact see things or believe them to be – but that does not mean that that part of the utterance is non-cognitive. The attitudinal function is a complex of many related functions. Expressions of pleasure, pain, fear, desire and so on are not expressions of how we see things or believe things to be, but our personal reactions to these states of affairs, whether voluntary or involuntary. The utterance *Rebecca's coming home tomorrow* may be an emotionally neutral statement of what we believe to be true, but if we say *It's a good thing Rebecca's coming home tomorrow*, or *I hope Rebecca's coming home tomorrow*, we are adding an expression of our emotional attitude to the state of affairs as we see it. We may equally be intending to mislead, of course. Or, if we say *Rebecca may be coming home tomorrow*, or *Rebecca can't be coming home tomorrow*, we are adding our assessment of the probability of a state of affairs. This may have an emotional content in it (it depends on our relations with Rebecca) but it is principally a statement of the degree of confidence we personally have in the truth of our perception of the state of affairs. Again, we may be intending to mislead. Judgements on the probability, likelihood, possibility or certainty of the propositional element of an expression are often called the modal element of an utterance. We may say *Rebecca, come home tomorrow!* Clearly, we are here expressing a desire for a certain state of affairs. Inasmuch as all these different utterances express emotion at, confidence in or desire for some state of affairs, they all have an element in them which tells the hearer something about the speaker. They all have an attitudinal element in them. We can ask now: Is it possible for there to be utterances which only have attitudinal function, that is, which lack any propositional or cognitive element? What propositional element has *Hullo!* or *Good-bye!* or *How do you do?* They can scarcely be said to express a perception of a state of affairs, although their utterance may presuppose such a perception. If we look at such utterances, we find that their occurrence is fairly predictable, and that they are formulaic in structure, and, for this reason, more like the calls of animals in character. Some people have called them, therefore, 'language-like' behaviour. Their function is clearly attitudinal, though they may do no more than establish a feeling of solidarity or friendly relations between speaker and hearer. But the great majority of utterances are not of this formulaic sort and do contain a propositional element in them. Perhaps that is why tradition has picked out the prime or only function of language as 'the communication of thought'.

Speech acts

Most utterances do have a cognitive element in them, but this does not mean that the function of language is simply the expression of that element. All language has an attitudinal element, that which is related to the intentions of the speaker, by which he conveys something of his state of mind, his activity and why he is speaking at all. This attitudinal element may, of course, not be overtly expressed, as we have seen. Not every utterance begins with the word *I*, but any utterance can be prefaced with some such words as *I want, I wish, I order, I deny* or any one of literally hundreds of the verbs which express intentions, wishes, beliefs, assertions, without changing in any way the meaning in a particular context. We can say that for every utterance there is a paraphrase possible in the circumstances which starts: *I . . . that . . .* Thus, for example, for even such a minimal and 'neutral' statement as *two and two is four* we can propose a paraphrase *I calculate that two plus two equals four*; or for *what time is it?*, *I ask you to tell me what time it is?*; for *come here a moment!*, *I command you to come here!*; for *this car must be washed this afternoon*, *I demand that someone wash this car this afternoon*; for *that will be Bill now, I predict that this is Bill*; or *let's go to the cinema, I suggest we go to the cinema*. There are certain speech acts which, in specific circumstances, require that the nature of the act be explicitly described in the utterance for it to count as an act of that sort. The setting for such acts are typically legal or religious and the utterance is usually part of a ritual. For example, in the 'naming' of a ship participants in the ceremony would feel the act had not been 'properly' performed unless the words: *I name this ship . . .* had been used. Similarly we should not feel an infant had been properly christened if the priest said: *Let's call him Archibald, shall we?* We can say, with Austin (1955) that the uttering of a specific linguistic form is a necessary part of performing the act. This notion can be generalized for all speech. Uttering speech is *a way of performing* a certain act, it is not an act in itself any more than moving one's arm is an act; it may be part of playing a golf stroke, directing traffic, driving in a nail and so on. If we follow this line of reasoning, we shall find that there are as many different sorts of speech act as there are 'verbs of speaking' or *performative verbs*, as they are called by Austin, and this means hundreds; any verb which fits into the frame *I hereby . . . that . . .* is a performative verb.

But an account of the functions of language which simply lists all the named acts is too unwieldy to be very useful. We need to group these acts into classes which have some common functional characteristics. Thus, we should probably agree that the acts of *ordering*; *instructing*; *demanding*; *commanding*; *warning* all have some common quality, that of getting our hearer to do or not do something. They have a functional similarity. We might also wish to include in this class *asking*; *questioning*; *inquiring* which all have the intention of getting our hearer to *say* something. If we wanted to give a name to this category of speech functions we might follow Austin in calling them *directive* acts because they aim at regulating the behaviour of our hearer, or ultimately controlling our environment through the medium of other people. Austin divides all speech acts into five different categories. The names he gives these categories need not detain us; he himself apologizes for the shocking neologisms he coined. The first class was made up of those acts which constituted judgements on some state of affairs, estimations, reckonings, appraisals, fundamentally those of giving a finding as to something; a fact or a value. The second constituted acts exercising some power, influence or right, such as appointing, voting, ordering, advising or warning; the third class of acts committed the speaker to some course of action: *promising*; *undertaking*; *announcing intentions* or *declarations of belief or faith*. The fourth had to do with essentially social behaviour: *apologizing*; *congratulating*; *condoling* or *challenging*. The fifth involved taking a stance with respect to something: *argument*; *reply*; *concession*; *assumption* or *supposition*.

Now this may look very much like the sort of classification of sentences into declarative, imperative, interrogative and exclamatory with which we are familiar in our grammar books. And so, up to a point, it is, except that it is more detailed and is based not on an analysis of linguistic forms alone, but on what these forms are used for or 'count as' in actual speech situations. For example, are we to group together *That paint's still wet* and *You shall have my answer tomorrow*, simply because they are grammatically declarative in form? In many situations the first will be interpreted as a warning and the second as a promise. It is true both could in particular contexts and spoken with appropriate intonation be taken as assertions of fact, e.g. *I hereby assert the paint is still wet* and *I hereby assert you shall have an answer tomorrow*. It needs some ingenuity, however, to imagine a situation in which we should say *I hereby promise you that the paint is still wet* and *I hereby warn you that you shall have my answer tomorrow*, but none to imagine the contrary: *I hereby warn you that the paint's still wet* and *I hereby promise you that you shall have my answer tomorrow*. The fact that we can, however, imagine this, merely reinforces what I have already said, that there is no one-to-one relation between a class of speech acts and the grammatical form of an utterance, and that it appears that almost any utterance can have almost any function in some context and situation. It is thus not only the *form* of the utterance which determines how we understand it, but the characteristics of the whole speech situation. This is what makes it so difficult to categorize speech acts in a systematic and scientifically valid way, and why we have to fall back very largely on *ad hoc* criteria which are based on common sense. One of the great unresolved problems in linguistics is to discover what the relations between the formal features of the utterance and the situation are which lead to a particular interpretation of that utterance as *a warning, a promise, an assertion* or an example of some other class of speech act. We would dearly like to give an explanation of that commonly heard remark: *I understand what you are saying, but I don't know what you mean*; sometimes shortened simply to: *I don't get you*.

Speech functions

One way we can tackle this problem is to start from an analysis of a speech situation. To begin with there must be, of course, at least two *participants*, the *I* and *you*, a speaker and a hearer, or 'sender' and 'receiver'. It is necessary to insist on this even where, as in communication in writing, the participants will normally not be physically present at the same time and place. Every writer is writing *to* someone or *for* someone, however unspecifically he may visualize his readers. I have already referred to the case where we talk to ourselves and suggested that such activity is connected in some way with our thought processes or has an auto-regulatory function, but we are here concerned with communication, that is, with the social function of language. Talking to yourself is not a social activity in adults, though the distinction in young children may not be so clear (Piaget, 1926).

For communication to take place, *contact* must be established between the participants. Just the physical nearness of two people does not establish a speech situation; we have to get people to give their attention. Indeed a deliberate refusal to give one's attention in certain situations, what we call 'cutting someone', is a significant act in itself. We can usefully make a distinction between *establishing* and *maintaining* contact. The first is achieved by acts which attract the attention of a hearer and make clear that it is him and not someone else we wish to engage in conversation with. Such acts are called '*calls*' of one sort or another, e.g. *Hey, Bill!, Excuse me, sir!* We can call this physical contact. But not only must physical contact be established, a channel of communication be opened, it must be maintained. We often 'test the channel', by such expressions as *can you hear me?* or encourage it – *speak up*. But contact is not just physical, it is also psychological. We must maintain *rapport* with our hearer, keep him interested, friendly and cooperative, keep the conversation going. We do this by what is often called 'small talk' – the weather, inquiries about health, giving praise and encouragement. We also test our psychological contact with our hearer: *Do you get me?*; *If you follow me.* . . . And we help our hearer to do so by organizing our discourse in a logical fashion: *First of all* . . .; *What I mean is* . . .; *my next point* . . .; *Now I want to explain* . . .; *As I have already pointed out.* . . . This is a sort of 'signposting' of our discourse.

Conversation or communications between people do not take place in a vacuum, but at a particular time and place, in a physical and temporal *setting*. They may be sitting or standing, walking or driving along in a car. They may be in a crowd or alone together, among friends or strangers, in a room, a cathedral or a street. All these factors may play a part in what goes on in the conversation, but they are not what it is *about*. Where we are, who we are with and at what time may limit what we talk about and how we talk about it, but they are not, for that reason, the *topic* of our conversation. Of course there are places and times for talking about certain things as also for not talking about them. The topic of discourse is obviously an important element in the speech situation. Whatever the function of an utterance may be, it will nearly always be about something, it will have what I have called a propositional element in it. There may or may not be some direct relation between the setting of a speech episode and the propositional element in the speech, but there will always be a connection between the topic of the discourse and its propositional content, even if it is about purely imaginary things like fairies, goblins or unicorns.

We may establish contact with another person and yet be unable to communicate with him any further through language. This can happen if we do not share the same set of verbal conventions, if we have no linguistic *code* in common. The formal features of the language shared by the participants are themselves an important factor in the speech situation.

When we communicate with someone we communicate something, a message. The ways in which we do this may be constrained by the situation in various ways: if it is noisy, we may have to shout; if extensive, we may have to abbreviate; if formal, we will select a different set of words from those we might select in an informal situation. But even after we have taken all these things into account, the same message can still be communicated in a variety of different ways. The form of the message is itself a factor in the speech situation; it can be manipulated so that it communicates something.

Each of these seven factors – the speaker, the hearer, contact between them, the linguistic code used, the setting, the topic and the form of the message – may be the focus of the speech act, the element in the situation to which the activity is oriented. With each of these factors a different function of speech can be associated. If the orientation is towards the speaker, then we have what has been called the personal function of language; it is through this function that the speaker reveals his attitude towards what he is speaking about, and eventually reveals something of his personality to his hearer. It is not just that he expresses his emotion *through* language, but his emotion *at* what he is talking about. As hearers, it is merely informative that our interlocutor is angry or sad or happy, it becomes communicative when we associate his emotional state with what he is talking about, that is, *why* he is angry, sad or happy.

Hearer-oriented speech is that in which the function is directive. It is the function of controlling the behaviour of a participant, not only to get him to do something, act or speak, but to behave in general according to some plan or system to the speaker's liking. This may be done by command, request or warning, or by some general admonitory statement such as *People generally do (or don't) do this or that*; or *You mustn't do this or that*, by invoking the legal, moral or customary sanctions of society.

Where the focus is on the contact between the participants we find speech which functions to establish relations, maintain them, promote feelings of goodwill and fellowship, or social solidarity. These are typically formulaic, or ritual: leave-takings, greetings, remarks about the weather, inquiries about the health of the family. These functions, sometimes called *phatic*, are also performed by gesture, physical contact, facial expression, such as waves, shaking hands or smiles. They 'soften up the target' and keep it 'soft'.

The topic-oriented function of speech, often called the *referential* function, is that which looms largest in most people's minds. It is typically realized by the propositional element in the utterance. As we have seen, it is this function that gave rise to the traditional notion that language was for the communication of thought, for making statements about how the speaker perceives the way things in the world are.

We now come to the two functions associated with the code and with the message. In some ways these are the most difficult to pin down. When people communicate with each other, they must be satisfied not only that they have established contact by 'testing the channel' as it were – *Can you hear me?* – but also that communication is being maintained, by testing their mutual understanding – *Do you follow?*; *Do you see?* This is what we can call the contact-oriented function. But the best way of ensuring that communication is successful is to see to it that the participants really do share the conventions of the code. When two people play a game like chess it is not usually necessary to check before they start whether they agree about the rules, because they are known, well-established and unequivocal. But when people play the 'language game' they are constantly having to make sure that they are playing it according to the same set of rules. This is the function of definitions. A definition is a statement of a rule in the language game which the speaker invites the hearer to accept so that the conversation may proceed. Science has been called a way of talking about the world, and if we look at it this way then a science textbook is a rule-book for the language of talking about the world. This function of language has been called the *metalinguistic* function, or language about language, and is the principal one in learning and teaching.

Where the focus is on the message, we have to do with the *imaginative* functions of language. Here we must make quite sure that we do not confuse two things: the use of language to express original or unusual thoughts or ideas, feelings, fantasies or what have you, and the imaginative use of language to express what may be mundane, matter-of-fact things or pure nonsense. The two, of course, occur together and may become inextricably bound up. But by the imaginative function of language I mean the second of these two. Language may be manipulated for its own sake, for the pleasure it gives speaker and hearer. Nursery rhymes or jingles may not be 'about' anything; or, if they are, not about anything interesting or even important. Their function is achieved through their sound, their rhythm, their tunes. They are just one sort of language use whose function is imaginative. *Pat-a-cake, pat-a-cake, baker's man* is not intended as a recipe.

The analysis of speech functions given in the preceding pages follows fairly closely that given by Hymes (1968) and it is not difficult to see how it fits, at a certain point at least, the classification of speech acts. Clearly the social acts have to do with establishing and maintaining contact while the acts of exercising rights and powers are related to the directive function of language. Similarly, the referential function of language is largely carried on by means of those acts which adopt a point of view with regard to some state of affairs real or hypothetical. In the at-present primitive state of our knowledge in this field we need both accounts even though there may be some overlap between them. But what both accounts insist on is that any single utterance may have a multiple function or represent more than one act. An utterance may assert some state of affairs *and* demand some action of the hearer, it may have both a referential and directive function. *Fetch me that book*, for instance, both *asserts* the existence and location of an object, *names* it and *directs* the hearer to do something with it.

Language teaching and the function of language

We do not know for certain whether all the speech functions just outlined are to be found in all cultures. What is certain is that the relative importance of these different functions may vary from culture to culture; their distribution may vary. There are some cultures in which the contact function of language, the use of language to establish and maintain social contact and goodwill, appears to be more important. Some people believe, for example, that the relative frequency of thanking is different in America and Britain. This sort of difference leads to judgements that in certain classes, countries, social groups, etc. people are more 'polite'. In Britain, for example, we do not have a ritual reply to an expression of thanks, as in America, *You're welcome*, or France, *Je vous en prie*, or Germany, *Bitte*. But this does not mean that there is no appropriate verbal response in such a situation – only that its form is less predictable. In some cultures the asking of questions is considered unacceptable in certain roles, in others the poetic use of language is greater.

For anyone to participate in the social life of the community he has to be able to communicate and be communicated to. That is why the learner is learning a language. Leaving aside the case of a learner who studies language simply as a means to educational advancement and then proceeds to neglect it, anyone who learns a language does so, or is required to do so, so that it may become functional or useful in some way. This does not mean that the range of functions aimed at will be those at the command of a native speaker. The functions may be highly restricted. A language learner may know very exactly what he wants the language for, or he may have no clear idea at all. As we saw in chapter 1, for any language-teaching operation we need to specify its aims. These aims can be expressed in terms of what we want the learner to be able to do at the end of the course. These might be formulated in terms of what intentions he must be able to communicate, what classes of speech act he must be able to perform or what speech functions he should command. Or we can approach the matter in a different way by specifying what roles he is going to fulfil in the society. A social role is a cluster of rights and obligations and involves a certain range of behaviour more or less clearly defined, depending on the nature of the role in question. In most societies, the learner will never be integrated into it as a full member with all the multiple roles that a member of that society may achieve or have ascribed to him. He is likely to have ascribed to him the role of 'foreigner'. This role has certain expectations associated with it, very often a great tolerance of deviation from the various norms of behaviour, both linguistic and non-linguistic. How often do we hear the oddness of a foreigner excused with words like: *You can't expect him to know that, he's a foreigner*. However, it is very probable that the expectations of foreigners, that is, the role-behaviour of 'foreigner', may be defined very differently from culture to culture. For example, it is widely held that the French are less tolerant of linguistic deviation in a foreign speaker than the British. Unfortunately, we still know very little about what the role of foreigner is in different cultures in terms of rights and expectations. The evidence we have is largely anecdotal and subjective. While the learner has, as it were, the role of 'foreigner' thrust upon him, there may be many other roles – occupational, such as scientist or salesman; independent, such as tourist or sportsman – which he may also wish to assume. With each of these roles there is associated a range of speech functions which he must command.

There is a lot of interest nowadays in what has been called scientific or technical language, and the need to teach it. I shall return to this in later chapters, but it may be more useful to take the view that what we are teaching the learner is not 'scientific' French or German, but to equip him to assume the role of 'visiting scientist' in France or Germany. This is by no means the same thing. The role of scientist goes well beyond the ability to conduct scientific discourse. But even if we were to specify the teaching aims in terms of the types of discourse in which a learner was preparing to participate, the notion of language functions is still relevant. Much of the research into so-called 'scientific language' has concentrated on the formal properties of the language used by scientists, the grammatical structures used and their relative frequencies, the nature of the vocabulary and the relative frequency of different words (Huddleston, 1971). It has turned out that the differences between such discourse and non-scientific discourse have not been as great as might have been expected. A more promising approach might be to analyse scientific language in terms of its functions. We might find, for instance, that it was, as has been already suggested, predominantly metalinguistic, or that there was a great preponderance of predictive or referential speech acts and a virtual absence of directive acts, or that it had little personal and no poetic function. Syllabuses for language teaching operations have tended to be expressed in terms of a list of linguistic forms to be learned. Perhaps too little attention has been directed to what these forms are to be used for. One hears frequent complaints from teachers that learners seem to be able to cope with the language while in the classroom, but fail to make use of it satisfactorily outside. This suggests that the learners have acquired speech functions appropriate to the classroom or the role of 'language learner', but no other.

Until we know a great deal more about the relation between linguistic forms and their function in speech we shall have difficulty in drawing up a 'functional' syllabus in formal linguistic terms. We may teach the learner to form interrogative sentences, and fail to teach him how to ask questions in an appropriate way. Until we know more about this relationship, we cannot teach linguistic functions in a systematic way. Looked at from a functional point of view, there is a large learning task for the learner which the teacher is relatively powerless to help with. It is a situation which we shall meet with frequently in this book. Language learners, if we are lucky, eventually learn a great deal that we do not, or cannot, teach them, because we have an inadequate description of it. This is the case with learning the functions of language – to use language to some purpose. The only solution we have to offer at present is that the learner be exposed to as a large a quantity and variety of duly contextualized language as possible. He must hear and see 'language in action'. This does not mean just listening to it. The whole speech situation must be presented. He cannot, for example, tell from the sound alone whether *That paint's wet* is a statement or a warning; whether *You'll come back* is a prediction or a command. At least then the data will be available to him from which to discover the rules and conventions of verbal behaviour for himself. We are concerned with teaching him not just to produce grammatically acceptable strings of words, but also to use language to some purpose, to communicate and be communicated to, to assume certain roles.

Chapter 3
The Variability of Language

Language and languages

When we hear someone referred to as a 'good linguist', it is more than likely that what the speaker means is that he has a command of several different languages. Similarly, those who are called 'modern linguists' are people who study 'modern languages'. It is only within a small academic community that 'a good linguist' is a person who is good at 'linguistics' or a 'modern linguist' is contrasted with a 'traditional linguist'. The ambiguity of the term 'linguist' reflects the difficulty which most people have in conceiving of the study of language as something different from the learning of, or study of, *a* language or languages. Now, in a sense it is true that one cannot study human language as such without examining linguistic data, i.e. utterances made by people. But what the linguist is trying to do is to find out what are the particular characteristics of human language. He does this through a study of human language in all its myriad manifestations. It is not so long ago, however, that linguists despaired of ever being able to make general statements about all human language. They thought that the best one could do was to investigate the nature of some limited body of utterances drawn from some particular group of speakers.

The difficulty that people have in conceiving of the study of language as such is not surprising. They are aware that human language presents itself in such a vast array of different forms, sounds, tunes, rhythms, that they cannot believe that there is anything in common between all these manifestations, other than that they are produced by the same organs as they themselves use to talk with. Considering some of the peculiar sounds they hear they may even suspect that this is not universally the case.

The other thing that strikes one is that people from different parts of the world obviously do not always understand each other when they speak. If there were anything common to all their means of linguistic communication one might at least expect some degree of *mutual intelligibility*. This expectation is all the more reasonable since people know that they can make themselves understood for fairly basic purposes by means of gesture and facial expression when they go abroad. On the other hand, they all know that there are lots of people, generally those who live around them, with whom they can communicate through language. They also know that there are many people elsewhere in the world with whom they cannot communicate with through language, but that these people have living around them others with whom they can communicate.

All these obvious facts give rise to the notion of different 'languages' and 'language communities'. A language community is, on this account, simply a group of people who communicate by means of a 'common' language. There is, however, a serious snag to this definition. Unless we can define *a language* in terms other than of the people who speak it, or *a language community* in terms which do not include a mention of a common language, we are in a circularity.

Let us attack this problem by considering how we might define a language independently of those who speak it. We might start by saying that a language is characterized by having a more or less unitary grammatical, lexical and phonological system. In other words, we would judge whether any particular utterance which was presented to us was or was not an utterance in that language by examining its formal characteristics. To do this we should have to have available, of course, a grammar and dictionary of that language. But grammars and dictionaries are based upon a body of data drawn from a language. They *presuppose*, therefore, that we know what a language is before we start. Again we are in a circularity. The descriptive linguist *as linguist* is not able within his discipline to *define* a language. As Haugen (1966) says, 'There is still no calculus that permits us to describe the difference between languages in a coherent and theoretically valid way.'

We can attack the problem in a different way. We can say that people who speak one and the same language can understand each other, that they are mutually intelligible. A speech community is a group of people who can all understand each other when they speak. This is quite a promising argument, so let us pursue it. The first thing anyone notices about the speech of people he regularly interacts with is that it is different from his own in a number of more or less insignificant ways. They use some words he never does, their accents are slightly different perhaps and they may use forms which he calls dialectal or 'bad grammar'. This does not seriously impair communication between them. However, he may sometimes meet people whose speech is sufficiently different from his own actually to make it difficult for him to understand and be understood at first hearing. Less often he may meet people with whom he has the greatest difficulty in communicating, so greatly does their speech differ from his own. Finally, he will, of course, meet people with whom, with the best will in the world, he cannot communicate through speech at all. At what point along this continuum of mutual intelligibility do we draw a line and say that we are concerned with different languages? And is mutual intelligibility a simple function of formal linguistic difference? Let us take the example of the Swedes and the Norwegians. Linguistically, their ways of speaking are quite similar and they understand each other quite readily, and yet they *are said* to speak different languages, and they themselves *claim* to speak different languages. Or to take another example: the Scottish crofter and the Jamaican smallholder do not readily understand each other, and we can easily show that their speech is linguistically more different than Swedish and Norwegian, and yet they are both said, and claim, to speak the 'same language'. The question then is, how formally similar must two manners of speaking be to be considered merely varieties of the 'same language', and how mutually intelligible must people be for us to regard them as speaking the 'same language'? Quite apart from the difficulty of *measuring* in any rigorous and meaningful way both the mutual intelligibility and similarity of two different forms of language, the decision is bound to be essentially *arbitrary*.

Let us take one more example. Wolff (1959) reports the case of the Nembe and the Kalabari of the Eastern Niger Delta. They speak forms of language which are linguistically so similar that linguists agree that they are essentially forms of the 'same language'. The Nembe, furthermore, recognize this similarity and say that they have no difficulty in understanding the language of the Kalabari. The latter, on the other hand, maintain that Nembe is a very different language and that they cannot understand it at all, except for a few odd words here and there.

There is, therefore, no clear, simple relation between linguistic similarity and mutual intelligibility. We must conclude that there is some *subjective* social–psychological dimension in mutual intelligibility. We seem to understand those we are prepared to or expect to understand, and do not understand those we do not expect to. Mutual intelligibility depends, in part at least, on the *attitudes* we have towards our own and others' manner of speech, and these are closely connected with the attitudes we have to the community to which they belong, their political and social relations with us, and our and their view of the relative statuses of our two communities.

The outcome of this discussion is that linguistic similarity and mutual intelligibility are connected, but not directly, and that neither provides us with a criterion for defining a language. What is left, then, of our concept of a speech community if it cannot be defined in terms of mutual intelligibility or linguistic similarity? The clue has already been given. The concept of 'a language' is a matter of social psychology. A speech community is made up of people who *regard themselves* as speaking the same language; it need have no other defining attributes. In other words, a speech community is defined in terms of *its beliefs*, not its language. This avoids the circularity in definition I referred to earlier. Of course, a speech community usually shares many other beliefs about itself; it also usually has a common history, literary tradition and writing system. An English speaker, then, is a person who regards the language he speaks to be English; in doing so, he tacitly accepts some *norm*. By this I mean that he has in his head some abstract notion or 'ideal' of the language. He may not always 'live up to' this ideal in his actual behaviour. But people sharing the same norm agree in general terms what are and are not the formal features of the language (Labov, 1970b) and, particularly when they are writing or speaking carefully (when they are selfconscious, about their language behaviour, as for instance on formal occasions), their performances will tend to become more alike and will shift towards the norm. As Labov says, 'Social attitudes to language are extremely uniform through a speech community.' This explains why a Norwegian, whose speech is formally similar to that of the Swede and is intelligible to him, is not a Swedish speaker. He does not regard himself as a Swedish speaker and the norm he accepts is different from the norm accepted by the Swedish speaker. It also explains why the Scottish crofter and

Jamaican smallholder, whose speech is most of the time formally very different and mutually unintelligible, nevertheless speak the 'same language'. They accept the same norm. They both regard themselves as English speakers.

Dialect and idiolect

Although members of a speech community may have extremely uniform attitudes to their language, their actual individual language behaviour is very variable. The speech of each individual is different in some variable degree from every other speaker. While he may accept some forms of the other's speech as being part of their 'common language', these forms may not feature at all in his own usage. He may even stigmatize some of them in such terms as 'sloppy', 'vulgar', 'dialectal', 'nasal' or 'guttural'. The language of each individual is unique and peculiar to himself. This language we call his *idiolect*. For certain purposes – speech therapy, psychiatric diagnosis – there may be reasons for studying the language of individuals. But what the linguist is usually interested in is making general statements about 'a language'. What the sociolinguist, on the other hand is interested in is what Fishman (1968) has called the 'patterned covariation of language and society', the way that linguistic structure is related to social structure. This is what he calls the *Sociology of Language* to distinguish it from the study of speech functions, which he calls *Sociolinguistics*.

Although people are unique in their use of language, they may, nevertheless, be classified together in various ways linguistically and socially. A linguistic classification would be that of people whose dialects had some major part of their linguistic features in common, who shared a common code or norm. A sociological classification would be that of people who shared similar education, belonged in the same income brackets, had similar occupations, or were related in a kinship group or lived in the same area. There are, of course, many different sorts of sociological classification based on different criteria. What we wish to relate is the linguistic classification and the social classification. There are two dimensions in which it is usual to make such a connection – geographical and socio-economic. Language can be said to show variability according to geographical and social space. Variability in a geographic dimension is called, following tradition, dialectal. Variability in a social dimension is also often called dialectal; but I shall follow more recent terminology and call it 'sociolectal' when I wish to make a distinction between geographical and social dialects (Fishman, 1971). The actual points along the continuum of variation at which the boundaries between one dialect or sociolect and another are established is essentially arbitrary. We can put this another way: both sociolectal and dialectal varieties 'merge' into one another. Since this variability is two-dimensional we can illustrate the relationship diagrammatically as in Figure 1. Within this space the idiolectal repertoire, 'the totality of linguistic forms regularly employed in the course of socially significant interaction' (Gumperz, 1964, p. 137) of any individual or any group we care to isolate sociologically can be plotted. The point of intersection can be regarded as some sort of a 'norm', although the degree to which any *randomly selected* group of speakers would agree upon the characteristics of such a norm is uncertain. If, however, we select a group of speakers having some set of sociological characteristics in common, e.g. education, social class, geographical residence, the degree of agreement about where the norm lay might be greater. Nevertheless, as studies of *acceptability* have shown (Labov, 1966; Quirk and Svartvik, 1966) even in these circumstances, there is not as much agreement as one might expect.

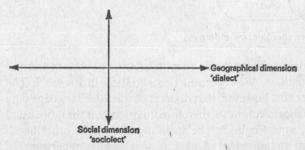

Figure 1 Social and geographical dimensions of variability

However, careful investigation of the speech of individuals does not show a consistent use of 'one unitary idiolectal system'. When a person talks he will vary his performance in both the sociological and geographical dimension in response to the social situation in which he finds himself – 'who he is' in relation to 'who his hearer is'. Equally

Figure 2 Dialect or sociolect switching (a)

important will be the degree of 'attention' which he pays to how he speaks. He will shift backwards and forwards along these dimensions in the direction which he perceives as the 'norm' or the standard. This behaviour has been called 'dialect switching' or 'code switching'. From the sociolinguist's point of view a better name would be dialect or code *shifting*, since, as I have suggested, the distinction between one dialect or code and another is essentially an arbitrary one. It is here that we must recognize openly that the linguist and the sociolinguist differ in their objectives and hence in their accounts. The linguist must have, if he is to construct a theory about language, a *well-defined* or 'homogeneous' set of data on which to base his description. He calls these data the utterances *in one and the same language* or one and the same dialect.

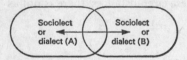

Figure 3 Dialect or sociolect switching (b)

A speaker can be said, therefore, to switch from one code to another in different situations. We represent this situation in Figure 2. The linguist will concede, however, that dialects of the same language may have characteristics in common, therefore this picture is the more usual one of overlap, as in Figure 3. The sociolinguist, on the other hand, prefers to regard an individual speaker as possessing a 'repertoire' of forms, or a 'sheaf of grammars' as Hockett (1967, p. 220) has called them, within which he shifts about, picking his language here and there; more as in Figure 4. Labov (1970b) suggests that a language can best be described not just in terms of one set of invariant rules, but partly in terms of *invariant* rules and partly in terms of *variable* rules. For example, an 'invariant' rule in English would be that a definite article and a possessive adjective cannot occur before the same head-

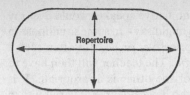

Figure 4 Shifting within the repertoire of a speaker

noun, e.g. *the my book*. An example of a 'variable' rule would be to say the word *soften* could be pronounced [sɔftən], [sɔfən] or [sɔfn̩], depending upon certain specific characteristics of the speech situation. Or that the message: 'He told me nothing' can be expressed in the form *He didn't tell me anything* or *He didn't tell me nothing* in different situational contexts. As we shall see in the next chapter some descriptions of the vocabulary and pronunciation of a language do attempt to incorporate this sort of variability. The drawback of such a proposal is that we must first have a developed theory about social structure and speech situations in order to categorize and describe all the relevant features of a speech situation which correlate with different linguistic forms. We are far from having such a theory or description at the present time, although certain sociological variables can already be related with certain linguistic forms. When this can be done, we can speak of the linguistic forms which relate to these sociological variables as linguistic 'markers'. Thus it is possible to relate certain linguistic markers with differences in social class, or with differences in regional residence. Labov (1966) has related such shifts in pronunciation with such variables in performance as speaking casually, paying attention to how one is speaking, reading aloud, pronouncing isolated words or speaking pairs of words which are very similar in form.

From an applied point of view we do not need to take one or the other point of view. Given their objectives, both approaches are equally valid. If we are thinking of how we are going to select the material for teaching, the linguist's account is obviously relevant. If we approach our task as a problem of what sort of situation the learner is going to have to participate in we shall want to make use of the notion of 'repertoire', and in that case the idea of variable rules is of great relevance. Teachers are often asked by their pupils 'Is it right to say this or that?' They expect to get a clear answer. Sometimes the choice is between something which no native speaker would ever say and something some native speakers might say – in some situations. In that case the answer can be a categorical *yes* or *no*. But often such a question has the answer: *both are right*. The teacher will then have to describe the context in which one or the other is appropriate. It is sometimes surprising that learners who have a degree of variability in their own mother tongue should expect there to be no such variability in the second language.

The fact that the distinction between different dialects cannot be sharply drawn does not make the concept useless or invalid. A dialect has just as much social–psychological reality as a language. If members of a community recognize the existence of dialects and sociolects in their language by their behaviour and the way they talk about their language, then they exist. Where this is the case, we can speak of the community as being bi-dialectal or multi-dialectal. Similarly, where a political or other social group or community uses more than one different language, we speak of that community as being bilingual or multi-lingual. It is, of course, the rule rather than the exception for political states to be multi-lingual. Britain is no exception in this respect.

Where we do find two or more dialects or languages in regular use in a community we have a situation which Ferguson (1959) has called 'diglossia'. He has observed that in diglossic communities there is a strong tendency to give one of the dialects or languages a higher status or prestige, and to reserve it for certain functions in society, such as government, education, the law, religion, literature, press, radio and television. The prestige dialect is often known as the *standard* dialect, it is the one most frequently described by linguists as 'the language', and represents, particularly in communities with highly developed educational systems and long histories of political unity, the 'norm' of language recognized by most speakers. Some countries have set up institutions, such as l'Académie Française in France, to regulate and codify the standard dialect. The process of codification is sometimes called 'language standardization' (Ray, 1963). But even when no such regulatory body exists we find situations where high and low varieties are widely recognized and accepted, and have fairly clearly defined differential functions in the society. Such is the case in Switzerland, where 'Schwizerdutch' and 'Hochdeutsch' subsist side by side, or in Greece with its Demotiki and Katharevoussa, or in the Arabic speaking countries in their well-defined distinction between classical and demotic Arabic. In these countries the language situation is relatively stable. This is not the case in most newly independent states in Africa (Spencer, 1963) or the Indian subcontinent; there the functions of the various indigenous dialects and languages are not so well defined, and there exists what Le Page (1964) has called a 'national language question'. Decisions about what languages and dialects to use for what purpose in the community is a political matter for governments to decide. These decisions may be based on no more than political or racial prejudice, or they may be based on a careful survey of the various functions which the different languages and dialects actually fulfil in the community. Investigations into matters of this sort are the central concern of the sociology of language, and planning the most efficient arrangements of language function in such communities is a branch of applied linguistics often called *language planning*.[1] Where the questions concern which dialect to select for teaching, then we call it the 'problem of the model'. For example, there have been discussions as to whether the 'model' of English to be taught in West African countries should be a British or a West African dialect (Prator, 1968). The reader will see the relevance of this work to the planning of the total language teaching operation. It bears on the question of which language or languages to teach in the schools of the country and at which level and to whom these languages should be taught. This matter will be taken up again in chapter 9.

I have said that within a language community – a group of people who consider they speak the 'same language' – there may exist one or more socially recognized forms of the language which correlate with the social and/or geographical structure of the community. The individual's idiolect is not a well-defined thing; his speech varies up to a point according to the social and geographical situation in which he happens to find himself. Each member of the community acquires some degree of ability to 'shift' his manner of speaking along either of these dimensions. It is largely through formal education in the school that he develops this ability. When a child first acquires language, the particu-

1. The term 'language planning' is sometimes also used in the sense of 'language standardization' as described above. They are, of course, different but related operations.

lar form he learns is, of course, the one he hears in his home environment, especially the speech of other children of the same age. This will be a particular dialectal form, whether standard or non-standard. The educational system will most probably make use of some form of the standard dialect. A particular dialect selected for educational, administrative or governmental purposes is often called a 'superposed' variety of the language. In some places it might better be called an 'imposed' variety. On going to school, then, the child is faced with the problem of learning a new form of his language. The standard form may vary quite markedly from the form he has acquired as his 'mother dialect'. We have then in most countries a situation in which the great majority of children, on entering the educational system, have a learning task which is similar in many respects to the learning of a 'second language'. The magnitude of this task will vary from child to child, of course, but the task is a very real one and not sufficiently recognized by most teachers (Labov, 1970a). This is the state of affairs we find quite regularly in our large industrial cities in Britain, and it is most obvious and acute where West Indian children are involved. The fact that the language they have acquired in the home is called 'English' must not obscure this fact. Of course for immigrant children from the Indian sub-continent the language of the school is not just a 'second dialect'; it is a 'second language'.

The distinction between a second language and a second dialect is quite clear. But a further distinction is often made between the learning of a 'second' language and a 'foreign' language. As far as the learner is concerned both are equally strange, but it is a useful distinction and has to do with the function that the language has in the community. English is a second language in the Welsh speaking parts of Wales, or in Nigeria, because it fulfils some function in the life of the community of the sort that has already been discussed. A foreign language, on the other hand, is one which has no such functions in the community. Thus, French is a foreign language everywhere in Britain, as English is in France.

Speaking from the point of view of the school pupil we find a continuum of 'strangeness' in the language he may meet in the school system. His home language may be the same as that of the school, in which case he has the least problems. He may be a native speaker of some non-standard dialect which varies to a greater or lesser extent from the norm of the school. In this case he has to acquire a second dialect. This includes the Glaswegian child as well as the West Indian child. He may be a native speaker of Welsh or Urdu, in which case he faces a second language. Although these differences appear to be differences of *kind*, it is probably wiser to regard them as psycholinguistically differences of degree, in the light of what has been said about the relations between dialects and languages. The difficulties the learner faces will be determined as much by his *attitudes* to the language of the school as by the formal linguistic differences between it and his home language. In other words, the problems he faces are as much social, cultural and psychological as linguistic.

Code and use of code

The dimensions of variability in language which we have been discussing so far, and have called dialectal, have been related to social characteristics of the speaker. They have been what Halliday, Strevens and McIntosh (1964) have called *user-related* features. The dialect or range of dialects, social and geographical, possessed or acquired by someone is a function of *who* he is in society. When we first meet someone, it is very largely on the basis of how he speaks that we 'place' him socially. But there are other dimensions of variability in language which are, to some extent, independent of who the speaker is socially. Who we are in terms of our social class and regional origin does not, for example, determine (although it may influence) what we talk about, how much we rely on written language or the sorts of people we interact with. These other dimensions of variability in language are related to the situations in which we use language; they are *use-related* varieties. At this point it is important not to confuse these differences in the use of language with what were called speech functions in chapter 2. We make bets, or requests, or issue challenges *whoever* we are. These acts are independent of the dimensions of dialect or sociolect. Of course, the linguistic *form* of the bet will vary according to who we are, but it will also vary according to who we are making the bet with, making the request of, or issuing the challenge to. It will also vary according to whether the bet, request or challenge is written or spoken. Furthermore, what the request is for, what the bet is about, what the challenge is to do, depends upon the situation. We do not challenge a lawyer to run a race with us in his role as lawyer, but we may challenge him to name the author of some obscure work on property law in this capacity.

We can identify in what has been said so far at least three dimensions of variability in language use, or use of the system or code as I shall call it in the next chapter. The first is related to the *relative social status* of speaker and hearer. Social status is related to social role. Thus we would expect to find the language used by a teacher speaking to a pupil to be different from that used by a pupil speaking to a classmate, or a judge speaking to a prisoner or to a counsel. This status-related dimension of variability is called *style*. A well known illustration of it was given by Joos (1962) where he arbitrarily divided up the continuum of variability into five stages of formality. An amusing illustration of these five 'styles' has been given by Strevens (1964):

Frozen: Visitors should make their way at once to the upper floor by way of the staircase
Formal: Visitors should go up the stairs at once
Consultative: Would you mind going upstairs right away, please?
Casual: Time you all went upstairs now
Intimate: Up you go, chaps!

In some communities a shift in style is associated with a shift in dialect or a switch in language. Rubin (1962) reports on the situation in Paraguay where two languages, Spanish and Guaraní, are both current. He identifies six social parameters in the speech situation which seem to control the selection of one or the other language: formality, intimacy, seriousness of discourse, mother tongue of speaker and sex of speaker. Only the latter two are social characteristics of the speaker; the rest refer to features of the speech situation. Gumperz (1966) also has investigated the factors in speech situations in Norway which appear to correlate with selection of dialects and styles of speech.

The second user-related dimension of variability is what we can call *medium*-writing or speaking. We do not need to enter here into the question of the linguistic relation between them, which I have called the primacy of speech. What is certain is that written and spoken language differ linguistically from each other in a number of significant ways in terms of their grammar and vocabulary. The reasons for this are twofold. Firstly, in writing we cannot make use of the information carried by features of the voice such as intonation, rhythm and stress or voice quality. We must therefore compensate for this by various alternative linguistic devices. Secondly, we use written language in different situations from speaking; for example, we do not have a 'hearer' present in time and place, indeed we may not have a specific hearer or group of hearers in mind as we must do in a speech situation. Of course, writing with a pen or pencil is not the only sort of writing; we may use a chisel on stone. This introduces rather severe limitations which are obviously reflected in the nature of the language. Another limitation on written language is illustrated by the cost of transmitting the message (e.g. 'telegraphese') or the shortage of time for self-editing (e.g. 'journalese').

There is one further important dimension of use-related variability: what we can call *role-related variability*. I have already introduced the notion of role in connection with *style*. Every role in society has a status given to it by society. Thus, we speak of the role of a judge as being 'high' status, whilst the role of policeman is of a higher status than that of convict. Some roles are of less determinate status. What is the status of a sick person, for example? Sociologists speak about roles in different ways and classify them variously, e.g. *ascribed* roles, such as sex and age, *achieved* roles, *occupational* roles, and so on. We find most clearly a dimension of variability of language use associated with occupational roles, although in some communities sex roles are associated with variability in language, as was the case in Paraguay. Thus we identify religious language, legal language, medical language or, more exactly, priest language, lawyer language and doctor language. To use once more our previous illustration, we would expect a bet, a request or a challenge issued by a lawyer *in his professional role* to differ linguistically from the bets, requests or challenges he may make in his role as a father or president of the local football club. We must, therefore, allow for a dimension of variability in language use which is *role-related*.

Any attempt by the linguist to isolate and describe a religious, legal or medical code of language (or *a fortiori*, formal, casual or intimate code) is an arbitrary proceeding. It is even more arbitrary than regarding sociolects as well-defined. They do not normally have social–psychological reality; people are not consciously aware of the dimension of variability and do not have names for different varieties as they do in the case of dialects. For this reason, it is preferable to speak of people's use of language in different contexts as being 'marked' by certain linguistic features, rather than to speak of them using one or another variety of language. It is one of the tasks of the sociolinguist to identify such markers. Perhaps one of the most readily recognized markers are the forms we use to address people: *sir, Mr* or *Mrs, dear, darling, old man, Brown* or *George*. These indicate fairly reliably the social relation that we feel to exist between us and our hearer. Brown and Gilman (1960), for example, have studied the way the people whose language possesses a distinction between second person singular and plural pronouns, as in French *tu/vous* or German *du/Sie*, use these forms in different situations. They were able to relate these markers to situational features which they called power and solidarity.

Finally, it is necessary here once again to note that shifts in any of these dimensions of variability – medium, style, role – may be associated with a shift or switch in dialect or language. Thus, in some communities certain aspects of the use of language in religion or law may involve a switch of language, whilst a shift from speech to writing will often bring with it a change from non-standard to standard dialect, as will a shift in style.

Language functions and language teaching

The individual in his mother tongue has a 'repertoire' or 'sheaf of grammars', standard, non-standard, written, spoken, formal, informal and so on, from which he selects the appropriate forms according to the situation. Native speakers vary greatly in the size and range of the repertoire they have available, which depends upon their social background, their interests, their membership of various social groups, their education or occupation. A speaker's freedom of social action is dependant upon the range of his repertoire. His lack of a command of some code or style will seriously limit his freedom in certain directions. We may, for example, refuse an invitation to dinner just as much because we don't command the appropriate style of speech as because we don't know which knife and fork to choose. Limitations on our linguistic repertoire may produce social insecurity in just the same way as limitations in other aspects of our social skills (Labov, 1966).

Our ability to participate as members of social communities and groups depends upon our controlling the range of linguistic and other behaviour considered appropriate by those communities and groups. The learner of a second language is preparing to use that language for certain purposes, in certain roles and in certain situations. I have already spoken about his linguistic needs in terms of the roles he may assume, and we have seen that he is likely to have ascribed to him the primary role of foreigner, in which his communicative needs are normally going to be much more restricted than those of a native speaker. In preparing a teaching programme we have to take into account what his needs may be, and we will do this in terms of the social situations he is going to have to participate in and the social groups he may aspire to be accepted by, perhaps not as a 'full member' but as a 'foreign associate'. This will enable us to set about specifying the linguistic 'repertoire' which he will need to command. It is this proposed repertoire which forms the basis of a syllabus for a learner.

A language can be regarded as a 'constellation of dialects'. These dialects are related to each other linguistically by possessing a major part of their grammatical systems in common. I shall refer to this as the *common core*, which forms the basis of any syllabus. It represents what anyone who learns the language for whatever purpose *must* acquire; it does not constitute all that he *needs* to acquire. The possession of the common core alone does not enable the learner to behave appropriately in any particular situation; to do this he needs to know those parts of the code appropriate to that situation *not* included in the common core. We can illustrate this by taking an example from Arabic. Here we find an extreme case of diglossia where the classical and demotic codes are strikingly different, the classical being principally a written language and the demotic a spoken language. A person who has acquired only those forms of the language which are common to both classical and demotic Arabic will not be able to communicate adequately in either speech or writing. To do one or the other he will have to learn an additional set of linguistic forms. Which particular set of additional forms he must learn will then depend upon whether he wishes to speak or write Arabic, or both. In more general terms, it is the situation of language use that he will have to cope with that will determine which features of the language outside the common core he will have to acquire. Lyons (1968, p. 47) speaks of lexical items as having 'a greater or lesser centrality' in the vocabulary of a language. By this he means that a particular item is 'more frequent' or occurs in a larger number of situations of language use. In the framework of description I have been using, the notion of 'centrality' could be applied to linguistic items or systems which were common to a larger or smaller number of the constituent varieties of a language. On this scale the 'least central' material is that which is part of only one code. The second degree of centrality is assigned to items which are found in two or more codes, and the most central items are those found in the common core. This notion of centrality is applicable to the 'language as a whole'. But as we have seen, this is an abstraction. No native speaker commands a knowledge of any language 'as a whole', he possesses a repertoire, or set of overlapping codes. No learner needs, or can aspire to, a knowledge of the 'language as a whole'. The notion of centrality, however, is often introduced into discussions of what to teach, under the guise of 'the relative frequency' of linguistic forms – though usually in connection with vocabulary. The utility of such a notion is rather doubtful. If, for example, a learner wishes to converse with lawyers in a foreign language, then those items which are part of

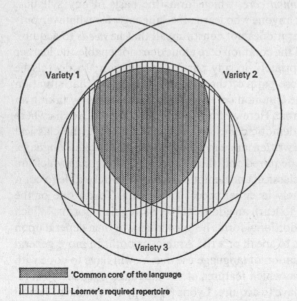

| | 'Common core' of the language |
| | Learner's required repertoire |

Figure 5 Centrality within a language and the learner's required repertoire

legal language are *central* to his needs; many of them, however, have very low 'relative frequency' in the 'language as a whole'. We shall return to the problem of relative frequency and its relevance to teaching language in more detail in chapter 9. Meanwhile, we need only say that for every speaker or learner, the 'centre of gravity' of his repertoire will be shifted in one or another direction from the central core of the 'language as a whole'. All learners must acquire what is central to the language, but that is only part of what is central to their needs.

The common core forms the basis of a general syllabus for all learners; it does not represent the whole of a syllabus for any learner. We can illustrate all these notions diagrammatically as in Figure 5.

Chapter 4
Language as a Symbolic System

Language and culture

In the last chapter we saw how dialects or codes were associated with social groupings of one sort or another. These groups were identifiable by having other characteristics than merely the possession of a common linguistic code. The members of the community share sets of beliefs, political or ethical, they share to a large extent the way they construe the world, how they classify objective phenomena, what meaning they give to this classification. Communities share a common history and agree about what is or is not important to them, a common value system. They agree about the right and wrong ways of getting things done, of dressing, eating, marrying, worshipping, educating their young and so on. All these things are their culture. It is not that some communities don't have beliefs about things or value things, or don't do things like dress and eat, or educate their young, but that they possess a distinctive way of doing them. They also possess a distinctive way of communicating through language. What is the connection between language and culture? Is it, for example, always and necessarily the case that languages and cultures go together? May communities with different cultures use the same language? Or may a culturally homogeneous community use different languages? We can answer these questions by referring back to the distinction we made between *dialects*, which we defined as the languages of some independently identifiable social group, and *languages*, which were associated with a speech community whose only characteristic was that its members called the language they spoke by the same name. As Sapir (1921, p. 214) says,

Most of us would readily admit, I believe, that the community of language between Great Britain and the United States is far from arguing a like community of culture . . . A common language cannot indefinitely set the seal on a common culture when the geographical, political and economic determinants of the culture are no longer the same throughout its area.

Historically speaking, it seems to be the case that when two groups of what was a single cultural community lose physical, economic and political contact with each other they begin to diverge. It may be that they start to differ culturally more quickly than linguistically. But this may well be only a superficial view. It is probable that their linguistic codes do, in fact, diverge also, but in rather subtle ways. On the other hand, when two culturally different communities come into contact and develop common economic and political systems there appear to be several different things that can happen. They may eventually merge, they may remain culturally distinct whilst being politically and economically a unit. Their languages may coalesce, one may supersede the other, or they may both continue side by side suffering some degree of mutual influence (Weinreich, 1953). Bilingualism, diglossia, superposed variety, are all terms that have been used to describe the various possible outcomes.

Quoting Sapir again (1921, p. 215): 'Language, race and culture are not necessarily related. This does not mean that they never are.' The difficulty of interpreting this statement is that of knowing what is meant by 'language' in this context. We can say, however, that there is a necessary connection between a community possessing a distinctive culture on the one hand and the nature of *its* language, that is, its *dialect*, on the other. This is a powerful reason for regarding *dialects* as functionally more important than languages (see chapter 3). It is also a reason for regarding the concept of *a* language as too vague to be useful for most practical purposes. The unitary nature of '*a* language' may be much more apparent and superficial than is generally supposed. As we saw in the last chapter, whatever linguists may say, they do not, in fact, describe languages, they describe *dialects*. The descriptions of what we call English are, in fact, descriptions of what we have called the standard dialect, that which has the widest distribution and highest social prestige. As J. R. Firth said (1957, p. 29), 'Unity is the last concept that should be applied to language. Unity of language is the most fugitive of all unities, whether it be historical, geographical, national or personal. There is no such thing as *une langue une* and there never has been.'

A community possesses both a culture and a language of its own. But what is the relation between them? Before suggesting an answer to this question we should note one important fact: it is largely, though not exclusively, through the language of the community that the child acquires the attitudes, values and ways of behaving that we call its culture. Learning these is the process of socialization, and is principally carried out through language, first in the home, later in the school and in the life of the community at large. Thus we can say that language *mediates* between the individual and the culture. But to do this successfully it must possess certain specific properties which qualify it for this task. For example, it must have *codifiability*, an economical and easily learned way of referring to objects and events which that culture classifies together, or regards as useful or important. To take a specific example, if it is regarded as socially valuable, i.e. important for the maintenance of social structure, that a *father's sister's son* should be distinguishable from a *mother's brother's son*, then the language of that community will *encode* that information in an economical and readily memorizable form, e.g. in single words. Or, to take another example, if it is economically or technologically important to a society that distinction should be made between different types of hawk, as it was in medieval Britain, then these distinctions will usually be reflected in the language in a set of simple and easily perceptible distinguishing names: goshawk, falcon, falconette, etc., rather than by adding a set of adjectival qualifications to the name *hawk*. In this sense, the language of a community, a dialect, will reflect the culture and serve the needs of that community by making it easy for it to realize distinctions where these are important and useful, whilst disregarding distinctions where they are not important or socially relevant. If, then, languages do reflect cultures, it is easy to see that where there are cultural differences between communities these will be reflected in differences in their linguistic systems. The structure of a language is often said to 'mirror' the structure of the world as it is seen by a particular community.

I have said that language mediates between the individual and the culture of his community, because it is largely through language that he acquires the cultural patterns of thought and behaviour of his community. Now the question arises: does the nature of the language *necessarily condition* the way the child, and, of course, ultimately the adult members of the community, sees things? In other words, does language *determine* culture? Or does it work the other way? Is language immediately responsive to cultural change? Is it as it is because that is the way its speakers structure their world conceptually? Or may there be some intermediate state where language and culture are mutually influential or mutually interdependent? To refer back to one of the examples: if the language has no single distinct expression for *father's sister's son* does it mean that the child cannot recognize such a class of kin, or does it only mean that he has more difficulty in forming a concept of this sort? Or does it make no difference? These are crucial questions to which we shall return in later sections. We need only note here that we have introduced such terms as *concept*, *memorization*, *perception*, *classification*, all of them psychological terms. It is in this area of relations between language, thought and culture that the psychological and sociological approaches to language converge. The psychologist is concerned with the relations between the formal system of language (the code) and the conceptual system (or cognitive structure) of the individual, i.e. language as a symbolic system. The sociolinguist, on the other hand, is concerned as we have seen, with the relation between the linguistic code and the culture of the community. We can illustrate these relationships diagrammatically, as in Figure 6. Thus, the psychologist is concerned with relation (A) and the sociolinguist with relation (B). The point of common interest is how the relation between the individual conceptual system and society's cultural system is developed (relation (C)), maintained, or perhaps constrained through the operation of language. Societies and their cultures change more or less slowly over time. But, on the same time scale, the

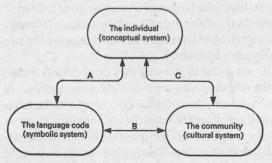

Figure 6 Relationship between the individual, the language and the community

individual is here today and gone tomorrow. The individual can have little influence on the development of society and its culture, nor can he significantly influence the structure of language. Any attempt to do so by using the language in an unconventional way, that is, by breaking the code, leads to a failure of communication. In spite of the fact, noted by Weinreich (1966) that we all seem to have an inbuilt tendency to try to make sense of utterances which do break the rules of the code, the ways in which we can do so seem themselves to be severely constrained by the nature of language itself. Poets, typically, are members of society who have licence to bend the rules, but there are rules for breaking rules. We even have names for them: metaphor, metonymy, zeugma, personification, transferred epithet – what are often called 'figures of speech'. It is also true that what was a 'permitted' breach of the rules at one time may, eventually, become part of the code; but this is rarely, if ever, the work of an individual. We come back then to the question posed before: if the individual cannot change the code, does the code mould the individual, does it necessarily constrain the way he thinks or 'sees the world'?

Codifiability

So far we have been considering largely the relations between a code, an individual and a culture. We have been working *intralinguistically* or *intraculturally*. But in the context of the learning and teaching of foreign languages we must also consider the problem *interlinguistically* and *cross-culturally*. This means asking the question: do the evident differences between the cultures of communities make it difficult, or impossible for people to learn the language of another society? Or, to put it rather differently: is the difficulty of learning another language directly related to the degree of difference to be found between the two cultures with which they are associated?

Languages evidently do differ in the way they symbolically reflect the world, that is, in the way they *categorize* or *codify the experience* of their speakers. As we have seen, the way they do this reflects the interests, needs, concerns and preoccupations of the community they serve. Where a society needs to recognize distinctions readily and economically, the language will reflect this need. This is most clearly seen in the *lexical encoding* of experience. Thus we would expect to, and do, find differences in the vocabularies of two different languages. Where language A has a single name for some phenomenon, language B has no such word and has to resort to periphrasis to express the same notion. German has the term *Gemütlichkeit*; English has to resort to a whole phrase or conjunction of terms, such as *kindly, easy-going, good-natured*. French has the simple term *entamer* for which the English is a whole phrase such as *to make the first cut in*. On the other hand, French has to resort to periphrasis in the case of the English *to kick, to punch: donner un coup de pied, donner un coup de poing*. The linguist would say that the semantic features which are realized in one language in one lexical item are in the other 'syntagmatically' distributed. In a sense, the semantic 'structure' of *kick* is more 'opaque' than that of *donner un coup de pied*. The semantic 'content', however, is equivalent. There is no need to multiply instances of this sort, which are common knowledge to anyone who has learned a foreign language. A slightly different situation, but just as familiar, is where language A has a single term for some phenomenon and language B has, perhaps, two or three terms covering the same area of experience, and therefore making distinctions which language A does not. Thus, English has the single generic term *horse*, where Arabic has a whole series of different words for different breeds and conditions of horses, but no word for horse as such. This does not mean that the English speaker is debarred from expressing the distinctions, only that he has more work to do: *spavinned horse, racehorse, piebald horse, skewbald horse*, and so on. The upshot of this discussion seems to be that it is easier to refer to certain phenomena, or to express certain distinctions within some field of experience in one language than in another. Languages vary, therefore, in the ease with which they permit codification. We can also note that what is lexically coded in one language may require both lexical and grammatical means in another, since circumlocution involves grammatical relations.

It would appear, then, that the answer to the question whether the difficulty of learning a foreign language is related to the degree of difference between two cultures is, up to this point, a qualified *yes*, inasmuch as certain concepts are more readily codifiable in one language than in another. But this is not necessarily the final answer. So far we have been dealing with cases where the speakers of one language have had to find an equivalent expression for the *same concept* in the second language. But might there not be cases in which the concept itself was not available in the culture of the second language? In such a case, there would be no way of expressing it in that language. The difficulty here is showing that the concept itself was not available. The fact that it was not encoded in some simple way in the language does not prove that it does not exist, or cannot be acquired by speakers of the second language. To test this it is necessary to investigate how these speakers behave *non-linguistically*, i.e. to study indirectly their capacity to form concepts for which there is no available symbol in their language code. The best known experiments in this field have been done in the field of colour discrimination. The colour spectrum provides a continuum of experience which has no language-independent, 'natural' divisions. The way different cultures divide up and encode the spectrum linguistically appears to be arbitrary. Roughly speaking, the behavioural test of linguistic determinism would be to get speakers of different languages to perform tasks which require breaking up the spectrum conceptually into 'colours' which do not correspond to the way their language does it (Brown and Lenneberg, 1954). Studies of this sort have been few, but the tentative conclusion is that people are able to conceptualize such fields of experience as colour in ways different from that of their language, and show this by their non-linguistic behaviour. So far as concept formation and lexical encoding is concerned, then, it appears that, whilst the semantic structures of languages do exercise some effect on concept formation, they do not have a totally determining effect. We can say tentatively, then, that there is as yet no evidence that the differences between cultures are of such a kind that they *preclude* the learning of foreign languages. The differences between cultures are ones of degree not of kind. The members of different cultures live in 'the same world' but they categorize it differently.

The Whorfian hypothesis

The linguist who really started people thinking rigorously about the problems of linguistic determinism or *linguistic relativity*, as the study of relations between language, culture and thought is called, was Benjamin Lee Whorf. He expressed the extreme view, which has already been hinted at in the previous sections, that our view of the world, the ways we can categorize our experience and conceptualize our environment, is effectively determined by our language. His ideas were led in this direction by Sapir, with whom he studied. He started the most important of his several essays on the subject with this quotation from Sapir (Whorf, 1956):

Human beings do not live in the objective world alone, nor alone in the world of social activity as ordinarily understood, but are very much at the mercy of the particular language which has become the medium of expression for their society. It is quite an illusion to imagine that one adjusts to reality essentially without the use of language and that language is merely an incidental means of solving specific problems of communication or reflection. The fact of the matter is that the 'real world' is to a large extent unconsciously built up on the language habits of the group. . . . We see and hear and otherwise experience very largely as we do because the language habits of our community predispose certain choices of interpretation (Sapir, 1921).

But Whorf himself went even beyond this qualified statement. Perhaps the most famous of the expressions of his point of view is this:

Formulation of ideas is not an independent process, strictly rational in the old sense, but is part of a particular grammar, and differs, from slightly to greatly, between different grammars. We dissect nature along lines laid down by our native languages. The categories and types that we isolate from the world of phenomena we do not find there because they stare every observer in the face; on the contrary, the world is presented in a kaleidoscopic flux of impressions which has to be organized by our minds – and this means largely by the linguistic systems in our minds. We cut nature up, organize it into concepts, and ascribe significances as we do, largely because we are parties to an agreement to organize it in this way – an agreement that holds throughout our speech community and is codified in the patterns of our language. The agreement is, of course, an implicit and unstated one, *but its terms are absolutely obligatory*; we cannot talk at all except by subscribing to the organization and classification of data which the agreement decrees. . . . We are thus introduced to a new principle of relativity, which holds that all observers are not led by the same physical evidence to the same picture of the universe, unless their linguistic backgrounds are similar, or can in some way be calibrated.

This is a very powerful claim, and goes well beyond the limited version of *linguistic relativity* discussed in the previous section. There we were concerned with interlinguistic *lexical codifiability*. But Whorf extended the argument to grammatical structure. Sapir warned, as many others before and after have done, that we should not make the mistake of 'identifying a language with a dictionary'. The grammatical categories, too, codify experience. The difference is not essentially one of kind, but rather in the degree of abstraction involved. Such aspects as tense, aspect, gender, number, case and so on with which we are familiar in European languages also have meanings, and relate to non-linguistic features of the external world as we perceive and conceptualize it. It is also perfectly true that the grammars of some languages have categories not found in other languages. Thus, Burmese, for example, has nominal classifying particles which indicate whether the class of objects referred to is conceptualized as a weapon or as a long object. Carroll, in one of his experiments (Carroll and Casagrande, 1958) refers to a feature of the Navaho grammar which modifies the stems of verbs of *handling* differentially, according to the *shape* of the object being handled, whether it is long and flexible, long and rigid, or flat and flexible. Similarly, Whorf refers to the fact that Hopi requires the speaker to specify by grammatical means whether his statement is based on observed fact, on memory, on expectation or on generalization. The only translations possible, as he thought, of the Hopi sentences into English show contrasts of *tense*. Thus, what in English was apparently regarded as a matter of *time*, is in Hopi a matter of *modality*, modality here being the name for those systems in grammar which express the speaker's degree of confidence in the factual truth of his message.

As we saw, it was difficult enough to investigate experimentally the validity of the linguistic relativity hypothesis in the matter of lexical codifiability. When it comes to the conceptually more abstract notions expressed by grammatical categories, it is even more difficult. But we can note one interesting fact. If, indeed, we are imprisoned within the conceptual system imposed on us by our language, how does it come about that Whorf himself was able to express *in English* notions which he implied were untranslatable? The probability is that, as in the case of *lexical encoding*, it is a question of relative ease or difficulty of encoding certain more abstract concepts in one or another language, rather than the flat impossibility of doing so, and certain languages make it easier or more difficult to discriminate within these fields of experience.

Linguistic relativity and language teaching

If languages reflected differences in *kind* between cultures, that is, encoded radically different ways of seeing the world, then translation between languages would be impossible. If the differences are only ones of degree, then translation in certain areas of experience may be more or less difficult. The evidence from language learning experience and from bilinguals is that the latter is the case; certain conceptual fields, particularly those which are generally encoded in the grammatical categories of languages will present such difficulties. The degree to which cultures resemble each other, *cultural overlap*, as it is called, are reflected in language as similarities of semantic and syntactic structure. The learning of a second language does clearly involve some degree of recategorization; how great this will be will depend on the two languages involved. Or, we can put it another way round, learning a second language does involve learning to see the world as the speakers of that language habitually see it, does involve learning their culture. But this is not an impossible task, only more or less difficult. Learning a new language is emphatically not a question of acquiring a new set of names for the same things; it is not just the learning of an automatic translation device, the internalizing of a bilingual dictionary. On the other hand, learning a language does not involve learning a new 'world view'.

The linguistic approach to language, which we discussed in chapter 1, provides the means of showing how and in what degree languages possess the same semantic (lexical) structure, the degree to which words in the two languages which usually 'translate' each other, or *translation equivalents*, have the 'same' meaning. Or, in the field of grammar, it shows the degree to which grammatical categories such as tense, case and gender are equivalent in different languages. These matters will be taken up again in chapter 10, where the methods of making linguistic comparisons between languages for applied purposes are looked at in greater detail. Such comparisons have the objective of identifying in general terms those areas of a second language where coding differences are greatest and consequently where the greatest learning problems for the student are likely to be found.

Part Two
Linguistics and Language Teaching

Chapter 5
Linguistics and Language Teaching

Macro-linguistic studies

In chapter 1, I said that language was such a complex and many-sided thing that there was at the present time no all-embracing theory which brought every aspect of the problem within a single coherent and mutually consistent set of propositions. The study of language as a phenomenon of the individual was part of general psychology and the descriptive categories used to account for the individual's linguistic behaviour were those used to account for his other non-linguistic behaviour – thus such terms as *learning, memory, skill, perception* were as applicable to language as to other behaviour. The study of language as a social phenomenon, as an event, similarly was part of general sociology, and the descriptive categories used to account for language, *social-structure, culture, status, role*, were used in general sociological descriptions of human society, its structure and institutions.

What distinguished the 'linguistic' study of language or 'linguistic linguistics' was its autonomy or independence of other disciplines. Linguistic linguistics (or as it has recently been called, 'theoretical linguistics') establishes its own categories and terminology which it does not share with either of the other approaches.

However, as we saw, there has been a general tendency in recent years for these separate approaches to recognize that what they are all trying to explain is in some sense a unitary phenomenon. Consequently, a process of 'bridge-building' has been taking place with the emergence of what can be called 'hybrid' disciplines, part linguistic and part psychological (psycholinguistics), and part linguistic and part sociological (sociolinguistics). The actual 'status' of the new studies is not clear, their aims are not well defined and their theoretical apparatus and methods are not yet firmly established. Is sociolinguistics a branch of sociology or a branch of linguistics? Are we to see a new super-linguistic theory, a science of semiotics, 'the science of the life of signs in society', as de Saussure called it, which will include and reconcile all these different approaches to language, or will the previously hard-won autonomy of linguistic linguistics in particular disappear and will linguistics merely become part of general psychology, as Chomsky suggests (1968a, p.1) when he says that theoretical linguistics is a 'branch of cognitive psychology'? It is too early to give any answers to these questions. All one can say is that there is now an increasing awareness amongst some psychologists, sociologists and linguists, that each has something to say about language which is significant to the others and that, if he does not take into account what the others are saying, his own statements can only be regarded as a partial explanation of the nature of language. The present unstable constellation of disci-plines concerned with language is what I have already referred to as macro-linguistics. The contrasting term micro-linguistics is sometimes used to refer to what I have been calling 'theoretical' or 'linguistic' linguistics.

Theoretical linguistics: the scientific study of language

Linguistics, or, to be more specific, theoretical linguistics, is often called the 'scientific study of language'. This was indeed the title chosen by Professor Lyons when he became Professor of General Linguistics at Edinburgh University for his inaugural lecture in 1964 (Lyons, 1965). The implication of this frequently-used definition of 'linguis-tics' is that there is, or was, an *unscientific* study of language. One might jump to the conclusion that what was being described in this way were the approaches to language which I have called sociological and psychological. But this would be a mistake. Both sociology and psychology make claims, similar to those made by linguistics, to being sciences. The contrast between scientific linguistics and unscientific linguistics is roughly that between modern and traditional linguistic studies, the traditional studies being regarded as unscientific. Now, this is not the place to go into a discussion of the history of linguistic thought. It is true, however, that linguistic studies were, until recently, subservient to, or in certain respects distorted by, the standards of the other studies with which they were closely associated, or indeed considered part of: logic, philosophy or literary criticism. Modern linguistics, or *structural linguistics*, as it is sometimes called, to distinguish it from traditional linguistics, claims to be scientific because its methods and philosophical orientation are those which are generally described in that way. These claims, and the attempt to live up to them, have led to the *autonomy* of linguistics – specifically, autonomy from logic, philosophy and literary criticism, but not so clearly from psychology and sociology, which had their own problems of asserting their autonomy from philosophy at much the same time as linguistics. Now that the linguist has won his freedom, he is quite happy to collaborate with the philosopher on equal terms in studying those problems they have in common.

The difficulty of establishing the validity of the claim of linguistics to being scientific lies in the fact that the term *scientific* itself has been subject to various interpretations, not only in the past, but at the present time. There is general agreement that the characteristic of a scientific approach is its objectivity, its logical coherence or rationalism, and the requirement of verification. But these terms themselves are subject to different interpretations. This is clearly not the place to go into a discussion of the philosophy of science, but it is necessary to draw attention to the two main ways that the term 'scientific' has been interpreted, since it is relevant to discussion not only of linguistics but also of the psychological approach to language and consequently, to notions about how language is learned.

One account of the scientific method proposes that its starting point is observation of the data. On the basis of this observation, hypotheses about the nature and regularity of the phenomena under investigation are formed. Using these hypotheses, predictions are made about the phenomena, which by further, now controlled, observation or experiment, are confirmed or falsified. A hypothesis, confirmed by experiment, becomes a theory about the matter in hand. The reader will recognize the process as one which is called *inductive generalization*. Indeed, Bloomfield (1935) specifically asserted that, in linguistics, the only 'useful generalizations are inductive generalizations' (p. 20). On this view a theory is what is arrived at as the *end point* of a set of scientific procedures and is *determined* by the data which were the starting point of the process. The implication of this account is that the scientist starts with an entirely 'open mind' about the whole matter, including presumably an open mind about what data to observe and which aspects of the data selected are relevant and significant, and which are not. The difficulty is that, in order to decide what data are relevant and what to look for in the data, you have to have some *preconception* about what you are looking for. In the case of linguistics, for example, some preconceived notion of what language is, and what are or are not linguistic data. As we have seen, this is not as simple as it might appear at first sight. Inasmuch as you *select* some data and *reject* other data, or accept one sort of regularity and reject another, you are *applying* some sort of theory about the subject. In other words, data are not *given* at all, but *taken*. The act of selection is the *result* of a theory about the subject, however informal, vague and ill-formulated this may be. This notion was well expressed by de Saussure:

Far from being the object that antedates the viewpoint, it would seem that it is the viewpoint which creates the object. Besides, nothing tells us in advance that one way of considering the fact in question takes precedence over the others or is in any way superior to them. (de Saussure, 1961, p. 8)

Or, as Allen (1966, p. 16) says:

Linguistics is a creative not an observational activity; it creates its elements out of the continuum of human speech; it does not observe units unfolding themselves in time, but selects from the continuum such data as are relevant to the characterization of the elements it has established.

This criticism of the *inductive view* of scientific procedure, suggests that theory, far from being the end point is, in fact, the starting point of a scientific investigation, and the data is used to confirm, disprove or improve the theory. In the case of linguistics, this would mean that we start out with some notions about what language is and what to select as data and what to look for in those data. This alternative account of the scientific process is known as the *hypothetico-deductive* approach (cf. Popper, 1959).

The linguistic study of language

What distinguishes theoretical linguistics from the other approaches to language is not, then, its scientific status, but its goals – what aspect of language it sets out to describe and explain. It is on the basis of what its goals are that it selects its data. What then, we may ask, differentiates the linguistic study of language from the psychological or sociological study of the 'same' phenomena? Linguistics may have achieved autonomy from logic and philosophy; has it also achieved autonomy from psychology and sociology? Certainly it aims to do so, and it does this by limiting very severely what it considers to be its data. The linguistic study of language confines itself to a study of the verbal utterances of human beings. Its aims are to describe the structure of these utterances and to do so by setting up a theory of linguistic structure – grammar. This means that it does not concern itself with the motives of the speaker, what he is trying to achieve through using language; it does not concern itself with the differences between speakers and hearers or the fact that no two speakers are identical in their verbal behaviour, that the society from which the data are taken cannot be regarded on some counts as homogeneous, or that people, when they speak, make mistakes or false starts, forget the thread of their arguments. The linguist is not concerned (or some claim not to be) with the situational context in which his data were produced, the relations between the speakers and hearers, their social characteristics, what is happening while they talk, the results of their speech, the accompanying paralinguistic behaviour, and so on. The linguist's data are, when reduced to the bare essentials in this way, of two sorts: (a) sequences of sounds, or more accurately, an acoustic wave form; and (b) certain sorts of judgements on these sequences, e.g. their acceptability, their similarity and difference (see page 231). These are his data, and his job is, by the application of some notions about them, to reduce them to some sort of order, to discover some sort of regularity in them in spite of their apparently heterogeneous nature.

One might think that, after the partial catalogue of all the things the linguist does *not* regard as part of his data, what is left is scarcely worth bothering with. This might seem to be particularly the case when we consider the usefulness of such an approach to language teaching. It almost looks as if everything we are interested in has been left out of account. And yet it is precisely because the linguist has in the past so severely restricted the range of what he attempts to account for that structural linguistics has such remarkable achievements to its credit, and why, of all the linguistic disciplines, it has constructed such a sophisticated and rich theory. This reason alone would make it necessary to take account of what the linguist has to say about language and, as I have already suggested, it is because of the richness, coherence and detail of the linguist's descriptions of language that they offer the best means available of characterizing what we teach. Let me repeat here, however, that whilst linguistics gives us a means of *describing* what we teach, it does not provide us with the means of *determining* what to teach.

The goals of a linguistic theory

I suggested in the previous section that there is a reciprocal relation between goals and data. What you have selected to observe constrains what can be said. Similarly, what you want to say determines what data you select in the first place. By so severely restricting his data the linguist also restricts what he can say about language. But even then there are considerable differences between the goals that different linguists have set themselves which have affected not only the nature of the data they have worked with, but also their attitudes to those data. Some linguists have set their sights no higher than to provide a *method* for describing the structural characteristics of some *finite* body of data, or a corpus. The motivation for doing this was particularly strong when the need was to describe languages or dialects on the point of dying out, as was the case in North America at the beginning of this century, or elucidating written but partially incomprehensible texts. All that was asked of linguistic theory and description at this level was that it should provide a means for describing exhaustively the sets of limited data with which it was concerned, that it should have as its end-point a comprehensive 'description of the language' of the corpus. Inasmuch as it does this, such a theory and associated description can be regarded as *observationally adequate*. The ideal of such a way of approaching linguistic data would be to have an automatic process, an algorithm, or a set of rule-of-thumb procedures which, when applied to the data, would churn out the grammar of that corpus, 'untouched by human hand'. The difficulty which arises here is that there are in principle an indefinite number of possible ways of doing this, all of which turn out an observationally adequate description of the data. In case this is not clear, consider various ways in which the data in a corpus could be described and classified. One could do what a dictionary does and classify all sentences in the corpus according to the letter of the alphabet with which they started. Or one could classify sentences according to the number of words they contained, or again, according to the part of speech with which they ended. This would yield three totally different and observationally adequate descriptions. One could think up a very large number of such criteria for the classification of sentences. If all one wished to do was to make generalizations about the data to discover regularities in the data, there would be no reason for choosing between one and another criterion or set of criteria, except the simplicity, elegance or economy of the resulting description. These may appear to be absurd proposals, but they have served their purpose if they show that in fact what matters in a description is starting off with the *right* criteria, and making the *relevant* generalizations. Unless one approaches the data with some notion of what is relevant, what it is one is trying to explain, there is no reason for preferring one set of criteria to another. In fact, of course, those linguists whose object was to describe the characteristics of their data did start off with a set of criteria. The only thing is that these criteria were not explicit. What the 'right' and 'relevant' criteria for making a description are depends on the goals you set yourself. I shall return to this point shortly.

The other problem is that the data drawn from living languages and dialects are not limited. People go on talking and writing. One cannot arbitrarily say 'Stop! while I complete my description!' Any useful or adequate description of a language must not only cope satisfactorily with what has been written or said, but also with what may be or could be written or said in that language. It must be *projective* (or predictive). Such an approach regards the data as a *sample* of the language. And the description must not only account adequately for the data on which it is based, but must also predict the nature of any other data which might be gathered from the same source. It deals, therefore, not only with 'actual' sentences in the language, but also 'potential' sentences. Descriptions of languages, or grammars of languages (as I shall now call them following the traditional and also the most recent use of this term), which have the characteristic of being projective, are in technical terminology called 'generative' grammars.

One outstanding characteristic of human language that differentiates it from animal communication is its *creativity*. This means that we all have the ability to construct and understand an indefinitely large number of sentences in our native language, including sentences we have never heard before. Indeed, most of the sentences we produce and hear are 'new' in this sense. When we teach someone a language we clearly wish him to have this same capacity to understand and to produce, at will, sentences he has never heard before but which will immediately be understood by his native speaking hearers. A description of a language which is projective is, therefore, a necessity for language teaching. Traditional grammars are, in fact, projective in this sense.

Another quality which we must seek in any adequate grammar of a language is that it is *vulnerable*, that is, that it can be proved wrong empirically. Clearly such a grammar must be predictive in the sense already outlined. If a grammar predicts that a certain sentence is possible and it turns out that this is not the case, then that grammar is inadequate, or, on the other hand, if it says that a certain sentence which has been observed is not possible, then similarly that grammar is inadequate. For a grammar to be vulnerable, it must be explicit, i.e. it must not leave anything unstated for the reader to fill in from his own knowledge. If it is not explicit, then any of its failures correctly to predict or to stigmatize can be conveniently blamed on the reader and not the grammar. The quality of explicitness is also important to language teaching. After all, if the learner were able to supply from his own knowledge what the grammar omitted or did not express clearly and unambiguously, then he would not need to be learning the language in the first place! Traditional grammars failed in the requirement of explicitness. Grammars, then, must be both explicit and projective if they are to meet the criterion of *descriptive adequacy*. Some linguists, including Chomsky, maintain they must be more. For a general discussion of adequacy in linguistics, the reader may care to consult Chomsky (1965, pp. 30–37).

We must now return to the question of the criteria for preferring one explicit, projective, that is generative, grammar to another, for selecting one grammar out of several as the 'right' one. The answer is quite simple but has far-reaching consequences: that grammar is 'right' which accords with the native speaker's intuitions about his language. This is why I said that the native speaker's judgements about his language are part of the linguist's data. To give just two examples of what this means: traditional grammars have always recognized that active and passive sentences were related to each other in some fairly simple way, e.g. the object of the active sentence is recognized as having the same function as the subject of a passive sentence:

The adder bit *Tom* – *Tom* was bitten by the adder

although physically the two sentences are obviously very different. In this respect traditional grammars accounted for the intuitions of the native speaker. But traditional grammars did not so clearly recognize that, in spite of the physical similarity of the following two sentences, the native speaker does not feel that they are as simply related as are passive and active sentences:

James is easy to please
James is eager to please

To check this we need only note that *It is easy to please James* is an acceptable paraphrase of the first, while *It is eager to please James* is not a paraphrase of the second. Although the elements of which both sentences are composed belong to the same 'parts of speech' in the same order, the relations between these elements are evidently not the same. In the first sentence we understand that it is James who is being pleased, whereas in the second it is James who is doing the pleasing.

The consequence of requiring that a grammar should accord with a native speaker's intuitions is that we must accept a different goal for linguistic theory. Whereas, before, we were content if a description of a language accounted in an adequate fashion both explicitly and projectively for any data from that language we cared to submit for scrutiny, that is, we were concerned with describing 'language', now it looks as if we are describing what native speakers *conceive* to be the nature of their language. The emphasis has shifted from the nature of language data to the nature of the human capacity which makes it possible to produce the language data. This is how Chomsky (1968a) puts it:

The person who has acquired knowledge of a language has internalized a system of rules that relate sound and meaning in a particular way. The linguist constructing a grammar of a language is in effect proposing a hypothesis concerning this internalized system. . . .

and later:

At the level of a particular grammar he (the linguist) is attempting to characterize knowledge of a language, a certain cognitive system that has been developed – unconsciously, of course – by the normal speaker–hearer. . . . Linguistics so characterized is simply the subfield of psychology that deals with these aspects of the mind. (pp. 23, 24)

Competence and performance

Some linguists, Chomsky among them, would claim that the objectives of the linguistic study of language have always implicitly been the characterization of the internalized code or set of rules used by a speaker–hearer when he uses his language, and not a description of the utterance produced by speakers of a language. Surprisingly, perhaps, the latter aim is regarded by some as being too ambitious, since it involves all those factors of a nonlinguistic nature enumerated in the section above, which fall within the domain of psychology or sociology. Linguists, according to this point of view, do not study what people *do* when they speak and understand language, but seek rather to discover the *rules* underlying this performance. This is what Chomsky (1966a) calls their *competence:*

A distinction must be made between what the speaker of a language knows implicitly (what we may call his *competence*) and what he does (his *performance*). A grammar, in the traditional view, is an account of competence. It describes and attempts to account for the ability of a speaker to understand an arbitrary sentence of his language and to produce an appropriate sentence on a given occasion. If it is a pedagogic grammar, it attempts to provide the student with this ability; if a linguistic grammar, it aims to discover and exhibit the mechanisms that make this achievement possible. The competence of the speaker – hearer can, ideally, be expressed as a system of rules that relate signals to semantic interpretations of these signals. The problem for the grammarian is to discover this system of rules; the problem for linguistic theory is to discover general properties of any system of rules that may serve as the basis for a human language, that is, to elaborate in detail what we may call, in traditional terms, the general *form of language* that underlies each particular realization, each particular natural language. (p. 9)

Now this distinction between competence and performance derives from and is certainly related to the distinction made by de Saussure between *langue* and *parole*. De Saussure (1961, p. 18) used the now famous analogy between the score of a musical work and its performance, to clarify this distinction. Each performance of a musical work is unique, not only in the sense that it takes place on a particular occasion, but that it shows many differences from other performances which derive from the idiosyncrasies of performers, audience, conductors, instruments, concert hall. Looked at in another way we would say that the score is an *abstraction* from all the different performances. A skilled musician could 'reconstruct' the score, if he was unfamiliar with it already, from hearing a number of different performances. In the same way, it is suggested, a skilled linguist *infers* the rules of the language from a study of the data of utterances. Actually, this analogy is faulty. The relation between score and performance is much closer to the relationship that many modern linguists draw between sentence (score) and utterance (performance). Utterances are instances of *parole*; they are situationally conditioned realizations of sentences. The concept of *langue*, a socially shared system of rules, a code in the sense we have been using it, or grammar in the linguist's sense, corresponds more closely to the system of rules which the composer follows to *create* scores, e.g. rules of sonata form, rules of harmony, rules of counterpoint, rhythm, etc.

The native speaker's competence, then, can be characterized as a set of rules for producing and understanding sentences in his language. The grammar of a language, thus, in its linguistic sense is a characterization of the native speaker's competence (see chapter 2). Now, as we noted in chapter 3, all speakers of a language vary slightly in the rules they follow, as well, of course, as in their performance. For this reason it is necessary to make a further abstraction. The grammar of language is, according to Chomsky, the characterization of the competence of the *ideal* native speaker–hearer in a *homogeneous* society. Thus, unless the linguist for some special reason (see chapter 12) proposes to describe the competence of some individual speaker (idiolectal competence) the grammar of a language does not factually represent the rules followed by any particular individual when he speaks or understands a language. The 'competence' which the linguist describes is thus an idealization or an abstraction.

The competence of a native speaker is made apparent and can be investigated through his ability to detect ambiguities in sentences, e.g. to recognize two or more possible meanings in such sentences as:

She is a beautiful dancer

to distinguish grammatical from ungrammatical sentences:

The dog looks terrifying
The dog looks sleeping

to recognize relationships between sentences:

James came home yesterday
James didn't come home yesterday
It was yesterday James came home
What James did yesterday was come home

to be aware of paraphrase relations between sentences:

James knocked in the nail with a hammer
James used a hammer to knock in the nail
James hammered in the nail

Now clearly, competence, in this sense of being able to recognize and produce grammatical sentences in a language and recognize the meaning relations between them, is something a learner, and also a native speaker, must have. Furthermore, it is a reasonable goal for linguistics to try to elucidate the nature of this capacity; but the description of a speaker's competence in this sense falls short of a full account of what a speaker must know in order to communicate. It is for this reason that an increasing number of linguists believe that this goal for linguistics is too limited. A native speaker must not only be able to produce and understand grammatically *well-formed* utterances, he must also be able to produce and understand utterances which are *appropriate* to the context in which they are made. It is just as much a matter of 'competence' in language to be able to produce appropriate utterances as grammatical ones. It is thus that the concept of *communicative competence* has come into being (Wales and Campbell, 1970, p. 249; Hymes, 1972). To give just one example: the sentence *Rebecca is the girl in blue* can be spoken with the principal stress on either *Rebecca* or *blue*. This yields two 'different' sentences which are certainly semantically equivalent, i.e. mean the same thing or refer to the same 'state of affairs':

Rebécca is the girl in blue
Rebecca is the girl in blúe

But only the first is an appropriate answer to the question *Who is the girl in blue?* and the second to the question *Which is Rebecca?*

It is probably unnecessary to point out that when we are teaching a second language we are trying to develop in the learner not just *grammatical competence* in the Chomskyan sense, but *communicative competence*. We are teaching him not only what we call 'the formation rules' of the language, but in addition what Hymes has called 'the speaking rules'. The learner must, it is true, develop the ability to produce and understand grammatical utterances, he must be able to distinguish grammatical from ungrammatical sequences, but he must also know when to select a particular grammatical sequence, the one which is appropriate to the context, both linguistic and situational. His utterance must be situation-related. Or to put it in another way, he must not only learn to talk grammatically in the target language, he must also talk coherently and to the point. Much of the 'teaching of grammar', particularly the drills and practice routines indulged in in modern teaching methods aim at developing simple grammatical competence and no more. The complaint, already referred to, which teachers often make, that their pupils perform well in practice in class but can't use the language to any purpose outside can be explained by reference to the distinction between 'grammatical' and 'communicative' competence. They have acquired the one without the other. The only pedagogical solution available at the present time is to ensure that the language data to which the learner is exposed be presented 'in context', i.e. as part of continuous discourse or dialogue, and in a situational context, if necessary, simulated. So long as linguistic theory is concerned only with the internal structure of sentences, as it has predominantly been over the centuries, the sort of descriptions the teacher needs in order systematically to develop communicative competence in his pupils will be lacking. Linguistic theories simply do not exist at the present time which give more than an anecdotal account of the relations between sentences in discourse or dialogue or the way in which utterances vary systematically in relation to differences in the situational context. Until such theories of communicative competence are much better developed the teacher will have to work on a principle of hit-and-miss exposure, hoping that the learner will discover on his own the discourse rules or 'speaking rules' of the language as we have called them.

Levels of analysis

The task of a linguistic theory is often said to be to state the systems of rules which relate meanings to sounds. This relation is a very complex one and linguists have always found it necessary to break down this relationship into a number of steps or stages. The stages, or *levels*, which they have set up to do this have varied from time to time and from one theoretical orientation to another. What all linguists have agreed about, but not always explicitly, is that at least two stages are necessary. This means that all linguists agree in finding at least two fundamentally different types of organization in language. This is sometimes called the *double articulation* of language. For there to be patterns there must be basic units which enter into formal relations with each other. The two sets of basic units corresponding to the two types of structure are what we can call words on the one hand, and sounds or letters (where the language has an alphabetic writing system) on the other. The first or primary units, words, are meaningful in themselves, whilst the secondary units, sounds, are not. There are, of course, problems in defining what a word or a sound is; the definition depends upon the particular linguistic theory or 'frame of reference'. 'Word' will be defined differently in different theories. There is no 'theory-independent' definition of 'word' or 'sound', or indeed any one of a host of other linguistic terms. The layman may think he uses such terms in a consistent fashion, but a little investigation will show that this is far from the case. For example, he may say that *worked* in *he worked his passage* and *he has worked his passage* are instances of the 'same' word because both are spelled the same. There is nothing odd about asking someone: how do you spell the word *worked*? They are, in linguistic terms, *orthographically* (and *phonologically*) one and the same word. But, in the sentences: *He can't read this word* and *he has just read the word*, the word *read* has the same spelling. Is it then to be regarded as the 'same' word, because of the spelling or two different words because of the pronunciation? Again, in the sentences: *he has gone to market* and *he went to market*, the words *gone* and *went* are often called 'different forms of the "same" word', the one that appears in the dictionary as *go*. That is to say, while they are phonologically and orthographically different words, they are instances of the same 'dictionary' word, or 'lexical' word. When we look up a word in the dictionary it is given in the grammatically 'unmarked' form. On the other hand, is *put* in *he put his pen down* and *put that pen down*, whilst lexically, phonologically and orthographically one and the same word, the same word grammatically? We would say that one was a past tense verb, and the other an imperative. These grammatically different forms are usually clearly distinguishable, e.g. *he dropped his pen* and *drop that pen!* Let us look at three more examples: in *I can't bear it* and *he was mauled by a bear* we have a word which is orthographically and phonologically one word, but grammatically and lexically two words. What about *use* in *use this knife!* and *what use is this knife?* Orthographically and lexically one word, but phonologically and grammatically two. Finally we come to a difficult example. In what sense are we to regard *ear* in *an ear of corn* and *a blow on the ear* as the 'same' word? Orthographically and phonologically, yes; they are both nouns, so grammatically, perhaps, yes. But are they lexically the same word? The dictionary regards them as distinct (their historical derivation is quite different), but as far as meaning is concerned, many people regard the *ear of corn* as a metaphorical extension of *the ear on your head*. This is the sort of problem dictionary-makers are constantly running into. What makes *works, worked, working* all instances of the same lexical word is that they all have the same 'meaning'. The problem the dictionary-maker (and the linguist) has to grapple with is: how different does the meaning between two physically identical forms have to be to count as two distinct lexical items. And conversely, may it not be the case that two physically different forms are really cases of the same lexical item: *go/went, contempt/despise*.

Table 2

	Phono-logically	Ortho-graphically	Grammatically	Lexically
worked–worked	√	√	×	√
read–read	×	√	×	√
go–went	×	×	×	√
put–put	√	√	×	√
bear–bear	√	√	×	×
use–use	×	√	×	√
ear–ear	√	√	√	?

Table 2, page 95, summarizes this little investigation. A tick means 'the same' and a cross 'different', and we can note a general tendency for orthography and phonology to go together, but no such tendency in the case of grammar and lexis.

No satisfactory scientific theory could (in any of its technical terms) tolerate such multiple ambiguity as we have discovered in the case of the word, *word*. Consequently, linguistic theories are either forced to invent new terms (e.g. lexeme, morpheme, morph, etc.) and/or restrict the meanings of such terms as *word* and *sound* to only one of their 'everyday' meanings, where this is feasible. There is, of course, nothing peculiar in this to linguistics; every scientific or technical field is forced to do the same, but it unfortunately leads to the layman's uncomprehending charges of using 'jargon'.

This little exercise has, however, introduced a number of terms – orthographic, phonological, lexical, grammatical – which refer to different types of patterning in language, for which the linguist sets up different *levels of analysis* in order to relate *meanings to sounds*. The phonological (and orthographical) levels are those which correspond to what has already been referred to as the *secondary level of articulation* of language, and the grammatical to the *primary level of articulation*. Within each level we find, in most theories, further subdivisions. Thus, within the secondary level we may sometimes meet two further levels: *phonetics* and *phonology*, and within the grammatical level, *morphology* (or accidence) and *syntax*. Just how many levels and sublevels may be set up, and the way they are related to each other is a theoretical matter which need not concern us at the moment.

Whilst the establishment of different levels and their relationships is a theoretical matter, what the theory is concerned with is the structure of language; each level has a type of structure of its own, and a corresponding theory which establishes the relevant categories of units, such as *word* or *sound*. These categories will, of course, have subclassifications, familiar, in the case of *word*, as the different *parts of speech* or, in the case of *sound*, such categories as *vowel* and *consonant*. Furthermore, each level has a set of possible relations between its units and categories. Some of these also are familiar from traditional grammar: *subordination, coordination, apposition, modification, word order, subject, object* and so on. This is not the place to go further into grammatical or phonological theory.

The reader will have noticed that I have not yet mentioned a 'lexical' level of analysis. It will have been clear from the discussion of the 'word' that what was regarded as *lexically* one and the same word, was so regarded because of its meaning. Indeed we could call lexical words 'dictionary' words, because that is where we 'look up' the meaning of 'a word'. Now, we have just seen that the grammatical level of analysis has to do with establishing grammatical categories of, and relationships between words or other grammatical units. Similarly, though I have not illustrated it, the phonological level of analysis also has the same function in respect of sounds, syllables, etc. But what, we may ask, is the equivalent operation in the case of 'dictionary' words? In what sense does a dictionary, as we ordinarily know it, classify words and state relations between them? The dictionary is just a 'list of words'. The only structure it imposes on this list is alphabetical, but this is, from the point of view of meaning, quite irrelevant, though it is obviously very handy for using a dictionary (notice that the alphabet is, *linguistically speaking*, a randomly ordered list of letters; that is why we have to learn it by heart). Words which start with the same letter obviously have nothing common in their meaning or their use. An ordinary dictionary, in other words, does not overtly classify words. But it does give us information about the way the vocabulary of a language is structured, and it does this through its definitions. Since this is an important aspect of linguistic structure, it merits a separate section.

Meaning in linguistics

If we want to know about the grammar of a language we get a grammar book; if we want to know about the pronunciation of a language we get a book on the 'phonetics' of the language; but what is a dictionary for? It is usually thought of as the book in which we find out about the meaning of a language, or, at least, of the 'words' of a language. It does this by giving the 'definitions' of words. But what is a definition? It is simply a statement of 'equivalence' of some sort, or more precisely of implication. Thus, in defining *a cabbage* as *a type of vegetable*, what we are in effect saying is that every time we refer to a cabbage we are implying that we are referring also to a type of vegetable. We could perfectly well, though with a slight change of meaning, substitute *vegetable* for *cabbage* in the same sentence. Notice that the converse is not the case; when we use the word *vegetable* we are not necessarily referring to a cabbage. Thus there is a relationship of implication between *cabbage* and *vegetable*. Relationships of implication between words, or indeed sentences, are *semantic* relationships. And the study of these relationships is part of the study of semantics. In this way, a dictionary is a description, though a very partial and unsystematic one, of the semantic structure of a language.

Just as in the case of grammatical relationships, we traditionally distinguish different sorts of semantic relationships by name, e.g. *synonymy*; *antonymy*; or, in more technical discourse, *contrary*; *converse*; *complementary*; *contradictory*. Thus *good* and *bad* are said to be antonyms; *start* and *begin* synonyms; *red* and *blue* contradictory terms; *husband* and *wife* complementary terms; *buy* and *sell*, *borrow* and *lend*, *take* and *give* converse terms, and so on. Thus, the vocabulary of a language is bound together in an enormously complex *network* of different relationships. The ordinary dictionary states, by means of definitions, just a very few of the semantic relationships that a word enters into with other words. One part of semantic theory then is concerned with the relations between the lexical words of a language, the *sense* relations between words.

Now it is evident that a dictionary, quite apart from its incompleteness, is, as we have seen, rather haphazard about how it organizes its statements about meaning. Might there be a more explicit way of organizing and describing the lexical material of a language? One way in which this has been done is by imposing a hierarchical structure on the vocabulary of a language. The best known description of the lexical structure of English on this principle is *Roget's Thesaurus*. In it, the vocabulary of the language is structured in a taxonomic fashion, rather as in the familiar Linnean botanical classification. From a descriptive point of view such an organization is an improvement on the random ordering of the dictionary, but unfortunately it depends upon using a limited set of sense relations, principally those of superordinate to subordinate terms (i.e. more general to more specific; e.g. *coloured* → *blue* → *ultramarine*; or *plant* → *vegetable* → *cabbage*).

I have referred to the sense relations holding between the lexical words of a language as a very complex network, and when we consider the nature of definitions we see that each word is defined in terms of other words. The result, of course, is that the network is a *closed* network, that the sense relations of a language make up a sort of *closed circuit*. Semantics is circular. One might ask: how does anyone ever learn a language, how does he ever break into this charmed circle? The answer is that sense relations are not the only relations which words enter into; indeed, for many people possibly the notion of meaning is more identified with these other relations, those which link words with objects, classes of objects and processes in 'the world outside', that is, with relations of *reference*. If someone asks you the meaning of the word *cabbage*, instead of saying it is a sort of vegetable, you can, if you have an example of the thing handy, point to a cabbage and say: *that is a cabbage*. This is a different sort of 'definition' and it does not depend entirely on other words. It is an *ostensive definition*. It is by means of ostensive techniques of this sort we begin to learn our mother tongue, and many techniques of second language learning make use of this method to break into the closed network of the lexical structure of a new language. There are other ways, of course. You can use translation, but as we saw in chapter 4, translation has its dangers. They are, quite simply, that the lexical structure of two languages is most unlikely to be identical or, technically speaking 'isomorphic', though in those areas where the culture of two communities 'overlaps' there will be a greater probability of structural similarity. Let us give just one example: if you point to a herring and ask a Norwegian speaker what he calls it in his language, he will say: *sild*. Thus, *sild* is a translation of *herring*, and has the same referential relations in the outside world. Now every English speaker knows that herrings are a sort of fish. There is a semantic relation between the two words; the word *fish* is superordinately related to the word *herring*. Now ask the Norwegian how he translates *fish* into Norwegian. He will most probably say *fisk*. But in everyday Norwegian it turns out that *sild* and *fisk* are not semantically related in this way; in other words *sild* are not a sort of *fisk*! We can illustrate this graphically as in Figure 7.

So far I have spoken only of the meaning relations of words, or the lexical elements of a language. It is quite clear, however, that other units of language, such as the sentence, may have meanings which are not just the 'sum' of the meanings of their constituent parts. Thus, *the boy loves the girl* and *the girl loves the boy*, although their constituent words are identical, do not mean the same thing; the one does not

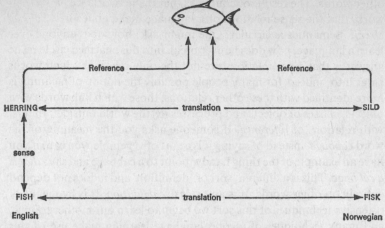

Figure 7 The semantic relations of *herring, sild, fish* and *fisk*

even necessarily, alas, imply the other. The difference in meaning is obviously connected with the different grammatical functions of *the boy* and *the girl* in each case. These functions are referred to traditionally as subject and object. So also, *the boy loved the girl* and *the boy loves the girl* do not mean the same thing, nor, alas, does the one necessarily imply the other. In this case the difference is related to a difference in the grammatical category of tense. Finally, *the boy loves the girl* and *Does the boy love the girl?* differ in meaning in respect of what, in chapter 3, we called *sentence function*, or in traditional terms, differences in *mood*. In every one of these cases the differences in meaning are *signalled* by some physical difference in the form of the sentence, either by a change in the order of the words, a change in the form of a word, or the addition of an extra word. It is necessary here just to add a note of caution. Whilst differences in meaning may be signalled by some physical differences in form, this is not *necessarily* the case. Hence the existence of ambiguity:

Mary is a beautiful dancer

Nor is it necessarily the case that differences in physical form always signal difference in meaning:

James used a hammer to knock in the nail
James knocked in the nail with a hammer

Acceptability

It is now time to return to a further consideration of the two key concepts of acceptability and appropriateness in the light of what has been said in the previous sections. When we teach languages we wish to turn out people who are capable of producing and recognizing utterances which are both acceptable and appropriate. After our discussions of the goals of linguistics and of the nature of linguistic analysis we can be somewhat more precise about these two notions.

I suggested that the goal of linguistics, which was to characterize all the actual and potential sentences of a language in a way which accorded with the intuitions of a native speaker about his language, was to give an account of what Chomsky has called the competence of a native speaker. The data on which such a theory is based are utterances of native speakers. In Lyons's words (1968):

An acceptable utterance is one that has been, or might be, produced by a native speaker in some appropriate context and is, or would be, accepted by other native speakers as belonging to the language in question. (p. 137)

But the reader will, by now, realize that there are certain difficulties in such a definition. Firstly, what is meant by 'the language in question'? The problems of defining *a language* have been dealt with in chapter 3. Is it possible to speak of native speakers of a language at all? A person is a native speaker of his own idiolect and no two people have identical idiolects. It might seem that the only way out of these difficulties was to do what Chomsky does and say that the linguist describes the competence of an *ideal* native speaker in a *homogeneous* community. However, in spite of the evidence of studies of acceptability already referred to on page 55 in which it has been shown that a group of native speakers did not agree about the acceptability or otherwise of a set of representative sentences, Labov's evidence does suggest that there is some norm which we all recognize – although it may include forms which we ourselves do not include within our code. It appears that the competence of the 'native speakers' is a somewhat variable, rather than a well-defined thing, that it is best characterized by sets of both variable and invariant rules. The grammar of 'a language' is thus seen as essentially *indeterminate*. If the descriptions of 'a language' appear sometimes to be well-defined and unqualified, then those qualities have been put there by the linguist, and they are not a feature of human language. But having said this we may again quote Lyons:

> To assert that the grammatical structure of a language is in *the last resort* indeterminate is not the same as to assert that no part of the grammatical structure is determinate. There are many combinations of words which all linguists will characterize immediately, not only as unacceptable, but also as 'ungrammatical'. (Lyons, 1968, p. 154)

For the language teacher this is just as well; he must be able confidently to stigmatize certain utterances of the learner as unacceptable or incorrect. But he must be able to go a great deal further: he must be able to say in what way they are incorrect or unacceptable (see chapter 11). It is here that our discussion of the levels of analysis comes in.

Utterances may be unacceptable at any of the levels of analysis. A foreigner may produce perfectly 'grammatical' sentences with a foreign accent. In such a case his utterance would be unacceptable at a *phonetic* level. No native speaker would pronounce it in the way he did. By 'speaking with a foreign accent', I mean no more than what, in the case of written language, would be called 'writing with a foreign hand' – no breach of the grammatical or phonological rules is committed. Then there are those foreigners, for example, who do not make a distinction between 'l' and 'r' in their pronunciation. Such an error is not merely phonetic, since it obscures the meaning distinction between such words as *lamb* and *ram* or *lice* and *rice*. The equivalent in writing would be precisely that of consistently using the letter 'l' to do the work of both 'l' and 'r' (at least at the beginning of words). The utterance of such a foreigner is *phonologically* unacceptable.

I do not need to illustrate unacceptability at the syntactic or morphological level since this includes all those utterances which we call in everyday language 'ungrammatical'. But it is important for the foreign language teacher to realize that what the native-speaking layman often refers to as 'ungrammatical', for example, 'double negative' sentences – *nobody told me nothing* – are not, of course, unacceptable except in a social sense or in terms of the grammar of a standard dialect. Learners do sometimes by chance produce sentences which resemble those produced by native dialect speakers, e.g.

He don't come here very often
I were talking to him
What was you saying?

But much more often the learner's erroneous sentences are of a form which probably no native speaker of any dialect of English would produce, e.g.* *he come very often here.* (We might note here that many of the 'starred' forms, i.e. examples of deviant, ill-formed or unacceptable sentences used for explanation and discussion by linguists, would never be produced either by native speakers or learners. They are simply artifacts in the methodology of linguistic research.)

Finally, we come to the level of semantic unacceptability. Here we are in some difficulty. Whilst no one would have any difficulty at one extreme in stigmatizing Chomsky's famous example sentence, *Colourless green ideas sleep furiously*, as semantically unacceptable, greater difficulty might arise with Mark Twain's equally famous statement: 'The reports of my death have been greatly exaggerated.' But in the case of a sentence like: *More than 100 per cent of the inhabitants suffer from malnutrition* we may wonder whether we have a case of semantic unacceptability or merely evidence of inadequate 'knowledge of the world'. At the other extreme, few would regard *these insects have only four legs* as semantically unacceptable; whilst we might say the speaker wasn't much of a zoologist or had bad eyesight, we wouldn't say he didn't know the language. It is between these two extremes we may have difficulty in deciding whether someone doesn't know what he's talking about or doesn't know how to talk about it. It is in this twilight area that much poetry seems uneasily to exist, and many of the 'cute' sayings of children and the erroneous utterances of language learners are found. There is a parallel between the poet's *a grief ago*, and the child's *We didn't go away for a holiday, we went away for a week*.

The difficulty is that when utterances like these occur we cannot, without further investigation, decide whether the speaker is breaking a sense–relation rule of the language or a reference–relation rule. If the former, it is a case of unacceptability, if the latter, a case of inappropriateness. It is, as we have agreed, just as necessary that a learner, child or foreigner, should learn the formation rules of a language as the speaking rules. Inappropriate language is a breach of the speaking rules of language. To appropriateness we now turn.

Appropriateness

Whilst the concept of acceptability is fairly well defined, at least at the phonological and grammatical level, appropriateness covers a multitude of relations, one of which, reference, has just been mentioned. Part of knowing a language is knowing the reference relations of lexical items, and as we have seen, it is through these relationships that we break into the closed network of the semantic structure of a language, and where differences lie in the way different cultures structure the world. We have also seen the consequent dangers that lurk in translation and the relevance of cultural overlap in language learning. We can call that *referential appropriateness*.

We have also seen that appropriateness is involved in the selection of utterances so that they relate to their linguistic environments in dialogue or discourse. We would call this *textual appropriateness*.

There is another sort of appropriateness which we can call, in general, *social*. This, too, has already been touched on in chapter 3 where we observed that the choice of language matches the social roles and status of the participants in any given interaction. Where the focus is on the relative status of the participants we can speak of *stylistic* appropriateness. As far as the lexical element in the language is concerned, a good dictionary will mark its statements of synonymy with some indication of the social situation which selects a particular item; thus, we often find in parenthesis (vulgar), (slang) after a particular word, and perhaps even (obscene), (blasphemous). I am told that naval men don't like their ships referred to as 'boats', although both words may name the same class of objects. We have to be a little careful here to make a distinction between referring to the same class of objects by different names in different social contexts and the use of technical terminology. In the latter case, we are often dealing with classes of objects unknown to the layman, or distinctions which the layman does not need to make. If he has occasion to refer to such an object he will have to resort to some vague circumlocutionary form, *the thingummy sticking out on the side of the whatsitsname – Oh, you mean the gudgeon pin*. The reader will recognize that we are back again here at something very similar to the differences between the way different cultures divide up reality. The football-playing British have, as I have said, a 'technical word' to *kick*, the French have to use periphrasis: *donner un coup de pied*. It is not an accident that the international 'technical' terminology of sport is largely of English origin. In this sense, a technical or scientific confraternity is a sub-culture with its own linguistic code. A good dictionary will indicate in which sub-culture a word is appropriately used (*tech.*), (*scientific*), (*naut.*), (*astron.*), etc.

Learning a language, then, is not just a question of learning to produce utterances which are acceptable, they must also be appropriate. Linguistics has a lot to say about the former. So far it has little to say about the latter.

Chapter 6
Psycholinguistics and Language Teaching

The psychology of language

In chapter 1 I described the approach to language which regarded it as a phenomenon of the individual, as psychological, and suggested that it was concerned with describing and explaining language as a matter of human behaviour. In chapter 4 one aspect of the psychology of language cropped up, the relation between thought and language, in which language is regarded as a symbolic system related to the conceptual system of the individual. The reader will remember that Whorf's famous essay was entitled *The Relation of Habitual Thought and Behaviour to Language*. This gives us a clue to a psychological study of language by introducing the terms *thought* and *behaviour*. The trouble with these two terms in 'everyday language' is their imprecision. In this respect they resemble the terms *word* and *sound* in the linguistic field.

We speak, as we have already noted, of *knowing* a language. Knowing something implies having learned it or discovered it; we aren't born knowing things. But we can scarcely speak of knowing some sort of behaviour such as walking; in such a case we speak of *knowing how* and *learning how*. There would be something rather odd about asking someone if he was learning *how* to speak French. The implication of such a question would be that it was a matter of muscular control, of 'getting your mouth round' some difficult sounds. The trouble is that the term 'behaviour' does not seem to do justice to language. This is because behaviour is usually thought of as something essentially physical and observable, and that, while much language has overt physical manifestations – movements of vocal organs with the production of sound, and movements of the hand with the production of traces on paper – any notion that this is all there is to language is obviously unsatisfactory. Thus, understanding speech has no obvious overt physical correlatives. This is why it is so difficult, without using language itself, to know if someone has understood us. Most people would feel that a great deal of language activity goes on 'inside the head', and that because this is unobservable by direct means, it does not mean that there is nothing going on. On the other hand, no one would deny that observable, measurable physical behaviour is the *data* with which the psychologist, as also the theoretical linguist, must work. The differences we find between the various psychological accounts of language derive to a large extent from the different philosophical approaches which their proponents adopt to the scientific method, their different attitudes to the role of data (cf. chapter 5, page 83).

The principal concern of the psychology of language is to give an account of the psychological processes that go on when people produce or understand utterances, that is, the investigation of *language performance*. But one of the ways of investigating this is to try and understand how people acquire such an ability. This is the study of *language acquisition*. It is important, if we are not to prejudge the issue, to make a distinction between *language acquisition* and *language learning*. Language acquisition takes place in the infant and the young child at a time when he is acquiring many other skills and much other knowledge about the world. Language learning, i.e. learning a second language, normally starts at a later stage, when language performance has already become established and when many other physical and mental processes of maturation are complete or nearing completion.

Language performance and language acquisition, then, are the two principal concerns of the psychology of language, or, to use the more recent term for these studies, psycholinguistics. The much intensified study of psycholinguistics in recent years has produced a considerable amount of literature and some significant advances in our understanding of language acquisition. The same cannot be said about the study of language learning. Surprisingly little fundamental research has been conducted into the processes of learning a second language. The consequence has been that most theories in this field are still extrapolations from general theories of human learning and behaviour or from the recent work in language performance and acquisition. This is not to say that there has been no valuable research on language *teaching*. But this has been concerned with the evaluation of different teaching methods and materials, for example, the use of language laboratories, the use of language drills, the teaching of grammar by different methods. Now, such research is difficult to evaluate for two reasons. First of all, experiments in language teaching suffer from the same set of problems that all comparative educational experiments suffer from. It is virtually impossible to control all the factors involved even if we know how to identify them in the first place, particularly such factors as motivation, previous knowledge, aptitude, learning outside the classroom, teacher performance. Consequently the conclusions to be drawn from such experiments cannot, with confidence, be generalized to other teaching situations. The results are, strictly speaking, only valid for the learners, teachers and schools in which the experiment took place. Secondly, it is not possible to draw any general conclusions about the psychology of language learning from 'operational' research into language teaching. The discovery that learners do or do not learn, or learn better or worse, under certain conditions, does not tell us *directly* about the process of learning itself. It is true it may give us 'hunches' which could be followed up by experiments in learning. For example, we might note that a teaching method which included practice in translation produced learners who were better at translation than a method which did not. (This is not by any means an obvious result, incidentally.) But the result of such an experiment in teaching would tell us that 'practice', something which could be rigorously defined and described as a *teaching procedure*, is relevant to teaching translation. It would not tell us, however, what is meant by 'practice' as a *learning process*. Similarly, we might find that drills involving 'imitation' promoted learning. Imitation can be rigorously described as a teaching procedure. But this does not tell us what this sort of behaviour is in the learning process. Is it just a question of repeating the physical movements which produce the same set of sounds – a sort of 'parrotting', or is it some much more complex process going on 'inside the learner'? Ultimately, of course, we need to correlate teaching *procedures* with learning *processes*; we need to be able to say what procedures are a *necessary* condition for certain learning processes to take place. We can, however, never say that certain procedures are a *sufficient* condition for certain processes to take place. You can take a horse to water, but . . .

It is, then, most important to maintain a distinction between language teaching and language learning. And of these two it is the learning processes which have priority for investigation. Until we have a much better idea of what these are we cannot, on a systematic and principled basis, create the necessary conditions for optimal learning; we can only do what we have largely been doing, that is, work on a hit-and-miss basis. It is as well to admit that at the present time we lack any clear and soundly-based picture of the learning process, and that our teaching procedures are founded, if they are founded on anything other than trial-and-error, upon general psychological theories of learning, and on what extrapolations may be speculatively made from theories of language performance and language acquisition, and from the little experimental laboratory-scale experiments with second language learning.

Language acquisition and language learning

There has been no lack of people who predicted that there would be nothing to learn from a study of language acquisition which could be of relevance to language learning. They pointed out that there were so many differences in the conditions under which learning and acquisition took place that there could be no transfer from one to the other. Language acquisition takes place during the period when the infant is maturing physically and mentally, and necessarily there must be some connection or interaction between the two processes:

We must assume that the child's capacity to learn language is a consequence of maturation because (1) the milestones of language acquisition are normally interlocked with other milestones that are clearly attributable to physical maturation, particularly stance, gait, and motor coordination; (2) this synchrony is frequently preserved even if the whole maturational schedule is dramatically slowed down, as in several forms of mental retardation; (3) there is no evidence that intensive training procedures can produce higher stages of language development, that is, advance language in a child who is maturationally still a toddling infant. However, the development of language is not caused by maturation of motor processes because it can, in certain rare instances, evolve faster or slower than motor development. (Lenneberg, 1967, p. 178)

Secondly, the *motivation* for learning in each case cannot be equated. Indeed it is not clear in what sense we can use the term *motivation* in the case of language acquisition. Congenitally deaf children develop a means of nonverbal communication which appears to satisfy their needs at least in the earlier stages, so that it does not appear that young children *must* specifically acquire *language* to cope with their environment. Yet we observe that all children whose physical and mental capacities lie within what we can regard as a normal range do learn language. All we can say is that 'it comes naturally' and not as a result of the discovery of its practical utility.

Thirdly, the data from which an infant acquires language are different. He is exposed to samples of the language on an unorganized basis. His data are not just the utterances which are addressed specifically to him, but any language he is exposed to. Furthermore, whilst the utterances which are addressed to him may be modified or simplified in some unconscious way by the adults who speak to him (Snow, 1972), he cannot be said to be exposed to a carefully planned or logically ordered set of data – he is not submitted to a 'teaching syllabus' in any ordinary sense of the word. If there is a learning 'programme' then it is an 'internal' one, a product of his normal cognitive development. It is indeed the main object of studies of child language acquisition to discover what the nature of this 'programme' is.

Fourthly, whilst people do learn second languages without being taught, that is, without having the language data organized for them by some teacher, second language learning for most people takes place under formal instruction; the exceptions are those people who pick up a foreign language in the country they happen to visit or live in. Now, in the case of language acquisition, whilst the language data to which the infant is exposed are certainly not organized, it is not clear to what extent he is exposed to 'teaching', if by that we mean a particular sort of behaviour by parents and others whose object is to promote the child's linguistic development. There are many reactions to a child's speech on the part of adults which have apparent counterparts in the classroom, but this does not mean that the parent is behaving in this way *in order to* teach the child. For example, a parent will often repeat the adult form of what he conceives to be what the child has attempted to express in his language:

CHILD Table hit head
ADULT No: the head hit the table

This looks like a form of 'correction'. An adult will often 'expand' a child's two or three word utterance into a full adult form. Or an adult may simply query a child's utterance by some such expression as *Eh?* or *What?* This could be interpreted as a directive to repeat what he has just said; however, it appears that it is more often interpreted by the child as a request to paraphrase his utterance, as this recorded exchange shows:

MOTHER Did Billy have his egg cut up for him at breakfast?
CHILD Yes, I showed him
MOTHER You what?
CHILD I showed him
MOTHER You showed him?
CHILD I seed him
MOTHER Ah, you saw him
CHILD Yes, I saw him

It is true, of course, that some adults do deliberately attempt to correct a child's non-adult utterances by some such remarks as: *No, say* ... But such attempts do not by any means always have the intended result, as the following example shows:

CHILD Nobody don't like me
MOTHER No, say: nobody likes me
CHILD Nobody don't like me
  (Eight repetitions of this dialogue)
MOTHER Now listen carefully, say: nobody likes me
CHILD Oh, nobody don't likes me
(McNeill, 1966, p. 69)

Or the adult may say: *That's not a* ..., *it's a* ... when a child makes a referential error.

Then there is a role of practice and imitation. That procedures which go under these names have always played a part in language *teaching* needs no mention; but, as has already been suggested, it is difficult to identify these unequivocally with processes in language learning or acquisition. Certainly the parent or adult, unlike the teacher, rarely attempts to get the child to imitate a spontaneous adult utterance and certainly never requires a child to 'practise' adult forms of speech. Where 'imitation' occurs, it is the child who selects what to 'imitate'. Whether imitation and practice are indeed processes of language acquisition is a matter of debate amongst those studying child language acquisition. The belief that imitation and practice are the fundamental processes whereby a child acquires language is, of course, a very ancient one, but it has only recently been incorporated into a specific language learning theory as the process of learning 'verbal responses'. In this theory the function of 'imitation' is regarded as the 'acquisition' of a response, and the function of 'practice' is to 'strengthen' it, i.e. to make it more likely to occur or render it more readily 'available'. The difficulty here is in the definition of a 'verbal response'. Is it 'formal' or 'functional'? We know that there is no one-to-one relation between these aspects of an utterance. As we have seen, children, like adults, rarely hear a formally identical utterance twice. How then are we going to reconcile satisfactorily the notion of a response as something which is imitated and practised with the fact that utterances are rarely formally identical? If, indeed, something is imitated and practised it must be something pretty abstract.

A careful study of infants' 'imitation' of adult utterances, which on some counts has been as high as 10 per cent of the child's recorded utterances (Ervin, 1964; Slobin, 1966), has shown that a child does not, in fact, spontaneously imitate a form it cannot already produce from the resources of its own grammar, and resists attempts to make it imitate forms which it cannot generate spontaneously. This suggests strongly that the child does not *acquire* new language forms by imitation, and that where imitation apparently occurs it fulfils some other function than learning. What about practice? The child's tendency to go through routines which resemble 'classroom' drills is well attested:

Take the monkey	Monkey [repeated three times]
Take it	That's a [repeated twice]
Stop it	That's a Kitty
Stop the ball	That's a Fifi there
Stop it	That's teddy bear and baby

(Weir, 1962)

In the light of what has just been said it may be doubted whether utterance sequences of this sort are practice in the sense of 'strengthening responses'. They may well be just another form of 'verbal play' fulfilling an *imaginative* speech function – the exercise of linguistic skills for their own sake (see chapter 2), i.e. a *use* of language, not a strategy of language learning. This is all the more likely since such practice sessions normally take place in the absence of adults, or at least unmonitored by them. We can compare this with the unmonitored 'practice' in second language learning, the learning value of which is in serious doubt. If, however, we do admit the role of practice in language acquisition, we must also allow the possibility that the responses being practised may be 'sub-vocal', since there is evidence from the study of psychotic children that, after appearing to have developed little or no language behaviour, they suddenly, after treatment or spontaneously, begin to talk fluently and at the stage of development appropriate to their age. A similar phenomenon has been observed with second language learners.

The main argument against language acquisition and second language learning having anything in common is that language learning normally takes place after language acquisition is largely complete. In other words, the language teacher is not teaching language as such, but a new manifestation of language. The language learner has already developed considerable communicative competence in his mother tongue, he already knows what he can and cannot do with it, what some at least of its functions are (Halliday, 1969). On this view, what the language teacher is doing is teaching a new way of doing what the learner can already do. He is attempting, therefore, to extend, to a greater or lesser degree, the behavioural repertoire, set of rules or ways of thinking of the learner.

This discussion has listed a number of features in which the circumstances of first and second language learning are different, but note that it is the *circumstances* (learner, teacher and linguistic data) in which learning takes place that are different. It does not necessarily follow for that reason that the *processes* of learning are different. The processes of relearning something are not necessarily different from the original learning process, and indeed, inasmuch as the child's grammar is constantly changing and developing, he could be regarded as in a constant process of relearning, and yet no one has suggested that the processes whereby a child acquires his first language change as he advances.

The main argument in favour of assuming that language learning and language acquisition are different processes is that the language learner is a different sort of person from the infant; that there has been some *qualitative* change in his physiology and psychology at some point in his maturation process; and that these changes in some way inhibit him from using the same learning strategies that he used as an infant, or make available to him some whole new range of strategies which he did not possess before. These notions are all included within what has been called 'the critical period' for language acquisition.

Lenneberg (1967) summarizes what is meant by the 'critical period':

Language cannot begin to develop until a certain level of physical maturation and growth has been attained. Between the ages of two and three years
language emerges by an interaction of maturation and self-programmed
learning. Between the ages of three and the early teens the possibility for primary language acquisition continues to be good; the individual appears to be
most sensitive to stimuli at this time and to preserve some innate flexibility
for the organization of brain functions to carry out the complex integration
of sub-processes necessary for the smooth elaboration of speech and language. After puberty, the ability for self-organization and adjustment to the
physiological demands of verbal behaviour quickly declines. The brain behaves as if it had become set in its ways and primary, basic language skills
not acquired by that time, except for articulation, usually remain deficient
for life. (p. 158)

The evidence for the critical period for the acquisition of language is very strong, drawn as it is from the extensive study of the mentally subnormal and from studies of aphasic disturbances. Whether the milestones in language acquisition correlate with other milestones in the child's development, such as learning to stand, walk and perform other tasks involving coordinated motor skills is still an open question, but there is some evidence that, if the latter developments are delayed for some reason, so are the developments in language, and just as the development stages in these other respects cannot be brought forward by training or teaching, nor can the regular development of language be accelerated. This does not mean, of course, that other sorts of human learning also are subject to a critical period. We go on learning many skills and acquire many other abilities in late adolescence, and indeed most of our learning capacities seem to go on unimpaired until later life. And obviously people *do* learn second languages at all periods in later life, though their ability to acquire a native pronunciation seems to be limited, at least for most learners, to the 'critical

period'. But learning a language is not just learning a pronunciation.

How does the notion of the 'critical period' bear on the question of the processes of learning first and second languages? Apparently we acquire language during a period when our brains are in a particular stage of their development. If language is not acquired then, there is some evidence that it is very much more difficult to acquire it at a later stage. If, however, we have acquired language, i.e. already possess verbal behaviour, then there does not seem to be any psychological or physiological impediment to the learning of a second language, if we want to. It cannot be too strongly stressed that 'learning a second language' is *not* the same as 'acquiring language again'. When we acquire language in infancy the particular 'outward' form it assumes is that of the dialect of the society into which we happen to be born. English infants acquire language in its English form, French infants in its French form. 'Learning a second language', after we have acquired verbal behaviour (in its mother-tongue manifestation) is a matter of adaptation or extension of *existing* skills and knowledge rather than the relearning of a completely new set of skills from scratch. We can conclude from this not that the process of acquiring language and learning a second language must be different, but rather that there are some fundamental properties which all languages have in common (linguistic universals) and that it is only their outward and perhaps relatively superficial characteristics that differ; and that when these fundamental properties have once been learned (through their mother-tongue manifestations) the learning of a second manifestation of language (the second language) is a relatively much smaller task.

Performance models

In the opening section of this chapter, I said that the two problems with which psycholinguistics was principally concerned were *language acquisition* and *language performance*. Miller (1970) has described the latter as 'The psychological processes that go on when people use sentences.' The term *use* here is, of course, neutral as between receptive and productive activity or skills. It has become customary in discussions amongst language teachers to talk about the inculcation of language skills. These are often identified as *speaking*, *hearing*, *writing* and *reading*. It requires, however, very little reflection to realize that this categorization is an entirely superficial one. These so-called skills are categories of more or less overt linguistic behaviour. They classify observable physical acts, but neither describe nor explain what is going on inside the head of the language user. It is also customary to group these 'skills' into two sets, 'active' and 'passive', thus implying that there is something in common between speaking and writing, on the one hand, and hearing and reading on the other. The names 'active' and 'passive' are justified only inasmuch as the 'active skills' have clear and unmistakable physical manifestations – movements of lips or hands, producing sounds or marks on paper – while the 'passive skills' have no such unambiguous overt signs. The holding of a book and the movement of the eyes or the inclination of the head and occasional nods and smiles are scarcely sufficient evidence that language activity is going on; they are all too easily simulated. For these reasons it is preferable to speak of productive and receptive performance.

Before looking at what component abilities are involved in productive and receptive performance, let us consider whether the language teacher is justified in talking about his task in terms of 'teaching speaking, hearing, writing and reading'. One answer is that he is not justified in doing so because his pupils can normally already do all these things in their mother tongue. It is true that there are second-language teaching situations where the pupils have not yet learned to read and write, and where the teaching of these activities goes on at the same time as the teaching of the second language. Notice also that learning to read and write *presupposes* (at least, in all normal people) the ability to speak and hear; in other words, it requires the possession of some verbal behaviour. Thus the language teacher is concerned *not* with teaching, speaking and hearing, etc. but *speaking in French*, or *reading German* or *hearing Italian*. This is only to repeat what was said at the end of the last section: the teacher does not teach language skills from scratch but rather modifies or extends these skills in some perhaps relatively superficial fashion. To take just the case of reading aloud, for example, there are recorded cases of children who have been able to read aloud to blind or illiterate grandparents (whose mother tongue was different from that of the child) in a foreign language they did not 'know' – at least to the apparent satisfaction of the grandparent. Most of us can 'have a stab' at reading aloud some unknown foreign language, so long as it has a roman alphabetic script. The chances are that an intelligent and literate native speaker will be able to make something of our performance.

This last illustration shows clearly that reading involves several different levels of activity or different kinds of skill. When we read to ourselves we are not just 'mouthing' vocally or sub-vocally a series of sounds (or 'barking at print' as it has sometimes been called), we are 'processing' the written material in a number of highly complex ways. Any normal meaning of reading includes (besides just recognizing the letters) at least recognizing the sentences and understanding the message.

The first thing one must be able to do in the case of speech is hear it. This is obvious. But strictly speaking, hearing is not 'doing anything'; it is something which happens to you. So it would perhaps be better to say 'listen', which implies 'giving attention' and is under voluntary control. It is an *act* – or better, activity – and involves 'directing one's awareness'. One must be able, in order to process speech or any other potentially informative noises which come to one – footsteps, car engines, bird song, music – to discriminate various degrees of *intensity* (or loudness), differences in *pitch*, *duration* and more particularly *changes* in intensity, pitch and duration. One must be able to detect differences in the *quality* of sound, that is, in the makeup of the frequency components of sound, the sort of discrimination which enables us to tell the sound of an oboe from that of a flute. There is obviously nothing specifically linguistic about these abilities. We need to develop these skills in order to make sense of the 'world of sound' in general. When speaking, we need the skill to control our organs of speech in such a way that all these 'parameters' of sound are under our control, and to do this we have to 'monitor' our own production – this process is called *auditory feedback*. The reason that the speech of a person who has become deaf often takes on certain peculiarities of sound is that the auditory monitoring process cannot operate. Deaf speakers have to rely on a rather less satisfactory and precise feedback mechanism to monitor their performance – information about the state of muscular tension of their organs of speech – *proprio-ceptive feedback*. Anyone who has undergone experiments in delayed auditory feedback – where information about the sounds he is making is delayed electronically by a fraction of a second – will know what havoc this can wreak on his ability to speak fluently and coherently. It tends to reduce the subject to a gibbering idiot. Similarly, anyone unlucky enough to possess a car with a virtually silent engine knows how difficult it makes decisions about changing gear. Good drivers depend very much on auditory feedback from the engine, unless they possess 'visual' feedback from the tachometer and speedometer.

The next set of operations in processing speech is at least partly linguistic. We can call it *recognition*. Its investigation falls within the general field of the psychology of perception. Perception is not just passive bombardment with sense stimuli, but an active process. Sense stimuli are fundamentally ambiguous, as Gregory (1970) puts it:

Perception involves a kind of inference from sensory data to object-reality. Further, behaviour is not controlled directly by the data but by the solutions to the perceptual inferences from the data. . . . So perception involves a kind of problem-solving – a kind of intelligence. (p. 30)

Problem solving involves, in its turn, the making or possession of hypotheses against which the evidence of senses is tested. These perceptual or 'object-hypotheses' are sometimes known as *perceptual schemata*. They are a sort of internalized abstract 'model' of entities in the world outside, including sounds, of course. Such object-hypotheses are learned and stored. We recognize some set of sensations as a car because we possess an object-hypothesis of what we call 'a car' and we do it by some sort of *matching* process between our schema and the incoming sensations. Recognition, then, is an active cognitive process and the schemata are learned inductively. Recognizing the sounds of speech involves such a cognitive process. When we 'listen' to a foreign language, we can distinguish variations of pitch, intensity, duration and quality in the noises we hear, if we pay attention, but we cannot 'recognize' them *as sounds* except inasmuch as we can 'match' them with some already learned schemata. We 'hear' foreign speech in terms of the perceptual schemata of our own language. Fundamentally this is why we pronounce foreign languages with an accent, at least until we have set up a new set of object-hypotheses. The reader will notice that there is a connection between the psycholinguistic process of 'recognition' with what we called in chapter 5 the secondary articulation of language.

The process of 'recognition' however, extends beyond the level of sounds, intonation patterns and rhythms of language to groups of sounds or lexical words. We also store object-hypotheses of words and even perhaps groups of words which habitually occur together (see the later discussion of habits). This is the theoretical justification for the 'look–say' method in the teaching of reading.

However, the processing of complete utterances must involve some other additional operations. The 'sounds' and 'words' of a language are finite in number; the number of sentences is indefinitely large and rarely do we hear the same sentence twice. There is no possibility that we can ever arrive at developing and storing a schema for every sentence in the language. Sentence 'recognition', if we can still call it that, must proceed by different means, it cannot involve a process of matching input data with stored representations. We could in any case not hold a list of all the sentences in a language in our head. An amusing calculation by Miller (1970) has shown that, assuming a vocabulary of 10^4 words in a language, just to utter all the acceptable twenty-word sentences of that language would take 10^{12} centuries, which is more than 1000 times the estimated age of this earth.

We have seen that, linguistically speaking, the sentences of a language can *most economically* be described in terms of a *finite* set of 'rules' (see page 90). Our strategy for recognizing sentences in a language must be through some equally economical procedure. By 'economical' I mean taking up the least possible 'mental' storage space. This means that we must use 'rules' rather than lists. In other words, we do not match the incoming data against some infinitely large set of object-hypotheses, but rather match the 'rules' which could produce the data against some learned set of rules.

It is most important at this point not to jump to the conclusion, as all too many have done, that the rules the linguist uses to describe the sentences of a language have psychological reality. We must not confuse the description of the process with that of the product. Broadbent (1970) illustrates this point most clearly:

I have heard somewhere that Michelangelo, when he called on someone and found them out, used to leave a visiting card containing nothing but a free-hand circle. The artist's ability to draw such a circle implies a quadratic equation relating the movement of his hand in one direction to the movement in the direction at right angles to the first. $y^2 = K - x^2$. It also implies, perhaps with even greater simplicity, that the artist's hand travelled over a succession of points on the paper all of which were equidistant from the centre of the circle. From our knowlede of human skilled performance, however, it is exceedingly probable that the relationship embodied in Michelangelo's nervous system was neither of these, despite their simplicity and mathematical elegance . . . A more plausible conjecture is that Michelangelo had learned a pattern of acceleration in two dimensions as a function of time, whose mathematical representation would be very complex . . . Mathematically such a description is apparently less tidy, but psychologically it seems more likely. (p. 89)

The account of the process of sentence recognition given above, or, as I shall call it from now on, sentence *identification*, in order to emphasize the point that different processes are involved, is sometimes called 'analysis by synthesis'.

It has one rather serious defect: it suggests that in order to 'identify' a sentence, we must first analyse it completely and then see if the structure of the sentence can be 'generated' by the rules of the grammar we have internalized. Such a process seems intuitively too cumbersome and slow (Thorne, 1966, p. 7). Consequently, some modifications have been suggested (Sutherland, 1966, p. 161) to the effect that we do not go through the whole process in its entirety, but 'sample' the incoming data and, on the basis of our sampling, *predict* the structure of the utterance and act accordingly; that is, go into the next phase of the performance. This modification of the 'analysis by synthesis' model is called a 'heuristic' model. It would account for the fact that we often do make mistakes in our receptive processing of utterances, and have frequently to 'backtrack' and do a more complete job of analysis of the incoming data. The heuristic model introduces the notion of *prediction* or *anticipation* which is found in all the cognitive accounts of perception, and very roughly covers what is meant by the saying, 'we hear what we expect to hear' (Bruce, 1956). The ability to anticipate is an absolutely fundamental skill in language use and language learning. It operates at all levels of comprehension – anticipating what a person is going to talk about in a situation, anticipating what a person's next utterance is going to be in a dialogue, what the next word in his utterance will be, down to anticipating what the next sound is likely to be after a given series of sounds. This is a very big part of what we have called linguistic competence. It is, in a sense, the sheer unpredictability of utterances in a foreign language which, at least in the earlier stages of learning, tends to be bewildering or indeed paralysing. If we have to process *all* the data down to the last detail the whole system gets clogged up and grinds to a halt. Any ability to anticipate or predict is based on a knowledge of rules. That is why language is often called 'rule-governed' behaviour.

If we want to see how this works in other fields of activity we need only think of driving a car. If we were unable to anticipate with some degree of certainty the behaviour of the other drivers we would be so paralysed that we would never venture out onto the road at all. It is because we and other drivers know the 'rules of the road', the highway code, that we are able to anticipate their behaviour within sufficiently narrow limits for us to dare to pass them, cross the lights at green and make all the other manoeuvres which involve other road users. Driving is, thank goodness, rule-governed behaviour and consequently to some degree predictable. (Most of us would like the behaviour of other drivers to be more predictable.) Language, however, is never *wholly* predictable. If it were, it would not serve for communication. What is wholly predictable is uninformative. Meaning implies choice and consequently whilst anticipation makes language performance possible, it is not the whole story.

It is not sufficient merely to *identify* utterances as grammatical. In linguistic terms, we have to internalize not only the grammatical but also the 'lexical' rules. These rules, as we saw, have to do with the semantic structure of the language, with its internal 'sense relations'. Utterances could be either grammatically or semantically unacceptable. Identification, therefore, is the process of recognizing utterances as grammatically and semantically well-formed.

It is at this point that I must introduce again the frequently-heard remark: *I understand what you say, but I don't know what you mean.* We can reinterpret this in the light of what has been said so far. It could be phrased as: *I identify your utterance as well-formed according to the rules of the language, but I do not understand it.* The reader will note that I have used the term *understand* differently in the two sentences; in the first, as equal to 'identify', and in the second as equal to 'know what is meant'. The second meaning is the one I used in the example in connection with a discussion of the 'function of language' in chapter 3. It meant there, as here, 'perceive the function of the utterance in its context', or 'perceive the intentions of the speaker'. The process of *understanding*, in this sense, involves, of course, 'understanding' the situation as well, and this relates the understanding of language to an understanding of the world. Readers will remember the functional ambiguity of *You must treat the river as an open sewer*. What is not at all clear is the extent to which the process of 'understanding' is a specifically linguistic part of the performance at all, or to what extent it can be regarded as a rule-governed activity. Labov (1970b) suggests that there are indeed what he calls 'invariant rules of discourse analysis'. He illustrates these rules from our use of *yes* and *no*. He says:

Given two parties in a conversation, A and B, we can distinguish 'A events' as things that A knows but B does not; and 'B events' as the things that B knows about but A does not.... The rule then states:

If A makes a statement about a B event, it is heard as a request for confirmation.

This rule contains the social construct of 'shared knowledge' which is not normally a linguistic rule. This is merely one of the many rules of interpretation which relate 'what is said' – questions, statements, imperatives – to 'what is done' – requests, refusals, assertions, denials, insults, challenges, retreats and so on. There are no simple one-to-one relations between actions and utterances. (p. 80)

In the terminology I have been using 'heard' and 'interpretation' would be expressed as *understood* and *understand*. We can illustrate this rule quite simply, taking *yes* and *no* to indicate that an utterance has indeed been *understood* as a 'request for confirmation'.

1. A. You're not feeling very well. (B event)
   B. No–Oh, yes I am. (confirmation–disconfirmation)

2. A. She told you she was coming. (B event)
   B. Yes–No, she didn't. (confirmation–disconfirmation)

3. A. I can see him quite well now. (A event)
   B. *Yes–No. (inappropriate)

As Labov points out, the rule operates so stringently that many speakers will not continue making a statement about a B event until a yes–no response has been forthcoming. On the other hand, as example 3 shows, statements about A events do not require or even tolerate a yes–no response.

The reader will by now have discerned the connection between the psychological process I have been calling *understanding* with the notions of 'communicative competence', 'speaking rules' and 'appropriateness', just as he will have connected the psychological process of 'identification' with 'grammatical/semantic competence', 'formation rules' and 'acceptability'. He will also have noted that there is a hierarchical ordering in these processes, such that *identification* presupposes *listening* and *recognition*, whilst *understanding* presupposes *identification*.

So far the discussion has been on the psycholinguistic processes of receptive behaviour. Can we simply reverse the order of events and say we have an account of speech production? The difficulty of talking about the process is well captured by William James (1890), quoted by Laver (1970):

And has the reader never asked himself what kind of a mental fact is his intention of saying a thing before he has said it? It is an entirely definite intention, distinct from all other intentions, an absolutely distinct state of consciousness, therefore; and yet how much of it consists of definite sensorial images, either of words or of things? Hardly anything! Linger, and the words and things come into the mind; the anticipatory intention, the divination is there no more. But as the words that replace it arrive, it welcomes them successively and calls them right if they agree with it, and rejects them and calls them wrong if they do not. It has therefore a nature of its own of the most positive sort, and yet what can we say about it without using words that belong to the later mental facts that replace it? (pp. 66–67)

Laver identifies five chief functions in speech production. These he describes as neurolinguistic. We would not expect them therefore to correspond on a one-to-one basis with the psycholinguistic processes of receptive behaviour already discussed. These are the *ideational* process which he says: 'Initiates the appropriate semantic content of any verbal message the speaker wishes to communicate' (semantic here must be taken to include the speaker's intentions); the permanent *storage* of linguistic information; the *planning* process 'which constructs an appropriate linguistic programme for the expression of the idea'; the *execution* of the programme which is the actual set of articulatory actions; and the *monitoring* function, about which I have already spoken. It is clear that these functions are not hierarchically ordered in the way the receptive psycholinguistic processes were. For example, the monitoring function must be simultaneous with the execution, and

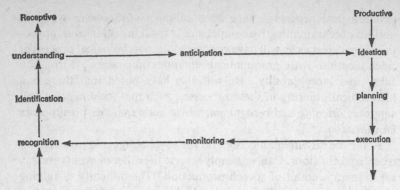

Figure 8 Processes in linguistic performance

the programme and the storage function describes a state rather than a process. We must not confuse the storage of linguistic information with the memory for particular utterances. These are certainly two separate functions (Johnson – Laird, 1970). Storage corresponds to the 'set of rules' and 'schemata' in the recognition phases of receptive behaviour. But there is sufficient correspondence to suggest that both accounts have a *three-tier hierarchy*: ideation is the counterpart of understanding, planning, of identification, and execution, the counterpart of recognition. Storage and schemata represent the 'learned element of linguistic information' whilst monitoring and prediction are complementary functions. This is shown in Figure 8. It is now only necessary to emphasize in the strongest terms the speculative nature of these accounts of the psycho- and neurolinguistic processes of performance. There is some experimental evidence to give them tentative support, but in default of any alternatives the applied linguist and language teacher must make what use he can of them.

Performance models and language teaching

The first thing to notice is that, in a three tier model, the extreme upper and lower ends of the hierarchy can only doubtfully be regarded as specifically linguistic activities. The lower end, *listening* and *recognizing*, i.e. matching incoming sense data with previously stored information, are certainly not specifically linguistic skills. It just happens that these general perceptual skills are also used in language. If we transfer the notion to written language the same is true. The ability to distinguish different shapes, whether 'natural' or man-made, a tree or a letter, or a written word, is a general perceptual skill. On the productive side the motor skills of manipulating the organs of speech, whether monitored by an auditory or a proprio-ceptive feedback system as in whistling, humming, or in eating, swallowing, clearing the throat, are not specifically linguistic. More obviously, the muscular control involved in writing is not peculiar to language. We need it for drawing, playing the piano, typing, tying up raspberries and a legion of manipulative arts of all sorts. The difference is that the control of the muscles of our speech organs is not under the same degree of voluntary control as those of our hands. They seem to have a greater degree of routine or pre-planning in their manipulation. It may well be necessary therefore in teaching pronunciation to develop in the learner some degree of 'conscious' control of the organs of speech – what we call a 'phonetic skill'. But notice that in doing this we shall also have to 'educate his ear'. Our eye is much more used to exercising a visual feedback function than our ear is to exercising an auditory one. It is certainly the case that most people are better able to perform a visual matching task than an auditory one. The use of the language laboratory for training the auditory-perceptual skills through self-monitoring is of very uncertain value. As we have seen, *recognition* requires a learned schema. The ability to use auditory feedback to control the organs of speech *presupposes* the prior existence of such a schema. Hence ear-training and pronunciation learning must *necessarily* proceed *pari-passu*.

For most learners, as we have seen, learning to form and identify the letters of the alphabet is a motor-perceptual skill they already possess. Learning to write in a foreign language therefore involves other skills, notably the acquisition of schemata of new letter combinations or 'written' words, i.e. spelling schemata. But already here we are entering into the domain of specifically linguistic processes. As every eight-year-old knows, there are 'rules of spelling'. In fact English spelling is a curious mixture of items which must be acquired 'as a whole', for which there must be a perceptual schema, and others which can be produced 'by rule'.

Turning to the other extreme of the hierarchy, it is virtually impossible to decide whether *understanding* and *ideation* are specifically linguistic processes or not. This is because the terms are still 'pretheoretical'. They have not yet been even provisionally defined in any psychological theory. I will remind you of William James' words:

The intention of saying a thing before he has said it is an entirely definite intention, distinct from all other intentions, an absolutely distinct state of consciousness, therefore; and yet how much of it consists of definite sensory images, either of words or things?

The language teacher, at all events, can scarcely regard it as part of his job to teach people what intentions they should have and wish to express, *what* messages they should formulate. His job is to make it possible for them to express their intentions and give their messages. He doesn't teach them *what* they ought to say but *how* they are to say it. But he does work on the principle that what they want to say can be said in the target language.

In between the extremes of the three-tier hierarchy are performance processes which, at least, provisionally we may accept as specifically linguistic: the recognition of sounds and whole words by matching with a stored schema, the heuristic processes of identifying sentences and planning their execution with the concomitant processes of prediction and monitoring and some part of the process of ideation and understanding. All these go to make up the general skill which has been called communicative competence. The learning of these skills is the central task of the infant acquiring his mother tongue. The task of the language teacher is the teaching of an alternative set of schemata, of rules of formation and rules of discourse.

Theories of language acquisition and learning

We have discussed in previous sections notions about what goes on when people speak and hear language, and looked at some of the circumstances under which language acquisition and second-language learning take place. What we want to know now is how do the child and the learner acquire these skills? Theories of language acquisition and learning (and we can still keep an open mind about the degree to which they are similar processes) are bound to be related to what one thinks goes on during performance. Now, since there appear to be several different sorts of process involved in performance, it is not at all unreasonable or inherently improbable that there will be different processes involved in learning them. It would be doctrinaire to suppose otherwise. But we have noted that some of the processes in productive and receptive language performance are probably not specific to language, notably the processes of recognition and articulatory execution. We called these processes motor-perceptual, and we could refer to a large literature on the acquisition of motor-perceptual skills (Vernon, 1962). Similarly we tentatively suggested that some part of the processes of *ideation* and *understanding* were not specifically linguistic. At this level experimental studies are fewer, and the disentangling of linguistic and more general cognitive processes is virtually impossible – but here also there is some information, notably on concept formation and acquisition (Bruner, Goodnow and Austin, 1956). What we are left with is the specifically linguistic skills of *identification* and *planning*. Our understanding of the learning of all these skills is still very limited, and theories of language learning must be approached in the same sceptical frame of mind as theories of language performance.

We can start by ruling out of court any notion that language learning or acquisition is merely a question of memorizing a set of *associations* between all possible sentences in the language, and a corresponding set of contextual stimuli. This somewhat naive notion was current at one time. Language learning was regarded as a process whereby 'Certain combinations of words and intonation of voice are strengthened through reward and are gradually made to occur in appropriate situations by the process of discrimination learning.' This is the 'associationist' theory of learning. Quite apart from the problem of 'storage capacity' since, as we have seen, the number of different sentences in a language is indefinitely great, there is the problem of the time factor. (As we have seen, to articulate all the twenty-word sentences in English would require 10^{12} centuries.) The speaker of a language is always producing novel utterances, ones which he has not heard before. Any satisfactory account of language learning must necessarily involve some processes of generalization and abstraction from the language data to which the learner is exposed, in order simply to reduce the quantity of what has to be retained. This raises in an acute form the adequacy of any account of language learning as *simply* the acquisition of habits, or dispositions to respond, if they are understood as sets of fixed responses to specific environmental stimuli, or in Mowrer's disapproving words 'fixed automatic, unconscious neural connections or bonds between some stimulus and some response' (quoted by Rivers, 1964). It does not rule out, however, the possibility of some of the performance processes being 'habitual' in the sense that they are eventually established as routines or sub-plans, or that some of the motor functions of articulation are not habitual or preprogrammed in a neurological sense. On the other hand, there is an obvious sense in which the learning of language must be related to the learning and knowledge of the world. Language has semantic links with the world outside language, but it does not follow that there is any simple one-to-one relation with internalized linguistic representation and 'situations'. Chomsky has said that language is 'stimulus-free', meaning that we have not yet been able, and perhaps never will be able, to relate in any simple way situational stimuli with linguistic responses in the form of whole utterances. If we should ever be able to do so it would rob language of meaning or its communicative function, since it would be wholly predictable from a knowledge of the situation. But this does not mean that there is no discernible relation between situations and utterances. If there were not, we could never learn language at all. It would be an entirely self-contained system into which there was no way of breaking.

Broadly speaking, current theories of language learning (I am not here concerned with the motor-perceptual skills of articulation and recognition) fall somewhere on a continuum between wholly *inductive* learning at one extreme and wholly *deductive* learning at the other. Inductive learning is the creation and storage of abstract internal representations (linguistic information) through a process of *generalization*, *classification* and *association*. *Deductive* learning is the discovery of the linguistic information to be stored by a process of applying to the data some inborn 'theory' about language, i.e. some set of 'ready made' inherited categories or concepts common to all human language ('linguistic universals'). This latter theory of language acquisition is known as the 'nativist' hypothesis and is based on three considerations: firstly, all human languages in spite of their obvious superficial differences do seem to show remarkable underlying similarities; secondly, the process of constructing a theory from the data, i.e. the inductive theory, would simply take too long; and thirdly, that the data on which it works is too distorted and partial for the purpose. The most famous statement of the nativist hypothesis is that of Chomsky (1965):

128 Introducing Applied Linguistics

A theory of linguistic structure that aims for explanatory adequacy incorporates an account of linguistic universals, and it attributes tacit knowledge of these universals to the child. It proposes, then, that the child approaches the data with the presumption that they are drawn from a language of a certain antecedently well-defined type, his problem being to determine which of the (humanly) possible languages is that of the community in which he is placed. Language learning would be impossible unless this were the case. The important question is: What are the initial assumptions concerning the nature of language that the child brings to language learning, and how detailed and specific is the innate schema (the general definition of 'grammar') that gradually becomes more explicit and differentiated as the child learns the language? For the present we cannot come at all close to making a hypothesis about innate schemata that is rich, detailed and specific enough to account for the fact of language acquisition. Consequently, the main task of linguistic theory must be to develop an account of linguistic universals that, on the one hand, will not be falsified by the actual diversity of languages and, on the other, will be sufficiently rich and explicit to account for the rapidity and uniformity of language learning, and the remarkable complexity and range of the generative grammars that are the product of language learning. (pp. 27–8)

The inductive theory of language learning, which is a modified form of stimulus-response learning theory, is based on the assumption that verbal behaviour is no different *in kind* from other behaviour (Skinner, 1957) and is acquired in fundamentally the same way: by processes of conditioning, imitation, practice, generalization and reinforcement, and that the infant starts learning with nothing more than the powers he possesses to learn anything. The deductive theory assumes that language is peculiar to human beings (we cannot extrapolate from animal learning studies to human beings); that they are born with a specific programme for acquiring it; that it is learned by some sort of data-processing device specific to language learning, proceeding by heuristic processes of hypothesis formation and testing; that language is a matter of rule-governed behaviour, not a matter of habit, and that what we learn is not responses but rules for making responses.

Rules, habits and holophrases

At this point it may be as well to say a little more about habits and rules, since there is a good deal of confusion about them. The fact is that many of our utterances do bear resemblances to each other, and that parts of them may be identical in the sense that the grammatical construction or string of grammatical elements, is the 'same'. For example:

The policeman warned the cyclist
The car entered the street

have an apparently identical grammatical structure, in terms of phrasal constituents, which can be described as: noun phrase + past tense verb + noun phrase. In terms of a phrasal analysis there are many utterances which are grammatically identical (whether a more sophisticated type of analysis would class all these as similar is a different matter). For example, in terms of phrases the following sentences would also have an identical structure:

Thick treacle covered the plate
John dropped the case
Bill loved Jane

If they are analysed in terms of their constituent words, however, they are all different from each other and from the first set. At some level of constituent analysis we are going to have to stop and say: 'This is a "basic" pattern which is learned as habit'. But the decision at which level to stop is arbitrary. No two teachers or textbook writers agree about what are the 'basic' patterns of the sentences of a language. If, however, we adopt a 'rule based' approach, all the sentences just given will have in their generation a number of rules in common, e.g. the sentences all consist of a 'noun phrase' and a 'verb phrase'. But the sentences in the examples differ as to which rule they select for the construction of the noun phrase, e.g. the noun phrase may consist of a proper noun *or* an article and a common countable noun *or* an adjective and a mass noun. Are we to say: 'All right, these sentences involve learning a number of different habits'? If we do that, we have destroyed the difference in meaning between 'rule' and 'habit'. Miller has said in this connection: 'I believe an implicit rule must be called a habit.' But this term stirs up as many problems as it solves. He settles for a compromise, and later talks about 'acquiring habitual linguistic rules'. This does not mean necessarily that the notion of habit in a more everyday sense is meaningless in connection with language learning. There are literally thousands of what we can call 'word sequences' which seem to operate as wholes or units, such as: *as a matter of fact*; *I mean to say*; *further to my letter of . . .*; *it has been said . . .*; *by and large*; *yesterday afternoon*; *for the sake of*; *waste not, want not*; *how do you do?* The reader will know of his own secret failings in this respect.

Now, some of these locutions would be called 'idioms', others proverbs or clichés, strings of words which habitually go together and which cannot be altered. Nor can they, all of them, be generated by the 'rules of the grammar'. They have to be learned as units, like single words. Are words habits, then? To suggest that would be to destroy again the value of the concept of habit. As we have seen, some words at least appear perceptually to be units. Are, then, any sequences of words which regularly occur together in the speech of an individual, whether they can or cannot be generated by the rules of the grammar, to be regarded as habits? The answer seems to be 'yes', if you like to call them that. The fact is that all of us develop what I have called sub-routines or 'ready-made sub-plans' (these are sometimes called *holophrases*) which are stored for shorter or longer periods as units of linguistic information, to which we have ready access and which we do not have to plan in detail 'by rule', even though linguistically they may be generable by the rules of the grammar. They are equivalent of the shorthand writer's phraseograms, and are an obvious means whereby the work of planning and recognition can be simplified. They are an economy measure, a sort of short cut. They may be learned as a unit, i.e. holophrastically, or they may originally be produced 'by rule' and later stored as 'useful phrases'. Notice, however, that what for the *speaker* may be a habitual sequence of words, may not be for his *hearer*. The hearer may have to operate on the sequence as if it were a new phrase. A speaker's cliché may be a hearer's flash of insight. 'Habits of speech' of this sort play an obvious part in language acquisition as the most superficial observation of children will show. They also play a most important part in second-language learning. Much language may be stored in the early stages of language learning as holophrases, and only be utilizable in that form to begin with, but these may later be analysed by the rules which the learner eventually acquires and cease to be 'holophrastic'. Thus many learners acquire the appropriate use of such phrases as '*would you mind –ing?*' '*how are you?*' long before they know the rules which generate them as regular sentences or constituents of sentences. One sometimes has the impression that the foreign waiter's English consists entirely of such holophrases. The old fashioned phrase book was based upon a similar system. One could learn to ask questions long before one could understand the native's answers! Our conclusions must be, then, that habit formation in its everyday sense does play a part in language learning but perhaps only a minor part. There can be no question of language learning being *simply* a matter of acquiring a 'set of habits'. If there are linguistic habits, they develop rather *after* language has been learned, though there may be 'temporary habits' formed in the process of learning.

Facilitation, transfer and interference

I have said that when people learn a second language they are not acquiring language, they already possess it. The learning of a second language is rather a question of increasing a behavioural repertoire, or learning a set of alternatives for some sub-set of the rules of the language they already know. The assumption, then, is that some of the rules they already know are also used in the production and understanding of the second language. This is what is meant by 'transfer'; learners transfer what they already know about performing one task to performing another and similar task. But the learner does not know what the full nature of the new task is; until he has learned in what way the two tasks are different he will perform the second task in the only way he knows, that is, as if it were the same as the first task. He will continue to apply the old rules where new ones are needed. And he will make mistakes of course. Making errors in the second language can, in part, be explained by the notion of transfer. It is sometimes called 'negative transfer' or *interference*. Where the nature of the two tasks happens to be the same, of course, this tendency to transfer is an advantage. This is called 'positive transfer' or *facilitation*. It is just as well that different languages do, in fact, have strong resemblances to each other. If they did not one might doubt whether people would ever learn a second language. On this account what has to be learned is what is different between the mother tongue and the second language.

Even a cursory examination of a learner's attempts to speak the target language will show that many of the forms he uses do bear a resemblance of one sort or another to that of the mother tongue. This is explained by the theory of transfer, the inappropriate use of the rules of his mother tongue in his performance of the target language. But we have to account for why certain aspects of the target language appear to be more difficult to learn. In the end a well-motivated learner will eventually master the grammatical rules of the target language. The same cannot be said about his pronunciation. There appears to be some difference of kind between the learning of pronunciation and the learning of the formation and speaking rules. These have been identified on page 117 with different behavioural skills – motor-perceptual skills on the one hand, involving processes of recognition and articulatory execution, and the 'organizational' skills on the other hand which we described as those of planning and identification. Articulatory processes do seem to be programmed in more or less fixed routines; once learned they become firmly established and resistant to modification or extension. Similarly, recognition processes, which depend upon matching incoming sense data with some already stored perceptual schema, also appear difficult to modify or extend. Motor-perceptual skills in other fields are well known to be resistant to change, and the term 'habitual' seems especially appropriate when applied to them. For these reasons, it may well be that the learning of motor-perceptual skills in language is indeed rather a process of classical conditioning than of discovery, and that imitation drill and pronunciation practice are consequently appropriate techniques for teaching them. Learning these skills in a new language may be more justly described as modifying or 're-shaping' existing behaviour than as acquiring a new set of rules. It may also be that, for this reason, it is rare, after the 'critical period' of language acquisition is past, for anyone to learn a native pronunciation. This appears also to apply to all complex motor skills – playing musical instruments, playing games like tennis or golf, perhaps riding bicycles, skiing or swimming.

The learner as a data processing machine

In the introduction I said that this book was concerned with applied linguistics in language teaching, and that the applications of linguistics were to be found principally in the design of teaching programmes and materials rather than in the classroom procedures. In its most general sense, by classroom materials we mean the language and non-language data to which the learner is *exposed*. If, for a moment, we use the analogy of the learner as a machine like a computer into which data are fed, then the materials of language teaching are the *input*, or, more accurately, the potential input, since we must make a distinction between what is *available* for putting in, and what the machine will actually *take in*. In technical terminology *input* is what the machine actually takes in. Without a much better understanding of the process of language learning and acquisition we do not know what parts of the material that a learner is 'exposed' to he can actually make use of at any particular stage in his learning process. Computers can store data until they are ready to use it. It is doubtful just to what extent learners can do the same. Now, obviously it is desirable that the learner should be exposed at any particular moment to precisely the data that he needs and is ready to process. For the efficient working of the machine, therefore, the organization of the input data is of the greatest importance. But no such organization is possible unless we know something about the programme which controls the machine. This is where the psycholinguistics of language learning comes in and is relevant to the applied linguist, because theories of language learning are theories about the programmes which control the processes inside the machine.

The output from the machine is the 'formation rules' (grammar) and 'speaking rules' of the language. These are stored in the 'memory' of the machine. They have to be accessible because they have to be continually revised. We can illustrate this diagrammatically as in Figure 9. The input to such a device must have certain properties. It must consist of a finite number of well-formed utterances in the language, also a finite set of deviant utterances *with an indication that they are incorrect*. It must also comprise general information about the world of perceptual objects and events and the particular circumstances in which these utterances were produced. The programme of the machine would include instructions to discover regularities, patterns, rules of some sort in the data. We have already seen in chapter 5 that where the data is finite, i.e. a corpus, there is a theoretically unlimited number of

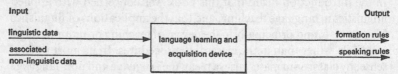

Figure 9 Processing linguistic data

solutions to this problem. Therefore if the machine is going to come up with the unique 'correct' solution there must be some built-in restriction on the way it processes the data and what it is programmed to accept as a solution. The psycholinguist is trying to find out what is the nature of these built-in restrictions and programmes in the case of the infant. It is these restrictions that Miller was referring to when he spoke of 'habitual linguistic rules' as quoted earlier. The big debate amongst psycholinguists is as to whether these innate characteristics are language specific or more general cognitive limitations on learning.

If we now apply the analogy to the foreign language learner we can see immediately where the differences lies. The language learner has already incorporated into his programme a full set of formation and speaking rules for language. He 'knows', not only what language is like, but also the rules of a particular manifestation of language – his native language. Thus, the output from the device has now been incorporated into the programme of the device; it already has a full specification of what the grammar of a language is like. If the learner knows some other second language, the grammar of this will also be incorporated into the device. The assumption is that this will make the new task easier, he will possess a larger number of *useful* hypotheses to work with, instead of having to construct some of his own which will have later to be rejected. At the present time the hypothesis that knowing several languages facilitates the learning of new languages, whilst widely believed, has not yet been investigated scientifically. The theories here proposed would make it seem probable, however.

Language learning and language teaching

The development of language-teaching methods (if we can properly call change, development, since this term implies direction) has in fact been empirical rather than theory-directed. This has been so in spite of the fairly widespread view that language is largely a matter of 'habit formation'. The observation of teachers' actual practice in the classroom suggests, on the other hand, that, whilst they may have paid lip-service to a somewhat naive version of this theory of language learning, they have in fact adopted methods of teaching which were not consistent with this approach. Thus, whilst teaching procedures of imitation, drill, formal practice and 'over-learning' of sentence patterns have continued to be used, they have regularly been accompanied by what some would consider the 'traditional' techniques of exemplification, rule-giving, description and translation, more appropriate to a deductive than an inductive theory of learning. One can only suppose this is the case because they have observed that these techniques yield results which are just as good as those achieved by the newer techniques of the so-called 'audio-lingual' method. The fact seems to be that teachers have 'followed their noses' and adopted a generally eclectic approach to teaching methods, and not, it would appear, without justification, in the absence at the present time of a much more solidly based and detailed account of language learning than I have been able to present here.

Chapter 7
Applied Linguistics and Language Teaching

What do we mean by 'application'?

I have used the term 'application' in several different contexts in the preceding chapters. I spoke about 'applying' a word or sentence to some object or situation in the world outside language; I also spoke of 'applying' the grid, or framework, of language to our experience of the world, and finally I spoke about a theory of language being 'applied' to language data, the corpus of utterances on which we base our descriptions of a 'language'. These uses of the term all have this in common, that they presuppose the prior existence of something – theory, term or framework – which is applied, and that the process of application *determines* or *defines* what it is applied to. As de Saussure said, 'It is the point of view which creates the object.' Following this analysis, the description of languages, dialects or varieties of a language is an application of linguistic theory. It is the 'primary' application of linguistic theory. As such it will be dealt with in the next chapter.

In a broader sense the applications of a science have to do with the use that is made of scientific knowledge to plan and draw up designs for some practical, everyday activity, whether it be building bridges, making electric toasters, brewing beer or mending broken bones. Language teaching, as I suggested in the Introduction, is such an everyday, practical activity or series of procedures. The process of planning and designing can be seen as the making of a series of logically interrelated and dependent decisions or choices. We can quite properly refer to these decisions as answers to specific questions, in which case the process of planning and designing can be broken down into a series of questions and answers, or, if we wish to put it another way, a series of problems and solutions. It is for this reason that applied linguistics has been called a *problem-based* activity. The problems are solved or the questions are answered according to the principles or knowledge derived from the scientific study of the structure of language, how it is learned and its role in society. There are three things to be said about this: when we use the term *problem* in this context we do not mean to refer only to specially difficult questions, but to any questions; secondly, we do not wish to suggest that all the questions which we must answer or problems we must solve can be answered or solved by reference to specifically linguistic principles or knowledge; thirdly, we do not wish to imply that the applied linguist is simply called in as a consultant when some particularly knotty problem turns up in the course of planning. There is, as I have already suggested, one phase in the planning and execution of a total teaching operation in which the application of linguistics is relevant: the stage at which the questions have linguistic answers.

How can we account, then, for those total language-teaching operations in which no applied linguist has been involved? The answer must be that what are essentially linguistic questions have been answered without benefit of scientific linguistic knowledge. The planner has, in fact, been taking decisions of a linguistic sort without fully realizing the nature of the problem or his solutions.

This suggests that the formulation of the questions, the identification of the problems and the specification of their nature *presupposes* linguistic theory. The nature of the problem is *defined* by the theory which is applied to it. The solution to a problem is only as good as the theory which has been used to solve it. Thus the formulation of the questions and the analysis of the problems which arise in the planning of a language-teaching operation are themselves part of applied linguistics. Asking the right questions means having the right language to ask them in. For this reason the applied linguist is not, as I have said, merely a consultant called in when difficulties arise; he is the man who has to ask the questions in the first place, who identifies the problems and specifies their nature.

It is a common experience for the specialist in any field to be asked to give his advice on some practical problem by the non-specialist. The difficulty the specialist nearly always faces in that situation is that he cannot understand what the exact nature of the problem is because the non-specialist cannot analyse and explain the problem in the specialist's terms. As we have seen, describing language scientifically involves inventing new terms or defining old ones very rigorously. It is not simply, therefore, a case of the non-specialist using alternative terms for the same things, but rather not having an adequate conceptual framework and appropriate language (i.e. theory) for talking about the subject at all. We could go so far as to say that if someone can talk adequately about something for some practical purpose he does not usually need to call in a specialist – he is one!

How then does the non-specialist know when he is faced with a problem at all? The answer must be: when the plans he makes, based as they must be on the knowledge he has, do not lead to the results he looks for. We visit the doctor when our own self-medication is ineffective. How much better to plan our good health on the best available principles in the first instance. The applied linguist is therefore not just a consultant but an integral member of the planning team for a total language teaching operation.

Two questions in language teaching

In a language teaching operation, once the political and economic decisions have been made – those concerned with whether to teach languages, which languages to teach and to whom to teach them – there remain two general questions: *what to teach* and *how to teach it*. These are the problems of content and method, or, using an industrial analogy, the problem of product and process design respectively. But formulated in this way they suffer precisely from the lack of precision referred to in the previous section; they are formulated in non-specialist terms. If an untrained person were to turn to an applied linguist and say: 'I have been given the job of teaching a class of beginners French; what am I to teach them?' the only short answer the specialist could give, other than 'haven't you got a textbook?' would be 'a knowledge of French.' This would be little help or comfort to the prospective teacher. He might go on to say: 'Yes, but what is meant by a knowledge of French?' At this point the specialist might himself ask a question: 'what do they want to learn French for?' By doing so he would be trying to analyse the problem of *what to teach* in terms of some sociolinguistic categories of role-behaviour, for example, to adopt the role of a French-speaking physicist. Or, alternatively, he might ask the question: 'what do your pupils want to be able to do in French?' In that case he would be analysing the problem in terms of the categories of speech functions, for example, to ask questions, issue challenges, pronounce judgements in French; or in some psycholinguistic terms of skills: to read, write or speak French.

It is, however, most probable that when the prospective teacher asked 'what am I to teach them?' he expected an answer in terms of some sort of linguistic categories, such as French grammar, vocabulary and pronunciation. And if he had got that answer he would then have gone on to say: 'yes, but what bits of grammar, what words, what sounds?'

It is clear from this discussion that there are as many ways of answering the question 'what to teach?' as there are ways of answering the question 'what is language?' Thus, what to teach can be described in linguistic terms, as sets of categories, rules, lists of lexical items, lists of sounds, rhythmical sequences, intonation patterns; or in sociolinguistic terms as lists of speech acts or speech functions, or in psycholinguistic terms as sets of skills or language activities. Our ability to answer the question depends upon our ability to describe language adequately in any of these terms.

The content and structure of a syllabus is related to the objectives of the learner or of society and these must necessarily be specified in the first place in socio- and psycholinguistic terms, i.e. what he wants or must be able to do in terms of social behaviour and linguistic performance. This is sometimes called his 'terminal behaviour'. This technical term was introduced in connection with the theory of teaching by 'programmed' materials and is associated with a behaviourist account of learning. If transferred from that context, it suffers from just the same sort of imprecision as the phrase 'what he is learning to do' does.

The same vagueness attaches to the question of 'how to teach?' First of all when we read books on 'how to teach languages' we find they often include the question of what to teach; they also deal with other aspects of syllabus structure such as in what order to teach things, as well as questions of method, such as presentational techniques, practice, testing and so on. In our discussion of language learning in the previous chapter, I suggested that there was a logical relationship between what goes on in the classroom and the preparation of syllabuses and teaching materials, that considerations of classroom teaching methods must influence the selection and organization of the 'content' of a syllabus. It is equally the case that decisions as to content will influence the methods of teaching. But ultimately, both relate to what we believe the psychological processes of language learning to be, and these latter are related to what we believe the various processes of language performance to be. If it is the case that there are several different processes involved in the reception and production of speech and writing, then it is logical to consider the possibility that the processes of learning these may be different. Consequently, the problem of how to teach does not receive a single answer but depends on how you answer the question: what is it we are teaching? This means that solutions to the problems of method are logically dependent on the solutions to problems of content. This point of view is seen at its clearest in the textbooks which not only present the data to be taught (in linguistic form) but are also accompanied by teachers' books specifying how the material in the students' book is to be dealt with.

We can say that any particular solution to the problem of what to teach, if it is embodied in a set of teaching materials, carries with it an implicit or explicit solution of the question of how to teach. For example, a well-known syllabus for the teaching of English as a foreign language, Hornby's *Guide to Patterns and Usage in English* (1954), which approaches the problem of content as a structural linguistic matter the solution to which is a list of 'grammatical structures', is closely associated with another text by the same author: *The Teaching of Structural Word and Sentence Patterns* (1959). Where, in the first book, we find an item listed as Verb Pattern no. 22A, described as 'Subject × Verb (be) × Subject Complement', we find in the second, instructions on how and when to teach one variety of this particular structure: *This is . . .* and *That is . . .*

1. The pronouns *this* and *that* will be taught during the first week, probably in the first lesson, with the verb *is*. There are three possible procedures:

(a) Names of pupils may be used:
   This is ↘ John.   That is ↘ Mary.

(b) Names of objects, preceded by the indefinite article may be used:
   This is a ↘ desk.   That is a ↘ chair.

(c) Names of objects preceded by a possessive may be used:
   This is my ↘ desk.   That is your ↘ desk.
   That is David's ↘ desk.

And later:

2. The first procedure does not need much description. The teacher either calls pupils to the front of the class, or he walks round the classroom. He touches, or (standing at their side so that *this* is appropriate) points to, a number of pupils in turn and makes statements:

This is ↘ Tom.   This is ↘ Harry. (Hornby, 1959, pp. 1–2)

Just what we may think is going on in the learning process is not here explicitly stated. The author does not say why this structure should be taught in this way. Nevertheless, we must presume that the method is based upon some psycholinguistic theory of language learning. It does, however, illustrate the point that if you define the content of the syllabus as a 'set of linguistic structures' to be learned this has consequences for how you teach it.

The linguistic contribution

However we determine the content of a syllabus – on linguistic linguistic, sociolinguistic or psycholinguistic criteria – whatever the aims of the learner may be in learning the language, the fact remains that we have no real alternative at the present time to *expressing* the syllabus in linguistic linguistic terms, since only linguistic theory is sufficiently well-developed and rich to yield descriptions of a language of a sufficiently detailed sort for the task. This does not, of course, by any means imply that we are yet approaching the day when we have a comprehensive and descriptively adequate account of any language. We must, therefore, conclude that since learners do evidently learn languages, that they do so at least to some extent without the benefit of systematic and deliberate teaching. We *teach* that part which we know how to describe. So long as we do not deprive the learner of the data which makes it possible for him to do so, he will learn on his own that part we cannot describe. The contribution of linguistic theory to language teaching is felt, therefore, in that vague area of *what we teach*. But this contribution is not a *direct* one and many theoretical linguists have quite explicitly stated that they do not see any way in which their findings can be useful in solving the problem of language teaching. One of the best known expressions of this point of view is that of Chomsky (1966b);

I am, frankly, rather sceptical about the significance, for the teaching of languages, of such insights and understanding as have been attained in linguistics and psychology. . . . it is difficult to believe that either linguistics or psychology has achieved a level of theoretical understanding that might enable it to support a 'technology' of language teaching. (p. 43)

If we read this statement with care we shall see that Chomsky is not saying that linguistics cannot be relevant, only that he does not see the relevance of what linguistics so far has been able to discover. He continues, however, later on:

Teachers, in particular, have a responsibility to make sure [the linguists'] ideas and proposals are evaluated on their merits and not passively accepted on grounds of authority, real or presumed. The field of language teaching is no exception. It is possible – even likely – that principles of psychology and linguistics, and research in these disciplines, may supply useful insights to the language teacher. But this must be demonstrated and cannot be presumed. It is the language teacher himself who must validate or refute any specific proposal. (p. 45)

Similar ideas to these have been expressed more recently by Thorne (1971) who said, in a radio interview, in answer to the question whether there were any lessons to be learned from linguistics of relevance to the teaching of languages:

This is the kind of question you should ask an applied linguist not a theoretical linguist. As a theoretical linguist, I would have thought no – not directly. All scientific advances always have, to use a fashionable word, spin-off, but it's usually the case that those engaged in work in the field never see what this is.

That is the point of view adopted in this chapter: the relevance of theoretical linguistics to language teaching is *indirect* and it is not the task of the theoretical linguist to say what relevance it may have. This is the field of applied linguistics.

The relation between linguistic theory and the actual materials we use for teaching in the classroom is an indirect one. Linguistic theory cannot alone provide the criteria for selecting, ordering or presenting the content of a teaching programme.

Orders of application

I have already called the activity of describing languages a primary application of linguistics – linguistic theory is applied to the raw data in a corpus of utterances and yields a linguistic description of those data. If the theory is projective, or 'generative', it will predict the features of any further data drawn from this same source. But we have already seen that the theoretical linguist cannot specify what is to be regarded as 'the same source'. This is a matter for the sociolinguist. It is he who establishes what 'a language' is. Thus, if a linguist claims to make a description of say, French, it is not he who determines what his data are. The linguist, as linguist, can only make arbitrary decisions about what to include in, or exclude from, his data. Thus, even at the primary order of application, other linguistic criteria than purely structural ones are involved.

We have seen that native speakers use more than one code or set of rules. Thus, the process of description must be carried out on more than one set of data if it is to be relevant to practical tasks like teaching. Furthermore, as we shall see, a knowledge of the nature of the learner's mother tongue is relevant in planning a language-teaching operation. Thus, linguistic theory must be applied to the data of that language as well.

Describing language, or parts of language, is, however, part of the processes of developing linguistic theory itself. The linguist must test or validate his predictions about the nature of language by applying it to a wide range of data drawn from different sources. There is, thus, feedback to theory in the activity of making linguistic descriptions. There are, however, linguists who would wish to make a distinction between the making of descriptions for purposes other than furthering our knowledge of language, i.e. theoretical aims, and the making of descriptions for use in some practical task:

The use of linguistic theory to describe language is not itself counted as an application of linguistics. If a language, or a text, is described with the sole aim of finding out more about language, or that particular language, this is a *use* of linguistic theory, but it is not an application of linguistics. Applied linguistics starts when a description has been made, or an existing description used, for a further purpose which lies outside the linguistic sciences. (Halliday *et al.*, 1964, p. 138)

The point of view adopted here differs from this one, for two reasons. Firstly, linguists do not, in fact, make 'complete' descriptions of a language in order to further linguistic science. It is a waste of time. Secondly, whilst later I shall distinguish between *pedagogic descriptions* and *theoretical descriptions*, at the level of application about which I am here talking, there is no difference *in kind* between descriptions made for 'applied' and 'theoretical' purposes. The differences (and certainly there are differences) are ones of *form*. How you say something depends on whom you are talking to, it does not necessarily affect what you say. A theoretical description takes the form it does because the hearer is a theoretical linguist. Other descriptions take the form they do because the hearers are teachers, learners or members of the general public.

As we have seen, there is no sense in which a native speaker can be said to 'know' the whole of his language. It is therefore an impossible objective to teach the whole of a language to a learner. Furthermore, we do not yet have descriptions of the 'whole of a language'. In any case, the linguistic needs of a learner of a second language will be more restricted than the needs of a native speaker. Thus the descriptions of a language which are the output of a first-order application of linguistic theory represent only an inventory from which a *selection* must be made in order to draw up the syllabus for any particular teaching operation. Figure 10 shows the processes in the first-order application of linguistics.

For some linguists the *sole* or at least main contribution to language teaching made by linguistic theory is in the description of languages.

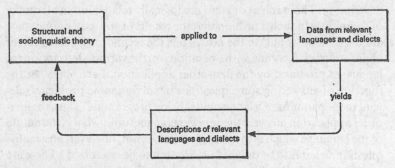

Figure 10 First-order applications of linguistics

Thus, to quote Halliday *et al.* again: 'The main role of linguistics and phonetics in language teaching is . . . to produce good descriptions of languages' (p. 170). This may be an acceptable point of view if, by linguistics, we mean only structural, or theoretical linguistics, but if it is taken to include sociolinguistics and psycholinguistic theory, it is evidently too restricted.

In the Introduction I said that language teaching was by no means the only practical activity to which linguistics had applications – I listed as other examples, speech therapy, psychiatry, literary criticism, communication engineering, translation and data retrieval. What all these fields of application have in common is the necessity for descriptions of the various languages involved. Speech therapy requires descriptions of the mother tongue of the patient as well as of his particular form of language. The same is true of psychiatric applications. Translation requires descriptions of both languages involved, and literary criticism may require descriptions of both the standard dialect and the idiolect of the writer. The first-order application of linguistic theory is common to all applications of linguistics.

Having introduced the notion of linguistic description as a first-order application of linguistic theory, it is now time to outline the general structure or hierarchy of applications of linguistics to language teaching, or, indeed, to any other practical activity. I said in the previous section that the application of linguistics to language teaching was not a *direct one*. By this I meant that there are a number of stages or steps in the application of linguistics to the practical activity itself. These stages, or steps, are represented by sets of different techniques of application, the first having already been identified as that of linguistic description. These stages or steps are logically related into a hierarchy of techniques in such a fashion that the results or 'output' of one stage are the data or 'input' to the next. Thus the second stage, or order, of application is concerned with operations on the various descriptions of languages produced by the first-order application. Each stage has the function of answering some questions or solving some problems relevant to the planning of a language-teaching programme. Thus, the first-order application answers the very general question: what is the nature of the language which is to be taught? It does not, however, answer the question: what is to be taught? or, how is it to be organized? These are questions which the subsequent orders of application aim to answer.

Second-order applications

The second stage, or order of application, is concerned with specifying the *content* of the syllabus. Its industrial analogy was product-design. We do not wish to teach the 'whole' of a language, even if we had a description of it, which we don't, any more than the design of a car incorporates every possible feature of automotive engineering. Learners, like cars, are designed for particular functions. We have even questioned whether the concept of the 'whole of a language' is itself meaningful. Out of whatever description of a language that the primary application of linguistics may yield, a *selection* must be made. Any process of selection is of course a matter of making comparisons according to some set of criteria. The criteria for selecting material for language teaching are various: *utility* to the learner, that is, selecting what he needs to know, his proposed *repertoire*. This can be interpreted in various ways: those codes and varieties of the language which will be useful to him, those speech functions which he will need to command, those parts of a language which he has not yet learned. Or we can invoke the criterion of *difference*. In a sense all parts of the second language are different from the mother tongue. But difference is relative. Some parts will be more different than others. The differences represent learning tasks and therefore are a basis for constructing a syllabus. For example, if the learner's mother tongue has no tense system in its grammar, the learning of such a system presents a learning task. There is a major learning problem. Where the learner's mother tongue, however, has such a system the size of the learning problem (that is, what has to be learned) will depend on the nature and degree of difference there may be between the tense systems of the two languages. A third criterion for selection might be *difficulty*. By this I do not mean the same as difference. There is evidence that what is different in the second language from the first language does not necessarily in all cases represent a difficulty. For example, at the phonological level, what is so totally different from anything encountered in the mother tongue that its recognition presents no real problems, does not seem to be so difficult to learn as something which is liable to confusion with some similar feature in the mother tongue. By difficulty, I mean only that there may be some features of a language which, while desirable to include in a syllabus, are nevertheless so difficult for a particular group of learners that it is uneconomic to attempt to teach them. To establish what *is* difficult to learn is a matter of empirical research and cannot be predicted on the basis of structural differences between the mother tongue and target language alone.

As I have said, the procedures and techniques involved in second order application of linguistics are *comparative*. It is by comparing the descriptions of languages, dialects, codes and varieties that we *select* what is to form the content of syllabuses. There are three different sorts of comparisons, each yielding different but important data. Each will be discussed at greater length in the third section of this book (chapters 9, 10 and 11). I shall here confine myself therefore merely to giving an outline of what is involved.

In order to determine the repertoire which we aim to incorporate in a syllabus we must compare dialects and varieties of the language to be taught. This I shall call *intralingual* comparison. The results of this form of comparison yield data about the *common core* and the *relative centrality* of the various linguistic items in the target language. If we know which codes, and varieties of the codes, the learner must have available, we are able to give the appropriate *weight* to a whole range of linguistic items in and outside the common core. This clearly has relevance to both the selection of material for the syllabus, as well as its sequencing in the syllabus. This matter will be discussed in greater detail in chapter 9.

The second type of comparison is *interlingual*, or, as it is more commonly called, 'contrastive' comparison. This is the process of comparing different languages. The languages involved are, in the first place, the mother tongue of the learner and the second language. But it may well be that we should also take into consideration any other languages the learner already knows. This activity yields an account of the differences between L_1 and L_2, or *predicts* learning problems or learning items. It has been suggested with a good deal of force that what the learner is concerned with is not so much acquiring the rules of the second language as learning the *differences* between his mother tongue and the second language. What is meant by *differences* will be discussed in greater depth in chapter 10.

The comparison of languages is, like the description of languages, part of the methodology of theoretical linguistics. The linguist is concerned with making statements about human language. This shows enormous variability. No one would suggest that we could give a satisfactory account of human language as such, merely by studying one of its manifestations – that is, a single variety of language. The linguist needs to study every manifestation he can gain access to. It has been a recurrent criticism of linguistics over the ages that it has been too ready to generalize about human language from too little data, that it has been *a priori* rather than empirical. The attempts of the eighteenth century grammarians to draw up specifications for a universal grammar were based upon the knowledge of a few ancient and modern European languages to which they had access, and a belief in the peculiar virtues of the classical languages. Even at the present day, some linguists appeared prepared to 'overgeneralize' about language on the basis of a rather restricted range of languages, in spite of the vastly greater array of different manifestations of language to which they have access.

The third type of comparison is often called *Error Analysis*. But this, while time-honoured, is a somewhat misleading name. The errors made by the learner may be an important part of the *data* on which this sort of comparison is made, but what is being compared in this case is not two existing and already known and described languages, but the language of the learner at some particular point in his course, with the target language. It may seem surprising to regard the learner as possessing a form of the target language *as a language*. But it can be so regarded in exactly the same way that an infant learning his mother tongue can be counted to possess a language of his own at each successive stage of his learning career. A learner's so-called errors are systematic, and it is precisely this regularity which shows that the learner is following a set of rules. These rules are not those of the target language but a 'transitional' form of language similar in many respects to the target language, but also similar to his mother tongue, or indeed any other language he may already command. The errors are part of the data on which a description of this transitional language of his is based. The process of comparison is a two-step operation. By the study of the learner's utterances we attempt to describe this transitional language or 'interlanguage' as Selinker (1969) has called it, and then we compare this description with the description of the target language. The differences we find represent the residual learning tasks of the learner.

We can relate error analysis and contrastive comparison in this way: the latter discovers the differences between the first and second languages and predicts that there will be learning problems; because they are problems the learner will make errors. Error analysis studies the nature of these errors and confirms or refutes the predictions of contrastive analysis. However, it would be a mistake to suppose that the data for comparing the learner's 'interlanguage' and the target language were only his erroneous utterances. Those who study child language acquisition do not confine their analysis only to those utterances of the child which differ from the adult's speech. All utterances of an infant, or a second-language learner, are relevant data, if what we aim to do is to give as full an account as we can of the nature of his 'interlanguage'. I shall return to these topics in chapter 11. Meanwhile, we can summarize this section in Figure 11.

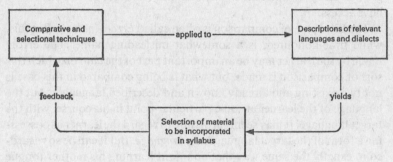

Figure 11 Second-order applications of linguistics

Third-order applications

As we move down the scale our applications become more specific to the practical activity to which linguistics is being applied. We saw that the process of description was common to all applications of linguistic theory; the process of comparison is not relevant to all applications though it is a necessary process, for example, in applications to speech therapy, where we must compare the patients' utterances with the normal subject, or in literary stylistics, where we want to compare the language of a particular writer with some 'norm' of language use. When we move to third-order applications the processes involved are wholly specific to the practical activity with which we are concerned.

The second-order of application yielded, as its output, lists of items which represented the learning tasks or content of a syllabus, whether we defined this in structural or sociolinguistic terms. But since we cannot present the whole content of a syllabus simultaneously, we must structure it on some principle or set of principles. This is one of the functions of third-order applications.

We may notice another thing about orders of application; the principles upon which each activity is based become more complex as we move down the scale. Thus, the problem of structuring a syllabus is not solvable by reference to any one linguistic approach. At this level many different variables are involved, sociolinguistic, structural linguistic and, at this point even more importantly, psycholinguistic. The structure of a syllabus is very much influenced by what we believe to be the psychological processes which take place in language learning.

One obvious requirement in sequencing material in any syllabus is that the learner should move from the known to the unknown, or, to put it in another way, we should make use of what the learner already knows in order to facilitate his learning of what he does not yet know. The desirability of this general pedagogic principle in language teaching is easy to assert but not easy to apply. It is not clear what is meant by 'known' in this context. In one sense the use of language is 'known', inasmuch as the learner already possesses language functionally for his communication needs. This knowledge 'facilitates' the learning of a second language, as we saw in chapter 6. Furthermore, and more specifically, there will be features of his mother tongue which resemble those of the second language more closely than others. I spoke of these 'differences' in the last section as forming the learning tasks on which the syllabus is based. But 'difference' is a variable matter. The features of one language differ more or less, not absolutely, from the features of another. Thus, the contrastive comparison is relevant also at the level of the third-order application in determining how much of the first language we can consider as transferable or facilitating in the learning of the second.

We may also consider structuring the syllabus on the basis of a gradual move from the more general to the more particular, a statement of a general rule to a statement of particular rules or exceptions. This would entail, for example, introducing verbs which formed tense or person forms by some very general rule before the irregular verbs.

Such an organization of teaching material would correspond to what we have called a *deductive* process. Alternatively, we can organize our material so that the direction is from the particular to the general. This form of structure is based on the assumption that the learning process is *inductive*, 'rule discovering' or heuristic. If we wished, we could characterize the deductive approach as being based upon structural linguistic principles whilst the inductive approach leans rather towards what we believe is a truer picture of the actual psychological processes of learning.

The inductive or deductive approach represent what are conceived to be extremes of organizational types, but say nothing about what is being organized, what are the items, elements, units which are being ordered. Here again, we can approach the matter in various ways. We can consider language learning sociolinguistically as the acquisition of the ability to perform different types of speech act. In such a case we would classify what had to be ordered as referential, directive, commissive or other classes of acts. Thus we might wish to say that pupils should learn to make certain sorts of statements before they learned to ask questions. Any rigorous application of such a criterion would have the effect of limiting rather severely the range of communicative functions a learner could employ at any particular stage of his learning.

Alternatively, we might wish to organize the syllabus on the more general sociolinguistic basis of types of situation that he could operate in, or roles which he could adopt in the second language. Such an approach can be seen in operation in many existing courses, where the material starts with home life, moves on to the classroom situation and then moves out of the school into the post office, the railway station, the grocery shop and so on.

A psycholinguistic approach would organize the syllabus on the basis of the sort of language activity to be taught, hearing before speaking, reading before writing; with dictation, relaying of messages, translation, précis as sub-varieties of these various activities. Such an approach might specify that the motor-perceptual skills of sound and letter recognition and production should be mastered before any specifically linguistic skills were taught.

The question, however, is: can we discover any logic in any of these different ways of organizing a syllabus? And if we can, does any one approach have natural priority over any other where a conflict exists between the criteria of different approaches. For example, the criteria of linguistic complexity might well suggest that learning to form interrogative sentences must follow the ability to form declarative sentences, whereas in terms of speech functions, both making statements and asking questions are complementary functions and should be learned together. Since interrogative sentences are often used to ask questions, there would be a conflict between linguistic and sociolinguistic criteria for organizing the syllabus. To take one more example, general pedagogic principles of good motivation would conflict with any psycholinguistic approach which held back the learning of linguistic skills until the motor-perceptual skills of sound recognition and production had been acquired. Few learners will tolerate learning and practising meaningless noises and making and recognizing meaningless marks on paper unless they are obviously associated with communicative functions. They resemble 'keep fit' exercises without any reason for keeping fit, or practising golf swings without ever playing golf. These and many other matters relating to the organization of the syllabus will be discussed in chapter 12.

We don't put syllabuses in front of learners. They form a guide which may be more or less detailed for those who actually prepare the teaching materials which are put into the hands of pupils and classroom teachers. Few teachers prepare, or are capable of preparing, syllabuses, but many, although a minority, prepare their own materials for teaching. However, even in these cases they accept the basic syllabus as laid down in the class textbook or ministry regulations. Their materials are usually additional to, or embellishments of, the usual class texts, particularly those parts of the texts which they have found by experience with their own pupils, deal inadequately with some particular point.

The process of turning the items selected for a syllabus into teaching materials for use by classroom teachers and learners is a separate process from the structuring of these items into a syllabus. Up to a point, of course, the way you present an item, what you say about it and how you practise it will be dependent upon what has gone before, but if we consider it as a psycholinguistic problem, that is, if we take into account *how* the item is learned, *when* it is learned is not of direct relevance. Thus, within the model of applied linguistic procedures adopted here the processes of syllabus structuring and *presentation* are both regarded as third-order applications.

We can, of course, analyse and classify teaching materials in a number of ways. We could categorize them into visual and auditory materials; we could go further and sub-categorize the visual in various ways – moving, still, three-dimensional, written. This is often done when the focus is on classroom teaching methods. Here, however, we shall not trespass in this field, but consider all teaching materials of all sorts as having the same function of teaching some item on the syllabus, whether by exemplification, description, illustration, practice, drill or any other procedure. The term sometimes used for all materials, whatever their more specific function may be, is *pedagogic grammars*. Some people have raised objections to this term on two counts: firstly, that grammar is, even in its broadest and classical sense, too narrow a characterization of what we teach, and secondly, the strong connection between the term grammar and *descriptions* of language, even if intended for pedagogic purposes, implies a method of teaching which is out of date or undesirable. Consequently, they would prefer to restrict the meaning of pedagogic grammar to 'the presentation of information about language for teaching purposes'. Thus, teaching methods which proscribe the making of descriptive statements about the target language to the learner would not place pedagogic grammars in the hands of the learner himself, but confine their use to the teacher. This is a perfectly good argument, but if such a restriction on the application of the term is indeed imposed, it turns out that very few pedagogic grammars have been written in recent years, or, alternatively, that all grammars which aim at comprehensiveness must be considered pedagogic, including those which are often called 'scholarly'. If the reader doubts the truth of this statement, I invite him to read the introductions to such works as Sweet's *New English Grammar* (1891), Jespersen's *Modern English Grammar on Historical Principles* (1921), Kruisinga and Erades' *English Accidence and Syntax* (1947), Poutsma's *A Grammar of Late Modern English* (1904), or Curme's *A Grammar of the English Language* (1935). This is even more clearly the case in the smaller versions: Jespersen's *Essentials of English Grammar* (1933), Zandvoort's *A Handbook of English Grammar* (1957), or Palmer's *A Grammar of Spoken English* (1924).

The problem which the making of pedagogic grammars or other teaching materials deals with is that of presenting the item to be learned in such a form that it will be more readily learned. This is a psycholinguistic problem. The form of teaching materials reflects the theoretical orientation of the person who prepares them, what he believes to be the language-learning processes. The problems of presenting linguistic material are dealt with more fully in chapter 13.

As in the case of first- and second-order applications we can illustrate third-order application in the form of a diagram as in Figure 12.

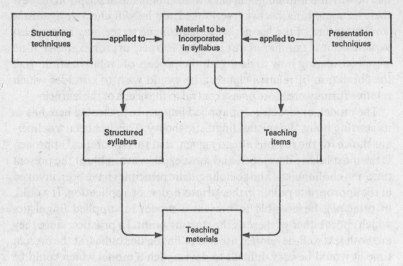

Figure 12 Third-order applications of linguistics

A model of applied linguistics

The application of linguistics to language teaching is an indirect one. It is not a single-stage operation. This is why many teachers, when first introduced to linguistics, see no relevance in it for their work and, conversely, why many linguists unacquainted with language teaching in practice disclaim any practical usefulness for their work. The fact seems to be that only those who are familiar with *both* linguistics *and* language teaching are in a position to discern the relation between the two.

I have, in this chapter, attempted to show the nature of this relationship as a series of logically related applications. In doing so I may have given the impression that the steps are wholly discrete and well-defined. This has been necessary in order to talk about them coherently. It is, however, in some measure a falsification as any generalization is liable to be. When someone is actively engaged in the task of preparing teaching materials he certainly does not start at the top and work downwards systematically; rather he switches or shifts, almost without being aware of it, up and down the scale. For example, when faced with the problem of how to present some linguistic items on his syllabus he will find himself going back to the linguistic description to see if there is something he has overlooked, or he will check it against a similar feature of the learner's mother tongue to see how he can best exploit what is familiar about it to the learner, or, for example, if he were considering how to deal with the process of 'relativization' (i.e. the formation of relative clauses), he would wish to consider which relative forms were more or less central to the needs of the learner.

The model, or structure, of applied linguistics presented here has as its starting point 'linguistic' linguistic theory. This has been a deliberate choice for the reasons already given, that this theoretical approach is the most highly developed and most explicit available at the present time. Psycholinguistic and sociolinguistic principles have been invoked at the appropriate points in the various orders of application. It would, in principle, be possible to present a model for applied linguistics which chose either of these as the starting point. In practice, since they are both less well-developed aspects of linguistic studies, at the present time, it would be very difficult to devise such a model which could be made to work. There would, however, be nothing theoretically objectionable about doing so. What we learn when we learn a second language is just as properly described in terms of language skills or social behaviour as in terms of linguistic categories and processes. What is certain is that whatever the starting point selected the relation between theory and practice is indirect. I shall content myself, therefore, with summarizing the content of this last section of the chapter in a conflated diagram: Figure 13.

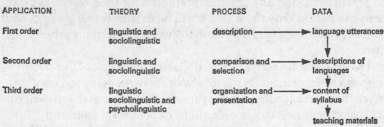

Figure 13 The ordered applications of linguistics

Chapter 8
The Description of Languages: A Primary Application of Linguistic Theory

The content and form of descriptions

I said in the last chapter that theoretical linguists undertook descriptions of languages to test their theories about the nature of language. To learn more about language they have to keep going to its manifestation, that is actual natural languages; they do not concentrate on only one language, but try and investigate the nature of as many different languages as they can. The descriptions of languages that linguists make for their own theoretical purposes tend to be very fragmentary and partial for this reason. They usually concentrate on some particular aspect of a number of languages to discover in what way they express some particular aspect of reality and experience. This use of description is internal to linguistics. If some feature crops up in some manifestation of language which cannot be accounted for within their theoretical framework then the theory must be changed. However, as we have seen, the goals of linguistic theory are various – the structural description of a corpus of utterances, the characterization of the native speaker's competence, even an account of the speaker's performance. These differences in objectives determine what the linguist considers relevant in the data – what he must account for in an adequate description. We can illustrate how this works. A linguist who is concerned only with providing a structural description of the sentences of a corpus will not need to take into account certain relations which can be shown to exist between sentences whose structure is manifestly different. For example, the relationship between active and corresponding passive sentences. For him there is no correspondence because there is not necessarily any superficial structural similarity. However, a linguist who wishes to account for the native speaker's intuitions about his language will have to incorporate in his description some principled account of this relationship since every native speaker is presumably intuitively aware of it. For the linguist who aims at accounting for the native speaker's performance it will not be sufficient to show that passive and active sentences are related, he will also have to state the contextual conditions under which one or the other form occurs or is likely to occur. In this way we can see how the goals of the theory make different aspects of the raw data relevant. The linguist *selects* from this data just those features which are significant and disregards those which are not. In this way, the theory determines what is said in the description, that is, the content of the description.

The *use* to which the description is put, on the other hand, whether to further theory or to serve some practical purpose such as language teaching, does not affect what is said in the description (i.e. the content) except inasmuch as certain theoretical goals may be more relevant for some practical purposes than others, but it does influence how it is said, that is, the 'presentation' of the description. For example, a description intended for linguistic ends may make descriptive statements in some sort of symbolic form, e.g.:

$$\Sigma \rightarrow NP + VP$$

This same statement may appear in a grammar intended for some applied purpose as 'Every sentence consists of a subject and a predicate.' To take another example: much criticism used to be directed at the definitions of the various parts of speech in traditional grammars. Thus, 'nouns' were usually said to be the names of things, people or places. The noun was defined in terms of meaning. This was regarded as inadequate because 'meaning' was a subjective and variable matter which could not be defined rigorously. Consequently, the attempt was made to define the noun in some more objective, rigorous and formal terms. When this was done, however, it appeared that more or less the same set of words turned out to be nouns as in the traditional description. What had happened was that traditional grammarians had in fact been using formal criteria all along, but when they came to present their descriptions they chose to define nouns in terms of meaning. The content of the traditional and modern grammars turned out to be very similar, only the presentation was different because the use to which they were to be put was different.

This explains, perhaps, why theoretical linguists so readily study the great comprehensive scholarly descriptions of languages, to which I referred in the last chapter. These descriptions embody many insights into the nature of language in general and languages in particular, even though their theoretical orientation is not generally explicit and even though they were written for various different practical purposes.

Idealization of the data – utterances and sentences

The goals of the theory determine what is regarded in the raw data of utterances in the language as relevant for the description. Utterances in the language are 'samples of performance'. Unless the objective of this description is to characterize linguistic performance – a goal which few linguists have as yet aspired to – the raw data will have to be purged of those aspects which are irrelevant because they are contextually determined. This process of eliminating contextually dependent features of the data has been called 'idealization of data' (Lyons, 1972). It is most important that this should not be confused with any idea of 'rigging the data' to suit the theory. It is, rather, a systematic process of selecting the relevant features, those which remain *constant* under all contextual conditions, and ignoring irrelevant ones.

There are three stages in the idealization of the data. The first is *regularization*. Real life utterances show a number of apparently adventitious features such as slips of the tongue, hesitations, 'searching for words', repetitions, changes of plan, 'structural blends'. They also show such 'continuity features' as *well*; *I mean to say*; *you know*; *oh*; *ah*; and expressions of emotion such as *hell, damn it*, etc. Some of these are signs of imperfections in the planning and execution of utterances and are of great interest to psycholinguists and psychiatrists since they give insights into the actual process of speech production (see chapter 6). They may be due to a number of causes: emotion, tiredness, lack of attention, drunkenness, drugs and so on. What is clear is that they have little to do with language as a system. They are not evidence of the speaker's knowledge of his language, though they may to some extent have to do with his performative knowledge of how to use his language, particularly such features as continuity and emotional expression.

If a tree is stunted or a plant has shrivelled leaves this is irrelevant for the botanist who is trying to make a systematic description of the plant world. He is interested only in good specimens. Bad specimens are of interest to the plant physiologist and pathologist. Bad specimens of utterances are of interest only to speech physiology and pathology.

There is normally no difficulty in carrying out the process of regularization. Speakers are well able to 'correct' their mistakes when their attention is drawn to them. They will also willingly eliminate continuity features and emotional expressions if asked to do so. Such expressions may be informative but they are not communicative in the senses used of these terms in chapter 2.

The next process of idealization is *standardization* or *normalization*. This process has already been discussed in chapter 4 in connection with the variability of language. The linguist concerned with describing language as a system must treat it as well-defined. His rules are absolute rules not variable rules. The process of standardization involves the elimination of all variability which derives from the personal and sociocultural characteristics of the producers of the data. This does not, of course, mean that linguists must necessarily choose one particular social or regional dialect rather than another to describe – only that the social source of the data must be homogeneous. The native-speaking informants must agree in matters of what is and is not acceptable. The linguist is interested, of course, in all manifestations of language and selects one rather than another variety of a language to describe not because it is linguistically more interesting or socially more highly valued, but for reasons which are practical rather than theoretical, such as availability of sufficient data, accessibility to informants, usefulness for application, its widespread use, or most likely because he speaks that form himself! The selection of the data for his description is thus, linguistically speaking, arbitrary.

The third process of idealization is what Lyons has called *decontextualization*. Of course, standardization also is a process of removing contextually dependent features from the data, those which relate to the *language user*. The process of decontextualization is that of removing from the data the features of *language use*. Every utterance is made in a particular context and interpreted in the light of the information 'supplied' by the context. The context may be situational or linguistic or both. As we saw in chapter 2 the form of an utterance depends upon the characteristics of the context in which it is uttered. It is traditional to say that utterances are often elliptical, i.e. the hearer has to 'supply' some information from his understanding of the context in order to interpret the utterance. This accounts for the judgement that is often made that utterances when taken out of context are incomplete in one way or another. For example, it is impossible to know just what the speaker means when he says '*I have*' unless one knows what utterances have preceded it in the discourse. It can, of course, felicitously follow an almost indefinite number of utterances; here are some examples:

Who's got a penknife?
Not many people have seen the sphinx
Nobody's been there
Has anyone seen Bill?
I don't suppose anyone's done their homework yet

The only feature which all these utterances have in common is that they contain some form of the verb *have*. There are evidently rules for ellipsis, for what can and cannot be 'omitted' in an utterance in a particular context without its becoming unintelligible. But these are discourse rules, or speaking rules, as we have been calling them, not rules of grammar or 'formation rules', as they have traditionally been understood. The process of decontextualization is one of 'putting back' into the data those linguistic elements which have been 'deleted' because they can be 'understood' from the context. Just how much reorganization or reconstruction is involved in the process of decontextualization is far from clear at the present time. Where the utterance *I have* followed the utterance *has anyone seen Bill?* the 'decontextualized form' would be *I have seen Bill*, and this is, of course, a perfectly acceptable response in itself. We can say that this is the *sentence* which underlies the utterance *I have* or the sentence from which the utterance is derived in that context. Clearly the utterance 'I have' may be 'derived' from an indefinite number of sentences, e.g. *I have got a penknife*; *I, too, have seen the sphinx*, *I have been there*; *I have seen Bill*; *I have done my homework*, etc., etc. The distinction made here between sentences and utterances accounts for the often heard statement that an utterance was incomplete or even 'ungrammatical', i.e. it had no subject: *coming?* or it lacked an auxiliary: *you coming?* or a verb: *Bill's*. It also accounts for the instruction to language learners to answer 'in a complete sentence' or 'use the short form'. Teachers thus implicitly make the distinction between sentences and utterances.

Linguistic descriptions which aim at accounting for language as a system or for the *grammatical competence* of the native speaker deal with sentences not utterances. On the other hand, the linguist who aims at accounting for the *communicative competence* of the native speaker, that is language performance, will not submit his data to the process of decontextualization since he is interested not only in the formation rules which generate sentences such as *I have seen Bill*, but also the speaking rules which 'reduce' such a sentence to the utterance *I have*. Notice, however, that in order to perform the process of decontextualization the linguist must in some sense 'know' the speaking rules of the language, otherwise he won't know what to 'put back' into the data. Since, at the present time, we have no systematic account of the speaking rules, the process of decontextualization is carried out largely on a subjective, intuitive basis, and that is why linguists rely so heavily on native speakers in making their descriptions.

That 'speaking' rules exist and can be discovered we saw in chapter 3. But it is worth investigating them here a bit further, because of their importance in applied linguistics. For example, in answer to the question *Who is that?* the underlying decontextualized response-sentence would presumably be *That is George*. This would be accepted as an appropriate response utterance (the 'long answer' in language-teaching jargon). But the acceptable 'short' response utterance would be *George*. On the other hand, neither *that George* nor *is George* would be produced by a native speaker in that context. Both these utterances are, however, regularly produced by learners of English and would be called 'ungrammatical' by most teachers. In view of what has been said, it would perhaps be better to call them 'uncontextual' or 'inappropriate' since both derive presumably from the same grammatical response-sentence. This illustrates a problem in applied linguistics which will be dealt with more fully in chapter 11: how do we know whether a learner's erroneous utterances are due to ignorance of the formation rules for sentences or the speaking rules of the target language? Let us consider one further example and see if we can discover some general speaking rule. As a general contradiction of the sentence *They are eating plums*, the following are the possible appropriate utterances:

(No) They are not eating plums
(No) They are not
(No) They're not
(No) They aren't

Presumably the first in the list is the 'nearest' to the contradiction-sentence. The following are inappropriate contradiction utterances:

*They not eating plums
*Not eating plums
*Are not eating plums
*They are not eating
*Are not eating

Any one of these is likely to be produced by learners of English in the context. The rules for turning a contradiction-sentence into appropriate contradiction-utterances appear to be, in the case of the above structure:

1. Verb + object (optionally deletable *as a unit*).
2. Are + not → aren't.
3. Subject + are → —'re.

It is interesting to note that these rules can be extended to account for answers to yes/no questions also. Thus, to the question *Are they eating plums?* the following are appropriate and inappropriate answers:

(Yes) They are
(No) They aren't
*(Yes) They eating
*(Yes) They eating plums
*(No) They not eating
*(No) Not eating
*(No) They are not eating

The process of idealization is applied not only to the grammatical structure of utterances but also to the pronunciation of individual words and syllables. The form of a word given in a pronouncing dictionary is the idealized form of the word and the one which forms the basis of a description of the phonological system of the language. And yet, of course, we know that there are as many 'deletions', 'weakenings' and 'changes' in the actual pronunciation of segments of an utterance as there are deletions and changes in its grammatical structure. For example, the utterances: *let's go!*; *haven't you been yet? what did you say?* would in a familiar style of speech appear in ordinary orthography as something like: *'Sgo!*; *'Vn' you bin yet?*; *'D'you say?* or in phonetic transcription: [s'gou]; [vnju'binjet]; [dju'se]. There are certainly performance rules for weakening and elision, some of which are described in the standard phonetic manuals. These are 'speaking rules' which must, of course, be learned by a language learner.

After this discussion of the processes of idealization we can now perhaps see more clearly the force of the statement by de Saussure, quoted on page 84 that 'it is the point of view which determines the object'. Different theoretical goals determine the nature of the data, and the sort of idealization which it is subjected to. At the present time, it is clear that we can describe more adequately the sentences of the language than utterances in the language. Many linguists maintain that you cannot do the latter until you can do the former. It is to a consideration of describing the sentences of a language, that is, its grammar, that we now turn.

Relevant criteria and observational adequacy

Having established by the processes of idealization what our data is to be – utterance tokens, utterance types, or sentences – we are once again faced with making decisions about what is important or relevant in the data and what is not. The same problem faces any scientist who sets out to make a systematic description of some aspect of the world. The layman, when asked to describe a type of plant, will probably select as significant the colour of the flower, when it blooms, whether it has a scent, where it grows, what uses it has, as the features by which he recognizes particular instances of it when he comes across them. Such a description often occurs in popular works on wild flowers:

Cowslip: gay, beloved with its fragrant, deep yellow flowers, widespread and locally abundant in grassland, mostly on chalk, thinning out northwards. April–May.

As it turns out few of these features are significant to the botanist who is making a systematic description of the plant world. He is concerned with stable, observable and measurable characteristics which reliably distinguish between species and enable him to relate species together in a classificatory system on the basis of genetic similarities and differences. For him some of the relevant features of the cowslip, couched in non-technical language are:

A downy perennial with leaves like a primrose but smaller and abruptly narrowing at the base. Flowers in umbels, drooping usually to one side on leafless stalks; calyx pale, green, inflated.

Size, colour, scent, location and use are none of them stable, predictable 'defining' characteristics of plants. They are too variable and contingent to be reliable for distinguishing between species. The features which are selected as criterial for scientific description must, in the first place, be *perceptually distinctive*, that is, we must be able to perceive the differences with our senses (and, of course, with sensitive instruments). They must also be constant in the sense that all instances of the object in question must show all these features.

In the case of language, the features which are selected as criterial for the description must in the last analysis have a physical basis in their articulatory and acoustic characteristics. Sound is measurable in the dimension of frequency, amplitude and duration. Thus, for example, assuming we regard such words as *kit, pit* and *tit* as made up of a sequence of perceptually distinct segments, or speech sounds, it can be shown that the initial segment in each case is both physiologically and acoustically different in various ways. There is, however, no purely physical justification for this assumption since the organs of speech are in continuous movement during the 'stream of speech'. Segmentation is part of the process of idealization. The 'k' sound is produced by a closure of the velum, the 'p' by a closure of the lips and the 't' by a closure made by the tongue against the ridge behind the teeth. On the other hand, they are all acoustically similar, in that there is a brief interruption of sound produced by a momentary stoppage of the air stream. They are also characterized by a temporary interruption of the vibration of the vocal cords. For this reason they are all regarded as examples of the same sort of sound – *stops* (or *plosives*). We can extend this analysis further and say that the words *contráct* and *cóntract*, although made up of similar (though not identical) sequences of sounds are acoustically and physiologically principally distinguished by a different placement of prominence or *stress*. At another level we should wish to say that the statement *Rebecca's here* and the question *Rebecca's here?* are also acoustically and physiologically distinct; in this case we should ascribe the distinction to a difference in the placement of the principal stress and a difference in the intonation, differences which correlate with differences in amplitudes and frequency of different components.

It does not, however, follow that all acoustic differences are criterial in every context. Thus the initial sounds in the sequences which we recognize as the words *poor*, *pit* and *pew* are all demonstrably different, both acoustically and articulatorily; the 'p' sound in *poor* is pronounced with rounded lips, and the 'p' sound in *pew* with a raised tongue. But these differences are not criterial in English in that context. In other words, they do not serve to distinguish different syntactic or semantic elements in the language. In our description, therefore, we have to differentiate between criterial and noncriterial distinctions, or, as it is sometimes put, between distinctive and nondistinctive features of sounds. The difference between the initial 'p' sounds I spoke about is nondistinctive, because whichever 'p' sound we choose to pronounce in any of these three words would not make any difference to how they were interpreted by the hearer (though he might think we had an 'un-English' accent). Sounds which are different in certain respects, but not in such a way as to affect meaning, are said to be in 'complementary distribution': none of them are found in the same phonetic environment. Our choice of one or the other depends entirely on the sounds which precede and follow. They could be called *contextually determined variants* of the 'same' sound. An important part of the description of the sound system of a language is to discover groups of sounds which are in 'complementary distribution'; such groups or classes of sounds are usually called *phonemes*. A phoneme, according to this theory, is a class of sounds which have both *phonetic similarity* and *functional identity*, in the sense that the substitution of one for another in the same context does not change the *phonological structure* of an utterance and consequently does not change its syntactic or semantic function, i.e. makes no change in its meaning.

Having established our inventory of speech-sound classes on a functional basis (i.e. inventory of phonemes) we can go on to list the permitted sequences of phonemes, and, on the basis of such lists, we can start to classify phonemes according to their potentiality of occurrence in such patterns. This is how we arrive at such primary classes of phonemes as consonants and vowels. They have typically different distributions in the structure of syllables or words. For instance, the English /h/ phoneme does not occur in word-final position, whereas the phoneme /ŋ/ (as in '—ing') does not occur in word-initial position. We can also group phonemes together functionally into classes according to their distribution in different phonological contexts. There is a class of phonemes in English /p/, /t/ and /k/ which occur in a word-initial sequence, or cluster, between an /s/ and an /r/, as in such words as *spray*, *stray* and *scream*. We can express this symbolically as a 'rule' (where ⧣ indicates a word boundary):

$$\text{Initial consonant cluster} \rightarrow \text{⧣}/\text{s}/ + \begin{Bmatrix} /p/ \\ /t/ \\ /k/ \end{Bmatrix} + /r/ + \text{vowel}\ldots$$

This rule allows us to infer (using ordinary orthography) that whilst the initial sequences in *spray*, *stray* and *scream* are acceptable, those in **sbray*, **sdray* and **sgream* are not. Note that /p/, /t/ and /k/ are all, phonetically speaking, 'voiceless stops'. So we could express this generalization in a rule for English:

$$\text{Initial consonant cluster} \rightarrow \text{⧣}/\text{s}/ + /\text{voiceless}/ + /r/ + \text{vowel}\ldots$$
$$\text{stop}$$

A different class of phonemes can occur in the initial cluster of a consonant followed by /r/:

$$\text{⧣}/\text{——}/ + /r/ + \text{vowel}\ldots$$

The members of this class are not only the 'voiceless stops', but also /b/, /d/ and /g/, which are all 'voiced stops'. This yields such clusters as *bray*, *dray* and *grey*. But besides these we also find the phonemes /f/, /ʃ/ and /ɵ/ (as in *frill*, *shrill* and *thrill*). We can express this as a rule too:

$$\text{Initial consonant cluster} \rightarrow \text{⧣} \begin{Bmatrix} \text{voiceless stop} \\ \text{voiced stop} \\ /f/ \\ /ʃ/ \\ /ɵ/ \end{Bmatrix} + /r/ + \text{vowel}\ldots$$

Now we can combine these two 'rules' into one:

$$\text{Initial consonant cluster} \rightarrow \text{⧣} \begin{Bmatrix} (/\text{s}/) + \text{voiceless} \\ \text{stop} \\ \text{voiced stop} \\ /f/ \\ /ʃ/ \\ /ɵ/ \end{Bmatrix} + /r/ + \text{vowel}\ldots$$

This is what we called a 'generative rule' in chapter 5. It allows us to generate twelve different word-initial consonant sequences or 'clusters'. This rule tells us not only that all those clusters already exemplified are acceptable but that such initial clusters as *mr—*, *sr—*, *lr—* are not. It does not state, however, the restrictions on the nature of the following vowel, a matter which does not concern us at this point.

The phonological structure of language, however, is not just a hierarchical organization of phonemes and sequences of phonemes, such as syllables, in 'higher' units. These higher units also have distinctive properties in their own right. To revert to our previous example, the sequence of syllables *con+tract* form two different units *cóntract* and *contráct*, representing different stress patterns: $|\diagup \cup|$ and $|\cup \diagup|$, which function in a different way syntactically, as noun and verb. In this respect the functional difference is not unlike that of *bit* and *beat*. Similarly, at a still higher level, at what some linguists call the 'phonological phrase', stress and intonation together serve to distinguish:

John isn't coming tonight (but Mary is)

John isn't coming tonight (but tomorrow)

We can say that, just as stress is a property of the phonological 'word', intonation is a property of the phonological phrase in English. Thus, for example:

‖ Rebecca's here ‖

with a falling intonation on and after the principal stressed syllable contrasts with

‖ Rebecca's here? ‖

with a rising intonation on the final stressed syllable. The semantic function of these two phonological phrases is different, although their syllable/phoneme sequences are similar. The reader will notice that I have not referred to these examples as 'sentences', but 'phonological phrases'. The sentence is a unit of grammatical structure, whilst the phonological phrase is a unit of phonological structure. There is no necessary coincidence of these two units. We can show this by another example: we can speak the same sentence as *two* phonological phrases:

‖ Rebecca's ‖ here? ‖

Both phrases have rising intonation with a meaning roughly: *Do you mean to say that you're talking about Rebecca and saying that she's here?*

I spoke in chapter 5 about the 'double articulation' of language. We can now discern how these modes of articulation interact or relate to each other. Ultimately distinctions in the sound structure signal syntactic and semantic distinctions. We can study the speech sounds (phones) of a language as acoustic and physiological phenomena in their own right: this is the study of phonetics; or we can study how sounds, stress, and intonation, function to make syntactic or semantic distinctions – in which case we shall be concerned with classes of sounds (phonemes), classes of phonemes, phonological words and phrases and permitted sequences of all these. This has been called 'functional phonetics' by Martinet (1946).

The approach I have just outlined regards phonological structure as hierarchical – phonemes combine to make 'phonological words', and phonological words combine to make phonological phrases, but none of these phonological units corresponds on a one-to-one basis with the grammatical units which I shall discuss in the next section. The 'secondary articulation' of language in this theory is, thus, 'autonomous', that is, it is independant of, or parallel to, primary or grammatical articulation. The only connection we have observed is that the substitution of some phonological element for another changes the syntactic (or semantic) function of that unit. In other words, the sequence /jus/ (use) (a noun) and /juz/ (use) (a verb) are different in the same way as /bit/ and /bid/ are. Both are 'minimal pairs' in that they differ in respect of only one phoneme. What this account fails to capture is that the first pair are semantically similar, while the second are not. The difference, in the first instance, is purely syntactic. There are hosts of pairs of words in English which differ minimally phonologically, but which have this semantic similarity, e.g. *leaf/leaves*, *life/live*, *diplomat/ diplomacy*, *please/pleasure*, *concede/concession*, and our original examples, *contact/contact*, *Rebecca's here*, *Rebecca's here?* We can illustrate the same phenomenon in French: *doux/douce, fou/folle, bon/*

ponne, or in German: *gross/grösser, Buch/Bücher*, etc. This particular phonological description fails to capture then an important generalization, what every native English, French or German speaker knows about his language. It is thus descriptively inadequate to this degree. What we need is a phonological description which somewhere expresses the generalization, and yet accounts for the difference in pronunciation between *leaf/leaves, fou/folle* or *gross/grösser* as a *process* or *derivation*. Now the relationship between *leaf/leaves* is a grammatical one of singular/plural, *fou/folle* of masculine/feminine, *gross/ grösser* positive/comparative. This suggests that we need a phonological description which is *dependent* on the grammatical description.

A solution which has been proposed is to regard the phonological structure of a language in somewhat the same way as the syntax, as having a 'deep' or 'inner' structure and a 'surface' or 'outer' structure. The latter would be a representation of the pronunciation in terms of the phones of the language. The deep phonological elements of a language would be 'sets of features' or 'systematic phonemes' as they have been called. Any phonological unit, such as a word, would consist of a permitted sequence of these 'bundles of features'. For example, the word *leaf* might be described as in Figure 14:

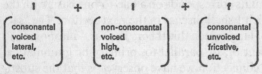

Figure 14 Phonological feature matrix for the word *leaf*

The process of realization of these sequences as elements of phonetic surface structure would be a series of 'transformation' rules which would have the effect of deleting, adding or substituting one 'feature' for another in such a way that when the derivation was complete (i.e. when all the applicable rules had been applied) we should have a specification in acoustic/articulatory terms of how the element was to be pronounced. This way of describing the sound system of a language is also 'generative' in the sense we used it in chapter 5. It is explicit and projective. The content of a phonological description would be a full list of all possible 'features', their possible grouping into 'systematic phonemes', the permitted sequence of these 'systematic phonemes' and a list of the transformation rules which 'mapped' deep phonological structure into phonetic surface structure.

To revert to our examples: *leaf/leaves, diplomat/diplomacy*. The native English speaker's intuition that these are 'semantically similar words' would be expressed by their having the corresponding parts being composed of the same sequence of systematic phonemes. The superficial phonetic difference would be the result of a process of differential 'transformational' derivation. We could say that they were 'phonological paraphrases'. Thus the native speaker might say, in informal description, that adding the plural suffix to *leaf*, i.e. *leaf* + '*plural*', had the effect of adding the feature of voice to the /f/ to yield *leaves*. This is evidently a pretty general process: *life/lives, knife/ knives, half/halves, calf/calves, loaf/loaves, thief/thieves*. It could be expressed formally in some such rule as this:

$$\begin{bmatrix} \text{consonantal} \\ \text{fricative} \\ \textit{voiceless} \end{bmatrix} \rightarrow \begin{bmatrix} \text{consonantal} \\ \text{fricative} \\ \textit{voiced} \end{bmatrix}, /\text{in the environment:} -+\text{plural}$$

A similar process would relate such pairs as *safe/save, use* (noun)/*use* (verb) and *advice/advise, wreath/wreathe, teeth/teethe*. Similarly we could suggest a general rule for French adjectives such as *fou, doux* and *bon*, which stated that the underlying or 'abstract' form in each case ended with a consonant, e.g. /fɔl/, bɔn/, /dus/, which, if not followed by a feminine suffix or by a word beginning with a vowel, was deleted by a 'transformational' rule with an attendant change of vowel quality: /fu/, /du/ and /bõ/. It is interesting that this account mirrors, to some extent, a historical process for which the orthographic forms in both languages are frequently evidence.

I have introduced the notion of 'distribution' in connection with the descriptive process of classifying phonemes and other units of phonological structure. The same notion can be applied in the classification of grammatical elements. Grammatical words which have the same potentiality of occurrence in a particular grammatical context are said to have the same function, or to be distributionally similar. They belong to the same 'form class', or, in traditional terminology, belong to the same 'part of speech'. For example, any words which will fit acceptably into the following contexts have the same grammatical function:

The — is good
I have a good —

Traditionally the words which have this function are called nouns. Thus, a definition of nouns would include the statement that they were a class of words which could immediately follow the word *the* but not immediately precede it in sequence. That is, they enter into a certain set of syntactic relations with other classes of words. A definition of this sort is called a *formal* definition since it is couched in terms of function or distribution and not in terms of meaning. If we say that the noun is a class of words which name things, people or places, we are attempting a *notional* definition.

By examining the actual functions of all the words in a corpus of data we can eventually arrive at a complete functional classification of all the elements in that corpus, and eventually draw up a list of all the possible sequences of categories found in the corpus; we can call these the 'sentences' of the language exemplified in our data. Any description which is based upon such observable and generally unequivocal distinctive features and arrived at by a process of distributional analysis, is called a 'formal description' to distinguish it from one which is based upon features which, in the present state of linguistic knowledge, are equivocal or unobservable, such as meaning.

If a description successfully meets these formal conditions, that is, if it nowhere states that some linguistic element or class has the property of functioning in a certain way which, by reference to the data (or an informant) it can be shown *not* to possess, or vice versa, if it denies that some element or class functions in a way that it actually does in the data, then that description is said to be *observationally adequate*. It accounts for the data in full and is nowhere contradicted by the 'facts', or as Chomsky has it, the description accounts for 'all and only' the grammatical sequences of the language under description. If a formal description is, in addition, generative in the sense used in chapter 5, it may achieve such a degree of observational adequacy that it can be used, when turned into a computer programme, to process and automatically analyse any further data from the language which are fed into the computer (Thorne, 1968). This is the most stringent test of the observational adequacy of a grammar. It proves that it 'works'. But, and this is a very big 'but', it does not follow that such a description tells us anything interesting. In other words, a test of this sort does not help us to decide whether the description is 'right' (for a discussion of this see chapter 5). Any scientific description of a language must 'work'; although this is a necessary condition, it is not a sufficient condition of a good description of anything. The object of a science is not just to describe but to explain. We must go back, then, to de Sassure's statement: 'It is the viewpoint which makes the object.' I said that criterial features must be observable, that is, perceptually distinct, but the selection of which observable distinctions to take into account was based on their functional significance. I extended the notion of functional significance to words and other grammatical elements, but not to permissible sequences of grammatical elements, or *sentences*, as I have called them. In other words, following the procedures outlined we finish up with simply *a list* of possible grammatical sequences of grammatical categories in the language, without any means of distinguishing between them functionally. Thus, for example, *John kicked the ball*; *The ball was kicked by John*; *John, kick the ball!*; and *Did John kick the ball?* are all examples of permissible, or well-formed, sequences (or sentences) in English, and that is all we can say about them, if we adopt this approach. This is essentially the sort of description which underlies many of the syllabuses used for language teaching at the present time, particularly those which are called 'structural syllabuses'. They consist essentially of a list of 'structures' which are to be taught, without any attempt to relate them to each other. These so-called structures are to be learned and 'overlearned' until they become 'automatic'. This last term gives a clue to the psychological viewpoint which underlies the material – an essentially behaviourist approach in which language learning is looked at as the acquisition of a set of habitual responses, each of which can be described in linguistic terms as a permissible sequence of grammatical categories, or 'structures'.

'It is the viewpoint which creates the object.' If one takes the view that the object of language is communication, what is significant as a criterion in description must be related to the communicative function of language. Traditional descriptions have always had, either implicitly or explicitly, the object of relating sounds to meaning, as we noted in chapter 5. The features that we select as relevant in the data must ultimately serve this purpose. Thus, when we saw that the difference between the various [p] phones in *poor*, *pew* and *pit* was not distinctive, what we meant was that they did not serve to make distinctions of meaning, and when we said that we classified words according to their distribution, what we were actually doing was to categorize them according to their function in signalling differences in meaning. This is why it was no accident that the traditional definition of nouns according to their meaning was not in serious conflict with the formal definition of nouns. A grammar that aims at more than just observational adequacy, a device for providing an automatic means of analysing the permissible grammatical sequences in a language must give an account not only of the structure of sentence but also of their function, how we interpret them – our linguistic competence. This is a much more demanding task. A grammar which succeeds in doing this has been called by Chomsky (1965) *descriptively adequate*. No description of any natural language has yet achieved this level of adequacy.

The making of a description

Making a descriptively adequate grammar of a language is an art. It involves hunches, insights and technical skills. It cannot be reduced to rules of thumb, or a set of automatic procedures. Enough has been said in the previous section to give an idea of some of the procedures involved: the discovery of the distinctive features of sounds, the establishment of the relevant descriptive units in phonology (e.g. phoneme, syllable), in syntax (e.g. word, sentence, etc.). To do this the linguist has to be able to understand the language, that is recognize differences and similarities in meaning, interpret its sentences, know when apparently similar structures may mean different things (i.e. detect ambiguities), know when dissimilar structures mean similar things (i.e. detect paraphrases), or have access to a native-speaking informant who can. For example, a descriptively adequate account of English must be able to show the various meanings expressed by the so-called possessive structure, as in *John's letter*:

The letter John wrote
The letter John received
The letter which is in John's possession
The letter which was addressed to John

Or, to take another example, the linguist must be able to recognize the various meanings expressed by the *subject* of a sentence, for example:

1. The person who performs the action, answering the question: what did John do? *John kicked the ball.*

2. The person to whom the event happened, answering the question: what happened to John? *John broke his leg.*

3. The place the event happened in: *The garden is swarming with wasps.*

4. The instrument which effected the action: *The key opened the door.*

5. The object involved in the process: *Cars sell well abroad.*

All these different meanings of a subject of a sentence are recognized in traditional grammars of English, and its native speakers are intuitively aware of them. A description of the language which merely lists the permitted structures of sentences does not, of course, systematically distinguish between them.

What is more demanding of the linguist is to discover 'facts' about a language which are not so readily available to the native speaker's intuitions, if at all. It often happens that what in one language is expressed by grammatical means is, in another, expressed lexically; it may, nevertheless, also be expressed grammatically, but more opaquely. Such is the case in so-called causative expressions. The educated native speaker in English is explicitly aware of the fact that so-called causative verbs may be derived grammatically from certain adjectives by the addition of a grammatical affix such as —*en*. Thus for example, *tighten, harden, weaken* are called causative verbs because they mean 'to make tight', 'to make hard', 'to make weak'. He also knows that this derivational process does not apply to all adjectives, e.g. *green, happy, poor*. In such cases we resort to lexical means of expressing causation: *make green, make happy* or *make poor*. But the native speaker is not generally explicitly or consciously aware of the fact that a large number of 'ordinary' verbs include in their meaning the notion of causation: *bring* (cause to come), *give* (cause to have), *make* (cause to be). Whilst a very large number of verbs may be either causative or non-causative, e.g. *stop, fly, open*, as in:

The train stopped
He stopped the train

The aeroplane flew
He flew the aeroplane

The door opened
He opened the door

This distinction is sometimes called a distinction in *transitivity*.

The real problem for the descriptive linguist arises when native speakers do not appear to be intuitively aware at all of some notion which is expressed in their language. This is where his hunches and insights come in. These insights are often derived from a study of other languages, which express notions for which no counterpart appears to exist in the language being described. For example, French speakers are intuitively aware that their language makes a regular grammatical distinction between the notions of *alienable* and *inalienable possession* that is between things you can dispose of if you want and those you can't. It signals this distinction by a contrasting use of articles, possessives and prepositions:

Alienable possession	Inalienable possession
Les chiens de Jean	*Les cheveux à Jean*
Jean a des chiens noirs	*Jean a les cheveux noirs*
Jean lave ses chiens	*Jean lave les cheveux*
L'homme avec les chiens noirs	*L'homme aux cheveux noirs*

But in English there is no formal contrast between the equivalent expressions:

John's dogs	John's hair
John has some black dogs	John has black hair
John washes his dogs	John washes his hair
The man with the black dogs	The man with the black hair

Of course, this does not mean that English cannot express the distinction between alienable and inalienable possession. It does so lexically. You cannot, for example, *mislay* something which you possess inalienably:

John has a long stick, but he's mislaid it
*John has a long nose, but he's mislaid it

Nor do we normally use the word *own* in connection with inalienable possession: **John owns red hair*
The question is: does English also make this distinction by grammatical means? The native speaker would probably say: no. But look at these examples:

John has a pain in the stomach
John was shot through the head
They kicked John on the shins

Here *stomach, head* and *shins* are necessarily interpreted as belonging to John. This is quite independent of the context. No possessive is necessary to signal this, though we may redundantly put one in if we wish:

John has a pain in his stomach
John was shot through his head
They kicked John on his shins

Consider, however, these sentences:

John had the dog put down
John had an accident in the car
John had a puncture in the front tyre

Here *dog, car* and *tyre* are not necessarily interpreted as belonging to John. The interpretation is dependent on context. We should have to substitute a possessive in order to signal possession unambiguously. Notice also that while we can say: *A car of John's* and *One of John's cars* we cannot say: **A finger of John's*
though we can say: *One of John's fingers*

Models of grammatical description

So far we have spoken about two measures of adequacy in the description of languages; observational adequacy, which is a measure of the degree to which the statements of a description accord with the observed relevant 'facts', and descriptive adequacy which is a measure of the degree to which the description succeeds in incorporating all the facts which the goals of the description consider relevant – in the case of a 'competence grammar', what the native speaker 'knows' about the structure of his language. We can now introduce a further notion, that of economy or 'power'. A description is more economical or powerful in the degree to which it accounts for the same facts with a smaller number of statements or 'rules', or alternatively, more facts with the same number of rules. These various measures are to some extent independent of each other. The statements in a description may be observationally adequate and yet not cover satisfactorily all the facts which are relevant, or alternatively the description may cover all the facts, but inexplicitly or faultily. In addition a description may cover all the facts and do so explicitly but in a clumsy or uneconomical way. But economy, while an advantage, is not an end in itself. We want a grammar to be 'elegant' and 'simple', but also to be elegant 'in the right way'. We want the generalizations to be *significant*, i.e. add something to our understanding of how the language works. For example, a grammatical description may give an observationally adequate account of the formation of both relative clauses and interrogative senences in English. But unless it shows that these two structures have a lot in common it lacks *significant generalization*. To do this it must make statements which are true of both structures, e.g. that interrogative and relative pronouns, adjectives and adverbs – *which*, *what*, *who*, *when*, *why*, etc. have the same form, that they come first in sequence in both structures and that they 'replace' phrases having the same functions, e.g. locative, reason, subject, object, time.

If we applied these various measures to traditional grammars, we might say that they rated 'good' on descriptive adequacy, 'fair' on observational adequacy, and 'low' on economy and explicitness. They missed many significant generalizations.

There is a connection between these measures. The more ambitious we are in our goals of explaining, the more difficult it is to achieve observational adequacy: in other words it is extremely difficult to 'formalize' our insights. If, on the other hand, we set our goals no higher than to list the permitted sequences of grammatical categories, i.e. sentence structures, we may achieve, as did the linguists who set themselves this principal aim, a high degree of observational adequacy. If our aim is to account for the native speaker's competence, it becomes much more difficult to attain observational adequacy, and if our goal is to describe the native speaker's performance, we can achieve, at the present, only a sporadic and minimal level of explicitness. Descriptions of languages show a constant compromise between these various levels of adequacy.

A great deal of theoretical research in linguistics is devoted to finding ways of accounting for the same facts with fewer more powerful statements, particularly with discovering significant generalizations. Much of the discussion about the form, nature and order of rules in modern grammar centres round this problem. This is why two descriptions which look very different superficially may yet be stating the same set of 'facts' about a language. Some of the 'modern' grammars of English ten to twenty years ago covered actually fewer facts than traditional grammars, but were more powerful and observationally adequate.

There is, of course, no doubt what the ideal grammar from a linguistic point of view would be: one that was descriptively and observationally maximally adequate and at the same time maximally powerful. The trouble with linguists, as with other scientists, is that they are always discovering new facts and new significant generalizations, so that they are constantly having to rewrite their descriptions or find new ways of formulating their statements whilst maintaining observational adequacy.

The models of grammar which we are now going to examine achieve quite different degrees of adequacy and power. I choose them because they all are, or have been, candidates for application to language teaching.

Linear models

The first model I shall call a *linear grammar*. This model of description treats the sentences of a language as a 'string' of grammatical categories like beads on a necklace, or alternatively as a series of 'slots' to be filled by words of the category appropriate to each slot. For this

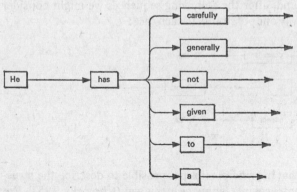

Figure 15

reason this model is sometimes also called a 'slot-and-filler' grammar. Description of this sort treats the structure of the sentence as a *linear* pattern, such that the choice of each successive category is *dependent* upon the category immediately preceding it. Of course, there is some range of choice at most points in the sequence; at some points the range may be large, at others there may in fact be no choice. For example, given the sequence: [he] → [has] → there are clearly a lot of possibilities, e.g. adverbs of manner, frequency, 'not', past participle, 'to', an article, etc.

If we knew what the next word was to be, that is, if 'dependency' worked in both directions this would, of course, cut down our choice considerably, e.g.:

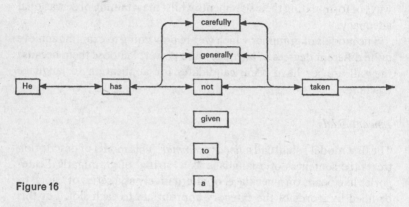

Figure 16

On the other hand, after the following sequences we might consider that there was only one possibility in each case:

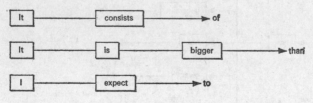

Figure 17

We now know that in principle it is not possible to describe the structure of *all* the sentences in a language in this way (Chomsky, 1957). But

180 Introducing Applied Linguistics

apart from this obvious inadequacy, this type of description has a number of other disadvantages and inadequacies both for theoretical and for applied purposes. First of all, it is obviously extremely clumsy and uneconomical. It lacks power, in that generalization is at a very primitive level; it is only one stage of generalization better than a list, the most inadequate of descriptions. It does not allow for various *degrees* of similarity or difference; either sentence elements are the same or they are treated as entirely different. For example, such a description must treat the following sequences as fundamentally distinct:

[These] → [boys] → [paint]
[This] → [boy] → [paints]

In other words it regards what, in traditional terms, have been recognized as similar categories – singular and plural nouns, demonstratives and verbs – as totally different categories, having no connection with each other. This is not only uneconomic but counter-intuitive to the native speaker. Therefore the model lacks power as well as descriptive adequacy. Furthermore, it cannot cope economically and adequately with dependencies which exist between categories which are not immediately contiguous – the relationship traditionally called concord. It cannot, for example, 'generalize' the two sequences in Figure 18 as in Figure 19:

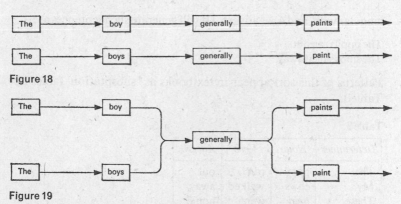

Figure 18

Figure 19

To do so would be to state that *The boys generally paints* was a permitted sequence, i.e. grammatical. In other words, the rule which every native speaker 'knows', i.e. that adverbs of frequency may be inserted between subject and verb, cannot be expressed in a description of this sort, without leading to observational inadequacy.

But the main objection to this model of description is that it does not differentiate between different sorts of relations between the components of a sentence; it treats them all as the same. It can do nothing to explain, therefore, how the grammar of a sentence enables us to interpret that sentence. Any grammar which aims at descriptive adequacy must attempt to relate sounds to meanings; a linear grammar tells us nothing about this.

The only reason for introducing a discussion of this particular model of description is that, in somewhat more generalized form, it has been used as a basis for producing language teaching materials. The best known example of it is Fries (1957). In this description the so-called 'basic' sentences of English are listed as 'strings' of constituent categories ('word order' patterns or 'formulae'). For example, Fries calls the following pattern Formula I:

$$D+1+2-d+4$$
$$\underset{-}{S} \ + \ +$$

(where D = determiner, 1 = plural noun, $2 \overset{\cdot}{-} d$ = past plural or
$$\underset{-}{S} \qquad\qquad + \qquad\qquad +$$
singular verb, and 4 = adverb.) It will generate such sentences as:

The pupils ran out
The ships sailed away

Patterns of this sort appear in textbooks as 'substitution' tables like Table 3.

Table 3

Determiner	Noun	Verb	Adverb
The	pupils	ran	out
My	cows	walked	away
These	men	went	home

This particular table will generate 34 perfectly grammatical sequences.

A more developed form of this table may attempt to take into account concord dependency:

Table 4

Determiner	Noun	Adverb	Verb	Adverb
These Some	boys men		walk	home away
		generally		
This A	boy man		walks	out

The pedagogical objection to this form of description, apart from its manifest descriptive inadequacy, is simply that, because of its lack of generalization, it implies that the learning of grammar is a question of memorizing a vast list of different and unrelated sequences, together with a very large list of different and unrelated categories. Now any description will need to distinguish between a fairly large number of primary grammatical categories, but one which fails to group together, for example, past and present forms of verbs, masculine and feminine forms of adjectives, singular and plural forms of nouns, definite and indefinite articles, places an unnecessary burden of memory upon the learner. There is, however, every reason to suppose, as was shown in chapter 6, that generalization plays an important part in learning. A description which is so devoid of significant generalization is ill-adapted to help the learner to discover these generalizations; it does nothing to explain how he is to interpret sentences.

Phrase structure models

If asked to group together the elements of a sentence which 'go together' in some sense, native speakers would have no difficulty in saying, for example, that in the sentence, *the man hit the ball*, *the* and *man* are more closely connected than *man* and *hit*, and *the* and *ball*, than *hit* and *the*. We can express this knowledge by bracketing the elements in this way:

(The man) hit (the ball)

rather than

The (man hit) the ball
The man (hit the) ball

If asked to perform this process of 'segmentation' one step at a time on this sentence, perhaps the majority of native speakers would do it as in Figure 20, though some might wish to make two 'cuts' to start off with:

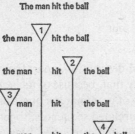

Figure 20 Successive segmentation

We could express the same series of procedures as a 'tree diagram' as in Figure 21. An analysis of a sentence by the process of successive segmentation is called *immediate constituent analysis*. Each successive act of segmentation divides up a single construction into two constituent components. This is not an arbitrary procedure, but based upon some 'feeling' for the relations that exist between the constituents. This 'feeling of relatedness' is clearly connected with how we interpret the sentence, but also, of course, derives from the formal characteristics of the language itself. For instance, *the man* or *the ball* are naturally felt to be single constituents because they can both be replaced acceptably by single words such as *John* or *you*. *Hit the ball*, similarly, is felt to be a single constituent because, it, too, can be replaced by a single word such as *advanced*. The possibility of replacement by a single word scarcely exists for *man hit* or *hit the*, for example. Furthermore, whilst we can conjoin *advanced* and *hit the ball* and *the man* and *John*, i.e.:

John and the man advanced and hit the ball

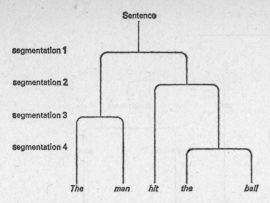

Figure 21 Tree diagram of *The man hit the ball*

we cannot do the same for *man hit* or *hit the*:

*The man hit and boy kicked the ball
*The man hit the and kicked the ball

Describing sentences in the way outlined is not only obviously more economical or powerful than the linear description, but also captures something of the way we understand sentences; it groups together those elements which function as meaningful units. Traditional grammars had names for the function of some of these constituents. Thus, in the example just given, the sentence constituent *the man* is said to function as *subject*, and *hit the ball*, as *predicate*. Similarly the constituent *the ball* is said to function as *object* and the constituent *the* as *noun modifier*. The next step is to name or label each constituent. We can do this by naming their functions – subject, object, etc. Or we can give them some arbitrary label like A, B. It is usual, however, to select a name which has a mnemonic value referring to the internal structure of the constituent, e.g. noun phrase, verb phrase, prepositional phrase, etc. This latter course is the one usually chosen in a grammatical description of this sort since we want to be able to keep separate our discussion of the internal structure of a constituent from our discussion of its function in the structure of other constituents.

If we apply these procedures to our example sentence, we might finish up with a *bracketing* and *labelling* as in Figure 22.

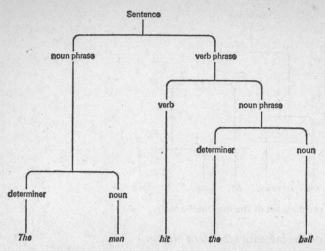

Figure 22 Labelled tree diagram

Each stage of this process can be expressed as a 'statement' about the grammar of the sentence:

1. The sentence is a sequence consisting of a noun phrase and a verb phrase.
2. The verb phrase is a sequence consisting of a verb and a noun phrase.
3. The noun phrase is a sequence consisting of a determiner and a noun.
4. Examples of nouns are: *man, ball*, etc.
5. Examples of verbs are: *hit*, etc.
6. An example of a determiner is: *the*.

These statements, of course, are not only true of the one particular sentence but of vast numbers of other different sentences, in which case we can regard them as 'rules' of sentence structure in English. They are powerful statements. They can also easily be expressed in a symbolic form:

1. Σ → NP+VP.
2. VP → V+NP.
3. NP → D+N.
4. N → {man, ball ...}.
5. V → {hit ...}.
6. D → {the ...}
(where → = 'consists of' or 'is rewritten as')

186 Introducing Applied Linguistics

A phrase structure description obviously incorporates more significant generalizations than a linear description. It treats as similar in function groups of sentence elements which are themselves different in internal structure, e.g. singular and plural nouns, past and present tense verb forms and so on.

Phrase structure descriptions of this sort underlie much teaching material. For pedagogical reasons clear distinctions are not always drawn between 'formal' and 'functional' labels for the various constituents in the hierarchical structure. An example of the use of this model can be found in the Hornby grammar already referred to on page 141. Thus Hornby gives as an example of what he calls Verb Pattern 18 the substitution table shown in Table 5.

Table 5

Subject and verb	(Pro)noun	to	(Pro)noun
He read	the letter	to	all his friends
He sold	his car	to	the man from Leeds
I have written	letters	to	most of my old pupils
etc.	etc.		etc.

Underlying this account is the phrase structure derivation given in Figure 23. The difference between this example and that given in Table 3 on page 182 is that here the analysis groups individual words or com-

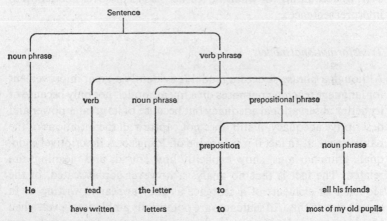

Figure 23 Phrase structure derivation

plete phrases together because they are functionally similar though formally different. The linear model would treat all these examples as different 'patterns' of constituent word classes.

The pedagogical advantages of the phrase structure model of description are obvious. By making significant generalizations, i.e. by treating as 'the same' those constituents, whatever their internal structure, which have the same function in the structure of the sentence – it helps the learner to understand how sentences are interpreted – in other words, it does something to show the 'grammatical meaning' of sentence constituents. Since it is also a more economical description, it places a smaller burden on the learner's memory – it does some of his work of generalization for him. Instead of memorizing a vast number of unrelated sequences, he has to learn a much smaller number of rules or significant categories and relations. But, and this is a big 'but', these categories and relations are more 'abstract', in the sense that they are not immediately apparent in the data. They have to be inferred from the data. There is some experimental evidence that some sort of 'immediate constituent' analysis of this sort forms part of the psycholinguistic process of interpreting sentences. Up to a point, therefore, a phrase structure grammar is psychologically more 'real' than a linear grammar (Johnson, 1965; Fodor and Bever, 1965). If it had no other advantages, this alone would recommend it as a model for application in language teaching. It goes only a very little way, however, to accounting for what the learner has to discover about how to interpret sentences.

Transformational models

Although a phrase structure model is evidently a great improvement for language teaching purposes on a linear model, not only because of its better observational adequacy but because of its greater power and descriptive adequacy, it still does not capture all the intuitions of the native speaker. In fact it is incapable of doing so. A descriptively adequate grammar must show explicitly how sounds and meanings are related. The fact is that no analysis, however sophisticated, of the sequence of elements of a sentence as they appear in writing or in speech can do this. All sentences are potentially ambiguous, even when 'decontextualized'. No phrase structure grammar, for example, can

show by differential bracketing and labelling that *John's letter* has four
different interpretations. Nor can it show, what every native speaker
knows, that active and passive and interrogative and declarative sentences share a major similarity of meaning. A phrase structure grammar
can, of course, generate these different structures, but not in a way that
makes clear their essential similarity. For example, there is nothing
evidently similar about the two analyses given in Figure 24. What we
intuitively want our description to say is that these two sentences are
'alternative' forms of the same 'sentence' or 'message', just as we
would wish to say that while *It was easy to please James* was an alterna-

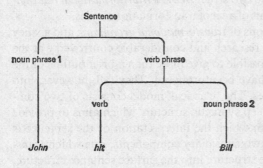

(a) Active derivation

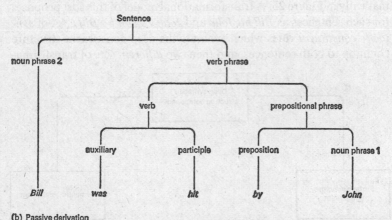

(b) Passive derivation

Figure 24 Active and passive phrase structure deviations

tive form of *James was easy to please, It was eager to please James* was *not* an alternative form of *James was eager to please*.

A transformational description aims to incorporate these sorts of insights. To do so, it finds it necessary to say that there must be two structures to any sentence, an *outer*, apparent structure, which is the linear structure we see on the page, and an inner 'abstract' structure which corresponds more closely to the semantic structure of the message – the meaning of the sentence – and that these two structures are related in a regular fashion. It is the task of a transformational grammar to state the nature of these two structures and relate them together. The relation between the two structures is a *transformational relationship*, and is stated in terms of a set of transformational rules.

There are many versions of *transformational grammars*, and as they are a field of intensive research and considerable controversy at the present time, it is not possible to give more than a brief outline of the various solutions that have been proposed. They fall, however, into two fairly distinct classes. The 'classical' model consists of two components: an inner, or deep syntactic structure which aims to provide all the information from which the interpretation of the sentence is derived, together with two subsidiary components, one which transforms the deep sentence structure into the surface sentence structure, and another which provides rules for interpreting the information provided by the deep structure categories and relations as shown diagrammatically in Figure 25. A transformational model of this sort proposes for such sentences as *Bill hit John* and *John was hit by Bill* a set of *syntactic constituent* rules which generate the deep constituent structure common to both sentences, and then two *different* sets of transforma-

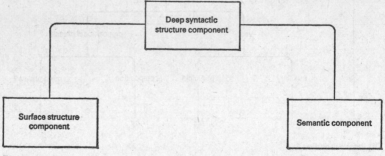

Figure 25

tional rules which produce the two different surface structures. One and the same set of semantic interpretation rules apply to the single deep structure underlying both different surface structures, thus ensuring that both sentences receive the same interpretation.

We can attempt to illustrate this in a very simplified form, leaving out such matters as tense, concord, etc. The deep structure component would, by a series of phrase structure or 'constituent' rules, generate the common deep structure of both sentences as in Figure 26. The active surface form of this deep structure would be relatively little transformed, whilst the passive surface structure would be generated by a set of transformational rules which (1) brought NP2 into 'subject position'; (2) turned NP1 into an 'agent' propositional phrase *by John* in final position; and (3) turned V into a 'passive form' *was hit*.

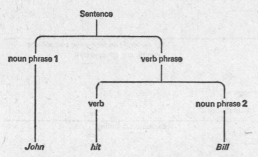

Figure 26 Deep syntactic structure of *John hit the ball*

The semantic component is of greater interest and would have rules something like those in Figure 27. (No one has worked out a reasonable set of semantic interpretational rules for any language.) This is in essence the model proposed by Chomsky (1965). From a language learner's point of view it means that instead of learning a large number of categories and the relations between them and a set of enormously complex but unexplained rules for interpreting these categories and relations, as in the phrase structure model, he would have to learn a much smaller number of categories and constituent rules and a large number of transformational rules, together with a smaller, and presumably less complex, set of semantic interpretation rules. Again, there is some evidence that this model has some degree of psycholinguistic validity (Miller and McKean, 1964).

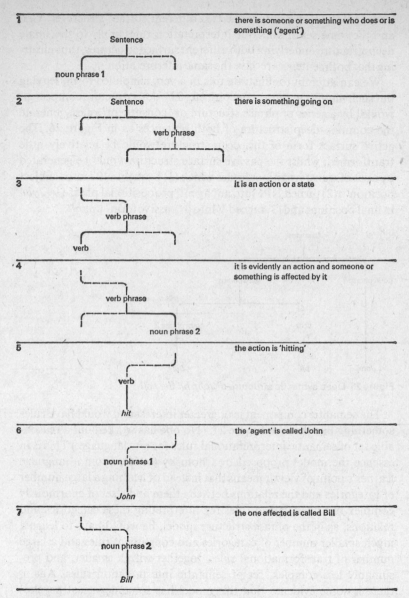

1 — there is someone or something who does or is something ('agent')

Sentence

noun phrase 1

2 — there is something going on

Sentence

verb phrase

3 — it is an action or a state

verb phrase

verb

4 — it is evidently an action and someone or something is affected by it

verb phrase

noun phrase 2

5 — the action is 'hitting'

verb

hit

6 — the 'agent' is called John

noun phrase 1

John

7 — the one affected is called Bill

noun phrase 2

Bill

Figure 27 The semantic interpretation of deep structural relations

It is most important at this point *not* to confuse the transformation exercises which are frequently performed in the classroom – turning active into passive sentences or declarative into interrogative sentences – as the application of the linguist's transformational rules. What is being overtly done in the classroom is changing one surface structure into another surface structure, whereas the linguist's rules transform an entirely abstract 'inner' structure into two alternative 'outer' structures. These two different processes are shown in Figure 28. The fact that, in this case, the surface structure of the active sentence happens to 'resemble' the common deep structure of both sentences is an 'artefact' of this particular description of English. There is nothing necessary about it; it is largely motivated by 'simplicity' or 'economy' of description.

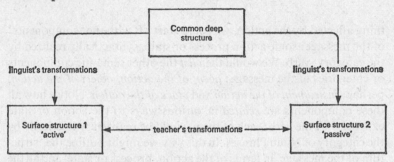

Figure 28 Linguists' and teachers' transformations

The second type of transformational description is called *semantic based*. Whereas the standard model starts with a *syntactic* deep structure of the *sentence* which is interpreted by a set of semantic rules, the semantic based model starts off with the structure of the 'message' which is then progressively transformed by a series of rules into surface syntactic categories and relations. A diagrammatic representation of this model would be that shown in Figure 29. No one has yet provided a description of this sort in any detail, but we can see in broad outline what is involved in doing so if we reverse the process of the semantic interpretation rules of the classic transformational model. In this case, instead of starting off with syntactic categories and relations, such as Σ and saying that this is interpreted as these being an 'agent'

NP1

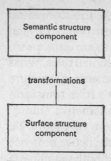

Figure 29 Semantic based model

and then moving on to, say, VP and saying that there is someone or

NP2

thing affected by the action, we could start off with the 'components' of the message: some action process or state, syntactically realized by the category: verb. We would then *list* the other semantic components or categories of the message: *agent of the action*, *object of the action*, perhaps *instrument of the action* and *place of the action*. Notice how all these components are *related* in various ways to the action or state expressed by the verb; each of them would be realized syntactically by the category of Noun Phrases. In this way we might outline the 'structure of the message' in terms of the action, process or state, and all the various things and persons – 'participants' in Halliday's terms (1970) – involved in that action or state, in various ways. This message structure would then, by a series of transformational processes, be actualized, or 'realized' in a number of possible surface structures. The particular relations between the noun phrases and the verb would be marked in surface structure by different case endings, prepositions or by the order of words. The particular model outlined above is called a 'case grammar' (Fillmore, 1968) and it is transformational in principle since it does attempt to relate the underlying 'notions' or 'case categories' to surface structure. It has not, however, reached the degree of observational adequacy of the classic syntax-based transformational model. Grammars of this sort present very great problems of 'adequate formalization'.

The main claim of a case grammar is that the array of message components or 'case categories' is relatively small and possibly universal to all languages. This is a claim which has yet to be proved, but is one that was never explicitly made for the deep syntactic structure of the syntactic based model, where only *similarity* in all languages is claimed for the deep or 'base' syntactic component. A transformational description of this sort is able in principle to recognize the essential similarity of the 'message' conveyed by such sentences as:

John opened the door with a key
The door was opened by John with a key
The door opened with a key
A key opened the door
A key was used by John to open the door

In all these sentences, in spite of their different surface structure, we interpret the phrase *John* as the agent, *the door* as the object affected by the action, *the key* as the instrument by which the action is effected. In the sense that this model incorporates the insights which the native speaker has into his language, it is, in principle, descriptively more adequate. However, as we have seen, raising one's sights in respect of descriptive adequacy usually results in losses in observational adequacy. Semantic based grammars at the present time have not yet solved this problem.

From the point of view of teaching, however, this sort of transformational grammar holds out prospects of great interest. When we learn a second language we are concerned with expressing meanings. Any account of how this is done is therefore relevant to our task. If it turns out that the rules for constructing messages are indeed universal to all languages, then they do not have to be learned by the learner – he already knows them. What he has to acquire is a partially new set of transformational rules which relate the *known* deep structure of his messages to the *unknown* surface structures of the target language. This is expressed in a diagram form in Figure 30. The task of comparing languages, then, becomes one of contrasting the two sets of different, or partially different, transformation rules. I shall return to this question in chapter 10.

The point of view adopted so far has been that the applied linguist must be eclectic in his choice of description. But this is not a point of view universally held. There are some who take the line that only the

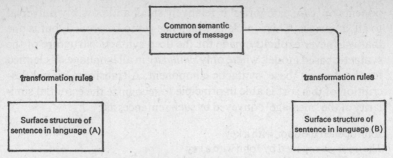

Figure 30 The relation between message structure and surface structure in two languages

best description – and that usually means, the latest – can serve as a starting point for the preparation of pedagogic grammars. Here is an expression of this point of view:

> If linguistics has any contribution to make to language teaching it is this: to make explicit in general and in particular what is learned. To the extent that transformational grammar provides the best description, it by definition also provides the best basis for application. It is incongruous to argue that some less adequate formulation can be successfully applied when a more adequate one cannot. (Saporta, 1966, p. 88)

On the face of it this arguments seems a good one. How can one deliberately reject the 'best description' or the 'most adequate' formulation and prefer some less good description or less adequate formulation? The answer hinges on the interpretation of 'best' and 'most adequate'. These are relative terms and presuppose some end or goal. Thus, 'best' implies 'best for some purpose' and 'most adequate' implies 'most adequate for some purpose'. The writer of the extract just quoted, by omitting to clarify the purpose for which the description is 'best' and 'most adequate', has assumed that the goals of linguistic theory and of applied linguistics are the same. But this, as we have shown, is not the case.

Criteria for judging the *validity* of a linguistic description are internal to linguistics. A description is valid if it describes adequately what it purports to describe. We shall meet this question of validity again in chapter 14 in connection with language tests. Validity is related to goals. It is therefore necessary to make a distinction between validity in respect of theoretical goals and validity for practical or applied purposes. I shall call this latter 'validity', *utility*. The test of the utility of a description is, then, whether it promotes more efficient language learning. The proof of the pudding is in the eating.

We do, however, know what some of the different goals of linguistics are: to make a structural description of a corpus of language, to characterize the competence of the native speaker, to give an account of linguistic performance. Which of the goals of description is likely to provide the applied linguist with the information he is most in need of? The object or goal of language teaching is to develop in the learner the knowledge and skills which enable him to play certain roles in another language community, to turn him into a *performer* in the target language, to give him a *communicative* competence. Does this goal match any of the goals of linguistics? The nearest is the linguist's goal of describing language performance. Do we have available any linguistic description of language performance? The answer is: no, none of the linguist's descriptions yet provides a systematic account of performance. We must judge then that linguistic descriptions fall short, by definition, of what is needed by the applied linguist. In these circumstances it seems inescapable that the applied linguist must be prepared to make use of any description which his knowledge and experiences of language teaching suggest to him may be useful, and that he should evaluate descriptions not in terms of their linguistic validity but their practical utility.

Part Three
The Techniques of Applied Linguistics

Chapter 9
Selection 1: Comparison of Varieties

The necessity for selection

No one knows 'the whole' of any language, or how to use it appropriately in all possible situations of language use. He acquires those parts of it which he needs in order to play his part in society. As he grows older, the roles that are ascribed to him or that he acquires change and develop, and as they change he learns more of his language (he may also forget some). He has a linguistic repertoire which changes and grows throughout his life. If no one knows the whole of any language then it cannot be the aim of language teaching to teach 'the whole' of a language; consequently there must be some process of selection in preparing the syllabus for a teaching course. It is obviously desirable that this process of selection should be carried out systematically and according to some principle. The second-order application of linguistics is concerned with the principles and techniques of selecting what goes into syllabuses, and since all selection implies comparison, I have called the second-order applications of linguistics *comparative application*.

Not only is it an unreasonable aim to teach the whole of a language; it is also an impossible one. There are two reasons for this: firstly, we haven't time. If it takes a native speaker the whole of a lifetime to acquire only a partial knowledge of his language, we are clearly not going to be able to teach the whole of a language in any sort of ordinary language teaching course. For this reason we are forced to make selections out of 'the whole of a language' to make up the syllabus. But, more important, we do not have descriptions of 'the whole of a language'. Indeed, as we saw in chapter 3, the concept of 'the whole of a language' is a product of complex social psychological attitudes, and we cannot teach what we do not 'know', or better, what we cannot describe. These two limitations are built-in, as it were, and the applied linguist has no control over them. His task is to make a selection out of such descriptions of the language as he can make, or has available – his explicit 'knowledge of the language' – which will most usefully fill the time that is at his disposal for teaching. The crucial word is, of course, *usefully*. This and the next two chapters are concerned with the principles and methods of making the most useful selection.

The objectives of language teaching and the motives of language learners

In government things go best when what the electors want and what the government does match up. So in language teaching we are successful to the degree that we achieve the best match between the objectives of teaching and the needs or demands of the learners. But we are faced with roughly the same problem as governments: that of finding out what the electors want. The applied linguist has, of course, no formal means of consulting his 'electorate', though, as we shall see, he may use something like an opinion poll to guide him. The trouble is that the language learning public, like the electorate, does not hold just one opinion or set of objectives, but represents a wide range of both, including no opinions or objectives at all.

The task of applied linguists is to devise syllabuses to meet all possible demands, or, where no demand is forthcoming, to provide a solution to the best estimates of the needs of the learner.

The objective of language teaching is to turn out people who possess sufficient skill in, and knowledge of, the target language for their needs – that is, the most relevant and useful repertoire in the sense used in chapter 3. To determine the linguistic characteristics of this repertoire we must be able to specify, in sociological terms, what functions the learner will require of the language, state in what domains and for what purposes he is going to need the language, in which social group and language communities he is going to operate and in what roles in these communities. This is a pretty tall order. How are we going to find all this out? Furthermore, we do not teach individuals; we do not produce custom-built syllabuses for each learner. Some varying degree of compromise is going to be necessary in devising any syllabus. Most people, as we have seen, start learning languages when they are still at school, before they have any clear idea of what their future careers will be and, consequently, what specific uses they will have for the language. There is nothing peculiar to language teaching in this; it is common to all but a few subjects taught in schools. At school, then, the motivation for language learning (where it is not solely concerned with passing of the examinations which open up further educational horizons) is likely to be influenced by the general climate of opinion in the students' home communities about language learning. This may or may not be favourable. The learner may come from a social background which regards language learning as a waste of time and of no practical value. On the other hand, he may come from a social group which accepts language learning as 'culturally' desirable, and the possession of a foreign language as a mark of 'the educated person', without specifying more exactly what the knowledge of a language is for. Or he may come from some community which values the knowledge of a second language highly, and regards it as a social, professional and economic asset. This is particularly likely to be the case where the language in question has some function in the society from which he comes, where it is a 'second' rather than a 'foreign' language (see chapter 3).

These three degrees of positiveness in attitudes to foreign language learning correspond roughly to the scale of motivation discussed by Gardner and Lambert (1959), where they distinguished between purely *instrumental* motivation and *integrational* motivation for language learning. By instrumental motivation they mean learning a language because of some more or less clearly perceived utility it might have for the learner, whilst integrational motivation means learning a language because the learner wishes to identify himself with or become integrated into the society whose language it is. The latter sort of motivation may occur at all levels of learning, where it exists at all, whilst instrumental motivation is commonest amongst adults. The difficulty in investigating motivation is that school pupils are rarely able to talk coherently about their motivation, and even when they do give reasons for their interest in learning a language, it is likely to be a 'rationalization'. Consequently motivation usually has to be 'inferred' from success in learning, rather than success in learning 'predicted' from known motivation. Investigations into motivation have therefore aimed at 'measuring' it rather than analysing it. The procedure goes like this (Pimsleur, 1963): we start by assuming that learning will not take place without motivation. Therefore, other things being equal, e.g. teaching methods and materials, intelligence and aptitude of learners, those who are most successful in learning, as measured on some standardized test, will be those with the highest degree of motivation. We then measure *indirectly* the motivation of the successful and unsuccessful learners by asking them questions about their and their parents' attitudes to the language being learned, the people who speak it, their degree of contact with them and their culture, and so on. We then compare their 'scores' in the questionnaire with their 'scores' in the language test to see what relation there is between them. We expect, and do generally find, a positive correlation between them, though not a very strong one. As a check on the validity of the results we then measure the motivation of a group who have not yet learned the language and predict on the basis of the results, who will and will not be successful. Motivation measures of this sort have proved to be fairly *reliable* but, of course, they do not tell us what the nature of motivation is. They tell us only that there is some connection between the expression of favourable attitudes to the language and its speakers, and success in learning it. For devising relevant syllabuses however, we need more precise information, particularly about the instrumental motivation of the learner.

Lambert has elsewhere gone so far as to suggest that the improvement in language learning which has taken place since the war is perhaps wholly ascribable to a generally increased 'interest' in language learning throughout the world, an interest which is perhaps a result of the war itself, rather than to any specific improvement in language teaching techniques and materials. Such a point of view may be a useful corrective to over-enthusiastic claims about the superiority of modern methods and materials over traditional ones. In view of the great difficulty of constructing well-controlled and valid experiments into the differential effects of different teaching techniques and materials, however, it is a hypothesis which is difficult to disprove or confirm. But it is just as plausible to suggest that the general increased interest in learning languages is a *result* of new methods and materials, and particularly of new and more relevant *objectives* in language teaching, such as the emphasis on spoken skills and on language as a means of communication.

If, then, the learner's motivations vary from a mere 'willingness' to submit to being taught a language to a positive intention to learn a language for some reasonably well-defined purpose, the applied linguist must be able to devise syllabuses which best meet the two extremes of demand. It has been customary, in fact, to speak of them as two separate tasks: the teaching of the 'everyday' language and the teaching of 'special languages', or, in more recent terms, the teaching of a language for general and special purposes. Whether in the light of discussions in chapter 3 these are well chosen terms we can pass over, but what is clear is that both extremes of this continuum of demand involve processes of selection.

The choice of a 'model'

Since it is a linguistic selection we are concerned with, it will be appropriate to adopt the linguistic approach to a 'language' as a constellation of well-defined codes, 'sociolectal' and dialectal discussed on page 56. The first decision that must be made is which of the various dialects from this constellation one should choose as the code from which a further selection is to be made to form the repertoire to be embodied in the syllabus. Any of the constituent dialects of the constellation is a potential candidate.

The factors which we must take into account are two-fold – *politico-social* factors, i.e. the attitudes of the language community whose language is being taught, and that of the learner's community to that language; and secondly, its *communicative potential*, i.e. the ability of the language to cope most adequately with the communicative needs of the learner.

Let me start by asking the reader what his reaction would be to a foreigner who spoke to him in a non-standard dialect? Assuming he did not simply ascribe the non-standard forms to an ignorance of the rules, that is, to a learner's error, I suggest the first reaction would be to wonder where he had 'picked up' the language. In other words, the first reaction would be to jump to the conclusion that he had not been taught but had simply acquired the language by living in contact with speakers of that dialect. This is quite a common phenomenon amongst immigrants, waiters or sailors, for example, whose main exposure to language data is likely to be of some non-standard sociolect or regional dialect, and whose communicative needs are generally rather restricted. We tend to assume, as native speakers, that the foreigner will have been taught a standard form of the language, and if he doesn't use some sort of standard form, then he can't have received formal teaching. This is an all the more reasonable attitude since it is the standard dialect which is taught in our own schools. Notice that we do not interpret a nonstandard dialect in the foreigner as any sort of *claim* to be accepted as a full member of some native social group. This is a different matter to which I shall return later. The use of a non-standard dialect in a foreigner is *socially acceptable*, at least in Britain. We do not attempt to correct a foreigner's nonstandard forms; we are not offended by them. This is not universally the case. The author was regularly corrected in Sweden for using non-standard though widely-used forms which he 'picked up' when learning Swedish. Evidently there are differences in the expectations which native speakers have in different language communities about what is acceptable behaviour in a foreigner and therefore a model for teaching.

The situation in the case of Swedish and English is different in other ways. English is a first or second language in many different countries all over the world, whereas Swedish is not. Where it is a first language, as in Britain, America or Australia, we have dialectal diglossia, one 'high' and a set of 'low' dialects and sociolects. Thus we find some degree of regional variability in what is regarded as the 'standard' dialect; in other words, there is some degree of variability in what is regarded by native speakers as a 'norm', particularly in matters of pronunciation. This is not so in the case of most other languages; though it will apply to Spanish and German amongst European languages. We therefore have in these cases at least a choice amongst standard dialects. This is where the attitudes of the learner's community must be taken into consideration in selecting a teaching model. Normally such decisions are political and based upon the interests, economic and political, of the territory. Thus, South American standards of Spanish are selected in America, and a metropolitan Spanish standard in Europe, whilst an American standard of English is frequently selected in South America and a British standard in Europe, though this may be changing in response to economic and political pressures.

Where the target language has certain functions in the community – where it is what we called a 'second language' – the situation is somewhat more complicated. Suggestions have been made that a deliberate selection of some local dialect as a model should be made in such cases, e.g. Indian English or West African English (Halliday, Strevens and McIntosh, 1964, pp. 172–3) on the grounds that it is more efficient for communication purposes, i.e. mutual intelligibility, to select a dialect which is the predominant form in the region, since the frequency of interaction between members of the community is greater than that between members and people outside – foreigners. Here the attitudes of the community to the language are determining. They do not normally accept the local dialect as a standard. In other words, they recognize the *same norm* as native speakers and regard any suggestions for establishing a local standard as being 'fobbed off' with some second best in typically 'colonialist' style.

We now turn to the communicative reasons for selecting a standard dialect as a model. These are three: first of all its 'coverage'. This can be understood in various ways. Sociolects and dialects do not all cover the same range of language functions in society; they do not all offer the same linguistic resources for dealing with all the communicative needs of the society. As we have seen, certain dialects are associated with certain language functions in a society. The standard dialect has the resources for coping with the widest range of language functions: government, administration, the law, education, science and technology, trade, journalism. Indeed certain of these functions are exclusively carried out by the standard dialect. Ferguson (1959) has exemplified this in a general way, where he shows the typically different functions of 'high' and 'low' varieties in a diglossic language situation as in Figure 31.

	High	Low
1 Sermon	√	
2 Instructions to servants, waiters		√
3 Personal letters		√
4 Political speeches	√	
5 University lectures	√	
6 Conversation with friends and family		√
7 News broadcast	√	
8 Radio 'Soap Opera'		√
9 Newspaper editorials; news stories	√	
10 Caption on a political cartoon		√
11 Poetry	√	
12 Folk literature		√

Figure 31 The function of high and low varieties of language in diglossic situations

The second consideration is that the stylistic variability of non-standard dialects is generally restricted, particularly at the more formal end of the spectrum. Furthermore, the writing system is normally best adapted to the standard dialect. This is most clearly shown in the technical difficulties, especially in spelling, of writing in non-standard dialects. (I am here thinking particularly of the problem of representing regional pronunciations.)

The objects of learning a language are to communicate, but not exclusively with native speakers of that language. Sociolinguists classify languages into those of 'wide dispersion' or 'major' languages, and of 'limited dispersion' or 'minor' languages. The reasons for learning French, Spanish or English, or for that matter Swahili, Hausa or Pidgin English, are not only to be able to communicate with native speakers but to have a common means of communication with many other people whose native language is a minor language; in other words, as a *lingua franca*. Maximum mutual intelligibility depends on, though it is not guaranteed by, formal linguistic similarity, that is, a common code. Since native speakers, particularly in the case of major languages, tend to share a similar 'norm', a standard dialect, it is logical that this should be the model for teaching. The acceptance by native speakers and learners of a common norm will help to keep in check the fairly general tendency to divergence inherent in language change.

The last and most practical reason for selecting a standard dialect as a model for teaching is simply that standard dialects are those which have been historically the object of linguistic description; in other words we 'know' much more about such dialects and are able consequently to produce better materials for teaching them.

Everyday language and neutral language

On page 204, I suggested that the best results in language teaching were likely to be achieved when the linguistic content of the course most closely approximated to the learner's functional needs. These needs varied between highly specific ones (language for special purposes) and very general ones, as in the case of the majority of school learners who could not be expected to be able to foresee their needs in anything but the most general terms (a language for everyday purposes).

There are two ways of looking at the content of a 'general syllabus': either as basic training in the language – *neutral* as between all the possible functions of the language – or a specific training for the use of the language in everyday situations. In the first case there is an obvious similarity with what we have been calling the 'common core' – those features of the language which are common to all dialects of the language. We saw that, whilst this concept was of interest to linguists and sociolinguists, it had dangers from a practical, applicational point of view – if you reduce the syllabus to only what is common to all codes, it has no 'surrender value' at any point. Similarly, the learner who knows only what is common to all uses of the code cannot use language appropriately in any situation; such a basic knowledge has been called *neutral language*. Neutral language is thus an abstraction – nevertheless it is an indispensable foundation for any functionally useful knowledge of language, whilst, in itself, it remains inadequate for any purpose. In this sense it is the *basis* of any syllabus; it is the minimum only which must be known for any purpose, whether general or particular, everyday or special. But there is another reason why one cannot *confine* teaching to neutral language alone. We teach language through 'performance'. Thus any language data which we place before a learner, if it is part of a discourse or contextualized in some other way, is an instance of 'parole' or 'language in use'. As such, it must, by definition, draw on material outside neutral language. If our teaching is not simply confined to the stating of rules and the giving of examples we cannot stay within neutral language and at the same time give examples of language which is appropriate in its use.

The term 'everyday language' is misleading. Language viewed as a *system* is neither 'everyday' nor 'special'. The use of the phrase 'everyday language' is to confuse the code with the uses of the code. The code is an abstraction; uses of the code are 'concrete'. It is the relation between sentences and utterances which was discussed in chapter 8. A particular word or grammatical structure is not more or less common in itself; it is a term in a system. To say that a particular word in a language is more common than some other word is like saying that the apex of a triangle in geometry is 'more common' than some other angle, or that diameters are 'more common' than chords of circles. The notion of relative frequency is not applicable to items in a language as a system, any more than it is in geometry. It is *instances* of the use of words or structures which are more or less common. For this reason it is preferable to talk of 'language for everyday purposes' or 'language for special purposes' rather than of 'everyday language' or 'special' or 'restricted' languages. Compare the absurdity of 'everyday geometry' with the sense of 'geometry for special purposes'.

What we select to teach the learner who cannot specify his precise needs, then, is 'language for everyday purposes'. This goes well beyond 'neutral language'. The notion of 'everyday purposes' suggests that there are certain situations and activities which occur more frequently in the experience of most people than others. This certainly seems intuitively true. Most people would probably agree that taking the population as a whole, 'shopping' is a more frequent experience than 'attending a horse race'; 'watching television' than 'going to the theatre'. It seems to make sense that we should equip the learner to cope with activities and situations which are more common than those which are relatively infrequent. There are, however, considerable difficulties in translating these notions into sociolinguistic terms, that is, in relating these activities to language needs.

The first difficulty is this: what I have called 'everyday situations' or 'activities' are sociolinguistically a range of rather different situations of language use. In terms of the categories of description used in chapter 2, shopping involves two distinct participant roles, buyer and seller, varying degrees of *contact*, great variety of *setting*, shop, garage, hairdressing salon, etc. They have in common perhaps only the *instrumental* function of language, achieving a purchase or sale of goods or services.

The case of television viewing is even more varied. It involves the role of viewer and a wide range of performers, actors, announcers, interviewers, commentators. The range of language function is equally wide, but involves only receptive activity. There can be no sense in proposing that we should teach the learner to participate as a viewer in all these various activities in the target language. We should clearly have to be highly selective and specific. We might even decide that, while television viewing was an 'everyday activity' in his home environment, it was likely to be a 'special activity' in the foreign environment.

This leads us to the second problem. What is an everyday activity for the learner in his home environment may not be so in another community. The question is: can we so classify everyday interactional situations in such a way as to identify those which the foreigner is likely to participate in and exclude those which he is not?

Gumperz (1966) has suggested the categorization of situations into *personal* and *transactional* interactions. He has shown how the language in these two types of situation varies. Transactional interactions are those in which the mutual rights and obligations of the participants are fairly well defined. The language which is found in such situations is consequently also fairly well defined and in some degree predictable. Transactional interactions are such as are found between shopkeeper and customer, doctor and patient, lawyer and client, waiter and diner. Personal interactions between friends, colleagues, acquaintances and relations are more informal, more fluid and varied. The language is consequently more variable and unpredictable. It seems probable that most of the interactions in which a foreigner will participate will be transactional. Personal interaction is largely conducted in the mother tongue. This is not, of course, to suggest that the learner will not enter into relationships which involve personal interaction, only that in terms of frequency, transactional interaction will predominate. In the learner's home environment the exact opposite will be the case – personal interaction will be more frequent. This categorization gives us an important principle upon which to base the content of a syllabus, by directing our attention to the varieties of language from which selection will be made.

The third point we must take into account is that we are preparing the learner at school to use the target language in the future rather than in the present. It is his needs as a mature adult that we must have in mind, as much as his needs as a child or adolescent. The social roles played by adults and consequently their language needs are very different from those of children. It is quite a common experience, for example, for people who were brought up as bilinguals in some foreign language community to return to that community as adults in later life only to find that their knowledge of the language, adequate as it was for their personal needs as a child, proves quite inadequate for the everyday transactional purposes of the adult.

It is here that we run into the problem of motivation. The objective of language teaching is to equip the learner to operate *as an adult* in the foreign community, and yet in the absence of instrumental motivation amongst school learners, we depend upon intrinsic motivation for success in language teaching. This means that the linguistic content of the syllabus must be relevant to the interests and language needs of the learner *at the time of learning*. Furthermore, a course which is based upon the linguistic needs of the adult will be not only intrinsically less motivating but probably unteachable, since the learner will not even possess the equivalent language behaviour and functions in his own mother tongue. We should then be attempting to teach him knowledge and skills in a foreign language for which he could not only have no use, but more seriously, no understanding. To some extent that is what traditional language teaching, particularly of the dead languages, attempted to do, with its principally literary emphasis, and its teaching of translation, essay writing, précis, composition of poetry and study of classical literary texts.

The general syllabus must, then, draw its selection from the language needs and skills of the learner as they exist at the age at which he is learning. This means investigating what these needs are, hence the importance of the work of such projects as The Child Language Survey, which was set up as part of the Nuffield Foundation Foreign Languages Teaching Project (now the Schools Council Primary School Modern Languages Programme. See Handscombe, 1969).

The conclusion of this discussion is that the objectives of a general syllabus is to lay the foundation of language use, to teach neutral language; to do this we must teach by means of language functions appropriate to the learner's age. In short, we teach a basic knowledge of the language system through that form of language activity which is appropriate to the learner at the time of learning.

Relative frequency and neutral language

In chapter 6 I said that the differences between codes was that there will be certain forms of the language which did or did not form part of a particular code. Linguistically speaking, codes were regarded as well-defined systems. When it came to the uses of the code, however, we saw that the question was one of probability, that is, there was a greater or lesser likelihood that some particular form would occur in a particular situation of language use. Differences between what we called varieties were a matter of statistics or relative frequency. Those forms which have a high probability of occurring in a particular type of situation were called the linguistic *markers* of the particular variety associated with that situation. These markers, of course, could be grammatical, lexical or phonological. We can all think, offhand, of markers which we associate with different situations of language use. Take, for example, the omission of definite articles in technical instructions (but note how they return when descriptions are given):

After steam ironing, unplug iron from mains and set push button to dry. Hold iron upside down and allow water to drain off filler hole. Failure to empty all the water from the iron will result in damage to the sole plate.

the absence of commas in legal documents:

This guarantee is given in lieu of and excludes every condition or warranty whether expressed or implied not herein expressly stated and is subject to the terms and conditions overleaf.

the frequency of passive constructions in technical writing:

In recent reports two new techniques have been added. Electricity is run through the needles, which may now be placed directly on either side of the surgical incision. A British GP describes a Caesarian section being carried out in a conscious woman in Shanghai involving long current-carrying needles which were placed in abdominal skin before laparotomy.

But this is seen most clearly in the selection of certain 'lexical' words, in contrast to 'grammatical' words (see chapter 5), in different varieties of language use:

Common Hornwort, found throughout Europe, has a dark green, lobed gametophyte, generally rough and without midrib. Each cell of the thallus contains a single large chloroplast. Embedded in the thallus are the female reproductive organs – archegonia. Rod-like sporophytes that rise from the fertilized archegonia split into two releasing the yellow spores and exposing a central columella.

It is the function of that branch of sociolinguistics, which is sometimes called *general stylistics* (to distinguish it from a specialized aspect of stylistic studies, literary stylistics), to establish the linguistic characteristics of different varieties of language use.

One method in general stylistics is statistical and aims to state the relative probability of certain forms occurring in certain social situations or types of language use. It is important not to confuse the concept of the common core with that of high frequency of occurrence in use of the code. The common core derives from a study of language systems or codes. It is a form of comparative linguistic study and statistics play no part in it, whereas the comparison of varieties is a sociolinguistic study of language use and is susceptible to statistical methods of study. There is, therefore, no necessary connection between the notion of the common core and that of high frequency of occurrence. There is, however, a clear connection between what I have called 'neutral language' and high frequency of occurrence *in general*, that is if we pay no regard to the differing types of situation in which the language occurs. Thus, those features of the code which occur in all or most varieties of use are likely to turn out to have high relative frequence when making a statistical study of large quantities of language data.

It is for this reason that statistical studies of frequency of occurrence, particularly of lexical words, have played such a part in establishing the content of syllabuses. It is important at this point to stress that what is being calculated is the *relative* frequency of words, not their *absolute* frequency, i.e. occurrence measured against time. The great mass of the words in a language occur with quite surprisingly low absolute frequency. Taking the figure of half a million words in the *Oxford Dictionary* it has been calculated (Miller, 1951, p. 89) that it would take three days' continuous reading to pronounce all these words. Given the amount of talking the average person does, *if every word had an equal probability of occurring*, it would be about three weeks before a word came up for a second time in his speech. In fact, we usually repeat some word on average about every four to five seconds. So words are far from equal in their relative probability of occurrence. It turns out that for many types of written material the first thousand most common word types account for about 90 per cent of all word tokens used, the second thousand words for about 6 per cent, the third thousand, 2·5 per cent and the rest of the vocabulary the remaining 1·5 per cent. In one of the first and most famous of all studies of word frequency (Kaeding, 1898), in which eleven million words of continuous written text in German were taken from fourteen different source types, no less than 50 per cent of the total of 258,173 different word types found occurred only once in the whole corpus.

The method of estimating the relative frequency of any feature of language is to take a large sample of language data and count the occurrence of tokens of whatever categories have been set up, and then express this in numerical form as a proportion of the total of the tokens of all categories established; thus, the famous Thorndike and Lorge *Teachers Word Book* (1944) took a sample of four million running 'words' from forty-one printed sources and expressed the results as a rank-ordered list of the 20,000 most frequent items. Dewey (1923) published *The Relative Frequency of English Speech Sounds*, having analysed 100,000 running words from a variety of written sources. Frequency studies of the occurrence of different tense forms, for example, have been made for French by Kahn (1954). There have been many word counts, not only of English but of several other languages, e.g. Dutch, Spanish, German and French.

Now, although the method as stated above seems on the face of it both objective and simple, there are a number of snags in it which considerably reduce the value for practical purposes of the information gained. The first problem is that of *sampling*. Clearly there is no sense in which one can use *all* the utterances in a language as data, since as we have seen these are infinite. A selection out of all available utterances must be made. For practical purposes the tendency has been to select written material. This is the first bias introduced into the investigation. Our knowledge of the differences between written and spoken language and, more recently, of the different language functions which writing and speaking fulfil, means that any sample which consists only of written material must be unrepresentative of the range of uses of the language as a whole. But this same problem extends to the selection of the written data itself. For a sample to be representative even of all written language it must be drawn from all different varieties of written material *in proportion to the relative frequency with which that variety occurs in language use*. Thus, for example, if it could be shown that people spent four times as much time writing personal letters as business letters, then the sample should contain four times as much data drawn from personal correspondence as commercial correspondence. Put this way, it is quite clear that we simply do not have, and probably never can have, any idea of the relative frequency *for the population as a whole* of different sorts of written language activity. Furthermore, from a methodological point of view a more serious snag is that proper sampling requires that we have previously categorized *all* the different uses of language into well-defined and readily recognizable varieties and that we know the relative frequency of the occurrence of such varieties. Chapter 2 will have made it quite clear that we are not yet in any position to do this. Up to now, therefore, we must conclude that all frequency counts are essentially subjective, since the samples on which they are based are subjectively selected. This can be shown quite easily by comparing the results achieved for the same item in different published accounts. For example, Horn (1926) places the words *approve* and *contract* in the first 500 of most frequent words, whereas Thorndike places them in the fourth and fifth 500 words respectively, whilst Horn places *bread* in the fifth 500 and Thorndike in the first 500. As with all quantitative statistical studies the results are as valid as the sampling procedure is valid. Up till now all statistical studies of language which aim to make general statements about language use are invalid. It follows, therefore, that if relative frequency calculations are to be any use for language teaching they must be based upon data which represent the same *range* of language use as that aimed at by the learner.

There is, however, another snag. A particular item may receive a high count either because it is found with a general low frequency but distributed evenly throughout component texts of the sample, or because it occurs with very high frequency in one component text of the data but not at all in the other components. In the first case we say that such an item has a wide 'range'. It is not, therefore, a marker of any variety, whereas in the second case the item has a restricted range and is a marker of one or another variety. For example, given that components A, B and C are all part of the sample and we are counting the items x, y and z, we might have a result like that in Table 6.

Table 6

	Occurrence in component			Total in sample
	A	B	C	
item x	50	50	50	150
item y	100	50	—	150
item z	—	—	150	150

Taking the sample as a whole, items x, y and z would be judged as having the same relative frequency of use in the language. Now, assuming that the samples A, B and C were correct for frequency of occurrence (in spite of what has just been said) the usefulness of these results would still be doubtful for drawing up a syllabus, since, as we have seen, the needs of the language learner are not equivalent to those of the native speaker. Let us suppose that text A was drawn from the Bible, text B from commercial texts, and text C from personal correspondence. Clearly item z would have greater utility to most learners than item x, and item x than item y, on the grounds that personal correspondence and commercial varieties of language are related to situations of language use which are more likely to be relevant to the learner than reading the Bible in a foreign language.

This does not, however, exhaust the methodological problems of statistical studies of language use. We have already seen that their validity depends upon setting up variety types upon some valid sociolinguistic theory of language use, and determining the relative frequency of tokens of these varieties. Similarly, the validity of statistical studies depends upon the validity of the linguistic categories, the tokens of which are to be counted. Here we must go back to the discussion of linguistic categories in chapter 5. For the purposes of counting them, what are 'words', 'sounds' and 'structures'? Different linguistic theories will yield different categories. Is there, for example, any use in determining the relative frequency of the articles, demonstratives, pronouns and other purely grammatical 'words'? The selection of these is determined by syntactic rules. Are we to count singular and plural forms of the same lexical word as separate categories? What about grammatical derivatives: *trust, trustful, trusty, mistrust, entrust, trustee, trustworthy, trusting*? To treat these as separate categories would be to treat the relationship between *cow* and *cows* as of the same *kind* as the relationship between *cow* and *horse*. What about prepositions whose selection is both grammatical and semantic? The selection of *in* and *on* in:

He persisted in doing so
He insisted on doing so

is wholly determined by the selection of *persist* and *insist*, whereas in the case of *He put it on/in the box* the choice is independent of the verb.

Even when we can agree upon a criterion for 'lexicality', how many different meanings are we going to assign to such items as *give*, *take*, *go*, *come*, *make* and *get*? What it boils down to is that when we make word counts we are covertly attempting to make 'meaning' counts. The practical value of word counts will be as good as our theories of semantics.

If the problems in the case of 'words' are so complex, how much more so are those in the case of grammatical categories. Even if we could establish some satisfactory criterion of similarity for sentence, phrase or word structures, we would still be faced, as we have seen in chapter 8, with the problem of multiple meaning. One and the same surface structure may have a number of interpretations, just as quite different surface structures may have similar interpretations. If it appears illogical to treat such items as *give* and *take* as belonging in only one category for the purposes of counting, it must surely be equally illogical to count ambiguous structures as belonging to only one category.

Relative frequency and functional load

When we turn to the relative frequency of phonological items, the problem is not very different. The setting up of categories for counting presents the same problem. We can, of course, choose a phonemic description of the language and count phonemes. This is in essence what Dewey (1923) did. But phonemes differ widely in their probability of occurrence in different positions in syllable and word structure. For example, the phoneme /h/ in English never occurs in syllable final position and the phoneme /ŋ/ in syllable initial. One might attempt, therefore, to classify syllables into various types and calculate their frequency of occurrence. This Dewey also did. But from another point of view the statistical study of phonological items is different in kind from that of grammatical and lexical items. This is so because of what we called the 'double articulation' of language. Phonological units are not meaningful in the sense that grammatical and lexical items are. As we saw, when we count lexical and grammatical units we are in a sense counting 'meanings'. This is not so in the case of phonological features, except intonational features perhaps. Phonological units are part of the system of realization of grammatical and lexical items. From a practical point of view it is of no direct consequence that the phoneme /h/ is relatively less frequent than the phoneme /d/ for example. In order to use English for any purpose whatsoever the whole of the phonological system of sounds must be learned. We cannot avoid or postpone the teaching of such a relatively infrequent phoneme as /ʒ/ for example, so long as we include in our syllabus any grammatical or lexical item in whose realization it plays a part, e.g. *occasion, measure, garage*.

There is, however, a much more compelling reason for disregarding the accounts of the relative frequency of phonemes in a language, and that is that they are abstractions required for linguistic description, not concrete entities. What we learn when we learn pronunciation is not abstractions but how to make the appropriate movements of the vocal organs – if you like, speech sounds – and phonemes are realized in a wide variety of ways, depending upon their phonetic environment. Perhaps, then, what we need is a frequency calculation of actual phones, as they occur in the speech of native speakers. To suggest such an idea is to reject it out of hand. Even if we could set up any meaningful system of classification of the almost infinite variety of phonetic realizations of phonemes in language use, the variation amongst individual native speakers is far too great, even amongst those who are said to speak 'with the same accent', for us to be able to come to any useful picture of the relative frequency of speech sounds.

From a language learning point of view it is not the relative frequency of sounds which is important, but the contrasts in meaning which differences in sounds signal. For example, *pin* and *bin* mean different things and differ phonologically in respect of their initial sounds. There are many words in English, mostly monosyllables, which are distinguished only by the 'opposition' of /p/ and /b/. Similarly *wreath* and *wreathe* differ in meaning because of the difference in their final consonants, /θ/ and /ð/. But there are very few words in English which are kept apart in meaning solely by this contrast. It is clearly important that the learner in English should be able to make a consistent distinction between /p/ and /b/ and not nearly so important that he should do so for /θ/ and /ð/. This is why, in chapter 10, I said that there was a sense in which what we learn when we learn a language is differences between things, i.e. relations. We say that the contrast between /p/ and /b/ has a high *functional load* in English, whereas the distinction between /ə/ and /ð/ has a low functional load. However, as with frequency calculations there are certain difficulties in calculating the functional loads of various contrasts in a language. First of all, it is evident that the functional load of a certain contrast will vary according to the different phonological environments in which it occurs, such as in initial or final position in a syllable. For example, the highest functional load of any contrast in English consonants in monosyllabic words in final position is /d/ – /z/, i.e. the contrast which distinguishes *had* from *has* or *bead* from *bees*, whereas in initial position this contrast, e.g. *zoo–do*, has one of the lowest functional loads; this is so, obviously, because so few English words start with the initial sound /z/. (*The Concise Oxford Dictionary* lists only seventy-four beginning with the letter 'z'; most are borrowings from Greek and all of them have a very low relative frequency of occurrence.) Table 7 shows a comparison of the relative functional load of some contrasts of English consonants in initial and final position in monosyllabic words – without initial and final consonant clusters (the highest load is counted as the base for comparison).

Table 7 **Relative functional load of certain consonant contrasts in English**

	Initial	Final
k/h	100	—
p/b	98	14
m/n	59	42
k/g	50	29
d/z	7	100
ə/ð	1	6
n/ŋ	—	18

The calculation of the functional load of contrasts in phonology has to do with the language as a system and not with the frequency of occurrence of items in language use and yet from a teaching point of view it is the relative functional load that is important in communication. Therefore the frequency of items must be taken into account. It might be the case, for example, that the functional load of a particular contrast was very low, as in the case of /ə/ð/, because the number of word types in the language which began or ended with one of these sounds was very small; however, if the tokens of these words were of very high frequency of occurrence then it would be important for the learner to be able to make this contrast.

However, even here there are problems. While it is important for the learner to be able to distinguish *has* from *had* for the purposes of communication, since they may occur in the same environment (i.e. are distributionally equivalent – belong to the same grammatical class), it is clearly not so important that he should be able to distinguish between *zoo* and *do*, since there is no environment in which one could be substituted for the other and still make sense. Confusion is only possible between words which belong to the same grammatical class. If we build this restriction into our calculation of functional load the results we are likely to come up with will be very different. No one has yet attempted to make such a calculation.

Finally, we must also take into account the situations in which contrasting utterances might occur. The contrast in English between /l/ and /r/ in initial position has quite a high functional load (eighty-three on the scale used above). It is also one which presents difficulties for many learners of English, especially from the Far East, but it is probably very rare that this leads to misunderstanding, precisely because, even where the confused words belong to the same class and are also of similar relative frequency, e.g. *lock* and *rock*, they will almost certainly not occur in the same lexical or situational environment with the same degree of probability. Compare, for example:

John locked the door
John rocked the door

There are very few objects which we are as likely to *rock* as to *lock* in any situation you can imagine. But while we might agree that

Pick up that lock!
Pick up that rock!

were both equally probable in general, it would be difficult to imagine any situation in which a misunderstanding was likely to occur. The hoary old joke about *flied lice* does not reflect any genuine or regular failure in communication.

Whilst the notion of functional load has obvious importance for questions of language teaching, we must conclude that at the present time we do not possess all the relevant information to make use of it in syllabus design and possibly in principle can never obtain it, dependent as it is on relative frequency and the use of language in different situations. The notion does, however, have relevance to methods of teaching, that is to the degree of attention that must be paid in the classroom to certain problems in pronunciation learning. To use language adequately for any purpose the whole of the phonological system of oppositions must eventually be learned, even though the possibility of misunderstanding is much less than is generally believed if it is not.

The utility of vocabulary control

The selection of vocabulary on the basis of relative frequency is often called 'vocabulary control'. It is worth considering whether some notion similar to that of functional load could be applied to the selection of lexical material for a syllabus. Phonology is a closed system; we cannot invent or introduce new phonemes or syllables into the sound system of a language, nor can we operate the language effectively if we omit any elements in the system. The functional value of each phoneme is determined relative to all the other phonemes in the system. It is a network of contrasting relationships and, as has been suggested, learning the sound system of a language means learning the whole set of these contrasts. But this is similar to what we discovered in chapter 5 about the semantic structure of language. It, too, is a closed network of relations. The learning of a lexical word involves learning the set of relationships into which it enters with other words in the language – what we called its 'sense relationships', such as synonymy, autonymy, contrariety, converseness and so on. Looking at the vocabulary of a language in this way suggests that simple or 'simple-minded' calculations of relative frequency may be of little value. When one is 'learning vocabulary' one is learning a network of relations. One obviously does not 'know' a word when one has learned only its pronunciation and its grammatical function. One knows a word when one has learned how to use it acceptably semantically and that means knowing its 'sense', and when one can use it appropriately in a situational context. In a true sense we do not know the *full* meaning of any word until we know the meaning of all the words with which it enters into semantic relations. It follows, then, that the control of vocabulary in a syllabus does not just effect a limitation on the *number* of words to be learned but, more seriously, a limitation on the ways those items can be used by a learner. We may, of course, be able to teach by ostensive methods the referential meaning of that part of the vocabulary which has simple relations of that sort with objects and classes of objects in the world outside, but this is only a part of the 'meaning' of a word. Furthermore, there are good reasons for believing that the more words one 'knows' the easier it is to 'learn' new words, because one has more 'associative' links available.

The reason that such emphasis was placed, in the past, upon vocabulary control in the syllabus was largely that 'words' presented linguistic objects which appeared to be readily recognizable. Their occurrence in texts could be counted and their presentation in teaching material could be readily controlled. But because you can do something apparently with ease is, of course, no reason for doing it, unless it happens to be the appropriate thing to do. I have now suggested that establishing the relative frequency of words may after all not be so easy as was first thought and that when you have done it what it tells you may not be very easy to interpret.

There still remains the question of the extent to which the principle of relative frequency is the right criterion for the selection of the lexical material in the syllabus. We want learners to talk about and understand the topics which are interesting and useful to them. Relative frequency of a lexical item in the use of the language in all situations is too crude a criterion. There will be many words which are central to the needs and interests of a particular group of learners which have low relative frequency. We must first establish the topics and situations in which the learner must use the language and then, and only then, does the principle of frequency begin to have a relevance – the most useful (i.e. frequent) words in the most useful fields.

Chapter 10
Selection 2: Contrastive Linguistic Studies

Preliminaries

In the last chapter we approached the question of the contents of a language teaching syllabus as a problem of selection. We were concerned with selecting out of the total repertoire of the native speaker of the language just those elements of the language which any particular group of learners might need to know in order to achieve the communicative purposes for which they were learning the language. Essentially, we were approaching the problem from a functional point of view, regarding language as communicative behaviour and defining the syllabus in terms of the communicative needs of the learner. In this chapter we approach the problem of the content of the syllabus in terms of what the learner has to learn. At first sight, *what the learner needs to know* and *what the learner has to learn* might seem to be synonymous. But this is not necessarily the case. Put more simply, it may be the case that the learner already knows something of what he needs to know before he comes to the classroom. Obviously we need only teach him what he does not yet know of what he needs to know.

There are a number of senses in which we can resolve this apparent paradox. Language teaching normally starts after the learner has already achieved a command of the 'formation rules' or code of his mother tongue; he has in most cases learned to read and write in his mother tongue. In doing so he has acquired an 'implicit' knowledge of the nature of human language, and to some degree even an explicit knowledge. As Lyons has said (1965):

Although linguistics is not a recognized school subject, there is a very real sense in which one can say that everyone . . . has inevitably done a certain amount of linguistics already by virtue of his having received formal instruction in reading, writing and composition, and what is perhaps more important, by virtue of belonging to a community in which certain beliefs about language are passed on without question from one generation to the next. (p. 6)

Furthermore, he has already discovered and makes use of a major part of the total range of communicative functions of language – directive, personal, contact, etc., and can perform a vast range of speech acts in his mother tongue. Depending, of course, on the age and social background of the learner he will already have become aware of, and able to exploit, some part of the social, situational and stylistic variability of his own language. From a functional point of view, then, the learner does not approach the task of learning the second language from scratch. We can put it this way: he brings to the task a large number of tacit expectations about what he will be able to do with the language, and presuppositions about the nature of human language.

The language teacher, as I said in chapter 6, does not teach language; he teaches a particular realization or manifestation of human language. It is his task to teach a *new* code, and those ways in which a selected range of already *familiar* functions can be achieved through its use – what I have called the formation and speaking rules of the target language. I think we can rule out the possibility that any learner will wish to use the target language for purposes and in situations which are not also included in that range of functions and domains for which he also uses his mother tongue. On the contrary, the gist of the previous chapter was that the range of functions and situations of language use needed by a learner will only be a selection out of the range he has in his mother tongue. In this sense, then, the learner already 'knows' a great deal about language which is as true of the target language as of his mother tongue. He does not have to learn what he can eventually do with it, that is, the range of communicative functions for which he can use it.

What the learner knows

The learner has to acquire a new code but it is used to achieve *known* ends. The real question is how new is 'new'. Can the learner in any useful or meaningful sense be said to know already something of the new code? This is another way of asking whether different languages resemble each other to any extent, or whether they are all totally different. Put this way it is immediately obvious that languages do, in varying degrees, share features in common; they are, in a linguistic sense, related. In the discussion in chapter 3 we saw the difficulties of deciding how we were to establish what 'a language' was, and saw also that this problem was not a strictly linguistic one, inasmuch as what, from a purely formal linguistic point of view, could be regarded merely as variants of the same code were, from a sociopsychological point of view, to be treated as separate languages because their speakers regarded them as such. Our conclusion was that treating codes as distinct and well-defined formally was something the linguist did. It was not 'a fact' inherent in the data, but a way of approaching the data dictated by linguistic theory.

Different languages vary considerably, therefore, in the degree to which they differ from each other. It is not only, however, a matter of degree but one of kind. Indeed, while speaking of languages as differing from each other to varying degrees is a common-sensical way of talking, there is, at present, no way of *measuring* the degree of differences in a rigorous or valid fashion. The most obvious way in which differences between languages show themselves is in the mutual intelligibility of their speakers; but here we must remember what was said in chapter 3, that mutual intelligibility was not just a function of the linguistic relation between languages, but also had an important sociopsychological component. The other way in which the degree of differences between languages is apparent is in the degree of difficulty the speaker of one has in learning another. Here also we must admit that it is a matter of subjective judgement. The ease or difficulty of learning something is not simply related to the nature of the task but has components of motivation, intelligence, aptitude, quality of teaching and teaching materials; more importantly it depends upon the expectations the learner has of success. Certain languages may be considered difficult to learn by members of a certain community. By being thought difficult they may *become* difficult. Believing oneself 'no good' at something is the surest condition for failure. As in the case of mutual intelligibility, so in the case of difficulty of learning second languages too there is an important socio-psychological factor.

Determining the formal similarities and differences between languages is something that has been central to linguistic studies in the past, notably in nineteenth-century Europe, under the title of 'comparative philology'. The object of this study was to establish *historical* or *genetic* connections between languages on the basis of their manifest similarities, or more generally *correspondences*, particularly between the forms of words having similar meanings, or *cognate* word forms. From these studies developed the notions of language families, groupings of languages which were more or less distantly related on the grounds of having developed over time from common origins. These studies represent the approach to language referred to in chapter 1 as language as an organism, and were principally concerned to elucidate the nature of linguistic change.

The historical development of two languages from some single common source is no guarantee that their formal characteristics will, in all, or indeed most respects, be similar. It is possible that languages which are unrelated may resemble each other in respect of some features of their systematic structure, whilst genetically related languages may differ quite markedly in the same features. Thus we may set up rather general criteria of classification which will assign languages which are not genetically related to the same class or type, and conversely assign genetically related languages to quite different types. How we classify languages will depend upon the criteria we choose – phonological, syntactic, morphological and so on. Perhaps the best known typology of languages is based on the morphological structure of their words, isolating, agglutinative or fusional. This sort of typology of languages is of a gross sort, and thus, while we might say that Turkish and Japanese are typically agglutinative languages and therefore 'similar' in this respect, they differ so markedly in many other respects that one cannot speak of any general similarity across all levels. Another criterion of interest to language teaching which has been used for classifying languages is the preferred sequential ordering of the main functional elements of their sentences: subject, main verb and object (Greenberg, 1963). Thus English belongs in the class of S(ubject) V(erb) O(bject) languages, whilst Turkish and Japanese are SOV and Hebrew and Welsh VSO languages. Typological studies of human language have as their ultimate objectives the discovery of the 'boundaries' of the variability within which human language manifests itself formally. Comparative linguistics is therefore an important part of the study of human language.

In language teaching we have to do with at least two languages: the mother tongue and the target language. These may fall into the same broad type as far as their morphological characteristics are concerned, but be strikingly different in respect of their syllable structures. They may differ markedly in their lexical structure, for example, in the semantic field of kinship terms or colour terms (see chapter 4) but yet be similar in many syntactic respects. They may or may not be genetically related. The fact is that linguistic similarity and difference cannot be asserted for 'languages as wholes' but only level by level, system by system, category by category. As Halliday, Strevens and McIntosh (1964) say in their discussion of 'comparative descriptive linguistics':

There can be no question of, say, 'comparing English and Urdu'. Each language is a complex of a large number of patterns, at different levels and at different degrees of delicacy: a 'system of systems', in a well known formulation. There can be no single general statement accounting for all of these, and therefore no overall comparative statement accounting for the differences between two languages. One may be able to compare, for instance, the nominal group of English with the nominal group of Urdu, or English clause structure with Urdu clause structure; but one cannot generalize from these two comparisons. In no sense can it be said that English clause structure is to Urdu clause structure as the English nominal group is to the Urdu nominal group. Each pattern comparison must be made independently and in its own right. (p. 113)

Furthermore, whilst we may arbitrarily decide what the characteristics of the target language are, we must remember that the notion of 'a language' is, in a linguistic sense, an arbitrary one, and the learner may have in his receptive, or indeed productive repertoire, a knowledge of 'his own language' going well beyond the standard form described by the linguist. For example, in Spanish the system of demonstratives can be described as a 'three-term' system: *eso–esto–aquel* and *aqui–alla–aca* referring respectively to three degrees of 'distance' from the speaker, whereas in standard English, we find a 'two-term' system, a single opposition between *this* and *that*, or *here* and *there*. There are, however, dialects of English which have a three-term system like Spanish: *this, that* and *yon*. If we make a comparison between the mother tongue system and the target language solely on the basis of some described standard we may be overestimating the learner's learning task. Similarly, if the target language has a pronoun system which differentiates between two second person pronouns, e.g. *Du–Sie* and *tu–vous*, this does not necessarily present a grammatical learning task to the English learner just because he does not make productive use of the *thou–you* contrast in his mother tongue. It certainly forms part of his 'recognition grammar'. I am, of course, ignoring deliberately the *functional* problem of the different uses of *thou*, *Du* and *tu*. Similar examples can be drawn from the field of pronunciation; the sound [χ] as in the Scottish word *loch* is certainly 'available' to many speakers of English, not only in the sense that they can discriminate between *lock* and *loch*, but because many actually produce this sound in their speech when what they think of as a 'k' sound occurs between vowels as an initial consonant in an unstressed syllable, e.g. as the 'k' sound in *worker*.

How then do we account for the observed fact that some particular language is easier for the speaker of another language to learn than some other second language? The answer must be that on balance it shares more features in common at various levels with the mother tongue than the other second langue. It is the object of applied comparative linguistic studies to find out what these features are. It follows that inasmuch as the two relevant languages share certain features, there is a sense in which the learner already 'knows' some part of the target language. This is why in chapter 6 I said that, perhaps, it was a useful way of looking at language learning to regard it as the task of discovering the differences between the mother tongue and the target language, i.e. what the learner doesn't know. The linguistic syllabus, then, is simply this set of differences. This is essentially the position adopted by Lado (1957) in one of the earliest serious works on applied comparative linguistics. He says:

We assume that the student who comes in contact with a foreign language will find some features of it quite easy and others extremely difficult. Those elements that are similar to his native language will be simple for him, and those elements that are different will be difficult. (p. 2)

Difference and difficulty

In Lado's words, however, there is the implication that difference and difficulty are synonymous. This is by no means self-evident. Indeed, many teachers will have been glad to find that what was identified as a difference and predicted as a difficulty turned out not to be so.

Because a particular feature of the target language is different from the mother tongue it does not necessarily follow that it is difficult to learn (Nickel, 1971). We must nevertheless assume that taken overall the time needed to learn a second language reflects the degree of differences there is between it and the mother tongue. I repeat the qualification 'taken over all', since it seems to be the case that we cannot assert that any particular feature of the target language which differs from the mother tongue is necessarily inherently difficult to learn. Indeed, there is evidence that something totally 'new' or different may prove easier to master than something which is only slightly different; for example, where a very similar sound exists in the two languages but in different phonetic environments, there may be a greater learning problem than in the case of a totally new sound. It would be wise, at this point, simply to note that difficulty is clearly a psycholinguistic matter, whereas difference is linguistic, and until we can relate the two 'measures' in some principled fashion we can only note the overall relation between difficulty and difference, but not measure the psycholinguistic learning difficulty of particular linguistic differences; e.g. is a 'new sound' more 'different' than a 'new environment' for an 'old sound'?

It is worth raising here the distinction between productive (encoding) and receptive (decoding) linguistic performance. The native speaker of English, I have suggested, may have an ability to discriminate between *loch* and *lock* when he hears the two words, but himself rarely produce the sound [χ] when he speaks. We have therefore to consider splitting up 'learning' difficulties into the difficulty of learning to use a language receptively and learning to use it productively. Whether these are different *types* of learning or merely different *degrees* of learning need not detain us now, but it does seem reasonable to suggest that what may be difficult to learn to use productively may present few difficulties to learn to use receptively. This is, of course, the distinction referred to in chapter 6 as 'passive' and 'active' knowledge. I shall return to this point in chapter 13.

Let me also hasten to point out that the learner himself, when he begins to learn, does not know what parts of the target language he already 'knows'. Nor can it be assumed that he will immediately discover correspondences by simple exposure to the data. He may all too readily assume similarities where they do not exist, because of a 'misreading' of the significance of what he hears or sees, e.g. where cognates occurring in genetically related languages are not translation equivalents: such as *actually/actualmente/actuellement* – the so-called 'faux-amis'. A linguistically sophisticated learner may do the opposite: he may assume (or fear) differences where they do not exist. The learner has to learn the differences between the two languages, but he must, equally, discover the similarities – this is also a learning task.

Similarity

Similarities between languages may be very general or abstract on the one hand, or superficial and trivial on the other; they are generally only partial, rarely complete. For example, the English learner cannot by inspection immediately discover that the number system of German is similar to that of English; namely, a two-term system in which all noun phrases are either singular or marked as plural. The reason is that the system of marking plurality in German is very different from English. Whereas English marks plural nouns with *–s* or *–es* with only few exceptions, German has a rich morphological system of plural marking, *–en*, *–er*, *–e*, *no mark*, and all of these with or without internal vowel change. But the marking of plurality in English and German is also connected with differences in the determiners (i.e. articles, demonstratives, possessives, etc.) which modify the noun. In English there is a series of determiners which unequivocally signal a singular noun phrase – *a*, *one*, *this*, *that*, *each*, *another*, and whilst some are ambiguous – *the*, *some*, *my*, *your*, *other*, *any*, only *these* and *those* are markers of plurality. The English determiners do not have a one-to-one relation with the German determiners, because of the 'interference' of the case and gender systems of German; thus *der*, *die*, *den* all co-occur with both singular and plural nouns. This is sometimes called 'morphological syncretism'. At a more general level German shares with English, and other European languages, the distinction between 'countable' and 'mass' nouns. The mark of the distinction in both languages is the restriction of their occurrences with certain determiners, thus in both English and German:

a child   but *a money
ein Kind   but **ein Geld*
each child but *each money
jedes Kind but **jedes Geld*

But what may make this correspondence difficult to discern is that particular lexical words which are translation equivalents in the two languages do not always belong in the same class of noun, thus:

ein Möbel   but *a furniture
eine Landschaft but *a scenery

This is only one example of a very general state of affairs that words which are semantically similar in two languages do not necessarily function syntactically in the same way.

If we now compare the number systems of French with English we find a greater degree of morphological similarity; written French marks its plural nouns with *–s*, or *–x*, in a way very similar to English, but in respect of the number system as a whole French differs more from English than German by having no vestige left of dual number, as does English in such phrases as *both men, either boy, neither girl*. Table 8 shows a comparison of these three systems:

Table 8 **Comparison of number systems in English, French and German**

			English	*German*	*French*
mass			some money	*etwas Geld*	*de l'argent*
			some furniture	—	—
count- able	plural		some tables	*einige Tische*	*des tables*
			some children	*einige Kinder*	*des enfants*
	non- plural	dual	both boys	*beide Jungen*	—
			either boy	—	—
		sing.	a table	*ein Tisch*	*une table*
			a child	*ein Kind*	*un enfant*

If we examine the operation of the system of dual number a bit further we shall see that German has greater similarity with French than English in that it resorts to 'periphrasis' in the same way as compared with English:

| both tables | *beide Tische* | *l'une et l'autre table* |
| either table (exclusive) | *entweder der eine oder der andere Tisch* | *l'une ou l'autre table* |

at either side of the street (inclusive)	*auf der einer und der andere Seite der Strasse*	*à l'un et l'autre côté de la rue*
neither table	*weder der eine noch der andere Tisch*	*ni l'une ni l'autre table*
at each side of the street	*auf beiden Seiten der Strasse*	*à chaque côté de la rue*
on each wall of the room	*auf jeder Wand*	*sur chaque mur*

In other words, the English dual system is 'richer', in that it incorporates in the word *either* both the inclusive and exclusive alternatives, whereas these do not form part of the French or German systems.

This small and relatively simple comparison of a small part of the grammar of these familiar and genetically related languages illustrates clearly two general points about comparison of languages: firstly, that within what is a broadly equivalent system in two or more languages the correspondences are very patchy and irregular, and consequently, it is only at a more general and abstract level that we can expect to find equivalence or identity between languages; secondly, that the absence of a systematically equivalent term in a target language does not in any way imply that the notions that are expressed by it in one language cannot be expressed at all in the other.

A basis for syntactic comparison

In the fragment of comparison I have just made between the number systems of German, English and French there were certain hidden assumptions which must be brought out to the light of day and examined critically. I assumed that there existed in each of the three languages a system that was comparable. But what basis did I have for making such an assumption? There are three possible answers:

1. That the noun phrases exemplifying the systems were translation equivalents, that is, there was an equivalence of *meaning* between the languages.

2. That the systems of contrast in each language were similar. We can call this *formal* equivalence between the languages.

3. That the terminology used for describing each language was the same, i.e. the 'number' system, singular, plural, count, mass, noun phrase, etc. This is equivalence of *nomenclature*.

Contrastive Linguistic Studies 233

Now it is, of course, obvious that in order to compare anything the dimensions or categories used must be applicable to both objects. We cannot meaningfully say that a person is 'angrier than he is tall', since 'anger' and 'height' are different dimensions or categories. We have available then three dimensions or categories for making comparisons between languages: nomenclature, form and meaning.

Let us take each in turn. We speak in English about high notes and high buildings, but we do not compare the height of a note with the height of a building. *Middle C is higher than the house opposite. Similarly we do not compare pleasure and light just because they can both be intense. Even more absurd would be to compare two people because they were both called Jones. What a thing is called is not a dimension or attribute of that thing. There is nothing 'Jonesy' about someone called Jones. For this reason one must be cautious about comparing categories in different languages because they are called by the same name. French is said to have a three-term tense system: past, present and future, while English has a two-term system: past and present. In what sense can we compare these systems? Just because they are called tense systems, and because some of their terms are called by the same name, past and present?

We have to ask how they came by these names in the first place. When we do this we discover, of course, that they are both called tense systems because they have to do with the expression of notions of time, that is because they both perform the function of expressing a similar set of meanings. We can compare apples and pears because, although they have different names, they are both fruit. Inasmuch as the two systems are both 'time-expressing' they are comparable. Identity of name does not, however, imply identity of function. Thus the 'past tense' in English does not express the same set of time notions as the 'past tense' in French. The name, past or present tense, may be misleading. This is one reason why many grammarians prefer to use names for grammatical categories which have no obvious semantic implications, e.g. preterite and non-preterite instead of past and present. To some extent the similarity of the names used in describing the grammars of different European languages is a legacy of the supremacy of Latin. Much of the criticism of earlier traditional descriptions of English and other languages was that they were made in terms of the categories set up for describing Latin and which, therefore, were not necessarily appropriately applied to other languages. The Latin categories of gender and case, for example, do not, at first blush, seem to be readily applicable to English. This criticism has some force, but not as much as used to be thought. A more careful examination of how these terms were used to describe other languages will often show that they were, in fact, used *in a different sense*. They were redefined for each language. The critics have frequently made the mistake of assuming that because the nomenclature was the same, the categories referred to must have been the same. We must therefore beware of committing the same fallacy in the comparison of languages.

This leads us to the second dimension of comparison, what I have called formal equivalence or similarity. Assuming for a moment that no question of similarity of meaning was involved, what might have been the basis for positing sufficient similarity between what we called the number systems of German and French and English to undertake a comparison? It must have been that there was a grammatical category which we chose to call Noun Phrases which was common to all three languages. How do we arrive at the categories we need in order to describe the syntactic structure of a language? Reference to chapter 8 will remind us that this is done on the basis of function. Those units which function syntactically in the same way are assigned to the same class. We are justified, therefore, in saying that in English *the boy* and *the boys* are of the same class because they occur in similar environments:

$$
\left.\begin{array}{l}\text{The boys}\\ \text{The boy}\end{array}\right\} \text{died}
$$

$$
\text{Do you know} \left\{\begin{array}{l}\text{the boys?}\\ \text{the boy?}\end{array}\right.
$$

The boy/the boys regularly alternate, i.e. are mutually exclusive in the same environments, and therefore are systematically related. We call this contrast a contrast of 'number' in English. We can perform the same operation for French and German.

$$
\left.\begin{array}{l}\textit{die Jungen sind}\\ \textit{der Junge ist}\end{array}\right\} \textit{gestorben}
$$

$$
\textit{kennen Sie} \left\{\begin{array}{l}\textit{die Jungen ?}\\ \textit{den Jungen?}\end{array}\right.
$$

$$
\left.\begin{array}{l}\textit{le garçon est}\\ \textit{les garçons sont}\end{array}\right\} \textit{mort(s)}
$$

$$
\textit{est-ce-que vous connaissez} \left\{\begin{array}{l}\textit{le garçon ?}\\ \textit{les garçons ?}\end{array}\right.
$$

So far we can say only that we have discovered pairs of items which are in contrast in similar (but not identical) environments in each separate language. What we cannot say is that the environments are formally identical in all these languages. They manifestly are not. They are different phonologically, lexically and syntactically. Thus, there is no phonological similarity between *died, ist gestorben* and *est mort*, and syntactically there appears to be a considerable difference between *do you know, kennen Sie* and *est-ce-que vous connaissez*. In what sense, then, can it be said that we have selected items belonging to one and the same category ('noun phrase') in all three languages in order to compare their mode of functioning in identical environments? If the environments in which they operate are syntactically different then the categories cannot be the same. It is clear that *unless we can impose a common, descriptively adequate, syntactic framework on any pair of languages*, the categories and relations used in the description of each language remain specific to each language and hence are not comparable.

So now let us consider whether there is a candidate for such a common syntactic framework for the description of pairs of languages. When I said that we were dealing with different and consequently not comparable syntactic environments in French, German and English for the items *the boy, der Junge* and *le garçon*, this was based upon an attempt to compare linear sequences of elements in the sentences of each language. The model of grammar I was using was what we called a linear model in chapter 8. In such grammars, you will remember, the classes of words or sentence elements are established according to their potentiality of occurrence in different sequential positions in a linearly ordered sequence of sentence elements. Items filling the same 'slot' belong to the same class, and consequently the word classes set up were for this reason specific to the language being described. Any attempt to relate the word classes of one language to another would therefore necessarily have to be made upon some non-syntactic criterion such as 'meaning', unless the grammatical sequences of one language could always be put into a one-to-one relation with those of another. Since this is manifestly not possible in the case of the great majority of sentences, we are forced to look for an alternative grammatical model.

There are good theoretical reasons for thinking that a transformational-generative grammar might offer a framework which would ensure that we had a common set of categories and relations for the comparison of two languages. A transformational model specifies that the grammar has two components, an inner syntactic component, and a transformational component which generates the outer or surface structure of sentences. Clearly the outer structure of our examples was syntactically different; but might it not be that they had the same underlying structure?

Chomsky proposes that (1965):

The function of (the base component) is, in essence, to define a certain system of grammatical relations that determine semantic interpretation, and to specify an abstract underlying order of elements that makes possible the functioning of the transformation rules. *To a large extent, the rules of the base may be universal and thus not, strictly speaking, part of particular grammars.* (my italics) (p. 141)

Perhaps we have here in a universal base component the identity conditions for comparison, namely that the rules which generate the

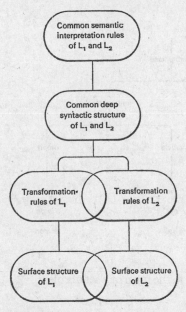

Figure 32

deep structure of sentences in all languages are the same, and that they differ outwardly or superficially, only because the same underlying structure has undergone a different transformational derivation. We can express this diagrammatically as in Figure 32.

This diagram is in essence the same as that in Figure 28 on page 193, which was proposed to account for such pairs of sentences within one language, sentences which had the same interpretations, such as actives and passives. In this case we are concerned with different languages, but the principle is the same. Thus, languages differ only in respect of having different sets of *non-comparable* transformation rules. The overlap in the diagram allows for the possibility that some of these rules may be the same in two languages. We can illustrate this by a simplified derivation of those sentences we have been using as examples. This derivation leaves out a number of steps or rules which do not affect the argument at this stage, e.g. matters of case, number, gender and concord. We can see that the rules of the base component will generate identical deep structures for the sentences in all three languages. This is shown in tree diagram form in Figure 33.

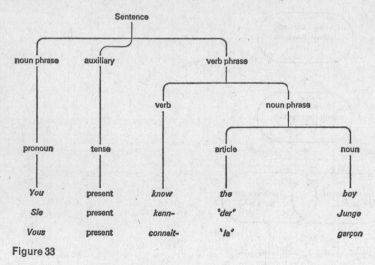

Figure 33

We can express the same information in the form of a set of rules:

1. $\Sigma \rightarrow$ NP+Auxiliary+VP.
2. VP $\rightarrow$ V+NP.

238 Introducing Applied Linguistics

3. Auxiliary → Tense.

4. NP → $\left\{ \begin{array}{l} \text{Pronoun} \\ \text{Article+noun} \end{array} \right\}$

5. Pronoun → {you, Sie, vous}

6. Tense → $\left\{ \begin{array}{l} \text{present} \\ \text{past} \end{array} \right\}$

7. V → {know, kenn–, connait–}

8. Article → {the, 'der', 'le'}

9. N → {boy, Junge, garçon}

It is when we come to the transformational rules which generate the obviously different outer surface structures in the three languages that comparison becomes 'relevant'. The rules which produce the English interrogative surface structure would require the following changes: permutation of *present* and *you* and the substitution of *present* by *do*.

Yes/no question transformations (English)
1. You+present+know ⇒ present+you+know—
2. Present+you+know ⇒ Do+you+know—

In German, on the other hand, the transformation would be a transposition of *Sie* and a combination of *present+kenn*:

Yes/no question transformations (German)
1. Sie+present+kenn– ⇒ present+kenn+Sie—
2. Present+kenn–+Sie ⇒ kennen+Sie—

Finally, the French transformation would require the addition of the interrogative marker *Est-ce-que* and the combination of *present+connait*– thus:

Yes/no question transformations (French)
1. Vous+present+connait– ⇒ Est-ce-que+vous+present+connait–
2. Est-ce-que+vous+present+connait– ⇒ Est-ce-que+vous+connaissez—?

On the face of it it looks as if we might have found an answer to our problem in a common set of categories and relations in the deep (base) syntactic component of a transformational grammar, since in our highly simplified derivation of these sentences in English, French and German we were able to show how different surface structures could be derived from an identical deep structure. But we should be unwise on the basis of the analysis of just one set of sentences to think we had found the answer. Let us remember that Chomsky said that: '*To a large extent* the rules of the base *may* be universal and thus not part of particular grammars.' Notice that this is not a claim that the base components of all languages are identical, only that they may have a large proportion of rules in common. In other words, he proposes only a *similarity* not an *identity* of the base component. It is, in fact, not too difficult to show that, as these have been formulated to date, they are not universal; furthermore, they are not even common to two such genetically related languages as English and German.

It is a fundamental requirement of a 'classical' transformational-generative grammar that all semantic interpretation is based upon the 'information' represented by the categories and relations in the base component. In other words, transformations do not affect meaning. Furthermore, there is no 'redundant' information in the base component, i.e. no categories or relations which do not contribute to the semantic interpretation of a sentence (Katz and Postal, 1964). If, then, we can show that two sentences in different languages have the same syntactic derivation but do not mean the same thing, or, alternatively, that two sentences which *do* mean the same thing have different deep syntactic structures, then we must conclude that the base components which generate the two sentences are not identical. Let us now look at two pairs of sentences:

1. *Ich arbeite hier jetzt drei Jahren*
   I have worked here now three years

2. *Ich habe hier voriges Jahr gearbeitet*
   I worked here last year

The sentences in each pair are assumed to be translation equivalents,[1] but clearly they do not have even a similar surface structure. The following pairs of sentences do, however, have very similar surface structures but are *not* translation equivalents. Indeed the English one of each pair is ungrammatical though perfectly easy to understand:

  1. I don't wish to go here into the problem of translation equivalence and identity of interpretation. Let us simply say that these two sentences 'have the same meaning'.

1. *Ich habe hier voriges Jahr gearbeitet*
   *I have worked here last year
2. *Ich arbeite hier jetzt drei Jahren*
   *I work here now three years

Now we can show the deep syntactic derivation of the verbal element in the two sentences (*I have worked* . . . and *Ich habe gearbeitet* . . .) are identical since they derive by identical rules in both English and German, i.e. with a slight addition to the rules given on pages 238–9:

1. $\Sigma \rightarrow$ NP + Auxiliary + VP + adverbial of time
3. Auxiliary $\rightarrow$ tense + (perfective)
6. Tense $\rightarrow \left\{ \begin{array}{l} \text{past} \\ \text{present} \end{array} \right\}$
6a. Perfective $\rightarrow$ have/hab– + participle formative

These are shown as a tree diagram in Figure 34. This, after obligatory transformation, having the effect of transposing participle formative to the appropriate position in relation to the verb and fusing them into one word, yields:

I have worked
Ich habe gearbeitet

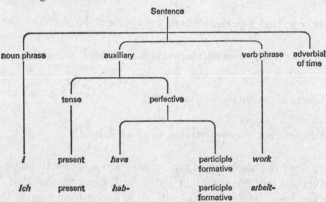

Figure 34

This same set of rules will generate *I work; I worked; Ich arbeite;* and *Ich arbeitete* as shown in Figure 35. It is not the rules for generating the verbal element in the two languages which are different, but the fact

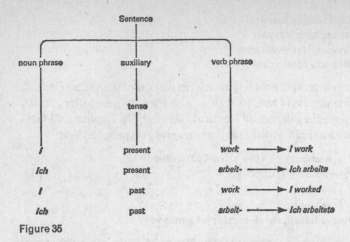

Figure 35

that the perfective form in German co-occurs only with an adverbial referring to past time, whereas the perfective form in English only co-occurs with an adverbial referring to *present* time. There exists, therefore, in the deep grammar of the two languages different co-occurrence restrictions, or what are called selection rules. These can be expressed in this form:

English: Aux → present + perfective/in the environment: adverbial *present* time

German: Aux → present + perfective/in the environment: adverbial *past* time

English ⎫
German ⎭ Adverbial present time → (now, jetzt)

English ⎫
German ⎭ Adverbial past time → (last year, voriges Jahr)

What determines the selection of the verbal form appears to be the class of adverbial and not the other way round, since we saw that *I work here last year*, whilst ungrammatical, is understood clearly to refer to past time, and *I work here tomorrow* to future time. Now the adverbials in English and German can readily be shown to be syntactically equivalent: *voriges Jahr/last year* and *now/jetzt*. They are also *semantically* equivalent, referring to past and present time respectively. Thus we must infer that the *formal* equivalence of the verbal element in

German and English hides a *semantic* difference. But this is contrary to the theoretical assumptions of the classical transformational-generative grammar, which asserts that if two deep structure derivations are identical then the semantic interpretation associated with them must be identical (cf. chapter 8, page 193). Therefore, assuming, as we have done, that the two sentences

Ich arbeite hier jetzt drei Jahren
I have worked here now three years

'have the same meaning', they ought, theoretically, to have the same deep structures. But I have shown that this is not the case. We are forced to conclude that according to a standard transformational grammar of the sort specified by Chomsky (1965), and Katz and Postal (1964), the deep grammars of English and German are not identical, only similar 'to a large extent'. They cannot adequately serve, therefore, as a basis for applied linguistic comparisons. If identity of structure exists between two languages then it appears it does so only at the more abstract level of semantic structure. This implies that it is only in terms of the meanings which can be expressed that two languages are identical. I do not wish here to go into this difficult problem except to say that unless we believed that by-and-large what can be expressed in one language can also be expressed in another, we should scarcely be interested in second-language teaching.

We shall therefore have to modify the diagram in Figure 32 in the way shown in Figure 36 to allow for the base syntactic components of different languages being different in some degree. But this model resembles very strongly the model illustrated in Figure 30 (p. 196) and discussed in chapter 8, page 193, where I talked about semantic-based grammars. I said there, in effect, that learners of a second language do not have to learn how to formulate possible messages, they only have to learn how to express them. What is universal, then, is the *semantic* structure of languages; that is, how possible messages are 'put together'. We may feel that the categories and relations involved in the deep syntactic components I have been talking about are pretty abstract. Unfortunately, they do not appear to be abstract enough to serve as a common base for the comparison of languages. We have to look for something even more abstract – the components of the messages themselves. What we need is what in chapter 8 I called 'semantic

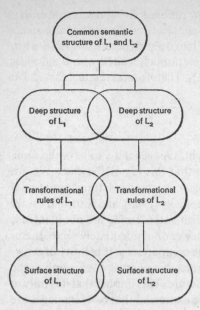

Figure 36

based' grammars. I also said that whilst linguists are actively engaged in research into such grammars, we do not yet have any which meet even the weakest demands on adequacy. It looks, therefore, as if we shall have to manage as best we can in applied linguistics with a notional comparison of languages, and with *ad hoc* descriptions of those parts of the languages which look as if they could yield to the inadequate knowledge we have.

The comparison of sound systems

So far our discussion of the comparison of two languages has centred on their syntactic structure. We must remember, however, that languages have what we called in chapter 5 'double articulation'; the secondary articulation being the organization of the sound resources of the language to make manifest or 'realize' the semantic and syntactic structure of sentences. Learning a language must therefore also involve learning the rules governing the organization of sounds in the target language. We may expect that languages differ quite markedly in how they utilize their resources of sound to realize their syntactic and semantic structures. As in the case of learning syntax, the difficulty of learning the pronunciation of the target language may also reflect the degree of difference in the ways the mother tongue and the target language organize their sound systems. Here, too, we are faced with the problem of finding equivalent categories in order to carry out our comparison.

We could make a start with the undoubted biological fact that the vocal apparatus of all human beings is anatomically similar, and that therefore the virtually infinite range of possible sounds, expressed in terms of variations of pitch, intensity, duration and quality which this vocal apparatus can produce, would be, in principle, equally available to all human beings. It is, however, a fact that the speaker of any particular language uses only a part of this total range of variation when he speaks. But we must also realize that no two speakers of any one particular language will in fact use exactly the same range of sounds. Indeed, strictly speaking, we should not speak of the 'speech sounds' of 'a language' at all, since pitch, intensity, duration and quality are *continua*, not scales with discrete steps. It is the act of physical measure-

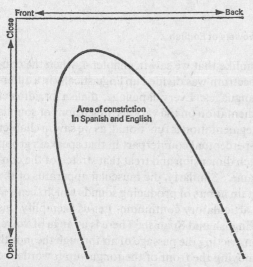

Figure 37 Front close vowels in English and Spanish

ment which imposes a scale on these attributes, e.g. decibels, cycles per second, duration in micro-seconds and so on. When we speak about the 'speech sounds of a language' we have already imposed a functional descriptive framework on a set of continuous dimensions, both acoustic and articulatory.

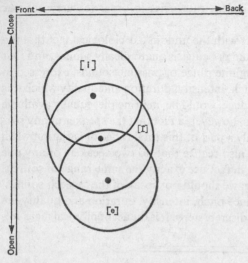

Figure 38 The front close vowels of English

The situation is not unlike that we saw in chapter 4, when the continuum of the colour spectrum was divided up linguistically in a different way in different languages. Every language, dialect or idiolect imposes a different segmentation on the various dimensions of sounds and articulation. This segmentation is functional, as we saw in chapter 8. But it has its motor-perceptual counterpart in that speakers group perceptually parts of each dimension and treat that stretch of the continuum as being the 'same'. Similarly, the muscular apparatus of the vocal tract acquires certain habits of producing sounds which 'centre' on certain parts of the articulatory continuum. Let us exemplify this from a comparison of English and Spanish. There is a range of vowel sounds produced by constricting the passage of air through the mouth in varying degrees by moving the front of the tongue up towards the palate. We can call them front close vowels. They may be modified

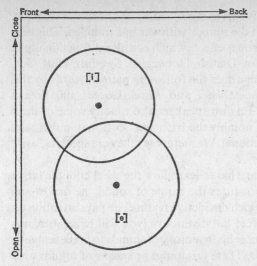

Figure 39 The front close vowels of Spanish

along other dimensions, e.g. they may be lengthened or shortened, or accompanied by rounding of the lips (labialized). Now, it is highly likely that the range of movement of the tongue in this space is much the same in the case of any group of English and Spanish speakers. This notion is shown schematically in Figure 37. The English speaker, however, groups the range of movement round three motor-perceptual 'centres', which we can label [i], [ɪ] and [e] (this is shown in Figure 38). Whilst the Spanish speaker groups them into two, which we can label [i] and [e], shown in Figure 39. Notice that the range of movements overlap. This means that the 'same' physical sound may be interpreted on one occasion as a 'sort of' [i] and on another as a 'sort of' [e], depending on context. Any one of this range of sounds may also be varied regularly on the dimension of duration, so that there may also be more or less regular association between the English [i] sound and an increased duration. This does not mean that there may not be contexts in which an English [ɪ] sound is longer than a short version of the [i] sound. Thus, for example, in many contexts the vowel in the English word *beat* actually lasts no longer than the vowel in the word *bid*.

Varying the duration of any of the sounds produced by the range of articulation is not the only sort of modification possible. For example, we can pronounce any of the sounds with our lips rounded. This produces an acoustically distinct effect, which is utilized functionally in such languages as German, Danish, Norwegian, Swedish. Thus, German systematically distinguishes the following pairs of words by this means: *liegen/lügen*; *lehne/Löhne*; and *Kissen/küssen*; and French *pie/pu*; *père/peur*. Many English speakers also modify some of these sounds in the same way, notably the Irish and Scots, but in this case, the distinction is not functional. We merely say they are speaking 'with an accent'.

The learner of a language has to learn how the speaker of the target language perceptually organizes the range of sounds he makes and hears into groups, and which distinctive features he pays attention to. What features were or were not distinctive, you will remember, was dependent upon how he uses his inventory of sounds to make semantic and syntactic distinctions. These groupings or classes of sounds were what we called phonemes. Put another way, each language has a range of sounds by which it 'realizes' its phonemes, and the 'same' sounds physically and articulatorily may 'realize' different phonemes in different languages. Thus, for example, the English speaker does not normally have to pay attention to whether his 'p' sound, in such words as *pit*, *spit*, *tip* or *tips*, is aspirated (i.e. followed by a puff of breath) or not. Aspiration in English, just as the velarization of the /l/, is entirely determined by the phonetic context and varies with the individual speaker. The distinction between aspirated and unaspirated sounds, however, is significant to a Hindi speaker, who uses it to signal differences in syntactic and semantic function in words. For him, [p] and [pʰ] are realizations of different phonemes.

We can see now that there are two ways in which we can compare the 'sounds' of two languages: (a) in physical, i.e. acoustic and articulatory terms; and (b) in functional terms. Clearly in the first case we have a set of criteria, acoustic and physiological, which is common to both languages. Thus, we can say that what the English regard as [i] sounds tend to be produced by a portion of the tongue which is higher and more forward than the Spanish [i] sounds, and that there is a tendency for them to be longer. Similarly we can say that what the Spanish regard as [e] sounds tend to centre on a position of the tongue which is higher than the English [e] sounds, though there is no systematic difference in length.

It is when we come to compare the way we *use* the sounds in two languages that problems of comparison arise of the sort we met when we considered the comparison of grammatical categories. We must here again warn against being misled by nomenclature. We have to label classes of sounds (phonemes) in order to talk about them and draw up rules for their use. These labels are usually chosen on the basis of articulatory categories. Thus, we have already spoken about the '/p/ phoneme' in English because it is typically realized by sounds whose articulatory features were *voiceless bilabial closure*. This phoneme contrasts functionally in many environments with the '/b/ phoneme' whose realization can be generally described in terms of the features of *voiced bilabial closure*. Now it happens that the Greeks have a single functional category which is realized by both voiced and unvoiced bilabial closures. Thus it is an arbitrary decision whether to give the Greek phoneme the label /p/ or /b/. What is called by the same name is not necessarily functionally identical. We saw the same problem in the case of such categorical labels as 'tense' in the grammatical comparison of French and English. The only common characteristic was that the category so named had something to do with the expression of notion of *time* in both languages, i.e. had *semantic* similarity. The situation is the same in the case of phonemes having the same label in two languages; they are generally realized by sounds which have some acoustic and articulatory characteristics in common, but this does not mean that they are otherwise comparable.

In chapter 8 an alternative approach to the description of the sound system was outlined, which approached the system in a rather different way. In that approach, instead of regarding the organization of the sounds in the language as an autonomous 'secondary articulation', the phonology of the language was described in such a way that it was dependent upon the syntactic description. It provided a means for accounting for the pronunciation of such acoustically different words as *decorate/decoration*, *wife/wives* so that their essential *lexical* identity was preserved in the description. This approach was called a generative phonology, since the sound system was described in terms of a series of transformational-type rules which mapped the inner ('abstract') sound structures onto the actual pronunciation in terms of sequences of phones in a regular way. It will be clear, however, that this approach similarly does not permit the sound structure of two languages to be strictly compared, since the sets of abstract sound elements, 'systematic phonemes', in the two languages cannot be classified in terms of a common set of categories.

The conclusion we arrive at then is that whatever phonological theoretical approach we adopt, it does not yield equivalent sets of categories for comparison. It is only in terms of the actual physical output of sounds, i.e. the physiological–acoustic terms, that we can make rigorous comparisons. Unfortunately, as we saw, the degree of variability in these sounds between different individual dialect speakers, and even individual speakers of the same dialect, makes even this comparison difficult. This is where 'idealization' comes in again. We have to set up an 'inventory' of 'norms' which represent some abstraction from the actual data of speech and treat these as the 'sounds of the language'. This is normally the form in which teaching materials are cast. The inventory of speech sounds for 'English' are to be found in such standard descriptions as Daniel Jones (1917), and Gimson (1964).

We can now apply the notions of *difficulty* and *difference* discussed above to the learning of the sound system and pronunciation of the target language. A learner must acquire the ability to produce and recognize the whole range of speech sounds (phones) used by the speaker of the target language. The amount of learning will vary greatly as between any two languages, since, as we say, the degree of overlap between the inventories may vary greatly. The overlap, however, may be much greater than the 'standard' descriptions of the languages suggest. Thus, the English speaker may already be familiar perceptually with the [χ] sound in German *Loch* because of the regional Scottish pronunciation of the word *loch*. He may be familiar with the pronunciation of the labialized close front vowel sound found in German *Küssen*, *Löhne* etc. because he uses these himself as a Scot or Irishman. He may, in his own accent of English, be used to producing all his 'l' sounds without velarization as in German.

But even where he apparently has no counterpart of some foreign sound in his own mother tongue accent, it does not necessarily follow that this presents a difficulty of articulation. What masquerades frequently as an apparent difficulty in making a sound probably derives as often as not from an unawareness of the relevant features of the sound in certain contexts. Thus, the often noted failure of Spanish speakers to distinguish two such words in English as *sheep* and *ship* has little to do with difficulty in articulation. The 'i' sounds in both words are found in the inventory of all Spanish speakers. It is the functional use of the sound which is unfamiliar to them. The task is, therefore, not learning *how* to make the closer and longer sound but when to use it. So the second learning problem in pronunciation is discovering which features of sounds are significant or distinctive (in this case closeness and length). Spanish does not use these features of the [i] sound to make functional distinctions either semantically or syntactically as does English, any more than English, as we saw, makes use of *aspiration* for this purpose, as do Hindi speakers. This learning task, then, is one of discovering the groupings of sound features into sets, i.e. the learning of the phonemes or functional sound units of the target language.

The third learning task is that of discovering the permitted sequences of these functional units. Whether this grouping of features is the same or slightly different in the two languages may not reduce this task very much. For instance, the 'nasal' phonemes of German and English /m/ and /n/ have similar sets of phonetic realizations, but their distributional characteristics are different. Thus, English has no initial sequence #/ʃ/+nasal+—, whereas this is a common sequence in German: *Schnee*; *Schmutz*. But English speakers have no difficulty in articulating a final /ʃ/ followed by an initial nasal, e.g. *fish market*, *fish net*. On the other hand, English permits an initial cluster, #/s/+ nasal: *snow*, *small*, whilst German speakers have no such initial sequence, although they have no difficulty in articulating a sequence of final [s] followed by an initial nasal, e.g. *Ich weiss nicht das weiss man nicht*. If the English or German speaker makes mistakes in pronunciation then it is certainly not an articulatory problem. It is a 'psychological' problem. He has not learned the phonological 'rules' of German or English.

The reader will have realized that there are essentially two ways of approaching the phonological structure of a language. Firstly, one may start from an inventory of speech sounds, describe how these are grouped into functional classes and then state how the classes function in systems. This is essentially the way one would start to describe some unknown language; it is the inductive approach. The other way is the deductive approach. In this one posits an inventory of abstract 'phoneme' symbols and then states the rules for their realization in terms of combinations of articulatory features or speech sounds. If one approaches the comparison inductively then one can compare languages in a language-neutral vocabulary, drawn from physiology, anatomy and acoustics. If, on the other hand, one approaches comparison deductively there are no common categories available. The inductive approach is the one that has served for most of the comprehensive published comparisons, e.g. Moulton (1962) and Stockwell, Bowen and Martin (1965) and others in the same series edited by Charles A. Ferguson. Nevertheless, recent work in phonological theory has tended to show that this approach is descriptively inadequate in various ways. The alternative deductive approach holds out better hopes of descriptive adequacy. Furthermore, it accords with some of the recent theories of how languages are learned. Unfortunately, it does not, because of the problem of common categories, lend itself readily to comparative techniques.

So far I have spoken about the differences between the sound systems of languages only in terms of their segmental features, phones, phonemes or phonological words. But languages also use duration, pitch and intensity in even more strikingly different ways. We saw in chapter 8 that the stretches of a language having very similar segmental structure could be systematically contrasted in respect of their rhythmical and intonational characteristics, e.g. *contract*, *contract*, or *Rebecca's here?* *Rebecca's here*. In English and other European languages patterns of pitch change are associated with longer stretches of language, phrases or sentences. But in some languages the movement of pitch is also associated with 'words'. These are the so-called *tone languages*, such as Chinese, Yoruba, Burmese. In these languages the same sequence of sounds in a 'word' may be spoken with a small range of contrasting pitch-patterns or tunes, e.g. high, low, rising, falling pitch, each one yielding a different meaning for the word. For example, in Adangwe, a West African language, *ma* spoken with one pattern means 'dough', with another, 'herring' and with a third 'nation'. Pitch patterns in tone languages serve two functions, that of distinguishing lexical items as well as such syntactic items as phrases and sentences, whereas in English or French pitch patterns only serve the latter function.

The learning problem connected with intonation then for any language learner is to discover with what sort of linguistic units pitch movements are associated – lexical or syntactic. The speaker of a tone-language has to learn that variations of pitch in a non-tone language are only used to distinguish different grammatical functions, e.g. declarative *v.* interrogative sentences, defining *v.* non-defining relative clauses, whereas the English speaker learning Chinese must additionally learn to associate pitch variation with lexical words. So fundamental are these different uses of the systems of intonation that it is not possible at the present time to express them in terms of a differential use of rules of the same sort in a contrastive analysis of the sound systems of two languages.

The use of variations in stress also account for major differences in the sound systems of languages. There are two separate problems here. The placement of stress in words of more than one syllable, and the regularity of stresses in relation to tune or rhythm. Languages vary considerably in the rules for placing stress within words. Thus, some languages have very simple rules, e.g. Czech, with the stress on the last syllable of all words, or Spanish with the stress normally on the penultimate syllable; whereas English or Russian, for example, have very complex rules for the placement of stress in words. In principle, however, it is possible to state these rules, although in English, as we have seen, as in some other languages, the rules are in part syntactically determined. Consequently, in the matter of stress languages are capable of being compared.

More fundamental is the question of rhythm. Rhythm of any sort means the regular occurrence in time of some particular phenomenon. We speak of the rhythm of the seasons, the rhythm of music, or the rhythm of running or walking. In the case of language it is the regular occurrence of some phonological feature which determines rhythm. Languages can be divided into two sorts, those in which it is the regular occurrence of the syllable which determines the rhythm *irrespective of stress*. Such languages are called *syllable-timed* languages. French, Yoruba and Tamil are examples. The other type of rhythm is where stresses occur at regular intervals *irrespective of the number of intervening unstressed syllables*. English, German and Russian are examples. We can illustrate these two sorts of rhythm thus as in Figure 40.

The bar lines indicate the equal time intervals and the large boxes the stressed syllables. Note how the stressed syllables in the English example occur at regular intervals. This is not true of the French example.

These fundamental differences in the two types of rhythm in lan-

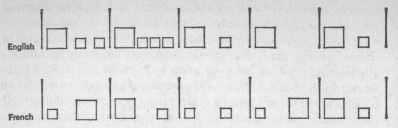

Figure 40 Comparison of the rhythm systems of French and English

guage have important consequences in pronunciation learning: they permit us to make fairly safe predictions about the learning tasks of speakers of one or the other type. For example, the English learner of French will have to learn to distribute the total 'stress energy' of his utterance more evenly over the whole utterance instead of concentrating it principally at one or two places. The effect of not doing this will mean that he will make the error of 'weakening' the vowels in the unstressed syllables to the point that he underdifferentiates them, giving them all some 'neutral' quality. The French learner of English, on the other hand, will tend to distribute his 'stress energy' too evenly over the utterance, and thus not weaken sufficiently those vowels which do not receive stress. Typically, these are found in the 'grammatical' words, like pronouns, prepositions, auxiliaries and articles, which in most contexts are pronounced with the 'weak' vowels [ɪ], [ə] and [ʊ]. No amount of practising the pronunciation of such words as *the*, *he*, or *for*, in isolation will make any difference, of course; on the contrary, it will worsen the situation. The problem lies in learning the rhythmical system of English, not learning to articulate particular vowel sounds.

Conclusions

The objective of theoretical linguistics is to provide a means for explicitly relating meanings to sounds. We saw that in the case of syntactic comparison of languages, it appeared that the only level at which we could find categories common to two languages – a necessity if comparison was to be undertaken rigorously – was that of semantic structure, the underlying structure of the meaning of two sentences. This was because we assumed, as we must, if language learning is to be regarded as possible at all, that there could be identity in the 'messages' which could be expressed in the two languages, even though the means for doing so were in some degree specific to each language. Much modern linguistic research at the present time is concentrated on finding a 'language-neutral' set of categories and relations to describe the structure of messages. The approach to this problem was sketched briefly in chapter 8.

At the other end of the scale – sounds – we saw that it was only at the level of phonetic realization (speech sounds) that we had already available a common 'language-neutral' set of acoustic and articulatory categories which allowed us to make rigorous comparisons of the speech signals of two languages. It looks, therefore, as if in the present state of linguistic knowledge, between the message and its physical expression in sound, there is a fundamental lack of common categories and relations available for really adequate comparison between two languages. Meanwhile we shall have to rely on 'suggestive' parallels and partial, unrigorous comparisons. This is all we can hope for in the absence of our 'identity condition' being met.

Chapter 11
Selection 3: The Study of Learners' Language: Error Analysis

Lapses, mistakes and errors

All learners make mistakes. This is not confined to language learners. We all make mistakes when we are speaking our mother tongue. They often cause a certain amount of merriment. Whether we bother to correct ourselves or not seems to depend on whether we think our hearers have noticed, and how urgently we want to get on with what we are saying. The important point for our present purposes is that we know how to correct them; we can recognize our own mistakes for what they are. This is not usually the case with mistakes made by a learner. Not only does he not always recognize his mistakes, but when his attention is drawn to them he often cannot correct them; he may even commit another error in trying to do so. Furthermore, the majority of learners' errors are linguistically quite different from those made by a native speaker.

We judge a foreigner's knowledge of our language by the number and sort of mistakes he makes. We are inclined to think he knows our language quite well if he does not make many mistakes. It does not usually occur to us that he may be avoiding taking risks and confining himself to doing only what he knows he can do right. The layman probably assesses a foreigner's ability in his language in the first place by how haltingly he speaks and by how good his pronunciation is, that is, in linguistic terms, but in its most superficial aspect. He tends to assume that one can equate a poor pronunciation with a general lack of knowledge of the language, and that a halting speech is confined to those who do not know the language well. The first judgement is without foundation; the second has some truth. However, these superficial judgements are usually revised after a longer exposure to the foreigner's speech. A person more experienced with foreigners knows that a good pronunciation does not necessarily go along with the ability to express oneself fluently or communicate readily in a foreign language. He also knows that fluency is a quality which varies both in foreigners and native speakers with the speech situation and the topic of conversation.

Whilst the nature and quality of mistakes a learner makes provide no direct measure of his knowledge of the language, it is probably the most important source of information about the nature of his knowledge. From the study of his errors we are able to infer the nature of his knowledge at that point in his learning career and discover what he still has to learn. By describing and classifying his errors in linguistic terms, we build up a picture of the features of the language which are causing him learning problems. In this respect the information we get is similar to that provided by contrastive analysis. Error analysis thus provides a check on the predictions of bilingual comparisons, and inasmuch as it does this, it is an important additional source of information for the selection of items to be incorporated into the syllabus.

The mistakes made by a native speaker and by a learner of his language are, as I have said, for the most part strikingly different. The mistakes a native speaker makes are of several sorts: one is changes of plan, where he starts an utterance, breaks off and starts another one with a different structure. For example:

It's a bit – it hasn't – I mean, I wouldn't really care to have one just like that. . . .

He may convert one structure into another without breaking off. These mistakes have been called 'syntactic blends'. Here is an example from a 'Letter to the editor':

One wonders . . . why this country should support foreigners in our already overcrowded prisons . . . for the non-payment of fines of which they had no opportunity to pay.

The redundant *of* appears to arise from a confusion of two constructions:

. . . no opportunity *of* paying
. . . no opportunity to pay

Then there is a class of mistakes which we call 'slips of the tongue' or 'slips of the pen'. These are the subject of investigation at the present time by linguists interested in language performance. Typical of such slips are the substitution, transposition or omission of some segment of an utterance, such as a speech sound, a morpheme, a word or even a phrase. Here are some examples:

It didn't bother me in the sleast . . . slightest
But those frunds . . . funds have been frozen
. . . of Peester Ustinov . . .

The object of these investigations is to discover the patterns of regularity in these slips, what the 'rules' for making slips are. By studying slips, linguists are able to 'infer the relevant properties of an unobservable system on the basis of its output characteristics' (Boomer and Laver, 1968). The breakdown of a mechanism gives insights into the nature of its normal functioning.

We are all subjectively aware that the likelihood of our making mistakes of this kind increases when we are tired, nervous, or in some sort of situation of stress or uncertainty, or when our attention is divided, or we are absorbed in some non-linguistic activity. We should therefore expect that someone trying to communicate in a foreign language or under the sometimes stressful situation in, and outside, the classroom would be particularly liable to such failures in performance.

What we less often observe in native speakers is speech or writing which we could call grammatically or lexically *unacceptable* in the sense used in chapter 8. It is true that we occasionally fail to observe such rules as those of the use of negatives, or subject–verb concord:

Nobody in his right mind would disagree that the Queen should not be paid enough to do her job properly

He will never be accepted so long as the most obvious aspects of his behaviour, his pronunciation, is foreign

Mistakes of this sort are breaches of rules of our code. But we must be careful not to assume a prescriptive attitude towards supposed errors of this kind in others, since, as we have seen, each speaker has a slightly different code or set of codes from every other. What is a breach of one man's code may be part of another man's rule. What are we to make of such utterances as:

That's a question which, if you were to press me, I wouldn't know how to answer it

Is this a slip of the tongue or a breach of the code occasioned by 'losing the thread' of the syntactic structure? Or what about this example:

I was able, luckily, to subsidize my wages from outside work

Is this an error of selection or is it part of the speaker's code?

Native speakers, then, frequently make slips or false starts or confusions of structure. I shall call these all *lapses*. They much more rarely commit breaches of the code, or *errors*. Both these sorts of mistake produce *unacceptable* utterances. But native speakers also produce *inappropriate* utterances. These are not so much lapses in performance as some sort of error of judgement. They are failures to match the language to the situation. The most obvious examples of these failures are 'social gaffes'; but they may be more subtle, the selection of the wrong term in some technical discussion. I understand the Navy do not like their ships to be referred to as 'boats'. Such *mistakes*, as I shall call them, are a case of the selection of the wrong style, dialect or variety, as they have been discussed in chapter 3.

Enough has been said to establish that ordinary speech and, to a lesser extent writing, is liable to breakdown or failure; that these breakdowns are not just random but systematic and arise from physiological and psychological causes or from imperfect knowledge of the linguistic norms of some group.

Whilst learners of a language are certainly liable to lapses and mistakes of the sort I have described, the great majority of their errors are of a different kind. They result in unacceptable utterances and appear as breaches of the code (what I have called *errors* in the case of a native speaker). They are not physical failures but the sign of an imperfect knowledge of the code. The learners have not yet internalized the formation rules of the second language.

I have referred to errors as 'breaches of the code'. This is a reasonable description of some errors made by the native speaker, since by definition they know the formation rules of their mother tongue. One of the features of competence as described in chapter 5 was the ability to recognize deviant sentences. Native speakers are able to correct their own errors, but learners cannot by any means always do so. It is therefore potentially misleading to refer to their errors as 'breaches of the code'. You cannot break a rule you do not know. We may be censured for not observing customs we did not know existed, we may even be prosecuted for breaking laws we are ignorant of, but we can scarcely blame the learner of a language for failing to obey a rule he has never learned.

We are in some difficulties here with our terminology. In contexts other than technical ones (for example Dogmatic Theology), the term 'error' tends to be reserved for wilful or negligent breaches of a rule which is known, or ought to be known or is thought to be known by the offender. None of these circumstances fit the case of a learner of a language. His situation is similar to that of an infant acquiring his mother tongue. He regularly produces utterances which are not those of an adult speaker. We accept the child's utterances as different because he is still learning, and we do not speak of them as erroneous. They are, in a very real sense, utterances in a 'different language'. The utterances of a language learner can, in the same sense, be regarded as belonging to a 'different language'. It is only when a child reaches school age that we begin to talk about his committing 'errors' in his speech. We can do this appropriately precisely because we send our children to school at an age at which an important stage in their linguistic and cognitive development has been reached, an age when they are believed to have mastered the major part of the formation rules of their mother tongue. They are by then considered to have acquired the adult code and consequently we feel justified in calling their unacceptable sentences erroneous.

What are we to say about the language of some poets? It often shows deliberate breaches of the code. Each poet may break a different set of rules. Do we speak about these breaches as errors? On the contrary, we accept them as a legitimate device of the poet to express what may be difficult to express in the standard code, to force the reader to see the familiar world through new eyes or to 'restructure' his picture of the world through a 'recategorization' of the language. It has even been suggested (Thorne, 1965) that the language of a poet should be regarded as an *idiosyncratic dialect*, but one which bears a regular relation to the standard dialect. It is fruitful to regard the language of a learner as an idiosyncratic dialect also.

I shall, in spite of what I have said, continue, for want of a better term, to follow the convention in language-teaching terminology and use the term 'error' to refer to those features of the learner's utterances which differ from those of any native speaker. I shall also distinguish learners' *errors* from *lapses* made by learner or native speaker. Lapses have no immediate relevance to the problem of language learning. I shall merely point out that it may not always be easy to distinguish between a learner's errors and his lapses.

The teaching of languages is not only concerned with the teaching of the formation rules of the language; it is also concerned with *appropriate* behaviour – the speaking rules (see chapter 5). Learners also make *mistakes* in the use of the code. But we do not in the case of the learner usually refer to his mistakes as 'gaffes', because we do not expect him to know the appropriate linguistic behaviour for all circumstances. We recognize him as a foreigner and assign to him a special role in which behaviour, inappropriate in a native, is socially acceptable. I shall return to this topic later when I deal with learners' mistakes at greater length.

Expressive and receptive errors

Chomsky speaks of the object of linguistics as the characterization of the competence of the native *speaker–hearer*. The code is neutral as between expressive and receptive behaviour. Both require a knowledge of the formation rules. Inadequate knowledge of these rules will therefore show itself in both sorts of behaviour. But it is much easier to detect imperfect knowledge in the case of expressive behaviour. Expression leaves traces transient, but recordable, in the case of speech, permanent in the case of writing. Receptive behaviour most often has no observable behavioural concomitants. The hearer does not always demonstrate unambiguously that he has understood fully what we say. Much speech and most writing requires no overt response from the recipients; some is satisfied with smiles, grunts or other paralinguistic behaviour; some demands specific non-linguistic activity: the executing of orders or the following of instructions, and only a small part expects linguistic activity: answers to questions, denials and agreements. It is only the last two types of response that enable a speaker to form some opinion about the adequacy of his hearer's understanding. Even here we must allow for wilful disobedience, disinclination to respond at all and other emotional and cultural constraints on the demonstration of understanding.

Even when we have reason to suspect a failure of comprehension, we still may have great difficulty in determining which particular linguistic features of our utterance have been misinterpreted. The beginner who,when asked, *What is your name?* replied, *I am twelve,* had understood no more than that he was being asked a question, and that it concerned himself, i.e. he reacted to the syntactic and phonological signals of interrogation and the pronominal features of reference, but nothing else.

Teachers are, of course, fully aware of the fact that errors in comprehension occur, and make regular use of the information from them in their teaching. Examinations and tests, for instance, normally include a component whose object is to test understanding, e.g. précis, translation and questions on a passage. But because of the difficulty of pinpointing the linguistic causes of failures in comprehension, many of these techniques can do little more than establish in general terms that comprehension of a passage or parts of a passage is incomplete. Furthermore, since examinations demand productive behaviour as well as receptive, it is no easy task always to determine that any inadequacy in the answer is a result of receptive rather than productive failure. It is possible to devise tests which provide more specific information of this sort and which require little or no productive performance in doing so. These matters will be raised again in chapter 14.

The consequence of all this is that we rely rather heavily in our studies of error on productive data. This is unfortunate but inevitable; unfortunate because, as we saw in our discussion of language performance in chapter 6, there may be reasons for believing that expressive and receptive processes are not mirror images of each other. Furthermore, there is a general belief amongst teachers that a learner's receptive abilities normally exceed his productive abilities, and that *recognition* of an item is easier than its *retrieval* in production. The difficulty of devising means of studying receptive errors has so far prevented us from confirming these general impressions or from establishing the qualitative or quantitative relations between them. It could well be that we overestimate the pupil's receptive abilities simply because we cannot so readily detect failures in comprehension. In any act of comprehension there is a major component supplied by the situation and the hearer. We may well be reading more understanding into the replies of the learner than is there in his language.

If, on the other hand, it were established that receptive and productive abilities were regularly unequal then it might be necessary to question the validity of the concept of 'competence' as neutral between expressive and receptive behaviour.

The errors of groups and individuals

It is the individual learner who makes errors and mistakes. The notion of knowledge of the formation and speaking rules is applicable to individuals not groups. Although it is individuals who learn, we usually direct our teaching towards groups; we cannot normally afford to teach an individual or modify our programme in response to the feedback from a single member of the class. Although each member of a class is initially different in some respect from every other member, programmes are designed on the basis of what is common to all the members of the group: their average intelligence, their common objectives, their common mother tongue and common experience of the second language. The information we get from the study of errors is in part used for constructing appropriate syllabuses and teaching materials. It is logical that when we have this practical objective in mind we make use of information drawn from the group as a whole. We take account, therefore, principally of those errors which are common to all, or a majority of, members of the group, and discount, for planning purposes, those which are peculiar to an individual or a minority. Just how small that minority must be to be disregarded depends on many local factors.

It may be that we cannot in the case of any particular group find any errors which are common to a majority. Furthermore, whilst we may find some common errors, it requires further investigation to determine whether, in fact, they are not merely superficially similar. The failure to use some form correctly may arise from a number of different causes. In this sense erroneous sentences are ambiguous. If well-formed sentences may frequently be ambiguous, i.e. be derived from different underlying structures, then ill-formed sentences similarly may show a variety of different derivations. We shall see, in due course, that this presents problems of description.

Collections of common errors have frequently been published for different languages. One theoretical justification for such collections might be that there are certain features of a language which are *inherently* difficult for anyone to learn. This is quite a different theory from that lying behind contrastive analysis, which only maintains that certain languages are more or less difficult for speakers of a particular language. Difficulty is a function of the relations between languages, not inherent in a language itself. It is obviously impossible to test the hypothesis that a certain language is inherently more difficult to learn for all learners, since each comes to the learning task with a knowledge of a first language which may make it easier or more difficult for him. The only evidence which might be relevant is that of the acquisition of different languages as a mother tongue by infants. At the present time the weight of the evidence from this source is overwhelmingly against different languages being inherently different in difficulty; but this does not mean that we must reject out of hand the notion of classes of errors which are common to a *heterogeneous* group of learners. There are other theoretical possibilities. It may be that certain normal and necessary processes in language learning, such as *generalization*, which are independent of the nature of the mother tongue, will, when applied to the data of a particular language, produce a set of similar errors. Such errors are discussed on page 289. It may also be that the normal processes of learning when applied *to a particular set of teaching materials*, or when the learners have all been submitted to a particular teaching technique, will yield a crop of similar errors, whatever their mother tongue. There is evidence that this does occur. Errors of this sort are also considered on page 291.

Nevertheless, most syllabuses are devised for homogeneous groups, and we would certainly not reject any collection of errors derived from such groups as irrelevant to syllabus planning.

In respect of what attributes is a group to be regarded as homogeneous? The most important aspect of homogeneity is the linguistic one, namely, that the group should be formed of speakers of the same mother tongue. If one wished to be rigorous in this requirement one would have to specify that the range of dialects and varieties they possessed was equivalent. Secondly, one would require that their knowledge of the formation and speaking rules of the second language was equivalent. Desirably, one would also expect some degree of similarity in their personal characteristics: intelligence, motivation, social background, experience of the world, age, maturity and so on. Homogeneity is a 'more-or-less' thing. We cannot, of course, expect full equivalence in all these dimensions. However, the ordinary school class group is normally fairly homogeneous in all these important respects. The widest divergence will be in motivation and personality. It is, therefore, with suitable qualifications, reasonable to regard them as a homogeneous group, a majority of whom will make the same errors, on the basis of the analysis of which we may plan our syllabuses.

Where the mother tongue, age, knowledge of the world and previous experience of learning languages, or the particular second language, are different, as may sometimes happen in the case of adult groups, then the errors produced by the group will be less homogeneous. If common errors are detected then they must arise from the normal process of learning interacting with the nature of the second language and the teaching materials.

The practical uses of error analysis

The most obvious practical use of the analysis of errors is to the teacher. Errors provide feedback, they tell the teacher something about the effectiveness of his teaching materials and his teaching techniques, and show him what parts of the syllabus he has been following have been inadequately learned or taught and need further attention. They enable him to decide whether he can move on to the next item on the syllabus or whether he must devote more time to the item he has been working on. This is the day-to-day value of errors. But in terms of broader planning and with a new group of learners they provide the information for designing a remedial syllabus or a programme of re-teaching. The matter, however, is not quite as simple as this. As we shall see in chapter 12 in the discussion of the structure of the syllabus there is no clear sense in which we can say that a feature or element in the language has been learned completely until the whole language has been learned. If we remember de Saussure's words that language is a 'self-contained system', in which each part is related systematically to another part, then the learning of some new item requires the relearning of all the items already studied; hence the necessity in language learning of a cyclical syllabus.

The theoretical uses of error analysis

The applied linguist wants to be useful, but in order to be so he has to understand what is going on when people learn languages. It has long been accepted that the application of a scientific discipline to the solution of practical problems provides feedback to theory. The applications provide confirmation or disproof of theory. In this respect they are like experiments which test the prediction of the theory. The study of learners' errors is such an application. The psycholinguist predicts that the nature of the mother tongue will facilitate or make difficult the learning of certain aspects of a second language. We make a comparative study of the two languages, we identify certain features of the second language as different from those of the mother tongue and predict that the learner will find them difficult, and will show this to be the case by making errors. Thus, the study of errors is part of an 'experiment' to confirm or disprove the psycholinguistic theory of 'transfer'. Of course, a predicted difficulty which does not show itself in errors in practice, or errors which are not predicted by the contrastive analysis do not (by any means) automatically disprove the theory. They may be the result of poor experimental method, i.e. they may derive from inadequate descriptive and comparative techniques. It would be a bold man who abandoned a theory on the basis of the analytic skills of both contrastive and error analysis as they have been developed up to the present time.

The theoretical interest in studies of error have therefore a feedback to both descriptive linguistics and psycholinguistics. But these cannot conveniently be separated. If the psycholinguistic theory of language learning incorporating some notion of 'transfer' is correct, and the data from error analysis do not confirm it, then we infer that the failure must be ascribed to the descriptive inadequacy of the linguistic theory, or our inability to apply the theory correctly to the language data. On the other hand, if we assume the linguistic theory to be correct and our descriptive techniques adequate, but the data from the error analysis do not confirm the psycholinguistic theory of transfer, then we infer that the psycholinguistic theory is faulty. In practice what happens is likely to be that both theories are partially confirmed. Some of the predictions are confirmed, some are not. Thus we infer that other factors than transfer are operating, e.g. the nature of the materials, the teaching and normal learning processes, and also we infer that had our linguistic theory and its application to the language data in both contrastive and error analysis been more adequate, the theory of transfer would have been more fully confirmed.

The study of learners' errors is part of the methodology of the study of language learning. In this respect it resembles very closely the study of the acquisition of the mother tongue. As we have seen, it is by collecting and analysing the utterances of the infant that the psycholinguist infers something of the acquisition process. He does this by logging the changes in the utterances of a single child over a period of time. He makes what are called *longitudinal* studies. By comparing successive states in the child's linguistic development he plots its increasing mastery of the systems of the language. But he is not justified, of course, in inferring that what one child does is typical of all children. He has to make a number of parallel longitudinal studies and then compare them. His initial hypothesis must be that there is something in common in the development of all children acquiring the same mother tongue, and, more ambitiously and generally, something in common to all human infants learning human languages. There would be no point in undertaking such studies at all unless some such hypothesis was adopted; there would be no point in studying the acquisition of language of a single child unless it was expected to contribute to an understanding of the whole process of child language acquisition. The parallel with linguistic studies is clear. There is little point in studying the nature of a particular language unless we believe that there is something to be said about human language in general. Child language studies and general linguistic studies both have fundamentally the object of discovering universals. The same is true of the study of the learning of second languages. The study of errors, then, is part of the psycholinguistic search for the universal processes of second-language learning. But we can go a little further. It is hypothesized, and some evidence is now available, that children do follow a similar course in the acquisition of their mother tongue. There are, of course, various factors involved, intelligence, social background, differential exposure to language data, etc., which may complicate the picture, but the assumption has solid foundations. What we would like to know is whether the same is true in the case of learning a second language. Is it the case that speakers of the same mother tongue learning a second language all follow the same course of development? Clearly the interfering factors are just as powerful in this case: motivation, intelligence, social background, knowledge of the world; but there is an additional interference factor in the case of the learner of a second language, namely, that he

receives teaching – he is required to follow an *externally* imposed syllabus. If we regard the course followed by an infant learning his mother
tongue as a sort of '*internal syllabus*', might there not also be an internal syllabus for learning a second language which would represent the
'psychologically natural route' between mother tongue and the target
language, determined by the inherent cognitive properties of the
human mind but conditioned by the particular properties of the two
languages involved? The answer is that we do not know. People do, of
course, learn second languages without a teacher and without a book
or set syllabus, 'on-the-job' as we might say. But no one has studied
them. It is clear, however, that if we could establish that there was a
'built-in', psychologically optimal, syllabus of this sort, and if we were
able to describe it in linguistic terms, it would be almost the most valuable bit of information we could have for the organization of syllabus
material.

Preliminaries to the description of errors

Meaningful speech is systematic, or (expressed another way) it is the
systematic nature of language which makes communication possible.
Learners use spontaneous language with the intention of communicating; whether they succeed or not is another matter. One must assume,
therefore, that their language is systematic. The assumption underlying the description of errors is that they are evidence of a system, not
the system of the target language, but a system of some 'other' language. To describe that 'other' language is precisely the theoretical
objective of error analysis. I have provisionally suggested that it could
be called an 'idiosyncratic' dialect, a peculiar personal code of the
learner. If communication, or intention to communicate, implies a
systematic code then the evidence for that code should be drawn from
data which were produced with the intention of communicating. But
not all language behaviour in the classroom has such an intention.
Drills and formal exercises are not intended to communicate, and
therefore one might be ill-advised to base one's description of the idiosyncratic dialect on evidence derived from such a source. In such circumstances the learner is not able to choose freely, but has imposed on
him a limited choice. The result must be that, unless he is already familiar with the system of the target language, his choice is random not

systematic. He guesses. It is for these reasons that error analysis is performed on language material produced by the learner *spontaneously* – essays, compositions, stories, free oral compositions and so on. This does not mean, however, that random guessing plays no part in such language behaviour; only that it is probably greatly reduced.

I have provisionally called the learner's language an 'idiosyncratic dialect'. This was done to emphasize the fact that it is a code which is not necessarily the code of any social group. We have, however, considered the possibility that other members of his class may possess a similar code, if the class is homogeneous. Whether they are to be regarded as a social group I leave to the sociologists. They do not naturally use their idiosyncratic dialects for communicating with each other; they usually have a common mother tongue for that purpose. In this sense it would be wrong to speak of the common core of all their idiosyncratic dialects as a 'language' or 'shared code' in the Saussurean sense. However, the salient characteristic of a learner's dialect is its *instability* – at least so long as he continues to learn. That is why Selinker (1969) refers to it as an *interlanguage*, thereby emphasizing its intermediate status between the codes of the mother tongue and the target language. Of course, we probably all have foreign acquaintances who, after long years living in our country, continue to make the same set of errors. They have ceased to learn, at least in certain areas of the language. Their interlanguage can be said to have 'fossilized' at some point in the past. Just why this is so is a matter of speculation, but one might hazard a guess that having found that they can communicate and understand well enough for all their normal needs, they have no motivation to eliminate these errors. If one examines the errors made by such people, one finds that they often involve 'redundant' features of language. Some linguists have reckoned that language may consist of up to 50 per cent of redundant features. The foreign speaker can well risk reducing that without running very often into serious failures of communication. One need only think of concord in English subject–verb relations, the personal endings of the verb in French, or the concord system of the determiner, adjective and noun in German, to see areas of redundancy very often exploited by the fossilized competences of foreign residents.

The instability of the interlanguage causes problems of description. It is difficult enough to collect enough data from one state of a learner's interlanguage to reconstruct its systems at any one time. The same problem faces the investigator of child language. The fact that the interlanguage *is* unstable is not a reason for abandoning the concept. After all, we speak of an *état de langue* in our historical studies of language change, though the decision as to what data fall within a particular *état de langue* is essentially an arbitrary one. It just happens that languages though, of course, also unstable, change slowly enough for us to collect enough data on which to base a satisfactory description.

The key, then, to error analysis is the systematic nature of language and consequently of error. No one would attempt the task unless he worked on this assumption. This is far from saying that all errors are systematic. Indeed, any teacher knows that this is not the case. There is, however, no way of describing or accounting for something which is not systematic. We must also remember that something may appear unsystematic only because we have no inkling of the nature of its regularity. For one thing, the single occurrence of an error is obviously insufficient evidence upon which to base any hypothesis of a system. We need a fair quantity of data before we can start hypothesizing; we need this to satisfy ourselves that the regularity we have observed is not a chance one. Nevertheless, it is probable that guessing does play a part in language learning. Just where the link between *random* guessing and *principled* guessing (or hypothesizing) on the part of the learner, lies may be difficult to determine. It is one of the explanations of errors, as we shall see, that they are evidence of principled but incorrect guesses about the rules of the target language.

The first thing that we observe in a study of errors is that they fall into two groups: those which are systematic, that is, can be predicted, and those which are unpredictable. But this classification is not adequate. The instability of the interlanguage means that prediction is an uncertain thing. A learner makes systematic mistakes in a particular area for a limited time. He eventually, we hope, gets the thing right, but the transition from wrong to right is not a sudden one; it takes some time and he may pass through intermediate stages, each of them having its own system. But most noticeable is the stage at which he sometimes gets a thing right and sometimes wrong. *He is inconsistent.* It looks as if he knew some rule but simply failed to apply it. This is what we would call the *practice* stage of learning. On the other hand, there is another stage in which he gets things wrong – most of the time, and only occasionally hits the right form, as if *by chance*. This is the stage of random guessing or pre-systematic stage. We could characterize this stage as one in which he is only vaguely aware, if at all, that there is something to be learned, that the target language has a particular system. Languages differ, after all, very considerably in the way in which they realize semantic categories. Thus, for example, there are languages that realize the concepts of time exclusively in adverbial systems, while others do this partly in the verb and partly in the adverb. A learner of such a language would have first to realize that the verb is marked for tense and aspect and then to discover which verbal forms related to which time notion. And yet, throughout his experience of the data of the language it would, of course, be showing tense and aspect markings. These would be inexplicable and apparently random characteristics until he discovered their *function*. During the first stage, the presystematic stage of errors, in that area of syntax, we would expect him to randomly affix tense endings to verbs. When he had begun to discover the function of these markings, he would enter the *stage of systematic errors*. He would be trying to discover how the system of tense endings worked, testing out various hypotheses. At a certain point he would discover the correct system but be inconsistent (for a period) in his application of what he knew. This is the *post-systematic stage* of errors, or 'practice stage' of learning. This is obviously a speculative account of the process of learning as it is reflected in types of errors, and is, no doubt, highly simplified. We must also remember that a learner is in a different stage of learning in respect of every different system of the language: pre-systematic in certain areas, systematic in others and post-systematic in others. We must also take into account the interconnectedness of the systems of a language, which make it difficult to speak of 'learning a system' or 'knowing a system'. We may learn to operate a system correctly within a defined range of contexts, but we have to relearn it or redefine it in order to operate it in a wider range of contexts. Hence the need for a cyclical syllabus already referred to.

The picture just given may serve as a first approximation, and is to some extent supported by informal empirical evidence. If a learner makes an error and we ask him to correct it, there are obviously two things possible, either he can or he can't. If we ask him why he made the error, or what he was trying to do, he can either give some reason, i.e. systematic account, or he can't. This assumes he has available either in his mother tongue, or the second language, the concepts and language for talking about what he is doing (i.e. some sort of linguistic knowledge). In the pre-systematic stage, since he has not yet realized that there is a system or what its function is, he can neither correct his error nor say what his problem is; in the systematic stage he cannot correct his error but he can give some explanation of what he was aiming at or trying to do; in the post-systematic stage he can both correct his error and explain what was wrong, i.e. that he had overlooked something, or simply forgotten to apply a known rule. These stages are summarized in Table 9.

Table 9

Error type	Correction possible	Explanation possible
1 Pre-systematic	No	No
2 Systematic	No	Yes
3 Post-systematic	Yes	Yes

The data for error analysis

You cannot begin to describe something until you are aware of its existence. This is a platitude. But recognizing that an error has been committed is not such a simple matter as it sounds. Experienced teachers become very expert in this, but the layman probably does not recognize half the errors made by a foreign speaker of his language for what they are. The first stage in the technical process of describing the linguistic nature of errors is to detect them. The difficulty in doing this lies in the fact that what looks or sounds a perfectly acceptable sentence may nevertheless contain errors. Of course, in many cases the sentence is not acceptable and then we know it is erroneous. Such sentences we can call *overtly erroneous*. Those which are erroneous, but not overtly so, we can call *covertly erroneous*. By acceptable, of course, I mean here, as elsewhere, a sentence such as the native speaker would accept as being superficially well-formed, and might himself utter on the appropriate occasion. That is precisely the difficulty. A sentence must not only be acceptable, it must also be appropriate, that is, relevant and inteligible in the specific context. The covertly erroneous sentences are those which are not appropriate in the context in which they occur. The student who wrote: *I want to know the English* wrote a perfectly acceptable sentence which, interpreted independently of its context, expressed unexceptionable sentiments. The context of the utterance showed, however, that his interest lay not in the people but in their language. Any identification of error, therefore, necessarily involves *interpretation in the context*.

The difficulty unfortunately does not end there. It is possible that a learner's sentence may be both acceptable and appropriate but nevertheless erroneous. After all, in any context there are always a number of different but appropriate things that can be said. We have additionally to satisfy ourselves that the learner's acceptable and seemingly appropriate utterance is, in fact, being interpreted by us in the way he intended, that he really is saying what he appears to be saying. Learners probably quite often say something acceptable and apparently appropriate, but which does not mean what they intend to mean. Such sentences would, of course, normally pass muster with the layman. Experienced teachers are unlikely to be so easily misled, since they have a pretty shrewd notion of what their pupils are or are not capable of saying. Sentences of this sort may be the result of the application of the wrong rules to produce, *by chance*, acceptable and appropriate results or, simply the repetition of something learned as a whole, parrot-fashion, i.e. holophrastically. We must certainly not rule out the possibility of a learner being right quite often for the wrong reasons (we have already envisaged this possibility in the case of pre-systematic errors). A learner who made no distinction, for example, between singular and plural nouns in English would produce acceptable noun phrases about half the time *by chance*, and quite often they would be appropriate in the context. An Indian immigrant girl wrote a short story in English in the present tense throughout (with two exceptions). But some parts of the story involved direct speech. These parts were both acceptable and appropriate, but would we be justified in regarding them as error-free? If we regard the systems of language as systems of binary, or multiple, but limited, choices, the production of a 'correct' form on an appropriate occasion can scarcely be regarded as error-free until we are satisfied that the learner is *also* capable of producing the contrasting form correctly on an appropriate occasion. The same Indian girl used just three past tenses, all correctly, *I said*; *he said*; *he broke* .... Were these to be regarded as evidence of her having learned the system of tense contrasts; or a case of 'parrotting' forms she had

The Study of Learners' Language: Error Analysis 273

obviously met in a story-telling context? They were almost certainly right by chance. The learner of German who consistently formed the attributive adjective with the suffix *–en* in all genders and numbers, produced a fine crop of 'right' forms, *die guten Bücher, meine besten Freunde, diese jungen Leute*. He also produced **viele anderen Frauen*; **wenige schlechten Fehler*; **einige ungewöhnlichen Sitten*; and **noch mehr unhöflichen Bemerkungen*. In this case he appeared to be systematic, but his system – a simple one – turned out a fair proportion of acceptable forms *by chance*.

The conclusion we must draw from this is that forms produced by learners are not properly to be regarded as right or wrong *in themselves*, but only as evidence for a right or wrong *system*. A wrong system may produce right forms sporadically and by chance. Which leads us back to our original statement about the purpose of error analysis. Its object is to describe the nature of the learner's interlanguage and to compare this with the target language. This is why error analysis is a brand of comparative linguistic study.

If we cannot begin to describe a learner's errors without first having an interpretation of what he is trying to say, the next question to ask is: how do we arrive at such an interpretation? If the learner is available, we can ask him to express his intentions in his mother tongue, and then translate his utterance into the target language, using whatever we can glean from his original attempt as a guide to the form he aimed at. This we can call an *authoritative* interpretation. It is an *authoritative reconstruction* of his utterance in an acceptable form; its appropriateness is guaranteed by the translation. In the learner's absence our problem is greater. We have to do the best we can to infer what he intended to say from his utterance, its context and whatever we know about him and his knowledge of the world and the target language. This can only be called a *plausible* interpretation. The corresponding reconstruction is only a *plausible reconstruction*. It is obvious we cannot place as much confidence in such reconstructions as we can when we can consult the learner himself. There will, of course, be occasions when the utterance is so incoherent that no interpretation of any sort can be achieved. Even though the following utterance was actually produced in conversation with an investigator, a plausible interpretation was difficult to arrive at:

If you want Indians very lovely, you will talk them

Incoherence may result from inadequate knowledge of the orthographic system in a native speaker who is learning to write; here is an extract from a composition on the Eskimo:

Fretheh hars to go owt to koki smi hodi for supper
Wili Mother is wo ta foor the fodi to maki own supper

In such cases the data has to be laid aside as useless until we know more of the learner's interlanguage. Teachers, in fact, become quite expert in understanding their pupils' interlanguage. In some cases they can actually speak it! Quite often an utterance is ambiguous; more than one plausible interpretation is possible in that context. Failing an authoritative interpretation such data also must be set aside. Ambiguity in erroneous utterances will be discussed on page 279.

Whether our interpretation is authoritative or merely plausible, we finish up with an erroneous utterance paired with a reconstruction of it in the target language; this, 'by construction', is a translation equivalent, or synonymous in the context. These paired sentences are the data for error analysis. The process I have described is presented in Figure 41 as an algorithm for producing the data for error analysis.

The linguistic description of errors

Error analysis is, as we have seen, a comparative process. We proceed by comparing synonymous utterances in the learner's dialect and the target language. In this respect it is a special case of contrastive analysis, which, as we have seen, makes its starting point the same message expressed in two languages. The difference lies in the fact that in error analysis we do not possess a description of the learner's interlanguage to help us make our comparisons. Error analysis, in this respect, is rather like the task a linguist faces when trying to describe a hitherto undescribed and unrecorded language.

At this point it is necessary to distinguish what I mean by description and explanation. Logically the one precedes the other. Description gives an account of what has to be explained. I have already suggested that one of the theoretical objectives in error analysis is the explanation of how errors come about. This is a psychological explanation in terms of the learner's strategies and the process of learning. But there is another sense to the term explanation – linguistic explanation – which

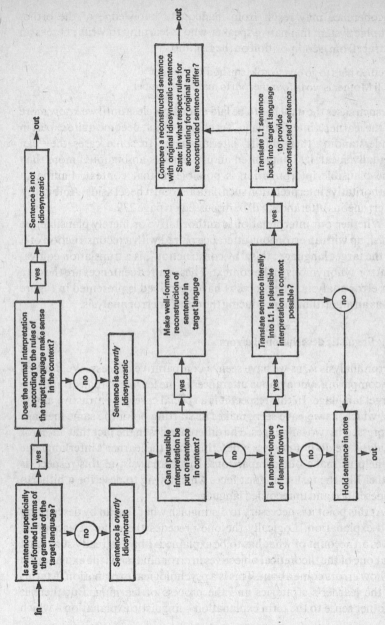

Figure 41 Algorithm for providing data for description of idiosyncratic dialects (after Corder, 1971)

is part of a total descriptive process. If, for instance, we say that the error in this sentence is the omission of a word:

I was told: there is bus stop

then we have in a sense described the error, but only partially. The omission of the article (in this case) is only the surface evidence for an erroneous or idiosyncratic linguistic system. A full description of the error involves 'explaining' it in terms of the linguistic processes or rules which are being followed by the speaker. We infer these from the evidence of this utterance, and from others from the same learner, in which articles are or are not present, whether correctly so or not. Systems and rules are an abstraction from the linguistic data. The omission of an article is part of the data for making such abstractions.

Linguistic explanations of this sort imply a linguistic theory in which the notion of deep and surface grammar play a part. Describing the error as an omission of the article has little explanatory power and is of little use to teacher or learner. Both want to know what the omission is evidence for – both linguistic and psychological. Of course, superficial description is a necessary condition for linguistic explanation but it is not a sufficient one, just as linguistic explanation is a necessary condition of psychological explanation but not a sufficient one.

The description of errors can be made, then, at various degrees of depth, generality or abstraction. The first and most superficial level merely describes errors in terms of the physical difference between the learner's utterance and the reconstructed version:

1. Original utterance: I was told: there is bus stop
    Reconstruction: I was told: there is the bus stop

2. Original: I have a great difficulty in ...
    Reconstruction: I have great difficulty in ...

3. Original: *Hier müssen Sie nicht rauchen*
    Reconstruction: *Hier dürfen Sie nicht rauchen*

4. Original: *J'aime le café beaucoup*
    Reconstruction: *J'aime beaucoup le café*

Differences of this sort can be classified into four categories: *omission* of some required element; *addition* of some unnecessary or incorrect element; *selection* of an incorrect element; and *misordering* of elements. We can take the first step to a deeper description by assigning

Table 10 Matrix for classification of errors

	Phonological/orthographical	Grammatical	Lexical
Omission			
Addition			
Selection			
Ordering			

the items involved to the different linguistic levels: orthographic/ phonological, syntactic and lexico-semantic. By doing this we are applying some theoretical framework to our analysis. A 'word', as we saw in chapter 5, is a unit at every level of description. To say that the 'wrong word' has been selected might mean that the 'right word' had been chosen from a grammatical or semantic point of view, but was incorrectly spelled, e.g. *He has three suns*, or that the right word has been chosen semantically, but the wrong grammatical form of it: **He have three brother*, or that the right word has been selected grammatically, but wrong semantically: *Er fing an zu schwören* ('He began to swear'). This analysis matches the various types of unacceptability outlined in chapter 5 and is explanatorily more powerful than a single statement of what is omitted or added. It yields, when combined with the superficial analysis, the matrix for classification shown in Table 10. But even then such a classification is only the necessary preliminary to a *systematic* analysis of the errors, the 'most explanatory' analysis. Relations, categories and rules are what are learned, not 'words' or other items, as such. Systems occur at each linguistic level. The learner who wrote *skrew* for *screw* did not just select the wrong item (letter) at the orthographic level, but showed that he had not correctly learned one of the rules for the formation of initial clusters of consonents in English spelling, e.g.

$$\text{Initial consonant cluster} \rightarrow \#\,s + \begin{Bmatrix} p \\ t \\ c \end{Bmatrix} + r + \text{vowel}$$

in ordinary language: the only consonant letters which can occur in the position between *s* and *r* in an initial consonant cluster of three consonants are p, c and t. The learner who said:

I am here since three o'clock

278 Introducing Applied Linguistics

did not just select the wrong grammatical item, but showed that he had not learned the function of the auxiliary system in English, e.g. the rule:

Auxiliary $\rightarrow$ perfective + tense + since + point-of-time noun

i.e. the verb is in the perfective form when collocated with the prepositional phrase of time: *since*+'point-of-time'. The learner who wrote:

They don't speak dialects: they speak languages

showed he had not learned a part of the lexico-semantic system of English: dialect and language are not in an *exclusive* but an *inclusive* relationship, i.e. dialects are a form of a language, as 'roses' are a sort of 'flower'.

Many erroneous sentences are ambiguous, as we have already noted. This presents a problem of interpretation and hence of description. The learner who wrote this ambiguous sentence:

If you don't know the meaning, ask a dictionary

may have intended:

If you don't know the meaning, ask *for* a dictionary

or

If you don't know the meaning, *consult* a dictionary

Both interpretations were equally probable in the context. We do not know whether to assign the error to an incorrect lexical selection (*ask* for *consult*) or an incorrect categorization of *ask*, i.e. that it is a member of the class of verbs which (in the meaning of *request*) requires a prepositional complement: ask *for something*. A similar problem arises with:

I want that you come here

Did the learner correctly choose the lexical item *want* but assign it incorrectly to the class of verb taking a *that*-clause object, or did he choose the right grammatical verb class but select the wrong lexical item, *want*, in place of *desire, require, demand*? Only an authoritative interpretation can resolve the ambiguity.

The learning of vocabulary as it is often called, is not just a question of learning the 'semantic properties' of items, but also their 'syntactic properties', that is, assigning them to correct grammatical classes. The learner who said:

I brought back three breads

made no semantic error. He incorrectly assigned 'bread' to the class of countable nouns. He selected, in other words, the incorrect *form* of the item. He should have chosen *loaf*, its semantic synonym. The learner who wrote:

He was filled with despise for her action

selected the right semantic item but its wrong grammatical *form*. He should have written:

He was filled with contempt for her action

Mistakes of performance

So far I have dealt only with errors resulting from an inadequate knowledge of the formation rules; but as I pointed out on page 261, the learner also makes mistakes in the speaking rules – uses inappropriate language. Native speakers also do this. I am not here concerned with *lapses*, but *mistakes* in relating language to the situational context or the world outside in general. These may be *referential* or *stylistic*. Reference is that relation which holds between linguistic forms and objects or events (or classes of these) in the world 'outside'. When a learner invites us to *climb that mountain* with him, and we can see only hills, his language is not erroneous or unacceptable, as we have been using these terms, but inappropriate. He has made a mistake of reference. It may be that he can use the forms *that hill, that mountain* correctly from the linguistic point of view that I have been discussing up to now, but he does not know how to apply them appropriately to objects in the world outside, he does not know to what they appropriately refer. Where this is not a joke or a simple mistake of perception, the most likely explanation is that he does not share with us our categorization of the world. Some of his 'mountains' are our 'hills'. It may, of course, also be that his knowledge and experience of the world does not include what we call mountains. In such a case the teaching of language is also the teaching of 'knowledge of the world'. This matter has been discussed already in chapter 4. The categories we need for describing mistakes are clearly not linguistic ones, they are philosophical (or psychological), those of 'material truth' or 'falsehood'. If we can, on any particular occasion, assume that a learner is not lying, then we can detect mistakes of reference (or application) by the criterion of truth. If a learner tells us he has three brothers and we happen to know that he has one brother and two sisters and is also familiar with the word sister and can apply it appropriately, then we judge he has made an inappropriate remark, that he does not know that *brothers* does not refer appropriately to what we call (in a technical variety of English) *siblings*.

Stylistic mistakes are, as we have seen, also made by native speakers. They account for one large class of jokes and comic effects on the stage. It takes quite a long time for the native schoolchild to learn to control appropriately the use of features of his mother tongue in relation to the social, technical, intentional and emotional differences in situations. One of the characteristics of the early written work of schoolchildren is the sudden and unpredictable variation in style within the same composition. It is not surprising then that this performance ability is one which is acquired by the foreign learner only at advanced stages, if at all. His awareness of this aspect of performance, learned first in relation to his mother tongue, no doubt helps him, as I suggested in chapter 5, to acquire the ability in a foreign language. But it is also the case that we do not expect or require of foreigners that they should be able to select the stylistically appropriate language with the same skill and control that the native speaker does. Indeed, it is often part of their role as 'foreigner' that they should not. We can even go further. The native speaker finds it *inappropriate* in certain situations for a foreigner to use the same style of language as he would do himself. We can take as an example those features which we call 'slang'. It is not only that the appropriate use of 'slang' requires great familiarity with, and sensitivity to, the social life of a people, unlikely to be acquired by a foreigner, but also that the use of *any* slang features by a foreigner is inappropriate. A foreigner can only use slang appropriately when he is no longer regarded as a foreigner. The use of certain stylistic features of language as of other behaviour can be regarded as a claim to be a member of some group, family, profession, caste, class, etc. A doctor may be offended or amused, for instance, when a layman uses medical terminology too freely. It is interpreted as an unwarranted claim to be treated as a member of the confraternity.

There exists, besides, the need for *consistency of performance or behaviour* (Goffman, 1959). Membership of a group requires of its members that all their behaviour shall conform to the norms of that group. Within language, too, we expect congruity. This means the selection of the linguistic features must be made appropriately *at all levels*. The use of the lexical and syntactic features of language called slang must be accompanied by the appropriate, in this case, native, pronunciation. There is nothing so incongruous as slang spoken with a foreign accent. A foreigner is unlikely even to be wholly integrated into some social group so long as the most obvious aspects of his behaviour – his pronunciation – is foreign. The selection of appropriate grammatical features must also be accompanied by congruent lexical ones. *Beware lest the dog tear the pants off you!*

The use of referentially inappropriate language is more evident in speech than writing. This is because checking the appropriateness of reference to features of the situation is only possible where speaker–writer and recipient are in the same place and time. Thus when a learner writes: *I had a steak for lunch* we cannot judge of its truth and so not know if his language was referentially appropriate or not. If he says: *I have a pencil in my hand*, we can. The detection of stylistically inappropriate language in the case of a foreign learner is still a matter of the hearer's *Sprachgefühl* or personal judgement. We do not yet have a grammar of style, nor do we have yet a sociological account of the role of foreigners or any hard facts about attitudes to, or expectations of, foreigners' linguistic behaviour in our own or anyone else's culture.

Some explanations of error

Linguistic theory provides the language for talking about the nature of errors, for comparing the language of the learner with that of the native speaker, perhaps even for describing the difference between what the learner did and what a native speaker would have done in the same circumstances. But linguistic theory does not provide a means of talking about *why* the learner makes mistakes or why he did what he did do. Such explanations are part of psycholinguistics, part of the theory of language learning discussed in chapter 6. I am concerned here with looking at learners' errors as evidence for such theories.

A learner acquires his knowledge of a second language and its use from *samples* of performance, i.e. utterances made available to him over a period of time. These samples may or may not be accompanied by descriptions or explanatory statements about them intended to help him 'process' them effectively. Errors may arise, on the one hand, as a result of the nature of the samples, their classification and presentation or, on the other, from the actual activity of processing the data. Teaching is concerned with the data and its mode of presentation; we can control and manipulate it in various ways. What neither the learner nor the teacher can do is entirely manipulate or control the learning process. This is part of human psychology.

Learning and teaching take place *over a period of time*. This is also something we can do little about. We certainly cannot make all the data available simultaneously, nor can the learner process them all simultaneously. Errors are a result of partial knowledge because the teaching–learning process extends over time. Language, as we have seen, is a self-contained system, all parts being interconnected, a system of systems. In a sense nothing is 'fully' learned until everything is 'fully' learned. Changing the grouping or sequencing of the data merely makes the nature and timing of the errors different in certain respects. It cannot eliminate them or reduce the total amount of error below some, at present unknown, lower limit.

However, both the learning and the teaching process may be less than optimally efficient. We may organize and present the data in less than the optimal fashion. In our ignorance we obviously do. This will increase the learner's difficulties. The errors he makes as a result are theoretically *redundant*. They do not need to happen. The learning process may also be less than optimally efficient. People are not all equally endowed with intelligence, do not all remember equally well, are not all equally motivated; they may be unwell, or tired, or emotionally upset or inattentive. Some of these factors lie outside anyone's control; others are part of the normal problems of learning anything. All may be the cause of redundant errors. The mark of effective syllabuses and teaching materials is the minimalization of redundant errors.

This analysis, then, categorizes errors into those which are *normal* to the learning and teaching process and those which are *redundant*, caused by faulty materials, faulty teaching and faulty learning.

It is generally maintained, and I have assumed it up to now, that many errors show signs of the influence of the mother tongue or other language possessed by the learner. When he is faced with the desire or urgent necessity to communicate with people who do not know his mother tongue, he has three possibilities: to remain silent, to use para-linguistic means of communication or to use his mother tongue. He probably uses a combination of all three. Even in a mother-tongue situation we are faced with the same three choices, but our linguistic ability reduces, to quite small dimensions, the amount of silence and gesture as a solution; it does not eliminate them altogether. There are always some things we feel we cannot communicate adequately with the linguistic knowledge or skills we possess. This may be the source of all great art and music.

Consequently, when in the course of learning a second language the learner is faced with the need to communicate something which re-quires knowledge or skill in the language which lies beyond what he possesses, he will have resort to silence, gesture or the mother tongue. The classroom situation does not permit silence or gesture, so we get a 'mixture' of the second language and the mother tongue (or any other language he knows). The learner makes up the deficiencies of his knowledge of the second language by recourse to the appropriate parts of the mother tongue. If you regard language as a matter of habit, then what he has resort to are the habits of his mother tongue; if you regard language as a matter of rule-governed behaviour, then what he trans-fers are rules. The phenomenon is undisputed but the explanations various. Of course, not all the rules or habits of the mother tongue will result in errors. It may be that even the major part of the transfer pro-duces no errors. It is the job of contrastive analysis to determine how far this is the case.

Our assumption all along (with certain reservations made in chapter 4) is that what can be said in one language can be said in another. It is in their way of expressing the message that languages differ, in the place and nature of the choices that they impose on the speaker. When the choices are similar and made at the same level of linguistic organ-ization, then the problems of the learner are smaller; when the choices, and where they are made, are different, the learner will make errors. The problem of the learner is to discover in what way the semantic ele-ments of his message are realized in the second language. The phe-nomenon of transfer will reveal itself in the attempt to realize in the second language the semantic features of his message in the same way as in his mother tongue. Let us take an example. We may wish to indicate the degree of certainty, or confidence, we have in a certain state of affairs. This is a semantic notion. In English this is expressed by the use of adverbs such as *perhaps*, *probably*, or 'modal auxiliaries' such as *can*, *may*, *might* etc. French also uses similar means but has besides a distinction between indicative and subjunctive forms of the verb which, taken with other features of the context, express the same notions. The English learner of French has to discover what those contexts are. In other words, he has a choice between two verbal forms which does not exist in his own language. The French learner of English, on the other hand, has no such choice but he has a different problem, of discovering in what way English conveys that particular semantic distinction. The English learner will make overt errors in French, while the French learner of English will not. He will, perhaps, sometimes fail to communicate his real intentions. If we are concentrating only for the moment on *overt errors*, then we can say that these will most likely occur where the learner faces choices in the second language *in a category* in which he has no choices in his mother tongue. These choices may be syntactic, like the one already illustrated, or lexical or phonological–orthographic. I shall illustrate the last two cases.

If we consider the concept of 'knowing', we might divide it into three sorts of knowing: cognitive or factual knowledge, empirical knowledge and performative knowledge. Lexically English makes no distinction between these; French, Spanish and German do make certain distinctions. These are shown in Table 11:

Table 11

	English	*French*	*German*
Empirical	know	*connaitre*	*kennen*
Cognitive	know	*savoir*	*wissen*
Performative	know how	*savoir*	*wissen wie*

We can see clearly where the differences lie, and will not be surprised at the following errors:

Est-ce-que vous savez M. Dubois?
Do you know to cook potatoes?
Er kennt nicht was er tun soll

Table 12

L_1	L_2	Error
No choice	Obligatory choice	Yes
Obligatory choice	No choice	Perhaps

Phonological choices, unlike lexical choices, are only indirectly connected with the meaning of the message. Word-final stop consonants in English may be voiced or unvoiced, e.g. *bed* or *bat*, *bag* or *back*. The phonological system in German prescribes, as we have seen, that all stop consonants in this position are unvoiced. The German learner of English is faced with a choice. The English learner of German with none. The result is that the German learner transfers his system to English and pronounces final stop consonants in English without voice whatever their spelling. The English learner transfers something different; he pronounces the German consonants on the basis of the English pronunciation of the letters with which they are spelled. The German says *bat* for *bad*. The English learner pronounces the German word *Bad* as *bad*. These relations and their attendant probability of error are summarized in Table 12. As a consequence of these relations between the systems of the two languages, erroneous sentences often 'look like' literal translations:

Sagen Sie mir, wie es zu reparieren   Tell me how to repair it
She thought to be a don   *Pensou ser profesor*

The examples we have discussed so far have been cases when the choice in the target language was obligatory. This was fully so in the case of the phonological choice, but the choice in the syntactic and lexical examples, since they involve meaning, could be avoided. They are treated as obligatory choices because descriptions of grammar are made on the basis of formal, not semantic oppositions, e.g. all finite verbs in English have either present or past tense form, but this does not mean that reference to present or past time must be realized by choosing one or the other. However, there are some formal choices which are not obligatory – they are optional. For instance, the semantic notion 'recipient' of an action of certain sorts may be expressed in English in two ways:

I gave John the book
I gave the book to John

The same semantic content has only one expression in French:

J'ai donné le livre à Jean

The French learner has therefore an optional choice in English. It is not surprising that he selects that which superficially resembles the form of his own language. But it does not necessarily produce an error, it merely restricts his range of expression. The English learner of French on the other hand, has to learn that one of his optional choices is not available. There is a probability, then, that he will sometimes produce an erroneous sentence:

*J'ai donné Jean le livre.

We can summarize this relationship also in a table.

Table 13

L_1	L_2	Error
Optional choice	None	No
No choice	Optional choice	Yes

It may be, however, that both the languages offer choices of one sort or the other within the same category. For example, whilst English makes the selection of singular or plural compulsory, Turkish permits the plural to be marked optionally. An English learner of Turkish will produce no errors in this area but merely redundancy of marking, whilst the Turkish learner of English will occasionally omit a necessary mark of the plural:

Table 14

L_1	L_2	Error
Optional choice	Obligatory choice	Yes
Obligatory choice	Optional choice	No

Finally we have the relationships in which both languages permit optional choices or impose obligatory choices in the same category. Thus both English and Spanish require obligatory marking of plural nouns and both permit an optional choice after 'verbs of sensation' of 'gerundive' form, although they are not completely synonymous:

I saw John $\begin{cases} \text{cross the road} \\ \text{crossing the road} \end{cases}$

Vi a Juan $\begin{cases} \textit{cruzar la calle} \\ \textit{cruzando la calle} \end{cases}$

Clearly this relationship, as the former, presents no serious learning problems and hence no errors of importance. We can express this relationship as in Table 15.

Table 15

L_1	L_2	Error
Optional choice	Optional choice	No
Obligatory choice	Obligatory choice	No

It is important to realize that the relationships we have spoken about refer only to those which bear some formal surface *resemblance* to, not identity with, each other in the two languages. Where systems are semantically equivalent but not superficially so in form, the matter becomes more complicated. There is no utility in such comparisons where the realization of a semantic property is formally very different. For example, the marking of interrogation by a 'particle' as in Russian or Turkish, bears no surface formal resemblance to the word order marking of interrogation in English. In such cases there is a learning problem in both directions which may be attended by a crop of errors. For a fuller discussion of these matters see Stockwell, Bowen and Martin (1965, pp. 282–91).

Not all errors resulting from the learning process are related to the nature of the mother tongue. When a child acquiring English says: *I seed him*, we say he is producing a form on the basis of analogy: *look–looked*: *see–seed*. We can put it another way: we could say he is over-generalizing the rule for the formation of the past tense, or applying the rule to a category to which it is not applicable. So-called exceptions to a rule are simply a subset of members of a category to which some general rule does not apply but on semantic and formal grounds might be expected to. Efficient learning certainly involves discovering the most powerful rules, but the search sometimes leads to the giving of too much power to a rule. Thus it would be true to say that learning not only means discovering rules, but also the exact categories to which they apply. This is the problem of *categorization*. The learner of German who wrote: *an der Nacht* had overgeneralized on the basis of: *am Tag, am Morgen, am Abend.* The learner of English who wrote: *witnessers and supporters* had overgeneralized the rule which derives agent nominals from verbs.

Now, learners presumably have some principle for thinking that a rule applies to a certain category. In the German example it seems to have been a grouping of nouns on a semantic criterion: 'times of day'. The English example appears to be a matter of syntax. The criterion for overgeneralization may also derive from characteristics of the mother tongue; the learner may assign an item to a class on the analogy of the assignment in the mother tongue. One would guess that this was the case of the learner who wrote:

I want that you come

since the commonest synonym of *want* in many European languages takes a finite clause as an object:

Je veux que vous veniez
Ich möchte, dass du kommst
Quiero que venga

One can only conclude that overgeneralization is an inevitable process in learning but that the criteria for assignment of items to classes may derive from either the mother tongue or the second language.

An interesting class of errors involving both analogy and the characteristics of the mother tongue concerns what are often called *faux amis* or false cognates. This is the incorrect choice of a word in the second language because of its physical resemblance to a word in the mother tongue. Where two languages have a number of such corresponding items, and where these are also so similar in both meaning and grammatical function that they are synonymous in most contexts, the learner by analogy assumes that all such physically similar items in the two languages are synonymous. Hence we get such unacceptable utterances as:

Actuellement, je ne le crois pas
Il n'avait pas realiséque les autres attendaient toujours
I assisted at the class since three years

or we may meet acceptable but inappropriate utterances, such as:

Ich brachte sie nach Hause

where the context clearly showed that the learner meant that he was bringing her to *his own* home and not *to hers*.

This process of generalization may even be extended to the invention of non-existing forms by analogy. An example of this produced by a learner of Spanish is this:

El pueblo indigenoso
Una venta muy profitable

And by a French learner of English:

A majestuous melody

Even adult native speakers may produce non-existent forms by analogy, e.g.

It was with a feeling of considerable unsurety that I...

The name 'false cognates' for these items is unsatisfactory. It may be true that the items confused derive historically from the same form, but this is irrelevant to the explanation of this phenomenon. Furthermore, there may be cognates which do not give rise to errors, simply because they do not physically resemble each other sufficiently. It is the physical resemblance which leads to analogical overgeneralization.

It will be clear by now that when it comes to accounting for particular errors made by a learner there is a large area of uncertainty and speculation. In very many cases there appear to be several simultaneous processes going on: transfer, overgeneralization, faulty categorization, not to mention lapses and syntactic blends, which operate in the planning and execution of an utterance. The learner's confusion is matched by the investigator's. Here is a final example of an attempt to explain an error made by a Portuguese learner of English:

She is a woman of hers fifty and odd

There are two possible sources in Portuguese and two possible reconstructions in English; there is clearly some correspondence between the paired sentences:

Portuguese 1. *E una mulher que tenia os seus 50 e tal anos*
  *She is a woman of fifty and something years
  2. *E una mulher que tenia os seus 50 e tal anos*
  *She is a woman who would have her fifty and something years

English 1. She is a woman of 50 years odd
  2. She is a woman in her fifties

When the unacceptable sentence is translated literally back into Portuguese it is still unacceptable:

E una mulher dos seus 50 e tal anos

The only conclusion one can arrive at is that the utterance was a syntactic blend of both English and Portuguese elements. The reader can puzzle out the sources for himself.

If it proves difficult, particularly at more advanced stages of learning, to account for the error, it is not surprising that it is usually very difficult to identify redundant errors whose source lies in the nature of the teaching and teaching materials (Richards, 1971), although these, too, may be easier to spot in the early stages. In the initial stages of teaching a language a good deal of time is usually spent on establishing the referential relations of lexical items by ostensive methods, by pointing to objects in the classroom and naming them in sentences of this form:

This is a table
That is a pencil

This is then practised by asking questions:

Is this a table?
Is this a pencil?

or by requiring the learner to point to things and name them. The majority of objects so named are not unique in the classroom, and consequently the name is most often accompanied by the indefinite article. In my illustration the learner in question spoke a language in which the system of articles was different from English, and something like an indefinite article was used only when reference was made to a specific but unidentified person or thing, as in:

A man came to my house last night

particularly when occurring as subject of the sentence. There was therefore no clear equivalent in the learner's own language of a word like an article in the sentence equivalent to *That is a . . .* In free composition this learner produced a crop of forms: *he is a sitting*; *the chair is a broken*; *today is a very cold*; *he is a eat a dinner*.

Since there is nothing in the learner's mother tongue which could alone account for this persistent error, the most probable explanation was that he had drawn the conclusion that an 'indefinite article' was part of the verb phrase, an idiosyncratic and functionless suffix of the verb *is*, to be affixed in all contexts whether the verb functioned as copula, or auxiliary in passive or continuous tense constructions. This was probably the result of passive overexposure to hearing the two words together in an identical context. It might perhaps have been avoided in two ways: by stressing the contrast between

This is a book
This is the floor

or by a greater exposure to other contexts in which *is* was not followed by the indefinite article:

This book is blue
It is lying on the desk

The teacher almost certainly was unaware of what was going on in the oral work and allowed the form to become well established, through lack of correction, before it became apparent in the written work, where it could scarcely pass unnoticed.

The correction of errors

The position taken in both chapter 6 and in this is that language learning is not so much a question of acquiring a set of automatic habits, but rather a process of discovering the underlying rules, categories and systems of choice in the language by some sort of processing by the learner of the data of the language presented to him by the teacher.

Errors are evidence about the nature of the process and of the rules and categories used by the learner at a certain stage in the course.

The technique of correction is not one of simply presenting the data again and going through the same set of drills and exercises to produce the state of 'overlearning'. It requires, on the contrary, that the teacher understand the source of the errors so that he can provide the appropriate data and other information, sometimes comparative, which will resolve the learner's problems and allow him to discover the relevant rules.

We have seen that the superficial description of errors as omissions, additions, wrong selection and ordering has little explanatory value, linguistically speaking, as an account of the rules and systems the learner is using. A technique of correction which merely draws the learner's attention to the *fact* of such omissions and wrong selection is unlikely to provide him with the evidence he needs to discover the right system. Knowledge of being wrong is only a starting point. Little better is the simple provision of a correct reconstructed form of the learner's erroneous utterance. It is improbable that he will be able to draw any useful conclusions from a comparison of the two forms. More useful might be a comparison of the reconstructed form with its translation equivalent in the mother tongue of the learner.

Skill in correction seems to lie in determining in any particular instance what are the appropriate data to present to the learner and what statements, descriptive or comparative, to make about it.

If knowledge of a language is in part a question of making choices in accordance with the rules of the language, then correction implies the provision of more data in such a form that the available choices can be readily perceived by the learner. If his error has to do with the present tense, merely giving more examples of the present tense will not necessarily help him. Choices are made within the same category; consequently 'knowing' the present tense implies a correlative 'knowledge' of the past tense.

Evidence from studies in concept formation show the importance of negative instances. A concept is achieved partly through the illustration of what is *not* an example of the concept, that is, through *negative instances*. The learner, through his errors, provides plentiful examples of negative instances, but they are not controlled by the teacher. There is a strong argument in favour of the controlled use of examples of incorrect forms so long as these are correctly labelled as such. The use of 'incorrect forms' has usually been condemned on the doubtful grounds that the learner might learn them. It will be clear from the view of learning adopted here that this is most unlikely. Language learning is not parrot learning; we do not 'learn' or 'practise' examples. They are the data from which we induce the systems of the language. Skill in correction of errors lies in the direction of exploiting the incorrect forms produced by the learner in a controlled fashion.

Chapter 12
Organization: The Structure of the Syllabus

The meaning of structure

The three previous chapters have been concerned with the principles for selecting the material which goes to make up the content of a teaching syllabus. They could be looked upon as an exercise in analysis – the analysis of what the learner must know or be able to do at the end of his course. The analogy in industrial processes is with the design of the product. In language teaching this is sometimes called the learner's 'terminal behaviour'.

As in the case of an industrial process, the product is made up of a number of different components each of which may be fashioned by a different set of processes. The problem in production engineering is to specify as exactly as possible the best way, i.e. the most efficient and economical way, of organizing these processes in time and space, so that components are ready when needed for sub-assembly and ultimately for final assembly in the finished product. Engineers have developed sophisticated methods of controlling the whole operation, and which have built into them allowances for possible hitches and holdups over which they have no control. Designs of this sort are called *critical path analyses*. While it is obvious that there are big differences between planning the production of some physical object like a motor car and that of teaching a human being, there is nevertheless sufficient similarity for an analogy to be usefully drawn between the organization of a teaching syllabus and the planning of an industrial process. In an industrial process, although the separate components of the finished product are all functionally related to each other, they can, in many cases, be produced simultaneously in different places. The methods of manufacture, the raw materials and the time needed for production may be different, but it is essential that a regular supply of components be available at the right time and place, if production is not to be held up. There is a complex logic in the structure of the whole operation.

A finished syllabus is the overall plan for the learning process. It, too, must specify what components, or learning items, must be available, or learned by a certain time; what is the most efficient sequence in which they are learned; what items can be learned 'simultaneously'; what items are available from stock, i.e. already known; and the whole process is determined by considerations of how long it takes to produce or learn, a component, or item. The process is under continual scrutiny by means of stock checks, or tests and examinations. The question of the actual manufacturing procedures for each component and the best techniques of assembly are matters of the most detailed planning. In the case of language teaching this is a problem of *presentation* and is discussed in the next chapter.

On the timetable in the classroom, language teaching appears as a linear sequence of lessons, but this does not mean that language learning is a matter of learning a sequence of more or less discrete items in a simple linear structure, any more than that the manufacture of a motor car is a question of starting with a lump of metal and by a series of discrete operations on the lump gradually shaping the finished product. The fact that lessons take place one after another does not mean that learning cannot be regarded as a number of simultaneous processes.

The task of organizing a syllabus is sometimes called 'grading'. This term implies a progression, and more particularly a gentle progression. It suggests that each step in the syllabus should be small enough for any learner to cope with at one time. It carries with it the useful notion of steps, items, components, but also, unfortunately, the notion of a simple linear sequence of items or groups of items. A simple linear sequence would of course be appropriate if the items or groups of items were, linguistically speaking, in some sort of logical relation of dependence to each other, or, alternatively, were all logically independent (in which case any sequence would be equally effective). But as we have seen from our discussions of linguistic structure, neither is the case. The structure of language is a 'system of systems', or a 'network' of interrelated categories, no part of which is wholly independent or wholly dependent upon another. Indeed, there is a good deal of truth in the saying that, in language, nothing is learned completely until everything is learned. If this is so, then no simple linear sequence for a syllabus is appropriate. A logical solution to this problem might seem to be a cyclic, or spiral, structure, which required the learner to return time and again to some aspect of language structure, language process, or domain of language use, in order to discover how it relates or is integrated with some different part of the language. Language learning is not just cumulative, it is an integrative process. In its most primitive form a cyclical syllabus means no more than the regular inclusion of 'revision' sections into a linear syllabus, where a rapid run through of the material presented in the preceding sections is performed. In its more sophisticated form, it means returning to some more general area of syntax or semantics, for example, or some domain of language use, developing a deeper or more extensive or more abstract understanding of the items, processes or systems involved, relating them and integrating them with the other material already presented and learned. This notion of a cyclical syllabus does not conflict with the idea already proposed of a series of parallel or simultaneous learning tasks. It is merely an alternative way of talking about the same thing, as can be seen from the schematic diagram in Figure 42. The spiral course 're-visits' at intervals the area representing different learning items, but each item remains 'on the programme', even whilst attention is being momentarily directed elsewhere. The industrial analogy is with the carpenter constructing a cupboard, for instance, who might work for some time on the legs, then on the sides, then on the doors, then back to the legs again. In the large-scale factory production all these processes would be carried out simultaneously by different men. This analogy illustrates the distinction between language learning and large-scale production processes. The learner is like the craftsman. It is a one-man job fashioning a knowledge of a language. Each learner creates his own

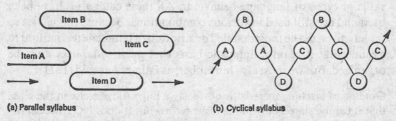

(a) Parallel syllabus   (b) Cyclical syllabus

Figure 42 Parallel and cyclical syllabuses

knowledge. There is no 'division of labour'. The syllabus is a guide or set of instructions to the learner about how he is to devote his time and what he should direct his attention and energies to.

A good description of a cyclic syllabus is to be found in Howatt and Treacher (1969):

Grading appears to be a 'linear' operation. That is, it seems to introduce points one after the other with the implication that each point is 'learnt' at the place in the course where it is introduced. This is misleading. Grading is better thought of as a 'spiral' or 'cyclical' operation where the continual reappearance of a language item in new contexts and exercises is more important than the place on the 'spiral' where the item is first introduced. The diagram (Figure 43), gives a better overall picture of the structure of the course than a description could do.

Since each stage revises the language of the preceding stage, the structure of the course during the three years will take the form shown in Figure 44 opposite.

Items and the grouping of items

The terms 'item in a syllabus' and 'ordering' have now been introduced. Clearly the crucial one, in the first instance, is that of 'item'. The time has come when we must be somewhat more precise about what we mean when we use the term 'item in a syllabus'. The three preceding chapters dealt at some length with the principles of selecting material for a syllabus, but it is probable that no very clear picture emerges from them as to the nature of 'an item'. This is not surprising since there is no simple answer to the question. Items may be categorized linguistically in either formal or functional terms; they may be categorized sociologically as speech functions, or situations of language use, or different classes of speech act, or, psychologically, as different skills or types of language behaviour. All these categories have been used and are still used in various combinations. Because linguistics so far has given us the most detailed description of language it is natural to assume that it is on a linguistic basis that most syllabuses must be organized. But we must also remember, as Palmer has said (1971):

Grading of teaching material is obviously a linguistic exercise in the sense that it can be stated only in linguistic terms. But it does NOT necessarily follow that the grading of the material can be determined wholly or even

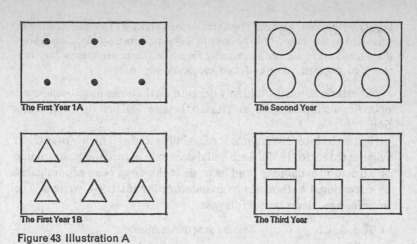

The First Year 1A   The Second Year

The First Year 1B   The Third Year

Figure 43 Illustration A

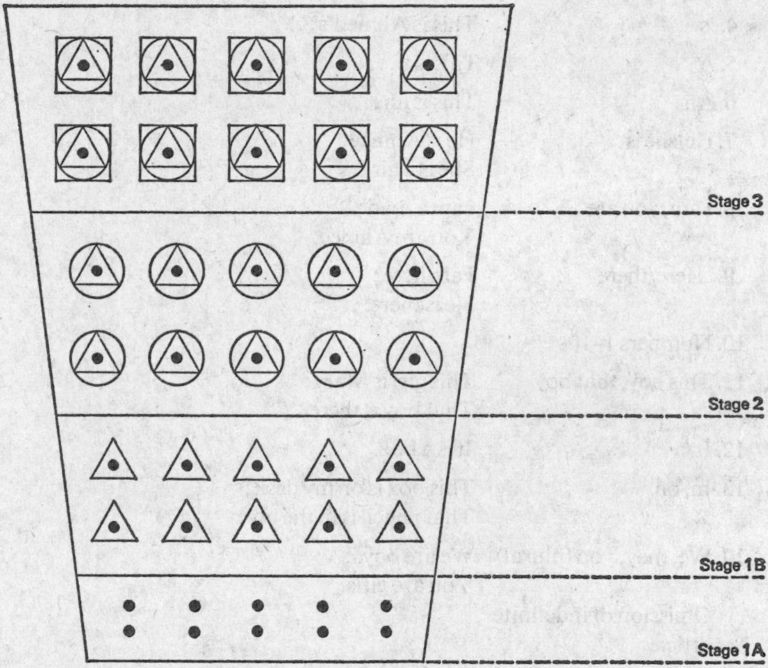

Stage 3

Stage 2

Stage 1B

Stage 1A

Figure 44 Illustration B

largely by iinguistic factors. This is an important point. The specification of what is to be taught can only be done in linguistic terms, but decisions about that specification are not necessarily linguistic. There are many other factors of educational, social and psychological kinds. (p. 264)

Nevertheless, the most highly organized syllabuses have been based upon linguistic principles, and it is to these we will first turn our attention.

First let us look at a fragment of an influential and highly organized syllabus (Mackin, 1955). Such syllabuses have earned the generic name of 'structural syllabuses' and have, as in this case, been promulgated by educational authorities as mandatory for textbook writers. The first nineteen 'items' are as follows:

1. This, that, is	This is John, that is Ahmed.
2. My, your	This is my/your ...
3. His, her	This is his/her ...
4. 's	This is Ahmed's ...
5. A	This is a ...
6. An	This is an ...
7. He/she is	He is Ahmed; She is a girl.
8. I am, you are	I am a man; You are Ahmed.
9. Here/there	I am here; He is there.
10. Numbers 1–10	
11. This boy, that boy	This girl is Mary; That boy is there.
12. It	It is a box.
13. In, on	This box is on my desk; That pencil is in the box.
14. We, they, you (plural)	We are boys; You are girls.
Omission of indefinite article	
15. These, those, they	These books are on my table.

16. And	You are a boy and she is a girl;
	Ahmed and Mary are there.
17. S v V	I am walking.
18. To, from	Ahmed is walking to/from my desk.
19. The	This is the floor;
	He is the headmaster.

(pp. 2–10)

If the learner has, in fact, learned the contents of the syllabus specified in this fragment we can express what he 'knows' of English, that is, the 'formation rules' he has learned, in the form of a phrase structure grammar of his transitional competence at this point. The following twenty-two phrase structure rules completely specify this grammar:

1. $\Sigma \rightarrow \Sigma + \text{and} + \Sigma$

2. $\Sigma \rightarrow \text{NP} + \text{VP}$

3. $\text{NP} \rightarrow \text{NP} + \text{and} + \text{NP}$

4. $\text{NP} \rightarrow \left\{ \begin{array}{l} \left. \begin{array}{l} \text{Pro(noun)} \\ \text{Det(erminer)} \end{array} \right\} + \text{Noun} \\ \text{Proper Noun} \end{array} \right\}$

5. $\text{Noun} \rightarrow \left\{ \begin{array}{l} \text{N}_{\text{sing.}} \\ \text{N}_{\text{plu.}} \end{array} \right\}$

6. $\text{Pro} \rightarrow \left\{ \begin{array}{l} \text{I} \\ \text{Pro}_{\text{sing.}} \\ \text{Pro}_{\text{plu.}} \end{array} \right\}$

7. $\text{Det} \rightarrow \left\{ \begin{array}{l} \text{Art(icle)} \\ \text{Poss(essive)} \\ \text{Dem(onstrative)} \end{array} \right\}$

8. $\text{VP} \rightarrow \left\{ \begin{array}{l} \text{Cop(ula)} + \left\{ \begin{array}{l} \text{Adverb of Place} \\ \text{NP} \\ \text{Prep(ositional) Phrase} \end{array} \right\} \\ \text{Verb} + \text{ing} + \text{(Prep Phrase)} \end{array} \right\}$

9. $\text{Pro}_{\text{sing.}} \rightarrow \{\text{he, she, it, this, that}\}$

10. $\text{Pro}_{\text{plu.}} \rightarrow \{\text{we, you, they, these, those}\}$

11. $\text{Poss} \rightarrow \{\text{my, your, his, her, proper N's}\}$

12. Dem $\rightarrow$ $\left\{ \begin{array}{l} \begin{Bmatrix} \text{this} \\ \text{that} \end{Bmatrix} / \text{\underline{\hspace{1cm}}} + N_{sing.} \\ \begin{Bmatrix} \text{these} \\ \text{those} \end{Bmatrix} / \text{\underline{\hspace{1cm}}} + N_{plu.} \end{array} \right\}$

13. Art $\rightarrow$ $\left\{ \begin{array}{l} \begin{Bmatrix} \text{A} \\ \text{the} \end{Bmatrix} / \text{\underline{\hspace{1cm}}} + N_{sing.} \\ \begin{Bmatrix} \emptyset \\ \text{the} \end{Bmatrix} / \text{\underline{\hspace{1cm}}} + N_{plu.} \end{array} \right\}$

14. Prep Phrase $\rightarrow$ Preposition + Det + N

15. Preposition $\rightarrow$ {on, in, to, from}

16. $N_{sing.} \rightarrow N + \emptyset$

17. $N_{plu.} \rightarrow N + s$

18. Cop $\rightarrow$ $\left\{ \begin{array}{l} \text{is} / \begin{Bmatrix} Pro_{sing.} \\ N_{sing.} \end{Bmatrix} + \text{\underline{\hspace{1cm}}} \\ \text{are} / \begin{Bmatrix} Pro_{plu.} \\ N_{plu.} \end{Bmatrix} + \text{\underline{\hspace{1cm}}} \\ \text{am} / \text{I} + \text{\underline{\hspace{1cm}}} \end{array} \right\}$

19. V $\rightarrow$ {walk, put . . .}

20. N $\rightarrow$ {girl, boy, pencil . . .}

21. Proper N $\rightarrow$ {Ahmed, Mary}

22. Adverb of Place $\rightarrow$ {here, there}

(Nothing has been said, of course, about the lexical element of this syllabus.) It is interesting to note that the number of rules needed to express the content of the syllabus taught so far is not very different from the number of items in the syllabus. But we can note also that the order of these items is not the same as the order of the rules. In fact, there is no simple relation between them. For example, the first item in the syllabus involves rules 1, 2, 4, 6, 7, 8, 9, 18, 21. This is why I said that it was difficult to define what is meant by 'an item in the syllabus'. Clearly learning *this* and *that* involves 'a lot of grammar' which is not apparent in the bald listing of the two words in the syllabus. Again, when one sees something as apparently simple as item no. 19 *the*, which is just 'one' word consisting of two sounds and dealt with apparently exhaustively in the grammar by rules 4, 7, 13, one might be led to think that there was nothing to the learning of the proper use of the definite article other than its position before a noun. How wrong one would be! The actual semantic function of *the* taught in this item of the syllabus, as we can see from the examples, is that often called 'unique reference', i.e. we use *the* to signal the fact that we are referring to an object of which there is only one of its class in the immediate situation of speech: *the floor*; *the ceiling*; *the sun*; *the moon*; *the postman*; *the headmaster*; etc. This is only one of many functions of 'the definite article'. A typical cyclic syllabus, as we have said, would return time and again to the definite article in order to teach another of its functions.

Similarly we could regard item 1 as teaching the 'simple present' tense. *This is John*. But this tense has quite a range of meanings, some of which are introduced in this syllabus, spread over the whole length of the course in the following way:

Item	1. Present state	This is John
	8. Habitual action	I come to school every day
	104. 'Timeless' truths	Cows give milk
	118. Verbs of perception	This mango looks good
	194. Timeless conditional sentences	I eat if I'm hungry
	222. Future reference	When I go to Dacca, I shall see my father

These examples merely illustrate the general point that a phrase-structure description of the sort just given says nothing about the meanings of the categories it deals with, or their appropriate use in speech. It provides only a set of rules for generating well-formed surface structures. This suggests that we might look to semantic functions as a criterion for establishing items. Thus, for example, it is quite usual to find 'conditional sentences' grouped together as a unit in a syllabus. Now, the only formal similarity in 'conditional sentences' is that they contain a conditional clause marked by such conjunctions as *if*, *unless*, *provided that*. A grouping of this sort is evidently a functional grouping, since conditional clauses all perform a similar semantic function, that of stating a condition under which some other proposition is true. The learning task in the case of conditional sentences is to discover the rules which govern the relation of the tenses in the main and subordinate clause, the so-called 'sequence of tenses' and the meanings expressed by these sequences: factual, hypothetical and counter-factual conditions, e.g.

If he comes, I shall tell him so
If he came, I should tell him so
If he had come, I should have told him so

Other sequences of tenses in conditional sentences are so unusual that they do not normally figure in syllabuses at all.

Nevertheless, sometimes syllabus designers have been misled by superficial formal similarities into including sentences of the following type along with true conditionals:

If you like swimming, there's a fine beach down the road

Clearly the presence of the beach is not conditional upon the hearer's love of swimming!

This example illustrates the general problem of deciding whether to include an item in a grouping on formal or functional grounds. To take another simple example: are we to include the following structure on formal grounds with imperative sentences expressing commands:

Play with that and you'll break it

or with conditional sentences on semantic grounds:

If you play with that, you'll break it

A typical example of this dilemma is that of the 'modal' verbs such as *can, may, will, must,* etc. Now, all these items have some syntactic formal similarity. For example, they are restricted in their tense and aspect forms, e.g. **he has could, *he is maying*; they do not add an *–s* in the third person **he cans, *he mays*; and they form their negatives as other auxiliaries, without the aid of *do*, e.g. *he cannot, he may not,*I don't can, *he didn't will*. But whilst they are syntactically and morphologically similar, each one is not a single semantic unit. For instance, *can* has the meanings of possibility, permission, physical or mental ability, or simply present time.

It can be cold in August
You can go now
She can count to a hundred
I can hear him now

The other modal auxiliaries show a similar range of meanings. Notice that we can generally express these same modal meanings in other ways by the use of 'modal' adverbs or adjectives, for example:

It's possible for it to be cold in August
You have my permission to go now
She is able to count to a hundred now
I hear him now

The problem which faces us in syllabus organization is whether to take the formal criteria as dominant, and group modal verbs together, leaving alternative ways of expressing the same ideas to some other part of the syllabus, or to base our grouping on semantic criteria, bringing all alternative ways of expressing necessity, obligation, possibility and probability, etc. together into separate single units. In other words, are we going to regard 'modal verbs', or alternatively 'the expression of obligation', as a syllabus item? For a discussion of this problem, see Wilkins (1972).

There is no simple answer to this problem. The more that investigation into linguistic structures takes account of semantic considerations, the more evident it becomes that the relationship between meaning and surface forms such as 'sentence structures', modal verbs, articles and even adjectives and adverbs, is a complex and indirect one. At a time when less attention was paid by linguistics to the whole problem of meaning, and language learning was thought of as a matter of acquiring the ability to produce automatically 'sentence patterns', it was perhaps logical to group materials in a syllabus on the basis of superficial formal criteria, but with the increasing emphasis on language learning as training the learner in communication, the relevance of semantic criteria in organizing the linguistic material increases too. Where, in structural syllabuses, the materials were, in part, grouped in formal categories – transitivity, double object structures, tense, modal auxiliaries, relative clauses, etc. – we are now coming to a point where we may wish to classify the linguistic material in terms of such more abstract semantic categories as time, anaphora, deixis, modality, possession, quantification, aspect, causation, etc.

Let us remind ourselves at this point that the object of linguistic grouping is to teach those things together which have some sort of relation to each other, either semantic or syntactic, because this enables the learner to discover underlying regularities, or, as we called them in chapter 8, 'significant generalizations'. One important set of associations in language which we identified in the same chapter were sentences which bore a meaning relation to each other, such as active–passive, interrogative–declarative, positive–negative. These relations, which we have called 'transformational', have always been recognized as learning items in syllabuses, and 'rules' for converting one 'sentence pattern' into another have regularly been practised. We could call this sort of item a 'syntactic process' item. In general terms, what is being learned is a relationship between sentences. But the items traditionally included far from exhaust the list of possible processes. Negative and positive forms of the 'same' sentence obviously differ in meaning, but what about those sets of sentences which have the same cognitive meaning and which we call paraphrases, e.g. active and passive sentences. There are a large number of syntactic processes whose prime function is to organize the surface structure of sentences so that they fit appropriately into the contexts of other sentences, which the learner will have to learn if he is going to be able to string sentences into an acceptable discourse. We called this function the 'textual' function in chapter 2:

There is a foglight on my car
My car has a foglight on it
I have a foglight on my car
What I have on my car is a foglight
It's a foglight that I have on my car

Various syntactic processes of this sort have been identified and named, e.g. *topicalization*, *thematization*, *focusing*, *clefting*, *extraposition*. They all have to do with expressing the same meaning in different ways appropriate to the context. They are all processes applied to one underlying sentence structure.

Another set of syntactic processes is involved in embedding one sentence in another. I have in mind such examples as *nominalization*, i.e. the process of deriving noun phrases or clauses from underlying sentences:

Arthur arrived late
Arthur arriving late is not to be risked
Arthur's arriving late disturbed them all

For Arthur to arrive late would be a disaster
Arthur's late arrival caused a commotion
The lateness of Arthur's arrival didn't worry us

or *relativization,* the process of embedding a sentence in a noun phrase:

Farmers grow tobacco.
Farmers *who grow tobacco* ...
Farmers *growing tobacco* ...
Tobacco-growing farmers ...
Farmer-grown tobacco ...

The general trend of what I have been saying suggests that the popular notion of a syllabus 'item' as a 'structure', or 'sentence pattern' – that is, one of a finite set of grammatically acceptable strings of surface grammatical categories (see the discussion of linear grammars in chapter 8) – is far too restricted and lacks the element of significant generalization which facilitates learning. Recent developments in syntactic research referred to earlier will certainly progressively transform what we think of as syllabus items and how to group them. We are moving from the view of what is learned as a static set of patterns towards the notion of a set of dynamic processes by which the patterns of surface structure are produced. Perhaps we shall soon reach the point where linguistic syllabuses are expressed as a list of finely differentiated verb classes based upon their potentiality of association with nominals in different sets of relationships – objective, agentive, locative, etc. (Anderson, 1971). But this is looking some way into the future. When this point has been reached, the distinction I have been making between formal and functional criteria for selecting syllabus items will have virtually disappeared.

Sequencing: linguistic-based logic

So far I have discussed the various interpretations of the term 'item in a syllabus'. We have seen that the systematic interconnectedness of language makes it unrealistic to think of any item as teachable or learnable in isolation, and that we should do better to consider an item in a more general or abstract way, i.e. as a syntactic process, or as some secondary grammatical category, such as tense or number. Simply to call all the items in a syllabus 'structures' is unhelpful and ultimately arbitrary. However we define an 'item' or a 'grouping of items', we still have the problem of ordering them, and as I mentioned in the first section, ordering, if it is not to be purely random, must be based upon some logical criteria. The ideal syllabus would be one in which the sequencing of items follows that of a system of deductive logic, in which each item taught logically derives from and presupposes the learning of some previous items. This is the principle which lies behind programmed instruction. It may be applicable to such subjects as mathematics and physics; whether it is applicable to language teaching is what we are concerned with here. The creation of such a logical syllabus presupposes the availability of a systematic and coherent description of the knowledge to be acquired. This is a necessary but not a sufficient condition. Let us remember that the descriptions of the structure of language are 'characterizations' of what the speaker of the language 'knows' about this language. They make no claim to psychological reality. We must be careful not to confuse a description of the product with that of the process. What, therefore, could be shown to be a logical sequence of items in terms of some linguistic description might not be logical in psychological terms. But learning is a psychological process. It was for this reason that I proposed the notion of the 'natural syllabus' or 'built-in syllabus' in chapter 11, the discovery of which I suggested was one of the objectives of error analysis. The fact is that at the present time we simply do not know to what extent linguistic categories have psychological reality, and therefore to what extent what might be a logical linguistic sequencing of items in a syllabus is psychologically logical, and therefore the optimum ordering from a learning point of view. Meanwhile, therefore, we may have to rely on whatever logic we can derive from linguistic descriptions. This is what Ferguson (1966) has to say on this matter:

Language teachers have long felt that the grading of material in terms of syntactic complexity is important in achieving maximum effectiveness in language teaching, and the current interest in programmed language learning is a new example of the traditional pedagogic concern with the question of what presupposes what in the language material to be learned. However, most grading of structures even when done by competent and experienced experts, has been based on impressionistic judgements and vaguely conceived theoretical principles or none at all. (p. 51)

Descriptions of language do give us some sort of logical account of the code or codes to be learned, that is, a characterization of the 'formation rules' of the language. But we are concerned with more than this in language teaching; we are concerned with performance ability. Linguistic description at the present time tells us about only part of what we need to know. Descriptive linguistic statements, if they are generative, describe the language in a set of partially ordered statements or 'rules' – phrase structure rules, transformation rules, phonological rules. There is a necessary order to these rules if they are not to generate unacceptable sentences. But, we may ask, can this logic be adopted in the structure of a syllabus? The answer must be: no. The data which we put before the learner are samples of performance, i.e. fully fashioned examples of utterances, the output or result of an application of the rules of the language. We cannot present as language data selected 'untransformed' basic strings any more than we can present 'redness' to a child learning the colours. Both are abstractions. We can only present him with *examples* of red objects, from which he will eventually 'abstract' the concept of redness. Any utterances we present to the learner to exemplify some particular syllabus item or process is a concrete, fully-formed bit of language. It is true that proposals have been made to base a syllabus on the teaching of each rule of the syntax as a 'syllabus item', but such proposals are based upon a fundamental misconception of the status of syntactic rules. It is true that we can, if we adopt a deductive teaching methodology, use the notion of 'rule' to teach an item in the syllabus, but this is a matter of *how* we present the item, rather than a principle for the organization of the syllabus. It will be discussed in its proper place in the next chapter. Saporta (1966) puts this succinctly:

All such discussions seem to be based on the assumption that somehow the order of presentation (in the grammar) determines the order of application, an assumption which is demonstrably false, since no one wishes to claim that one cannot learn to use the brake on a car before learning to use the starter. (p. 89)

Nevertheless, there may be some indications for sequencing the material of the syllabus from a study of the syntactic rules, and I have already suggested that there are some general types of syntactic processes, such as nominalization, relativization or thematization, which could be regarded as items in a syllabus, just as passivization, interrogativization and negation have long been so regarded. Linguistically speaking all these involve performing certain operations on the same deep structure from which superficially simple sentences derive. What is simple about simple sentences is, then, that they have undergone 'less' transformation; that they are, in a sense, 'closer' to the underlying structure. It has been argued that one should first learn such simple sentences. But we must remember that 'simplicity' in this sense is an artefact of the linguistic description. To use the notion of simplicity as a criterion for syllabus structure we should have to show that these 'simple' sentences were also psycholinguistically simpler to learn, remember, produce or interpret. This is what Miller and McKean (1964), and others since, have attempted to show. The results have been equivocal. 'Linguistic' complexity and 'psychological' complexity are evidently not the same thing, although there may be some connection between them (cf. the discussion of *difference* and *difficulty* in chapter 10).

The most usual claim for a linguistic logic in sequencing is made at the level of morphology. The argument goes like this: if, for example, the verbs *to have* and *to be* are used as auxiliaries in the formation of the perfect or progressive aspect of the verbal phrase then logically we must present and teach these verbs before introducing the formation of these aspects. This seems a good argument until we investigate what we mean by 'teaching' the verbs *to be* and *to have*. Learning any verb involves not only discovering the relations it enters into with nominals, whether it is transitive or copulative, for example, but also learning the morphological systems whereby tense, aspect, number and person are realized, together with their associated meanings: time, duration, frequency, etc. Of course one could resort to the old fashioned 'parroting' of conjugations: *I am*, *you are*, *he is*, etc. But this memorizing of meaningless forms can scarcely be dignified by the name of 'learning the verb *to be*'. The learning of something must surely involve the ability to use it acceptably, i.e. discover its functions. The function of the auxiliary *to be* in the progressive aspect, or passive voice, is different from that of the verb *to be* in copulative sentences (at least in most modern grammatical descriptions). To say that in teaching copulative sentences one is teaching the verb *to be* so that it can be available for later use as an auxiliary is to make a categorical error. Even if this were not the case, there would still be no cogent linguistic reason why we should not reverse the process and introduce the *forms* of the auxiliary *to be* in progressive verbal phrases as a preparation for their use as a copula in copulative sentences. The arguments in favour of the first course would seem to derive from some notions of the relative difficulty of learning the two different patterns of surface structure. But in fact it is not at all obvious why such sentences as *he is sleeping* or *they are talking* are more difficult to learn than *he is a teacher* or *they are clever*.

When one examines the arguments for a logical sequencing of grammatical forms in a syllabus, they usually boil down to some vague notion of relative ease or difficulty, without foundation in linguistic theory or description. This is not, of course, to deny that some items in the syllabus are not more difficult than others for speakers of certain other languages, as we saw in chapter 10. But relative difficulty may also be a result of the structure of the syllabus itself. We necessarily present new items in a matrix of known material, that is, we use known syntactic rules and lexical material as the context in which new items are introduced. The difficulty of the new item may depend upon the particular material which forms this matrix. But the matrix available is itself a product of the syllabus. Difficulty, therefore, is to some extent an artefact of the structure of the syllabus. Changing the structure of the syllabus may have the desired result of making certain items less difficult, but at the same time making others more difficult than they had been before. All linguistic syllabuses are therefore to some degree a compromise, where difficulty at one point is traded off against ease at another.

The phonological syllabus

All the discussion so far has concentrated on the problem of organizing the syntactic and lexical material of the syllabus, but the semantic and syntactic systems of the language are realized concretely in sound or in writing. Since we must teach these systems through actual examples of language – that is, utterances – the learner must be able to 'process' the data phonologically in order to be able to 'get at' the grammar and vocabulary. Logically, then, we should not even begin to teach the grammar or vocabulary of the language until the means to interpret and realize it in sound or writing, i.e. the phonological system, are available to the learner. Ought we then to teach the sound, rhythm and intonation systems of the language in their entirety before embarking on the grammar? To do this would be to attempt to follow the order in which the discovery of the systems of an unknown language proceeds in the hands of a linguist. As we saw, the phonological units of a language – phones, phonemes, phonological words and phrases – do not have cognitive meanings associated with them (though this is not true of the intonation system of all languages). Consequently it would seem that the teaching of the sound system could be undertaken in more or less total separation from the teaching of the rest of the system of the language. And indeed people can apparently do this up to a point. We are probably all familiar with the mimics on the music hall stage who can produce 'speeches' in 'foreign languages' which *sound* most convincing, but which are pure gobbledegook. Attempts have, in fact, been made in language teaching from time to time to teach the sound system before going on to grammar and vocabulary. Morton (1965), for example, experimented with a 'programmed' syllabus in which the first 300 hours were in effect devoted just to learning pronunciation and the phonological system (although he described what he was teaching as 'acoustic grammar'). Such attempts have failed, and for two reasons. Firstly, and most seriously, it is disastrous from a motivational point of view. As we saw in chapter 5, the ability to produce the phones of a language is a matter of motor-perceptual skill appropriately taught, perhaps by drill and repetition, certainly requiring fairly prolonged practice. If some given level of performance is to be achieved, it is going to take a fair amount of time. Morton evidently estimated 300 hours. For most school pupils, that is well over a year's work. How many learners are going to be prepared to spend so long mouthing what, to them at least, must remain meaningless noises? The object of language learning is to be able to communicate. The learner rightly expects to be able to use what he has learned for that purpose from the very beginning, however limited its range. As Newmark (1964) said, 'to teach the sound systems of the language before the grammar and the vocabulary is not in good agreement with our common sense feeling that it is more important to be able to speak a language fluently and say a lot of things in it than to have a marvellous pronunciation but not know what to say.' (p. 7)

Secondly, while it may be true up to a point that the linguist's 'discovery procedures' in describing totally unknown languages necessarily impose on him the need to start his work at the phonetic level, when we teach a language we start with a description ready made. The learner is not doing linguistic fieldwork. Furthermore, as we saw in chapter 8, modern linguistic descriptions do not in fact, all regard the phonological systems of the language as 'autonomous', but rather as dependent on, or at least related to, the syntactic and lexical systems. There is, therefore, not even a clearcut linguistic justification for teaching the phonological systems before, or independently of, the syntax. Both linguistic and pedagogical reasons, therefore, indicate that grammar, vocabulary and pronunciation teaching should proceed *side* by *side*. In other words, we need a *parallel* syllabus for the teaching of pronunciation. It is a curious thing that while simultaneous learning at the grammatical, lexical and phonological levels has always been understood and accepted by teachers, the notion of parallel learning of items *within* any one of these levels seems to be so difficult to accept.

Let us now turn to the problem of criteria for organizing such a phonological syllabus. We can start by reminding ourselves of the broad outlines of what the learner has to learn. He must ultimately be able to produce and identify the phones of the language. He must acquire the rhythmical scheme of the language – whether stress-timed or syllable-timed. He must discover over what stretches of language the pitch patterns extend, and how these are related to lexical or syntactic units, i.e. whether the language is a 'tone language' or not. And lastly he must learn how speech sounds are grouped into phonemes and the hierarchical structure of these into syllables, words, phrases, or alternatively in terms of the rules for the phonetic realization of the 'inner' phonological structure of the language.

The question we have to ask is this: is there any priority amongst these various learning tasks? Can we leave the learning of rhythm and intonation until the phonetic systems of the language and their realization in speech sounds have been acquired? It would be convenient if we could divide the problem of the learning of pronunciation into two main tasks: the acquisition of the motor-perceptual skills, that is, the articulatory problem, on the one hand, and the rule-learning problems on the other. The apparent logic would be to teach *all* the phones of the language before passing on to the rules for structuring them. This would be a logic derived from linguistic theory. Unfortunately, once again, we are up against the problem of the psychological status of linguistic categories. Because some linguists choose to describe the phonological component of language in a particular way, e.g. starting with speech sounds and then classifying them on a functional basis into phonemes, and then stating rules for the sequence of phonemes and so on, it does not mean that this is the psychologically logical way to teach pronunciation. Indeed, the fact that a Spanish speaker has difficulty in distinguishing between the pronunciation of *ship* and *sheep* in English is not just a question of his ignorance of the phonological rules of English, or, on the other hand, purely an articulatory problem of making the respective vowel sounds. As we saw, he probably possesses both in his mother-tongue repertory. Similarly the problem the German speaker has in pronouncing word-final voiced consonants in English is not purely an articulatory one; he can pronounce them perfectly well in other positions. Nor is it purely an ignorance of the rules. In other words, it seems legitimate to regard phonological structures and articulatory processes essentially as habits. To *tell* the German learner that he should pronounce his final stop consonants with voice in English will not immediately produce the desired result. He has to overcome a mother-tongue habit of never doing so. Certainly he has to discover the rule, but then he has to translate it into a new articulatory habit. The same goes for the learning of stress, rhythm and intonation patterns.

The general trend, therefore, of what I have said will lead one to the conclusion that there is, at least at present, no clear evidence of an inherent logic of a psycholinguistic kind which dictates a particular structure for a phonological syllabus. Certainly the learning of pronunciation requires controlled practice and plenty of it, particularly when there are speech sounds in the target language which are not available in the repertoire of the learner's mother tongue. All we can say is that all the phonological features I have listed – speech sounds, rhythm, stress and pitch patterns – require attention from the beginning. None can be left 'until later'. Again we are led to the conclusion that in the organization of a syllabus the question of when something should be taught is less important than for how long it should be taught or by when it should be known.

The lexical syllabus

I started off the discussion of the meaning of 'an item in a syllabus' with reference to syntax, the 'core' of a language as it has been called. Unless we achieve some mastery over the rules of syntax, we cannot claim to have any useful knowledge of a language, whereas most of us go through life without achieving anything like a native-like control over the 'secondary articulation' – the pronunciation of a second language. This lack of control does not usually seriously impair our ability to use the language for communication, it merely means that we are readily recognized for what we are – foreigners. This is because the units of the sound system of a language are not meaningful in themselves. The sound system is the means whereby the meaning-bearing categories and relations of the language – the grammatical and lexical elements – achieve physical realization in speech.

Since, however, we must teach language largely through actual samples of performance, that is, 'concrete' examples of language, the teaching of the grammar can no more proceed without a use of the phonological element of language than without a lexical element. It is true that in certain teaching procedures we may wish to explain a rule of grammar by referring to grammatical classes and functions without realizing them lexically or phonologically, e.g. we may speak about subject–verb–object or article–adjective–noun constructions, but we never present a dialogue in this form:

A: Interrogative adverb of time – auxiliary verb – pronoun – verb – adverb of place?
B: Adverb of time
A: Interjection!

Rather we exemplify the grammatical categories with lexical items and interpret the whole in phonological (or orthographic) form, thus:

A: When did you get here?
B: Yesterday
A: Fancy that!

In order to present and exemplify grammatical categories and processes we have to use lexical words. Does this mean that the teaching of vocabulary is logically dependent upon the teaching of grammar? Not at all. We could equally claim that the contrary was the case. We could decide what lexical material we wanted to present and then find a grammatical framework within which to present it. There is no logical dependency either way between the lexico-semantic system and the syntax. Indeed, in the most recent linguistic models the two interpenetrate to such an extent that the distinction between them is beginning to lose its significance.

This means that decisions made about the teaching of syntactic items necessarily involve decisions about the teaching of vocabulary, or, conversely, decisions about the teaching of vocabulary necessarily imply some decisions about grammar.

This provides us with another concept of grouping, which we could call lexico-semantic. An example of this is the co-occurrence of adverbs of past time, *yesterday, last week, three years ago*, etc., with past tense verbs; or co-occurrence of verbs of speaking and believing, *say, tell, cry, believe, hope, expect*, etc. with nominalized sentences (noun clauses) of different types. Nevertheless, lexical words are not all different from each other in their syntactic properties. It would be difficult to show that *cabbage, cauliflower* and *lettuce* or *lion, tiger* and *elephant* are examples of different noun classes, that is, that they each function syntactically in a different way. It is, of course, true that many vocabulary words are unique in their syntactic properties and therefore require to be taught in conjunction with some particular rule or set of rules in grammar. This would be true, for example, of the words *exact, own* and *very* in English. These are all called 'adjectives' in the dictionary, but they are rather peculiar ones. We can talk about *the exact time* being 3 p.m., but we can't say **the time was exact*, or **an exact time*. Similarly, *my own mother* but not **an own mother, *my mother was own*, or *the very moment* but not **a very moment, *the moment was very*. The more that investigation into syntax proceeds the more such single-word grammatical classes are found. Nevertheless, the structure of the lexical element in language is still sufficiently undetermined by syntactic constraints for us to consider the problem of the teaching of vocabulary as a separate operation. In chapter 5 a brief outline of the nature of the 'network of relations' which bind the vocabulary of a language into a structure was given. This showed that it was possible to isolate 'sub-fields' within the lexical structure of a language. Such groupings of lexical items bearing more or less close semantic relations to each other are called 'semantic fields'. Semantic fields provide 'natural' groupings of the vocabulary which could serve as 'items in a syllabus'. An example of such a 'semantic field' was often found in traditional textbooks 'Parts of the body'. Of course, this field includes much more than just the nominal elements, like *hand, neck, foot*, etc. It also includes many lexical words which would not be selected for teaching anyway, because they are not of importance to the learner for one reason or another. It would certainly include verbal items, such as *kick, grasp, slap, nod*, and more peripherally, *push, stretch, turn*. Semantic fields are not so much linguistically 'well-defined' areas of the vocabulary, as sets of items which are selected on non-linguistic criteria because they have to do with some sort of cultural social or scientific topic or *centre of interest* (Gougenheim, Michéa, Rivenc and Sauvageot, 1956). The grouping of vocabulary, and consequently to some extent the teaching of syntax, may be organized on the basis of some criteria of a non-linguistic sort. And to such criteria I shall now turn.

A functional syllabus

We teach language so that the learner may participate in a foreign society in certain roles and certain situations. This notion was discussed in chapter 9 at some length in connection with the selection of material for the syllabus. It provides us also with a set of criteria for grouping items in the syllabus and perhaps for sequencing such groups of items. We also saw in the same chapter that whoever our learners were and whatever their objectives in learning a second language were there was a core of linguistic material which was common to all learners. For groups of learners who have a fairly well-defined aim, the syllabus consists of this core plus a body of material which, while marginal or irrelevant for some other group of learners having different aims, is central to the needs of this particular group. In our discussion of the needs of the 'general purpose' learner, who represents, after all, the great majority of learners in schools, this distinction between 'core' and marginal elements was more clearly defined. This provides us with a fairly clear criterion for sequencing (which we can call utility): core items first and the more marginal ones later. But it doesn't give us any clear principles for organizing the material of the core.

Since the greater part of the language data presented must be samples of utterances – performance data – and since utterances occur in *situations* and have some *function*, e.g. *directive* (see chapter 2), perhaps these notions can provide us with a *learner-related set of criteria* for organizing the syllabus. The learner, as we have seen, wishes to use what he has learned for communicative purposes as soon as possible – most learners are not going to tolerate doing a lot of work which only has a pay-off after a considerable time. Thus, we have a criterion of *surrender-value* for the organizing of syllabus material. This means teaching those speech functions first which are the most useful to the learner, most central to his needs. Such an approach was used by the Nuffield Foundation Language Teaching Materials Project for their German course (Peck, 1971). For instance, it is clearly more useful to the great majority of learners to be able to *ask questions* than *to make bets*, to *signal agreement* than to *utter threats*. Related to the criteria of useful functions is that of *situations*. Some learners might wish to ask questions within an informal situation like the family environment rather than in a public situation like the town hall or the police station. For others the situation could be reversed; for example, for those learners who wish to use their language for tourist purposes. These proposals give rise to syllabuses which have been called *functional* or *situational*, in which the criteria for grouping the material are derived from the natural interests and objectives of the learner, and typically take the form of a series of 'centres of interest' or 'topics' such as: the house, the family, the school, the post office, the street, etc. These situations are culturally, socially or behaviourally coherent and obviously connected with the notion of semantic fields which was discussed in the last section. An example of such a syllabus design is the projected scheme for the Edinburgh English Course (Howatt and Treacher, 1969). I quote from the guide to the course:

The content of the course is woven round four major themes which are interpreted in different ways, depending on the age and level of the pupils at any particular time. These themes represent a division of the world into four basic areas of activity and interest:

Theme 1. Personal relationships within the family and among friends.

Theme 2. Social relationships, and activities of the community.

Theme 3. Cultural life – habits, customs, traditions, etc.

Theme 4. The natural environment, science, technology, etc.

All four themes are involved in the content structure of the course during all three years, but there is a shift of emphasis from Theme 1 to Themes 2 and 3 from the end of the first year. Theme 4 always plays a major part, though in different ways at different times. Thus, during the three years of the course, the overall pattern of content would be represented in the following diagram:

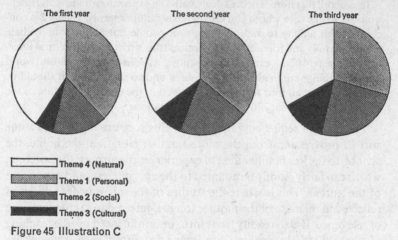

Figure 45 Illustration C

The themes may be interpreted in different ways to produce topics appropriate to particular age groups and also to suggest the language that could be used in those topics. For example, one aspect of Theme 1 is the expression of personal opinions on likes and dislikes. In the first year the language would be restricted to such statements as 'I like collecting stamps' or 'I don't like homework'. In the second year the same idea may be expressed a little more fully: 'I like collecting stamps because I'm interested in foreign countries'. By the third year the expression of opinion can become rather more complex: 'I used to collect stamps from every country in the world but now I want to make a special collection of American stamps. They're the most interesting'. Theme 2 in the first year is concerned with the simple set phrases of shopping, meeting people, and so on. In the second year the theme can widen out further into the community and bring in, for example, people's jobs, entertainments etc. and in the third year, social problems can be discussed in a fairly simple way. The third theme concerns such first-year topics as Christmas or London, and in the second and third years will deal with the basic points of interest about Britain, the United States and other English-speaking countries. Theme 4 in the first year raises such basic questions as time, counting, the weather, the calendar, animals and the colours. In the second year this language can be reapplied and developed to discuss simple activities such as making models or cooking and the main characteristics of things such as cars, ships or space rockets while, in the third year, the same language can be used again and further extended to describe, for example, car manufacturing, dock activities or space research.

In general, therefore, Theme 1 deals with the expression of ideas and intentions to people with whom you are on fairly familiar terms. Theme 2 is concerned with talking to and talking about people outside your immediate circle of family and friends. Theme 3 raises topics of a general cultural interest and Theme 4 involves all the interesting questions about the natural world and how things are made, how they work and so on. Finally, it should be underlined that all four themes are involved in the content structure of the course all the time, but with varying interpretations.

The logic of sequencing material of this sort usually follows some sort of progression from the more familiar situation, the home, the school, to the less familiar area of experience, the airport, the hotel etc. which can fairly readily be adapted to the age, interests and experience of the learner. This is where the studies of the interests of children as reflected in their use of the mother tongue, referred to in chapter 9, are of relevance. It also readily leads into, or is influenced by, the teaching of what are strictly speaking non-linguistic matters, such as the culture and way of life of the native speakers of the target language, or the study of the literature in the second language. These are traditionally part of what is called language teaching and to some extent used to be the *reason* for studying a language. They have, of course, important educational value, and the study of a language necessarily involves learning something about the society whose language it is and it's ways of seeing the world, as we saw in the discussion of cultural overlap in chapter 4. But it does not follow that these studies necessarily involve a study of the language, and they can indeed be (but rarely are) carried on without it. This even goes for the study of foreign literatures, in the earlier stages at least. For the more advanced study of literature, of course, where stylistic matters play an increasing part, a very advanced knowledge of the language is necessary – but is probably achieved by only a small number of learners.

A skills-based syllabus

Language performance is a psychological process. Learning a language is also a psychological process. Both matters were discussed in chapter 6. We can describe the 'terminal behaviour' aimed at by the syllabus in linguistic or sociolinguistic terms, i.e. 'rules' learned or 'function of language' mastered; but we can also attempt to describe it in 'behavioural' terms; the ability to understand or to produce language, or more specifically to read or write, take notes, translate, take dictation, interpret, relay messages, etc. – that is, in terms of what are often called language skills. But the reader will recall that these so-called skills were only the epiphenomena, or outward manifestation of a whole set of little understood psycholinguistic processes which go on when we perform receptively or expressively. They were, we concluded with Carroll, better called 'linguistic activities'. Can we then isolate out one or another of the specific psycholinguistic processes discussed in chapter 6 for teaching in isolation: identification, matching, recognition, ideation, and so on? A moment's thought will show that these processes do not occur in isolation but in some sort of sequence or coordination, when we perform linguistically, the one exception being what we called the motor-perceptual skills. These as we saw, are not unique to language behaviour and have in any case already been dealt with in our discussion of the phonological syllabus. Is it possible that we can at least teach productive and receptive activity separately? After all, many learners aim only at achieving receptive ability, e.g. reading. The answer again must be that even 'purely receptive activity' shares many common processes with productive activity. It does not follow, by any means, that in order to teach comprehension we must, or need to, confine ourselves to the practice of that activity. It may well be that the efficient learning of reading may also involve writing or speaking. One must not fall into an all too common confusion of ends and means. The end, for example, may be the ability to speak; this does not rule out receptive activity or exercise as a means to that end. Indeed, obviously some exposure to language is necessary in order to discover its rules, and consequently some learning of receptive skills must logically precede productive activity. We must learn something of reading before we learn to write, something of comprehension before we learn to speak.

But already we have said enough to make it clear that we are not any longer discussing anything that we could call in the narrow sense the structure of the syllabus. What we are talking about is learning and teaching strategies and these belong more appropriately in the next chapter.

Syllabus design – an art

In chapter 7 I warned that as one moved down the scale of application, more and more theoretical principles became involved in making decisions or solving problems. This chapter will have shown that the designing of syllabuses involves many different considerations, linguistic, pedagogic, sociolinguistic, psychological. We are clearly not yet able to give any firm answers about how to design a syllabus. One thing is certain: there is no such thing as a perfect, ideal or logical syllabus. The number of variables which are involved, particularly those relating to the learners for whom the syllabus is designed, are too numerous. Ideally, each learner requires a 'personalized' syllabus of his own. But we teach groups, not individuals. Any syllabus is bound, therefore, to be something of a compromise.

What we finish up with is some sort of integrated but parallel set of syllabuses: syntactic, phonological, cultural and functional and within each of these a parallel set of learning tasks. This is, in effect, only an admission that we do not possess any 'integrated' comprehensive theory of language, incorporating what are at present separate, structural, sociological and psychological accounts of language. It also reflects what is in fact the way that teachers look upon the syllabus when they walk into the classroom and say: 'today we will have a reading lesson' or 'a grammar lesson' or a 'pronunciation lesson', or 'today we will imagine we are in the Post Office'.

Chapter 13
Presentation: Pedagogic Grammars

Scholarly and pedagogic descriptions

When we talk to someone we adapt our way of speaking to our hearer. We also select what we are prepared to talk about in the light of who our audience is. The atomic physicist does not talk to his wife about atomic physics in quite the same way as he does to his colleagues, and unless his wife happens to be a physicist also he may be wise not to talk to her about it at all. The way we talk about something is obviously dependent upon the knowledge of the subject our hearer already possesses. We may judge that he possesses sufficient knowledge of a general sort to warrant our embarking on the subject, in which case we shall attempt to use some sort of everyday terminology, with a lot of explanation and qualification, and hope to get our message across to him. This is the task which the scientific journalist faces when trying to 'popularize' some recent discovery in science. If we judge our hearer simply does not have this general basic knowledge we don't even broach the subject. On the other hand, if we know our audience to be specialists we freely use what the layman calls our 'jargon', and in consequence get our meaning across more surely and economically.

The way the linguist, applied linguist or teacher describes the grammar of a language is determined by his audience. All are describing the same 'object' but the reasons they have for doing so are rather different. It is not only that their different audiences come with greatly varying knowledge of the subject, but that the result they are trying to achieve is different. We can approach the same problems from the point of view of the reader or 'consumer'. What does he read a description of the language for? There are a number of different sorts of consumers of grammars: linguists, students of linguistics, interested laymen, teachers of the language as a mother tongue, teachers of the language as a foreign language, students of the language as a foreign language. We might suppose that since the object being described is identical in every case, whoever is talking about it or whoever he is talking to, the differences in the descriptions would be rather matters of style than of content. But this is not quite the case. As we saw in chapter 5 it is the 'viewpoint which creates the object'; there are no 'facts' in language itself; it is the linguist who 'creates' them in his description; what is or is not relevant is determined by the theoretical approach adopted. What can be assumed or what must be explicitly stated depends on the knowledge of the reader, and what is included or omitted depends upon what the reader is meant to do with what he has learned.

A theoretical linguist writing a grammar of a language (or more probably a fragment of a grammatical description of a language) for other linguists, is trying to show his readers that that analysis, based upon the particular theoretical model of language he favours, reveals properties in human language, and, for that reason, in the particular language in question, which would not be revealed by some alternative and, in his eyes, inadequate theory of language structure. The object of the descriptive exercise is the evaluation or validation of a particular linguistic theory of language. This is explicitly stated in the Preface to Lees *The Grammar of English Nominalizations* (1963):

There are many different reasons for engaging in technical linguistic research on natural language, but we view the following motivations as especially compelling. Only by studying the grammatical details of particular languages may we gain a deeper insight into the mechanisms underlying that most characteristically human type of behaviour, man's ability to communicate by means of language. (p. xvi)

A similar object lies behind Nida's *A Synopsis of English Syntax* (1960):

The purpose of this analysis of English syntax is to demonstrate the application of descriptive techniques to the problems of syntax in the writer's own speech. (p. 1)

This introduction is followed by a section of twenty-seven pages listing the theoretical inadequacies of earlier descriptions of the language.

Since the object of such 'theoretical' linguistic descriptions is to validate a particular theory or aspect of a theory, or refute some altern-ative theoretical model, the linguist need only describe enough of the language in question to make his point. It is for this reason that we do not have any comprehensive theoretical linguistic descriptions of well-known languages at the present time. When a linguist does attempt to produce a comprehensive description we find that his objectives are significantly different. They are not so much to elucidate the nature of a particular language as to teach a particular linguistic theory to students. Such a book is Paul Roberts's *English Syntax* (1964). Its subtitle is *An Introduction to Transformational Grammar*. And although the author states that it is intended 'to give English speaking students a descrip-tion of the syntax of their language' (p. 403), a close inspection shows that it provides much less information about the subject even than any of the shortened versions of the grammars by the great grammarians, such as Curme or Jespersen. The work is, in fact, an introduction to a particular model of syntax, taught inductively through its application to a particular language. In other words, it is not a grammar of English so much as a textbook of syntactic theory. The difference between a work of this sort and those first mentioned is not one of objectives but simply of audiences; in the first case profes-sional linguists, and in the second case perhaps unwitting students of linguistics.

Most of what I have called the great scholarly grammars – Sweet, Jespersen, Curme, Poutsma, Kruisinga (see page 154) – addressed themselves to the educated general public. They were not writing for specialists. Their objectives were enlightenment of a general human-istic sort, the making systematic and explicit what every native speaker knows implicitly. These are summed up by Sweet (1891):

We study the grammar of our own language for other objects than those for which we study the grammar of foreign languages. We do not study gram-mar in order to get a practical mastery of our own language, because in the nature of things we must have that mastery before we begin to study gram-mar at all. Nor is grammar of much use in correcting vulgarisms, provincial-isms and other linguistic defects.

The native language should be studied from the point of view of general grammar. We then learn to compare the grammatical phenomena of our own language with those of other languages . . . so we are better prepared for the divergent grammatical structures of other languages. In this way the study of

English grammar is the best possible preparation for the study of foreign languages.

Lastly, grammar satisfies a rational curiosity about the structure and origin of our own and other languages, and teaches us to take an interest in what we hear and utter every day of our lives. (pp. 5–6)

Sweet even more clearly than the others had a didactic purpose in writing his grammar and this was of a rather specific kind.

But there is another class of comprehensive descriptions which have a more specific pedagogical objective. These are addressed not to the general interested layman but to some more narrowly defined professional group. For example, Owen Thomas (1965) addresses himself to the prospective teachers of the mother tongue:

It is my hope that teachers will learn something valuable about the nature of English from this text, and that this knowledge will improve their teaching and help their students.

I am personally and professionally interested in the problems of teaching English, and only peripherally interested in the problems of theoretical linguistics. To achieve my primary aim in the best way I know how I must risk offending those whose professional interest is in theory. I admire and respect them, but there is little I can do to enlighten them. (p. vii)

Similarly in Whitehall (1951):

... Intended primarily for teachers and students of English composition, it may serve other readers – particularly those interested in literary exegesis – as a succinct, elementary linguistic introduction to English syntax.

I should hasten to add, however, that this book was not written with my fellow linguists in mind, that certain distributional methods fruitful in technical linguistics are not used here, and that pedagogical simplicity rather than linguistic consistency determine the inductive approach to the subject matter. (p. iv)

The authors of these latter grammars, then, specifically reject the notion that they are trying to teach linguistic theory. Indeed, they admit that the theoretical framework they adopt may be open to criticism for that reason. They accept that it may be necessary, for pedagogical purposes, to be eclectic in their theoretical orientation. They take the point of view that these considerations override theoretical coherence. In other words, theoretical eclecticism may be necessary when the objective of the grammar is to teach something other than linguistic theory. This point of view has already been discussed at the end of chapter 8.

We shall find that this standpoint is even more apparent when the descriptions of a language are intended for teachers of foreign languages or their pupils. The linguist who makes descriptions of parts of a particular language for other linguists is expounding general linguistic theory, or as Sweet called it, 'general grammar'. The grammarian writing descriptions of a language for the native speaker of that language, whether educated layman, teacher or student, aims, on the other hand, to make explicit what every native speaker knows implicitly of his language. The writer of a grammar for teachers and students of foreign languages has rather different aims, to which I now turn.

Grammars for foreign language teachers

Foreign language teachers may or may not be native speakers of the language they teach. If they are not native speakers they are normally expected to have what is called a *near-native* communicative competence in the language. Grammars written for their use will in part have the same objectives as those written for the native speaker, but since they will have had to learn the language as a second language and studied it descriptively as part of their training, the objects of grammars intended for their use will be less to make explicit what they know implicitly than to present the 'facts' of the language in a form which will help them to present them to their own pupils. Pedagogic grammars of this kind, then, are in some degree textbooks in the methodology of grammatical presentation. However, because of the rapid advances in our understanding of the structure of particular languages which have resulted from recent linguistic research, we often find that these grammars also provide new information about the language besides indications of how to present it to their pupils. A good example of a pedagogic grammar intended for teachers of English as a foreign language which has already been referred to, is Hornby (1954). In his Preface he claims that the book is intended to 'provide information for those who are studying English as a foreign language' (p. v). However, two pages later he says: 'It is a sound principle not to present the learner with specimens of incorrect English' (p. vii). This clearly is addressed to the teacher and is a proposal about what I have called the methodology of grammatical presentation. The book is, as we saw already, accompanied by two volumes of methodological instructions on how to present the material described (Hornby, 1959).

But not all pedagogic grammars intended for teachers of foreign languages are so explicit in their methodological proposals. For the most part explicit suggestions on how to present syntactic data to the learner are found in books on teaching method. The methodological proposals in pedagogic grammar for teachers are more often implicit rather than explicit. In other words, the authors of such grammars have already organized the description or presented the data in a form which the teacher can use more or less directly in presentation to his own pupils. We could say that grammars of this sort present the facts of language in a 'partially digested' form. The amount of 'pre-digestion' will depend upon the amount of linguistic sophistication the author is presupposing in his reader. The reason that such 'pre-digestion' is necessary at all is not so much that the author wishes to help the teacher in his teaching, but that he judges the teacher will not be able to follow a rigorous linguistic presentation of the material. This accounts for the fact that we cannot always distinguish between those pedagogical grammars which are intended for teachers of the mother tongue from those meant for foreign language teachers, and, in extreme cases, from those suitable for the advanced foreign learner of the language. Only when teachers receive a grounding in linguistics as part of their initial training as teachers will the distinction between 'linguistic' grammars and pedagogic grammars for teachers disappear.

We can sum up the contents of these two sections in the table on page 329.

Grammars for language learners

All the examples of 'grammars' so far referred to have been more or less comprehensive descriptions of a language enclosed within the covers of a single book. This book has carried an explicit title such as *English Syntax*, or *A Grammar of English*. Older readers will remember, as learners of Latin or French (or some other language), possessing a 'grammar' book with some similar title, which was intended for reference purposes in addition, perhaps, to their regular textbook, or 'method': *A Course in Elementary French* or *A Latin Primer*. Some-

Table 16

Author	Reader	Object of 'grammar'
Linguist	Linguist	To illustrate and validate a particular syntactic theory
Linguist	Student of linguistics	To teach syntactic theory inductively through its application to a particular language
Applied linguist	Educated native speaker	To systematize in linguistic terms the implicit knowledge of the reader
Applied linguist	Teacher of the mother tongue	To systematize the implicit or explicit knowledge of the reader in a form which is pedagogically appropriate for his (native speaker) pupils
Applied linguist	Teacher of a foreign language	To systematize the implicit or explicit knowledge of the reader in a form which is pedagogically appropriate for his (non-native speaker) pupils

times the course book itself incorporated some part of the grammatical descriptions of the language and provided exercise material on it. Alternatively, the *Shorter Grammar of Latin* itself contained exercise material for practice in the application of the grammatical rules. Typically, however, a set of books for students of a language, particularly a dead one, consisted of a trio: dictionary, grammar and reader. This trio is associated particularly with a method of teaching usually known as the *grammar-translation* method, in which the main activities in the classroom were oral translation into English from the reader, the rehearsing of the conjugation of verbs and declension of nouns, whilst the main homework activities were written translations from 'unseen' passages in the target language. The theoretical presuppositions (that is, the framework for the grammatical descriptions, the various categories of a traditional 'general grammar'), were rarely discussed. The learner had, therefore, to discover for himself what was meant by such terms as: infinitive, participle, deponent verb, case, tense, number and so on. The teaching and learning of the theoretical foundations on which the description of the language was based was largely inductive and concentrated almost wholly on accidence and derivation. Very little was said about syntax. To this day I have only the haziest notion of the *function* of the 'supine' in Latin, though I can still spout the supine form of any verb you care to mention, regular or irregular. Reference to my dogeared copy of *A Shorter Latin Primer* (Kennedy, 1906) tells me that: 'the *verb* has (amongst other forms) two *supines* (verbal substantives)' and later, that 'The supines are cases of a verbal substantive: amatum, *in order to love;* amatu, *for* or *in loving*.' It turned out that there was another verbal substantive, the *gerund*. I did, it is true, eventually develop some functional concept of the verbal substantive, and discovered how to use the gerund somewhat tentatively. I have never, to this day, found any use for the *supine*.

With changes in language-teaching methodology in more recent years, the way that information about the target language is distributed in the teaching materials has changed. It is now less often so neatly divided into 'dictionary', 'grammar' and 'reader'. Sometimes all these are rolled into one textbook, so that instead of concentrating all the grammatical information in one place, all the lexical information in another, they are spread over the whole course in several course books, interspersed with reading passages and practice exercises of various sorts.

But redistribution is not the only change that has taken place, nor is it really the most important. Far more significant is the way that the information about the target language is now given. It would not be an exaggeration to say that there was little difference fifty years ago between a 'grammar' for learners of a second language and scholarly grammars intended for native speakers, except their scope. This is the distinction which Sweet proposed (1899):

As regards fullness of treatment, there is an obvious distinction to be made between a grammar which is to be assimilated completely so that the learner at least practically knows it by heart, and the one which is only for reference.
  The latter will aim at being exhaustive wherever reasonable and practicable and will, perhaps, give information on a variety of subjects which would be omitted altogether in the learner's grammar. (p. 137)

This is, perhaps, one of the earliest references in English to the distinction which has now become commonplace, between a scholarly or 'linguistic' grammar and a 'pedagogical' grammar. However, Sweet was a revolutionary in his own day in recognizing that it was not only in scope but also in presentation that what he called a 'practical grammar' should differ from a 'reference grammar'. He exemplifies this thus:

From the point of view of the practical study of languages, such a question as whether or not the prepositions are to be treated of in the grammar as well as the dictionary, and the further question whether all of them, or only some of them, are to be included in the grammar, must be answered by showing whether or not the acquisition of the language will be facilitated thereby. (p. 125)

Sweet clearly saw that the criterion for a pedagogic grammar for second-language learners, his 'practical grammar', was not 'theoretical purity' but practical effect. This is still the problem of pedagogic grammars: how do we present the information about the structures of the language to the learner in such a way that it helps him to develop his communicative competence?

Sweet speaks about 'assimilating the grammar completely' and 'knowing it by heart'. This might suggest the rote learning of paradigms and syntactic rules and their mechanical repetition. This was indeed part of the grammar-translation method at its most extreme. But a further reading shows quite clearly that by the notion of 'assimilation' and 'knowing by heart', he meant what would nowadays be called the 'internalization of the rules of the grammar' or the 'acquisition of competence', which shows itself as the ability to interpret and produce grammatical utterances. In other words it is quite clear that Sweet had realized that the rules and categories the linguist uses to describe the grammar of a language were only a 'way of talking' about what the native speaker 'knows' and not a description of psychological entities and processes. This means that our pedagogical descriptions of the target language must be devised to help the learner learn whatever it is he learns, but are not necessarily *what* he learns. Pedagogical descriptions are *aids* to learning not the *object* of learning; so long as we keep that firmly in our minds we shall not get confused by the ambiguity of the expression 'teaching grammar' which was discussed in chapter 1, page 29. The problem of devising an efficient pedagogical grammar is, then, more a psycholinguistic than a theoretical linguistic one. The form our pedagogical grammar takes will be dependent upon what we believe to be the psychological processes involved in language learning. These were discussed at some length in chapter 6. I suggested there that current theories fell somewhere on the continuum between pure deductive and pure inductive learning processes. If we apply the extreme inductive hypothesis to the learning of grammar, then pedagogic grammar would scarcely be distinguishable from reading materials or other 'textual' data, written or spoken. Or, to put it another way, all we should need to do would be to 'expose' the learner to plenty of uncontrolled, unorganized data for him to get to work on. This has been called the 'sunburn' method. In theory at least this differs little from simply sending the learner to live in a country where the language is spoken. Most people would hardly regard this latter course as a form of 'teaching', because what characterizes teaching is its methodical or systematic organization of the data for learning.

The classroom method in the most inductive approach, often known as the 'structural method', has in practice been associated with a very high degree of control of the data, usually in a much more organized and restricted form than in other approaches, to the point that the learner may even be so 'starved' of material to learn from that his progress is actually held up.

By rigid control of the data, I do not just mean the considerable degree of 'idealization' to which it has been subjected. Anyone who cares to compare the dialogue in a play or novel with actual everyday conversation will realize that even the most 'realistic' examples are still far removed from reality (cf. Abercrombie, 1963). The data supplied in pedagogic grammars and other textbooks under the rubric of 'dialogues' are even more idealized. By rigid control I mean, rather, the strict limitation of the data to a single syntactic structure to be presented at one time. This control derives from the belief that the learner must not be 'swamped' with too much data and that he must be given time to 'absorb' each new pattern or category or whatever, before passing on to the next item. This notion is often expressed as learning the pattern until its production becomes 'automatic'. The extreme inductive approach has in practice usually been associated with a 'structuralist' theory of syntax in which the structure of sentences is described in terms of permitted sequences of word classes rather than more abstract generative rules. A structuralist grammar of a language consists essentially of a long list of word classes and a list of permitted sentence patterns. Such a model of grammar (discussed in chapter 8, page 182) has also usually been associated with the psychological view of language as a habit structure and the learning of language as the acquisition of a set of habits (see chapter 6).

If this is the model of learning adopted there is not much that can be 'said' about grammar, because of the low level of generalization of its statements. Consequently, 'talking about' language is generally restricted or discouraged. A typical expression of this point of view is that of Fries and Lado (1957):

'Knowing' grammar has most often meant the ability to use and respond to some fifty or sixty technical names and *talk about sentences* in terms of these technical names.

The materials (in this book) rest upon the view that learning foreign language consists *not* in learning *about* the language but in developing a new set of habits. One may have a great deal of information about a language without being able to use the language at all. The 'grammar' lessons here set forth, therefore, consist basically of *exercises to develop habits*, not explanations or talk about language. (p. v)

Here we have a case where a 'pedagogical grammar' consists essentially of exercises rather than descriptions. Where these do occur they differ relatively little from those in 'theoretical' grammars of the same persuasion. Compare Fries (1957) with the work just quoted (Fries and Lado, 1957).

However, there is no necessary or logical connection between an inductive approach to teaching and any particular grammatical model. One may believe that the learning of the grammar is fundamentally an inductive process, and yet believe that the most adequate accounts of the grammar of a language are, for example, transformational.

The difference in that case will be the way the data is selected and organized rather than how it is presented. One may still decide that descriptive statements about the language do not help the processes of learning, and therefore exclude them from the teaching materials. However, in practice, it turns out that there has been an association between a more deductive approach to teaching and the adoption of some sort of transformational account of the grammar. In other words, there is a strong tendency for those who regard such a model as descriptively more adequate to believe that language is not a matter of habit, but rather rule-governed behaviour, and that inductive learning can be controlled or guided and made more efficient by statements, formal or informal, about the structure of the language – that is, by adopting a more deductive approach. Interestingly enough, Chomsky, who above all linguists is associated with transformational grammar, has taken the most extreme inductive stand in connection with foreign language teaching (1968b):

My own feeling is that from our knowledge of the organization of language and of the principles that determine language structure one cannot immediately construct a teaching programme. All we can suggest is that a teaching programme be designed in such a way as to give free play to those creative principles that humans bring to the process of language learning, and, I presume, to the learning of anything else. I think we should probably try to create a rich linguistic environment for the intuitive heuristics that the normal human automatically possesses. (p. 690)

The most extreme form of the deductive approach was undoubtedly the grammar-translation method. Here it was assumed that what was learned was neither more nor less than the rules and categories of the linguistic description; that there was a complete identity between the linguistic categories and processes and the psychological categories and processes. Therefore the rote learning and subsequent repetition of the rules of the grammar was regarded as evidence that 'internalization' of the rules had taken place. The learner who could best spout the conjugations and declensions, analyse sentences and parse words, must be the one who best 'knew' the language. Unfortunately, it didn't always work out quite as simply as that in practice.

The conclusion we can draw from this discussion is that there is no logical connection between a particular psychological theory of how grammar is learned and any particular linguistic theory of language structure. The two are separate dimensions in which teaching materials may vary. This is expressed diagrammatically in Figure 46.

There is, however, an undoubted *historical* connection between them, such that primarily inductive learning theories tend to be associated with 'structural' grammars and notions of language as a habit structure, and deductive learning theories with transformational models and the notion of language as rule-governed behaviour. We must, it seems, return to Sweet's essentially pragmatic approach to pedagogic grammars in which the nature and use of the grammar must be determined by 'whether or not the learning of the language will be facilitated thereby'.

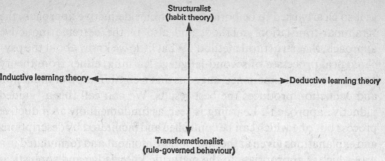

Figure 46

Data, description and practice

Learning the grammar of a language is acquiring the ability to produce grammatically acceptable utterances in the language, however we choose to describe that ability, whether as a matter of habit or skill or knowledge of formation rules. Any teaching materials which are designed to develop that ability are, pedagogically speaking, 'grammars'. We must not expect any longer that these materials should necessarily resemble what are traditionally known as 'grammars'. But, as we have seen, there is more to learning a language than acquiring its 'formation' rules. The learner has to be able to understand utterances in situations and himself speak and write appropriately. Not all elements in the teaching materials, therefore, have the function of teaching the grammar of the language. But with the distribution of the pedagogical grammatical element throughout all the teaching materials it is no longer so easy to isolate those parts which have purely grammatical teaching functions from those whose aims are the development of the general ability to communicate. The teaching of grammar is intricately bound up with the teaching of meaning. It is not sufficient merely to enable the learner to produce grammatical sentences; he must know when and how to use them. The distinction between competence and performance which was discussed in chapter 5, page 90, is no longer seen as relevant. Grammatical ability is only one element contributing to communicative competence. This means that there is now an insistence on understanding the meaning of grammatical forms, and that the teaching of grammar cannot be divorced from the teaching of meaning as it so clearly used to be both in the extreme deductive approach, the 'grammar-translation' method, and also in the extreme inductive approach, the 'structural method'. What little we know about the psychological processes of second-language learning, either from theory or from practical experience, suggests that a combination of induction and deduction produces the best results. We can call this a 'guided inductive approach'. Learning is seen as fundamentally an inductive process but one which can be controlled and facilitated by descriptions and explanations given at the appropriate moment and formulated in a way which is appropriate to the maturity, knowledge and sophistication of the learner. In a sense, teaching is a matter of providing the learner with the right data at the right time, and teaching him how to learn, that is, developing in him appropriate learning strategies and means of testing his hypotheses. The old controversy about whether one should provide the rule first and then the examples, or vice versa, is now seen to be merely a matter of tactics to which no categorical answer can be given. Giving a rule or description first means no more than directing the learner's attention to the problem or, in psychological terms, establishing a 'set' towards, or readiness for, the task; giving the examples or the data first means encouraging the learner to develop his own mental set of strategies for dealing with the task.

The learner must have data on which to base his hypotheses about the semantic or syntactic functions of each new 'item'. He may or may not benefit by explicit descriptions and explanations about how it works. He must, in any case, develop hypotheses and be given the opportunity to test their correctness. This means he must be given the chance to make decisions or choices and consequently run the risk of making errors. The function of the teacher is to provide data and examples, and where necessary to offer explanations and descriptions and, more importantly, verification of the learner's hypotheses (i.e. corrections). We can show the relation between these functions diagrammatically as in Figure 47. In the ordinary classroom lesson there is a constant switching from one activity to the next. In the same utterance the teacher may provide data and explanations whilst the learner may form a new hypothesis, test it and have it verified by the teacher. I do not, of course, suggest that these are all conscious or deliberate processes in either teacher or learner.

This analysis suggests, then, that there are up to four fairly well-

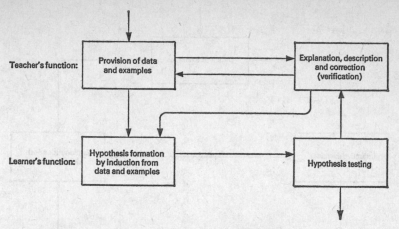

Figure 47 Teaching and learning activities in the classroom

defined elements in the grammatical component of teaching materials: data and examples; descriptions and explanations; induction exercises; and hypothesis-testing exercises. Each component has a function in the learning process, but the sequence in which they occur in the textbook cannot be prescribed for all cases. Descriptive and explanatory material may precede a full display of the data or it may follow it. It may follow or precede the largely mechanical exercises which are meant to promote the inductive processes. It may be omitted altogether from the textbook material and be carried out by the teacher in the classroom. The induction and hypothesis-testing exercises may be mixed together in the materials. A summary of the structure of the pedagogical grammatical element in teaching materials is given in Figure 48.

Explanations and exercises

We do not need here to go into a philosophical discourse on the distinction between explanation and description. In the classroom this is blurred by the fact that a description may often be used as an explanation, particularly when a learner wants to know why he has made a mistake (see chapter 11, page 283). It is a descriptive statement about a language to say that the verb agrees in number and person with the

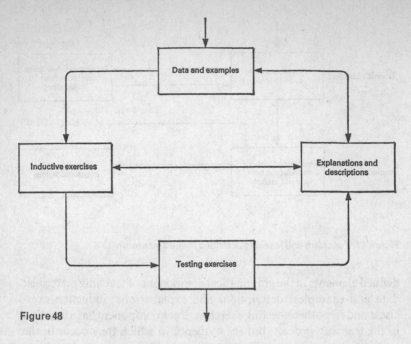

Figure 48

subject; when a learner makes an error of concord that description then becomes an explanation. It is an explanatory statement to say that concord marks a functional relation such as 'actor' and 'action'. What we are here concerned with is the form that explanations may take. One of the main objections to using descriptions of the language is that the learner has to learn the 'language used for making descriptions', he has to learn the meaning of such terms as subject, object, agreement, concord, person and number. This is regarded by some people as an additional learning task over and above that of learning the language. It is regarded as justified, on the other hand, by those who accept a guided inductive approach if it helps the learner to make precisely those conceptual generalizations he has to make anyway. The question then becomes not so much *whether* we should teach him the descriptive terminology, but *which* terminology. If he has to acquire new concepts anyway he might as well have some sort of a language for talking about them. The argument, then, is more about the nature of the terminology, its degree of formality or informality or scientific rigour, than about whether there should be any terminology at all.

I shall illustrate this problem by reference to a grammatical teaching 'item' in English: 'double object sentences'. This is a highly simplified account of the problem. There is an English sentence pattern which has two noun phrases following the verb, e.g.

I gave Mary a book

This can be generalized by stating the surface structure in terms of its grammatical constituents:

NP+VP+NP+NP

or their functions:

subject + verb + indirect object + direct object

We can call this Pattern 1. The 'meaning' of the constituents is usually expressed in this way: subject refers to the person who performs the action expressed by the verb; indirect object refers to the person who is a 'recipient' of the action expressed by the verb, and the direct object refers to the thing affected by the action expressed by the verb. There are alternative ways of expressing these relations between persons, things and the action, e.g.

I gave the book to Mary

We can call this Pattern 2. This sentence can still be regarded as a double object sentence because the meaning is the same, but it has a slightly different surface structure. The order of direct and indirect object is reversed, and the indirect object is realized by a prepositional phrase:

subject: NP + verb + direct object: NP + indirect object: to + NP

However, it depends upon which verb is chosen whether this alternative form of the sentence is possible. Some verbs are found with both patterns, some with only one or the other:

Give:	I gave Mary a book	Pattern 1
	I gave a book to Mary	Pattern 2
Ask:	I asked Mary a question	Pattern 1
	*I asked a question to Mary	Pattern 2
Explain:	I explained the problem to Mary	Pattern 1
	*I explained Mary the problem	Pattern 2

(Teachers of English as a second language will be thoroughly familiar with both these ungrammatical forms, which result from overgeneralization of a rule.)

If the indirect object is realized by a pronoun the grammatical structures are unchanged, but if the direct object is realized by a pronoun then only Pattern 2 is normally acceptable.

I gave a book *to her*	Pattern 1
I gave *her* a book	Pattern 2
*I gave Mary *it*	Pattern 1
I gave *it* to Mary	Pattern 2

Thus verbs which only occur in Pattern 1, e.g. *ask*, cannot occur at all with a direct object pronoun:

*I asked Mary it   *I asked it to Mary

Finally, only Pattern 1 has a corresponding passive form with the indirect object as subject:

I gave *Mary* a book
Mary was given a book (by me)
I asked *Mary* a question
Mary was asked a question

This means that verbs which occur *only* in Pattern 2, e.g. *explain*, have no corresponding passive form with indirect object as subject:

*Mary was explained the problem

These are the selected 'facts' about double object sentences, or, as has become evident, about verbs which take two objects. The question is: can these facts be explained to the learner in some fashion or other without using even this somewhat restricted terminology as in the foregoing account? The answer is: probably, yes; by setting out examples of these sentences in such a way that he will be able to infer the rules. But as I have already pointed out, he must first understand the meaning of the different forms, that is, he must be able to infer from examples of the different sentences which constituent refers to the action, which to the recipient of the action and which to the object affected by the action. He must, in other words, be able to *segment* the sentence and assign a function to each segment. This is what the textual data is for and also the purpose of any translations which may be given.

As we saw, we had three classes of verbs to deal with: those which occurred in both Patterns 1 and 2 and those which occur only in Pattern 1 or Pattern 2. Our exposition must therefore be such as to enable the learner to discover these sub-categories. We shall need a matrix of the forms shown in Table 17 to show this.

Table 17

	Pattern 1	*Pattern 2*
Verb class A	I *gave* Mary the book	I *gave* the book to Mary
Verb class B	I *asked* Mary the question	
Verb class C		I *explained* the problem to Mary

Needless to say, not all the information will necessarily be presented at one time. What is essential is that the *contrast* between the uses of verb classes A, B and C should be established. This will not be achieved by treating the *give* and *ask* classes, or the *give* and *explain* classes as one and the same. To do this would be to encourage precisely the overgeneralization which leads to the errors noted.

The establishment of a particular verb *class* can obviously not be done by using only one example, e.g. *give* or *ask*. It is the task of what I have called the 'inductive practice exercises' to establish the class membership of a number of verbs. This is usually done by several different sorts of exercise, basically all of a *substitution* type, in which the function may or may not be specified. Table 18 is a 'generative'

Table 18

Subject	*Verb (Class A)*	*Indirect object*	*Direct object*
John	gave	me	the book
I	lent	you	a letter
We	offered	Bill	a present
The men	wrote	the girl	the pencil
Someone	sent	my friend	some sugar

description in that it yields a large number of grammatically acceptable sentences. The learner can produce all of these by a process of selecting one item from each column in the sequence given. It is a pure-ly *mechanical* operation and if the lexical items are carefully chosen can be performed without any understanding. In the example given it will, of course, generate a number of semantically unacceptable sentences, e.g.

*I wrote Bill some sugar

In this form, then, *some* decisions of a semantic sort must be made. No syntactic decisions are needed. A most important substitution exercise in this pattern is the pronoun substitution exercise, shown in table 19. It can only concern the indirect object at this stage:

Table 19

Mary She	gave	Bill him	a present

There are, of course, a number of other types of inductive exercises. A substitution practice of this sort may lead on to a completion exercise in which the learner is asked to supply a semantically acceptable form to fill one of the noun phrase slots:

—— sent me a letter
I showed —— the papers
He taught the pupils ——

Notice again no *syntactic* decisions are required, only semantic ones. What we cannot do at this stage is allow the learner a *free* choice of verb, because this involves both a semantic *and* a syntactic choice, which he is not yet ready to make.

At this point we may wish to introduce the student to Pattern 2 in connection with the same class of verbs. This can be done by transformation exercises. Again these are purely mechanical, e.g.

She gave Bill a present   She gave a present to Bill
They sent us a letter   They sent a letter to us

(There are, of course, phonological problems here as well as problems about the appropriate use of these forms, but this is not part of the teaching of syntax.)

Two more sorts of transformation exercises complete a minimum list of inductive exercises on this pattern. The active–passive transformation:

She gave Bill a present   Bill was given a present

and the direct object pronominalization transformation which involves two operations, both purely mechanical:

She gave Bill *a present*   She gave it to Bill

What I have called inductive exercises are syntactically purely mechanical; they are what Dakin (1973) calls 'meaningless exercises' – they involve no grammatical decisions, at least as far as the particular 'item' being taught is concerned. (They may, of course, involve *some* syntactic choices, as in the case of the passivization exercise where appropriate tense, number and participle forms are concerned, but knowledge of these is *presupposed*. Similarly, the pronominalization exercises presuppose the ability to substitute *him* for *Bill* or *the man*, and *it* for *the present*, etc.) It would be legitimate to ask what use an exercise is which requires apparently no thought and which can be performed without any need to understand the sentence. The answer must be that any exercise which *demands* no decision of a semantic or syntactic sort may be of little value for the teaching of grammar – it may be useful as a pronunciation practice. But so long as *some* decisions are involved, even if they are only semantic or concerned with syntactic processes already supposed to be known, then the student is *forced*, to some degree, to understand what he is doing, and in the process discover something about double object verbs, even if only the sub-category to which the different verbs belong.

So far I have only outlined the inductive exercises relating to one sub-category of verb and one sentence pattern. Clearly the same procedures must be applied to the other verb categories and the other pattern, where they are applicable. But now the difficulty arises. In some respects each of these verb categories overlaps, i.e. *give* and *explain* both occur in Pattern 2 and *ask* and *give* in Pattern 1. How are we to make sure the learner does not overgeneralize and produce such forms as:

*I explained him the problem
*I asked the question to Mary

The answer is simply that he will surely do so, but that it is precisely the function of what I have called the hypothesis-testing exercises to overcome this. Hypothesis-testing exercises all have the characteristic that they force the learner to make syntactic choices, to differentiate what he has hitherto treated as the same, to make judgements about what is and is not acceptable. They are sometimes called *problem-solving* exercises for this reason. Dakin calls them 'meaningful exercises'. As I indicated on page 336, it is in these exercises that the teacher has an indispensable role to play. He, and only he, can provide the confirmation of the learner's hypotheses; only he can make judgements about the acceptability of the learner's sentences, the correctness of his choices.

Hypothesis-testing exercises simulate real life language, because when we speak we make perhaps hundreds of decisions a second, each one of which may have syntactic or semantic consequences, or be constrained in one way or another by the context. But choices are of two sorts. Those which involve making a decision between two forms which are given, and those which involve producing forms spontaneously. The former has some relation to the process of understanding language, the latter to producing it. So hypothesis-testing exercises are of two sorts. The first requires the learner to make choices between two or more given forms as to which is the acceptable one; these are called *recognition exercises*. The second type requires him to produce spontaneously the form which will make an acceptable sentence; these are called *production exercises*. The recognition type of exercise requires for success a less fully developed knowledge of the grammatical point being learned, and is therefore not such a stringent test of the learner's hypotheses or so full a confirmation of his knowledge. The productive type of exercise is the most demanding form and consequently is normally practised last in the series before completely free or unguided production practice.

The fundamental form of the recognition exercise is a multiple choice. In the particular example we have been using, the learner can be required either to fit the correct pattern to a given verb or to fit an acceptable verb into a given pattern. The former type is both easier to devise and is probably psychologically a more 'real' operation. The way the actual exercise is presented or 'wrapped up' will, of course, vary. But these are the types of choices involved:

John explained $\begin{cases} \text{the problem to me} \\ \text{*me the problem} \end{cases}$

The problem was explained $\begin{cases} \text{to me} \\ \text{*me} \end{cases}$

It was lent $\begin{cases} \text{*Bill} \\ \text{to Bill} \end{cases}$

The question was $\begin{cases} \text{*asked} \\ \text{*explained} \\ \text{given} \end{cases}$ him

What did you $\begin{cases} \text{*say} \\ \text{tell} \end{cases}$ him?

Production exercises typically require the learner to supply something, to complete a sentence in an an acceptable way:

I showed ——
What did you —— him?
Who did you —— the book to?

or to provide an appropriate response:

I've got a present
Who sent ——
I know a good dentist
Who introduced ——?

Again, what are fundamentally 'retrieval' exercises come in a great variety of forms in which varying amounts are to be supplied by the learner. In those illustrated, not only must a verb of the right sub-category be selected but also one which is semantically acceptable in the context. Or, alternatively, given a particular verb, not only must the correct pattern be selected but also semantically acceptable noun phrases.

Tests and exercises

If an exercise is largely mechanical and can therefore be done without necessarily understanding fully what is going on, it cannot serve as a test of the learner's grammatical knowledge (though it may test his vocabulary). If he makes a grammatical error it must, therefore, be due to carelessness, not to lack of knowledge. Furthermore, all mechanical exercises have one and only one solution. This means that they do not require the presence of a teacher to monitor the results. A machine which has the answer programmed into it can do the job. For this reason, exercises done in the language laboratory are typically mechanical induction exercises. On the other hand, the problem-solving exercises may or may not have a unique solution. Recognition exercises do, and can, therefore, also be performed in the language lab. or in programmed instructional material, but production exercises are open-ended; they have no unique solution. They require the presence of, or at least reference to, a teacher, and cannot be satisfactorily 'mechanized'.

I made a distinction between mechanical exercises which are intended to promote the making of hypotheses or the discovery of rules and the hypothesis testing exercises whereby the learner can check whether he knows the rules or how right his rules are. They tell him whether he still needs to work at the 'item' or not. But they also tell the teacher whether the learner has yet learned this 'item'. This is why hypothesis-testing exercises look like objective test materials. There is no difference *in form* between the two things, only a difference in function. Exercises of this sort are designed to tell the learner about his knowledge and thereby help him to learn. Tests are intended to tell the teacher (or researcher) about what the learner knows. It is of no consequence, therefore, whether the learner does or does not make errors in his exercises, they are not meant to *measure* anything. It may, of course, be of consequence to both learner and teacher if he makes errors in his tests. They are intended to measure his knowledge for various purposes. It is because of the similarity in form between tests and exercises of this sort that both teachers and learners have, particularly in the past, confused the two functions.

The teacher as a 'pedagogical grammar'

Any or all of the component functions of a 'pedagogical grammar' can be carried out without any printed or spoken teaching materials being imported into the classroom. In other words, the whole or any part of the teaching of grammar can be carried out by the teacher without the support of textual or recorded material. He can provide the data and examples orally or in writing. He can conduct the induction exercises orally, provide descriptions and explanations with the help of the blackboard, and carry out the hypothesis-testing procedures whether orally or in writing, providing correction and verification. The most difficult part for the teacher is to provide adequate quantities of well contextualized data. Hence the virtual indispensability of textual material written or recorded. A well-qualified, energetic and inventive teacher can be a 'living' pedagogical grammar; what he can't so easily be, curiously enough, is the generator of abundant and appropriate textual data, in spite of the love that teachers are said to have for the sound of their own voices! But unfortunately not all teachers are well-qualified, nor are they all endowed with unlimited energy and invention. This is one reason why they need the help of teaching materials. The question is: does the learner need a teacher at all if he has access to unlimited data and practice materials? In other words, can the live teacher ever be eliminated from the learning process? Apart from his general pedagogical and administrative duties, is the teacher indispensable? People do appear to learn languages by self-instruction, so the answer might appear to be: no. But a closer analysis of self-instruction will show that this is not the case. There is one function of the teacher which cannot be provided by any teaching materials yet devised. The one thing a self-taught student cannot get from himself or his learning materials is final authoritative confirmation about his hypotheses. This can only be provided by someone who possesses a knowledge of the whole grammatical system, who can make precisely those intuitive judgements about the acceptability of utterances which characterize the 'competence' of the native speaker referred to in chapter 5, page 91. The data available to the self-taught learner, however extensive it may be, can only be a sample of the language. Search as he may through it he can never be sure to find in the data the example which will unequivocally confirm every hypothesis he may make about the grammar of the language. In the last resort he must have access to a native speaker (or as near-native an informant as he can get). The minimal irreducible and indispensable function of the teacher is to tell the learner what is or is not an acceptable utterance. We can call this his *monitoring function*. A learner cannot, in thise sense, adequately monitor his own performance, whether receptive or productive. If he could, he would be a native speaker of the language!

Of course, producing acceptable utterances is not the whole of language learning. The learner must know when to select one or another in order to achieve his communicational ends. In other words, utterances must also be appropriate to the situation. This, too, requires monitoring. But the 'speaking rules' of language cannot yet be described. What we cannot describe we cannot teach systematically. Thus the learning of the speaking rules is still a wholly inductive process. A native speaker can tell whether an utterance is appropriate or not; this was what we called 'Sprachgefühl'. But he cannot say much about why a particular utterance is or is not appropriate. To acquire 'Sprachgefühl' a learner requires plentiful contextualized language data and he needs a native-speaking informant to make judgements about the appropriateness of his utterances. But teaching the speaking rules is not part of a pedagogical grammar. Perhaps one day it will be, when we know a little more about how language is used.

Chapter 14
Evaluation, Validation and Tests

Evaluation

The application of linguistics to language teaching is not just a descriptive activity but a prescriptive one. It is concerned not just with accounting for what happens when people teach and learn languages but with attempting to control and direct the process, with making it as efficient as possible. By 'making it efficient', I mean organizing things so that the learner learns a given amount in a shorter time, or with less effort, or learns more in the same time or learns it in such a way that he retains it better. Notice that in every case we are dealing with some notion of quantity – quantity of learning, or knowledge, and quantity of time. Efficiency can also be looked at from the teaching point of view. In this case it would mean teaching the same amount to more learners, or to the same number of learners with fewer teachers, or with less expensively trained teachers, or with less outlay in terms of space, teaching materials or technical equipment. Again we are dealing with quantifiable categories, ultimately reducible to sums of money. This is the cost-effectiveness approach. But whichever way we try to quantify efficiency, there is one element which is common to both approaches, and that is the 'quantity of knowledge or learning'. Although this is something which is not so easily measured as money or time or numbers of teachers and pupils, any discussion of efficiency in language teaching must always come back to the central question: what do we mean by knowledge of a language and how do we measure it? What we mean by knowledge of a language was the topic of the first section of this book. The problems connected with measuring this knowledge and the reasons for doing so are the topics of this, the last chapter.

Before we can improve the performance of some practical task in a systematic and logical way we have to understand it or describe it. We have seen already that we cannot teach what we cannot describe. So also we cannot systematically improve what we do not understand. Without understanding, any attempt to improve something can only be based upon intuition or trial-and-error procedure. This does not mean that having an understanding of a process necessarily guarantees an improvement; we still have to apply what knowledge we have in an appropriate fashion. In any case it will have become quite clear that our understanding of the process of language learning at the present time is far from perfect. This is all the more reason, of course, for experimental investigation and evaluation of the various factors, including the materials, involved in the teaching and learning processes.

But we are not only concerned to improve the efficiency of existing language-teaching tasks. The nature of the tasks that we have to undertake is continually changing. We are not only concerned in doing a better job with our old third form French class but with developing programmes of quite new sorts. New groups of people want to learn new sets of languages for a variety of new purposes. Furthermore, these programmes have to be planned and carried out with new types of equipment and aids, language laboratories, radio, television, computers, in new sorts of buildings and with new financial resources.

Whether we have to do with the improvement of existing programmes or the devising of new ones, we must have a means of evaluating our plans and their execution, a way of *monitoring* our activity. In other words, we need continuous information or *feedback* about our performance.

We can look at this in another way. When we plan some new activity or some new way of doing an old task, we are, in effect, making a 'prediction'. We are saying: if I do it in such and such a way, then I predict I shall get such and such a result. Now, few people are so sure of themselves, or so certain that they are right, that they do not feel the need to check their results or verify their predictions. Least of all applied linguists. Measuring the learning of the pupils by means of language tests is part of the process of verification of these predictions. There is no other objective and reliable way of doing so. Making predictions and verifying them by means of 'tests' of some kind is a sort of 'experiment'. It is scientific when it is conducted with a full control of all the relevant factors, and the results evaluated by the appropriate statistical techniques. The sort of predictions the applied linguist makes are about the effects on learning that the syllabuses and teaching materials which it is his job to design may have.

The materials for teaching are not the only factors which contribute to the effectiveness of language learning. The quality and nature of the classroom teaching clearly play a part. I shall refer to these factors as the contribution of 'the teacher'. And then obviously 'the learner' has something to do with it! His success may depend on a number of characteristics: his age, sex, intelligence, motivation and aptitude. Of these three factors, the 'teacher', the 'learner' and the 'materials', only the teaching materials are fully under our control. They happen to be the things with which the applied linguist is concerned. It is because we can, in effect, exercise relatively so little control over the other factors in the learning situation that rigorous scientific experimentation with classroom learning of languages is so difficult, and is one of the reasons why the results from those major studies that have been carried out have turned out so inconclusive (Scherer and Wertheimer, 1964; Smith, 1970).

Tests as measuring instruments

All scientific experimentation involves measurement. In the simplest case it is a question of all or nothing, yes or no; does the predicted event occur or not, how many of the predicted events occur, or with what degree of intensity, or how much change is observed in the test object? All measurement implies comparison; either with some other comparable object or against some arbitrary but conventional scale, such as length, weight, time, temperature or money.

Language tests are measuring instruments and they are applied to learners, not to teaching materials or teachers. For this reason they do not tell us *directly* about the contribution of 'the teacher' or 'the materials' to the learning process. They are designed to measure the learner's 'knowledge of', or 'competence in' the language at a particular moment in his course and nothing else. The knowledge of one pupil may be compared with the knowledge of others, or with that of the same pupil at a different time, or with some *standard* or norm, as in the case of height, weight, temperature, etc.

What we learn from such measurement and from such comparisons is of no interest *in itself*. It is what one can *infer* from it that is of interest and importance. This is the difference between measurement and evaluation. To know the air temperature somewhere is 45 degrees F has no significance until we know where and when the measurement was taken, say in Greenland (a sweltering hot day) or in Ghana (a bitterly cold day) or in Manchester on August Bank Holiday. To know that a learner knows just so much of the target language is to know nothing interesting or useful unless we also know, for example, how much he knew at some earlier point in time, how long he has been learning, where he is in the course, what materials and methods have been used to teach him, what his mother tongue is and a host of other facts about him, his teacher and the learning situation.

Measurement and evaluation are distinct but logically related processes. Measuring the learner's knowledge is a *means* of evaluating, not only the learner himself, but also the teacher and the teaching materials. The test results are neutral; they are merely the data from which to deduce something about any factor in the teaching situation.

Evaluation as a form of experiment

An experiment, in its scientific sense, is the process of testing a hypothesis, usually about some relationship of cause and effect. In applied linguistics this principally means the relationship between the teaching materials and their exploitation, and language learning. A typical hypothesis of applied linguistics takes this form; if we use such-and-such materials with a specific group of learners taught by a specific method, they will learn such-and-such an amount of the target language in a specific period of time. What we are investigating in this case is the effect on learning of certain types of teaching materials in a *specific learning situation*. The object of the experiment is to throw light on this relationship, and thereby evaluate the effectiveness of the materials. We would, of course, similarly evaluate the role of the other factors in the teaching situation, such as the 'teacher' (e.g. the relevance of his training and quality of his teaching methods), or the characteristics of the 'learner' (e.g. the role of age, motivation, intelligence or aptitude and so on), These are all interesting and important factors and ones we generally do wish to evaluate. However, making such an assessment, while a *task* of applied linguistics (i.e. involving applied linguistic techniques) is not an *evaluation* of the techniques of applied linguistics, or the contribution of applied linguistics to language teaching. In other words, applied linguists are involved in all experimental studies of language teaching, but not all experimentation in language teaching is an evaluation of applied linguistic techniques. What is common to all experiments in language teaching is the measurement of the learner's knowledge of the target language. This is done by tests, the making of which is an activity of the applied linguist.

Since experiments aim at discovering a single relationship, they are designed so that other possibly interfering factors are controlled in such a way that their influence on the results is minimized or eliminated as far as possible. In a language-teaching situation we believe that 'teacher', 'learner' and 'materials' all make a significant contribution to the progress of learning, but if we want to evaluate the influence of only one of these factors we must see to it that the contribution of the others is a known factor in our calculations, or is, as it is called, an *independent variable* in the experiment. For example, if we wish to assess the influence that the sex of the learner plays in the learning process, we should select a group of learners to be taught by one teacher with the same materials, who were all of the same age, intelligence, motivation, etc. but differed only in respect of sex. In such an experiment, the teacher and the teaching materials, the intelligence, age and motivation of the learners would all be independent variables. They would all have to be known, controlled and held constant throughout the experiment. Only the sex of the learners would be different, would be uncontrolled. In this experiment it would be the *dependent variable*.

Typically, experiments whose aim is to evaluate the contribution of applied linguistics to language teaching take the teaching materials as the dependent variable, whilst the teacher and the learner are the independent variables.

The difficulties which beset all evaluation procedures in education are twofold. The first is that we cannot treat teacher, pupil and materials as single variables. As we saw, pupils vary amongst themselves in respect of a number of characteristics, some of which, such as age and sex, are easily measurable and therefore controllable, but others, such as motivation, intelligence or aptitude present great difficulties in measurement. The same is true of what we have called 'the teacher'. Perhaps age and sex are less important, but intelligence and motivation certainly play a part. Moreover, the methods the teacher employs are almost impossible to describe, standardize and control for experimental purposes (Scherer and Wertheimer, 1964). We may be able to analyse, as we have done in previous chapters, the various techniques of applied linguistics which are involved in the making of teaching materials. But it is difficult, if not impossible, in most cases to disentangle these various components in an experimental evaluation. For example, if we wished to investigate the contribution of a syllabus, we should have to produce two or more alternative syllabuses each of which was realized in the same sort of teaching materials, or if we wished to evaluate our pedagogical grammars, we should have to have the same syllabus realized in two or more different sets of teaching materials.

The second difficulty is just as serious. Since evaluation necessarily involves comparisons of one sort or another, and since experimentation involves holding all factors under control except the one we are investigating, it would be necessary, when evaluating the teacher and his methods, for example, to have the *same* children taught with the *same* materials by two *different* teachers. But how can this be done? Since they cannot be taught simultaneously by two teachers (only successively) they will not be 'the same children' for the second teacher. They will already have been taught by the first teacher what they are also going to be taught by the second teacher.

This is a familiar problem in all scientific experimentation, but especially so in the educational field. It is expressed in the adage, 'You cannot jump into the same river twice'. All sorts of procedures have been devised to overcome it, and they all hinge on the notion of 'same'. Whilst we evidently cannot use the 'identical' teacher, materials or pupils for comparison, we can make an effort to find *equivalents* or *matches*. Instead of teaching the identical pupils a second time, we get a group which matches them in respect of as many independent variables (age, sex, intelligence, etc.) as we can. Or we find a set of materials which aim to teach a different part of the language, but one which is equivalent or matches it in difficulty. Or we look for teachers with equivalent skill in using different methods of teaching. But matching can never be perfect. For example, because we do not have any direct way of measuring teaching skill, or assessing the difficulty of sets of teaching materials, matching these can only be subjectively valid; or, in technical language, *unreliable*. I shall return to the whole question of reliability again in a later section.

I have already said that whatever factor in the teaching situation we may be evaluating, we can do so by measuring the knowledge of the learner, or, more exactly, the *amount learned* by the learner. But this does not mean that it is always the knowledge of the learner which is the 'dependent variable'. We must remember that testing is only part of the evaluation procedure. We need measurements of all the variables; teacher, learner and materials. Tests give us a measurement of one aspect of the learner. His knowledge *may* be the dependent variable in the experiment, that is, we may wish simply to point out how much each one of a group of learners has learned as a result of a particular teaching operation, in order to discover perhaps why some have learned more than others. On the other hand the learner's knowledge may merely be a *factor* in the experiment, i.e. an independent variable. In other words, what the learner knows or how much he has learned may not be *what* we want to find out, but measuring it may be *a way* of finding out what we do want to know. For example, if we want to evaluate some aspect of the 'teacher', e.g. the teaching method, then we get two teachers matched in all possible respects *except the methods they use*, to teach two matched sets of learners using the same materials. We measure the knowledge of the learners at the beginning and end of the course and compare the results to find out the amounts learned by each set, and then compare the two results. In such a case the dependent variable is the teaching method, and the independent variables, the 'learner' and 'the materials'. But the only measurement in the experiment, after setting it up, is that of the learner's knowledge of the language.

The discussion gives us means of classifying experiments according to what function they perform in the evaluation procedures. This is summarized in tabular form in Table 20.

Validity

Learners must, and do, learn all sorts of things about a language and to do all sorts of things with a language, which we cannot teach them. This is, as I have said, because we can only teach systematically what we can describe. The same is true of testing. We cannot test systematic-

Table 20

'Teacher' as variable	'Materials' as variable	'Learner' as variable	Information derived from experiment
independent	independent	*dependent*	ordinary practical information used by teacher for monitoring progress, diagnosing difficulties, selection of pupils, streaming, etc. Also learner's aptitude, motivation, intelligence, etc.
independent	*dependent*	independent	theoretical and applied research. Evaluation of applied linguistic techniques; syllabus content, structure and presentation.
dependent	independent	independent	typical pedagogical operational research into teaching methods; language laboratory, programmed instruction, teaching of reading and writing, etc.

ally any part of a language or type of performance in it which we cannot describe. This is why testing is a branch of applied linguistics and why ultimately our ability to do a good job of measuring the learner's knowledge of the language depends upon the adequacy of our theory about the language, our understanding of what is meant by 'knowledge of a language'. If our test is to do its job properly it must not, incidentally or accidentally, measure anything else, for example the learner's intelligence, his knowledge of the world or his system of beliefs. In other words the test must be *valid*. As Pilliner (1968) has said:

The validity of any examination or test procedure may be broadly defined as the extent to which it does what it is intended to do. (p. 30)

There is a considerable literature on the concept of validity in tests, and all sorts of procedures for assessing the validity of tests have been devised. For example, a test has one sort of validity if the questions in it, or the activities it requires the subject to perform, are those which he has been taught to answer or perform in the course of his study. This accounts for the strong resemblance there is between the forms of exercises described in the last chapter and certain test items and procedures. This is called *content* validity, and establishing it does not involve comparison with the results from other tests, but is a matter of 'expert judgement', and is therefore to some degree 'subjective' and 'unreliable'. A test also has another type of validity if its results can be used to predict the success of the test subjects in the performance of some other task which has been shown to depend upon a 'knowledge of the language', such as passing a traditional examination, or being selected to study the language at a university. This is called *predictive* validity. A test has a further type of validity if its results are confirmed by some different test whose object is to measure the same thing and whose validity has already been established. This is called *concurrent validity*.

The last two criteria of validity depend upon comparing test results with some other type of test, examination or selection procedure. In this sense they are essentially the same. Clearly the validity of a test cannot be shown to be greater than the validity of any of the tests with which it is being compared. We are thus in a circularity; Test A is validated by Test B, Test B by Test C, and Test C by Test A. The only way of breaking out of this circularity is to base the validity of our test on the best current understanding of what is meant by a 'knowledge of a language'. It is not a question of 'keeping up with the Joneses' but rather of being 'the Joneses'. But just as 'the Joneses' confidence in themselves is confirmed by having other people 'keeping up with them', so it is desirable that the results of tests which are based upon a theoretical understanding of the nature of language, which have what is called *construct validity*, should also, as far as possible, correlate well with results of other tests, examination and measuring procedures. If they do not we might well doubt the adequacy of our understanding of the nature of language.

Testing grammatical competence

A learner of a language is not only concerned with learning the 'formation rules' of the language but also its 'speaking rules'. We are trying to teach him what we called 'communicative competence'. But we also saw that our present knowledge of the nature of language was most highly developed in the area of language structure. We were able to pronounce firmer judgements about the 'acceptability' of learners' utterances than about their 'appropriateness'. As Perren (1968) says:

The real test of whether he can speak the language is whether he can say something which is understood by the listener *as relevant to a particular situation*. (my italics) (p. 112)

But to construct tests in whose results we can have confidence we have to be able to pronounce judgements of a categorical sort about the acceptability or 'correctness' of the learner's responses. These are judgements about which all native speakers would agree, and consequently tests of this sort are called *objective* tests. Because objectivity is a necessary, though not sufficient condition for having confidence in the results of a test, most tests at the present time are constructed to measure the learner's knowledge of the 'formation rules' of the language, that is, what we have called his grammatical competence, rather than his global communicative ability. But when we attempt to pronounce judgements about the appropriateness of the use of the language, as we must do when translation or précis or essay writing is used as a method of testing, we find, of course, that native speakers do not agree about what is right anyway. Appropriateness cannot yet be reduced to rules, and consequently judgements about it are necessarily subjective. Tests of this sort are therefore called *subjective tests*. It is obviously not because we do not wish to measure the learner's communicative competence that we tend to confine ourselves largely to tests of grammatical competence, but because we cannot yet test it objectively. When we consider that a learner has done a 'good' translation or a 'good' essay we do not know very precisely what quality or qualities we have measured, and are far from confident that our measure is a valid one.

If we consider knowledge of the formation rules of a language as the ability to carry out certain linguistic processes of sentence formation and interpretation, then, in testing it, we could be said to be assessing the correct working of a 'language-processing device'. This is rather a similar idea to the one we used in chapter 5 when we talked about the learner as a 'language-learning device'. It was an analogy derived from computers. By performing tests on it we are investigating the nature of the device, what it can and cannot do. By definition the native speaker's 'language-processing device' is fully developed and, consequently, if it is required to perform certain operations on certain data, we can predict with nearly 100 per cent certainty what the result will be. Using this computer model we can call the test instructions the 'programme' and the language material of the test the 'data'; the subject's responses are then the 'output' of the device. This is shown diagrammatically in Figure 49. It is from the responses of the subject that we *infer* something about the overall efficiency of the language-processing device, or 'the learner's grammatical competence'. The results of the test are expressed in terms of the numbers of right or wrong responses, his *score*. We finish up with an answer to the question: *how much* of the target language does the learner know? We do not necessarily finish up with the sort of information which will enable us to reconstruct the grammar of the learner's interlanguage (see chapter 11). Tests are designed as measuring instruments, not for finding out the nature of the learner's knowledge. This is the big difference between tests and what we shall call *elicitation procedures*. To find out *what* a learner knows, rather than *how much* he knows, different procedures are required. I shall say more about this matter shortly.

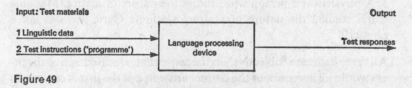

Input: Test materials

Output

1 Linguistic data

2 Test instructions ('programme')

Language processing device

Test responses

Figure 49

The difficulty in devising valid tests, that is, ones which only involve the 'language-processing device' and not some other component of the learner's cognitive capacities or knowledge, is the principal problem in test construction. In chapter 6 we saw, in our model of language performance, the difficulty of deciding where purely linguistic processes ended and other non-linguistic processes began, the difference between what one called 'understanding' and 'ideation' on the one hand, and 'identification' and 'planning' on the other, and between these latter two and general motor-perceptual skills, which are not specifically linguistic. If the test is to be truly valid we must avoid, as far as possible, testing such cognitive factors as general intelligence, knowledge of the world and the belief systems of the learner, or his general motor-perceptual skills. Language tests are not devised to find out the degree to which learners are deaf or blind, whether they know the name of the Prime Minister or whether they believe in God! One of the main criticisms of traditional ways of examining is that they do not satisfactorily disentangle these separate components. Our judgements on an essay or a précis are almost inevitably influenced by our opinion of its content or logical structure, or in an extreme case, whether we 'agree' with what the writer has said. This has not necessarily anything to do with 'objectivity', as we can see from the following examples: here are three 'multiple choice' test items:

1. A person who studies the nature of matter is a
(A) physicist
(B) physician
(C) materialist

2. Madame Curie was a
(A) physicist
(B) physician
(C) materialist

3. A physicist is a person who studies the nature of matter. Madame Curie studied the nature of matter, Madame Curie *was/was not* a physicist

All three items are 'objective', in the sense that educated native speakers would all agree about the correct answer, but the first is concerned solely with a knowledge of the language, whilst the second clearly involves both linguistic and non-linguistic knowledge. What does the third item test? However clever we are in devising test materials, we shall probably never succeed in eliminating entirely non-linguistic factors from our tests. Indeed, it may well be that it is impossible in theory, as well as in practice, precisely because linguistic abilities are not in fact clearly distinct from other cognitive capacities. We shall therefore have to make a small but significant addition to our model, as in Figure 50.

We should then say that the degree to which the test involves operations of a general cognitive nature is a measure of the invalidity of the

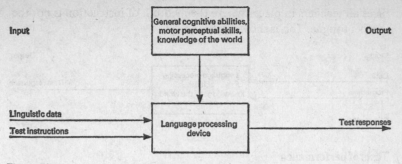

Figure 50

test as an instrument for measuring the learner's 'grammatical competence'. The ideal language test would eliminate entirely all general cognitive abilities, since their contribution to the results cannot be directly measured.

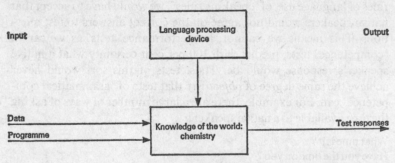

Figure 51

If we now compare language tests with tests and examinations in other subjects, we can see where the difference lies. If we are trying to measure the learner's 'knowledge of chemistry' then we are taking grammatical competence for granted, although it may be that, in this case too, the test is 'contaminated' by some element of linguistic ability (Figure 51). And if we are testing the knowledge of chemistry of a learner in some language other than his mother tongue, then the two components are inextricably mixed up. We have the greatest difficulty in deciding whether his relative failure was due to his lack of knowledge of chemistry or of the language. This is a problem which faces all teachers in places where the medium of instruction is not the mother tongue. This is shown in Figure 52.

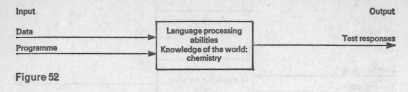

Input   Output

Data ──────────────────►┌─────────────────────┐
                        │ Language processing │
                        │   abilities   │──────► Test responses
Programme ─────────────►│ Knowledge of the world: │
                        │   chemistry   │
                        └─────────────────────┘

Figure 52

Tests of performance

I have said that most objective tests at the present time are concerned with measuring the learner's knowledge of the 'formation rules' of the language. Our object in teaching is to develop communicative competence. Can we devise tests which measure this global ability and what would they be like? First of all, for lack of adequate descriptions of the rules of language use, of 'speaking rules', we would have to accept that native speakers would not agree on the correct answers to test questions. This means we cannot, in 'performance' tests, as we can in 'competence' tests, predict with 100 per cent certainty what a native speaker's response would be. Thus, tests of this sort would never achieve the same degree of *objectivity* that tests of 'grammatical competence' can. For example, there are a large number of ways of asking the time available to a native speaker:

What time is it?
Have you the time on you?
What is the correct time?
How late is it?
What's the time?
Can you tell me the time, please?
What time do you make it?

Can the reader give any systematic account of the situational circumstances in which he selects one or another of these forms? He might be able to say in the extreme cases that he would very probably *not* say *What's the time?* to a stranger in the street, or *Excuse me, but would you mind telling me the time?* to his wife. But in between, there are clearly a number of possibilities which all seem to have a similar degree of probability. Any test of a learner's communicative competence, involving

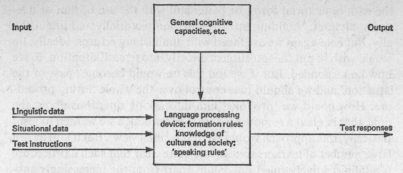

General cognitive
capacities, etc.

Linguistic data
Situational data
Test instructions

Language processing
device: formation rules:
knowledge of
culture and society:
'speaking rules'

Test responses

Figure 53

decisions about appropriateness must provide information about the situation in which the utterance is to be made. The difference between tests of 'competence' and tests of 'speaking rules' is not only in the degree of subjectivity in judging the results but also in the data we must 'put in' to the test material. Tests of communicative competence must provide situational as well as linguistic data. Furthermore, what is being tested is not just the 'language processing device', but knowledge of the culture and structure of the society whose language it is we are testing, not just a general knowledge of the world but a particular knowledge of one aspect of the world. We must again modify our test model as in Figure 53. But apart from the largely subjective nature of such tests, there is the purely technical problem of providing the non-linguistic data about the situation. We can do this to a limited extent linguistically by describing the situation in words:

If you were in a hurry and wanted to know the time, which of the following utterances would you use to a complete stranger in the street: What time is it, please? – Have you the time on you, by any chance? Excuse me, but could you tell me the time?

Most readers will hesitate to choose any one of these as being the most appropriate. They might wish to know more about the age, social status or present activity of the stranger: was he walking along, doing some particular task or just hanging about? Are we to write into our situational data all these possibly relevant bits of information? Clearly we are quickly reaching a point of 'diminishing returns' from the point of view of cost-effectiveness. An alternative might be to present the data in pictorial form, or better still with the use of film or television pictures, 'building up' the situation pictorially and linguistically. But here again we are faced with diminishing returns. Ideally, we would wish to put the test subject directly into a 'real' situation, to see how he responded. But if we did this he would become 'part of the situation' and we should lose control over the whole testing procedure. How could we 'provoke' him into asking questions about the time, that is, elicit a response within the area which we wanted to test? Basically, this approach would be 'test by interview'. But if you have a large number of learners to test, it is quite clear that such a procedure is administratively ruled out, quite apart from the increasingly subjective and unreliable nature of the results. At this point we can enunciate a general rule: the more ambitious we are in testing the 'communicative competence' of a learner, the more administratively costly, subjective and unreliable the results are.

It would be nice if we could show that there was a close relation between a knowledge of the formation rules of a language and its speaking rules. If such a relationship could be shown, of course, we could say that a high score in a competence test would predict a high score in a performance test. Unfortunately, there is no clear evidence yet that this is the case, and teachers certainly are aware that pupils who do well in their ordinary class tests and examinations are not necessarily the ones who seem to be able to use the language most effectively in the world outside the classroom.

Reliability

The term 'reliability' has cropped up on several occasions in the last few sections. It is now time to examine the notion in greater detail. We want our tests to measure as accurately as possible what they set out to measure. But if for any reason we cannot place our confidence in the results we get, then we can scarcely regard the tests as valid. We have therefore to do all we can to make our tests reliable. Nobody would place any confidence in the measurement of someone's height if the measuring tape used was made of elastic, nor would one have much confidence in a measurement performed by someone whose eyesight was so poor he couldn't read the markings on the scale. In language testing we seek to achieve reliability through what we have called objectivity. By this was meant that any group of impartial native-speaker observers would agree upon which responses were correct and incorrect. This involves casting our test items in such a form that there is only one acceptable response possible. If we can do this, then the matter of scoring the test can be reduced to a purely 'mechanical' procedure, which can literally be carried out by a machine.

But this eliminates only one source of unreliability, that which is introduced into the testing processes by *the observer*. It is the easiest source of unreliability to deal with. The second source of unreliability lies in the subject himself. People are not machines, even though we have been talking about them as if they were, in using such expressions as 'language-processing device' or 'language-learning device'. The fact is, of course, that our performance of any task, however familiar we are with it, or however skilled we may be in it, varies from time to time. Obviously alcohol, drugs and sickness have a serious effect on our performance, but there are many less powerful sources of interference: tiredness, emotional states, lack of attention or concentration. There is not very much we can do about these things except to try and create favourable conditions for doing the test in. This means administering the tests in pleasant, healthy, light, quiet surroundings with no distracting influences. We may have to resort to repeating the test or part of it on another occasion and average out the results. This sort of unreliability is called *subject unreliability*.

But these sources of unreliability are common to all testing operations, whether concerned with language or some other matter. Much more serious for our purposes, since it concerns applied linguistics, is the unreliability of the test instrument itself. Whether we are measuring the learner's 'communicative competence' or his 'grammatical competence', clearly we cannot examine his 'total knowledge', even if we knew what this might mean. There simply would not be time. So we have to *sample* his knowledge, hoping that this sample is a fair one, that it is representative of his total knowledge. We make, therefore, a selection out of our description of the language of a set of items which we regard as a fair or representative one, and then test his knowledge of these. To do this we have, of course, to have a model of some sort. The process of sampling depends on our 'construct', as we have called it in the discussion of validity. I shall say more about this in the next section.

Another approach to selecting test materials is that of Lado (1961). His argument runs as follows: a language learner finds certain features of the target language more difficult to learn than others. His errors reveal what it is he finds difficult, therefore we need test him only in those items, on the argument that what he does not find difficult he will have learned already. We can predict by a contrastive study of the mother tongue of the learner and the target language where the differences and hence the learner's difficulties lie. There are four problems here; all have been discussed in the preceding chapters. Firstly, contrastive studies are technically very difficult and we do not yet have any satisfactory accounts of the differences between languages; secondly, it does not appear always to be the case that a difference means a difficulty; thirdly, learners may avoid 'showing their hand' in spontaneous speech or writing. If they believe they do not know some aspect of the target language they will probably avoid, if they can, putting it to the test. 'Errors' do not, therefore, give a true picture of what the learner does or does not know. Lastly, we should have to make separate test instruments for every group of learners, depending on their mother tongue, but also, of course, depending on how long they have been learning. And what about heterogeneous groups of learners who all have different mother tongues?

Tests may be unreliable for reasons other than faulty sampling. These reasons are connected with the type of input: the language data and the programme (test instructions). The sentence we give the test subject to manipulate in various ways may contain unsuspected problems. A syntactic test item may contain vocabulary he does not know; the sentence may be ambiguous or involve knowledge of the world to interpret. Similarly, the instructions may be faulty. He may not understand them; they may be ambiguous or contain technical words he doesn't know. We must constantly remember that while we may be testing his 'grammatical competence', we can only get at it through his 'communicative competence'. He needs to make use of the very thing we are testing in order to understand what he has to do to show us that he has it! It requires considerable ingenuity to devise actual test items whose reliability is not vitiated by the subject's inadequate performance abilities. We can do this in various ways; for example, by giving him instructions in his mother tongue and by requiring no more than a yes–no response. But ultimately the only way of reducing this sort of unreliability is to test the test materials themselves by trying them out on a fair sample of the sort of learner they are intended for and eliminating any items which produce erratic results. This is called *item analysis* and is not unlike the process of 'debugging' a computer programme.

Tests and error analysis

Tests are meant to measure the learner's knowledge of the language, not to provide information upon which to build up a picture of the language learner's 'interlanguage' at any particular moment. The information we get from tests may help us to do this, but this is not what they are designed for. For example, as we have seen, it is a feature of objective test questions that they have one and only one correct answer. They are not 'open-ended'. We force the testee to choose one of *our* responses, not to produce spontaneously what his own form of the target language (his interlanguage) would suggest was right. It is not uncommon for a testee to wish to reject *all* the responses offered in a test question – even the correct one – because none of them are generated by the grammar of his interlanguage.

What we need, if we wish to get information about the nature of the learner's interlanguage, is a different sort of test. It has sometimes been called a *diagnostic test*. Such tests are not intended to measure anything. They are devices for provoking the learner into showing *what* he knows, what his interlanguage is. They are not really devised either, except incidentally, for finding out if the learner knows the rules of the target language. Whether the name 'test' is a suitable one for such procedures is doubtful. It is becoming more usual to call them *elicitation procedures*.

We have seen already that 'error analysis' has the object of describing the learner's interlanguage. We might ask, therefore, why we need elicitation procedures as well. The reason is simply that they permit us to sample the learner's language on a systematic basis, whereas error analysis does not. Error analysis is applied to what the learner produces as a 'byproduct' of the learning process, his composition exercises, précis, and so on. It is applied to what the learner *chooses* to say or write; that is, *his* sampling of what he can do, not *ours*. And it is reasonable to suppose that the sample is not a 'fair' or representative one, for the reason that most learners will shy away from using aspects of the language which they do not feel confident about, rightly or wrongly. It does not therefore give us a true account of what the learner knows. An error-free composition may delight the teacher's heart, but looked at coolly may reveal a very poor knowledge of the language. Elicitation procedures impose *our* sampling on the learner. They aim to 'put him on the spot'. Elicitation procedures are an 'error-provoking' activity, whilst spontaneous speech is an 'error-avoiding' one.

Regarded as scientific investigations, elicitation procedures and error analysis have their parallels in other fields of scientific investigation. The distinction is one between *experimental methods* and *clinical methods*. The clinical method is to wait until an example of the event to be studied occurs spontaneously under natural conditions, and then attempt to relate it to the observed circumstances. The experimental method establishes and controls the circumstances – independent variables – which it is predicted will precipitate the event – dependent variable – and then draws inferences about the relation between the two. Each method has its own strengths and weaknesses, determining the validity of the conclusions drawn.

The making of a test: content and form

We saw in chapter 5 that a native speaker revealed his grammatical competence by his ability to make judgements of various sorts about the 'acceptability' of sentences, to recognize ambiguity in sentences, and by his awareness of the relationship between sentences, such as paraphrase, contradiction, entailment, etc. Fundamentally, all tests of grammatical competence involve making judgements or choices. But because of the desirability of objectivity, these judgements are of a 'yes–no' sort: acceptable–unacceptable, same–different; not a 'more – less' sort. This is why objective test questions usually take the form of requiring the testee to make straight choices between a number of alternative responses.

We must now revert to the problem raised on page 365 about sampling and validity. In our discussion of acceptability in chapter 5 we saw that we could break down acceptability into various types, related to the linguistic 'levels of analysis'. Thus, a sentence might be syntactically acceptable but semantically not so, or vice versa, semantically acceptable but syntactically ill-formed. We could therefore imagine a situation in which a testee could make a high score in his judgements of semantic acceptability but a low one on syntactic acceptability. A test which only set out to measure the learner's semantic knowledge would not sample his whole knowledge and would therefore be invalid. Adequate sampling requires that the testee make judgements about acceptability and similarity at all linguistic levels. But we have seen that different linguistic theories apply different analytic frameworks to language. The problem of sampling is thus closely bound up with the adequacy of the linguistic model or 'construct' chosen.

When we set out to make a test, then, we must start out with some model of the structure of language. This provides us with the basis for sampling, that is, it helps us to establish the *content* of a test. At this point we can note the parallelism between the discussions in chapter 10 on the problem of selection for a syllabus, and the discussion here on sampling. This provides us with a means for making a distinction between two types of tests, *attainment tests* and *proficiency tests*. The content of a syllabus for a language-teaching operation is a *selection* from 'the whole language'. A proficiency test is one which aims to measure a person's knowledge of 'the whole language'. An attainment test, on the other hand, is one which aims to measure how much a learner has learned of what he has been taught. The content of such a test is therefore not a sample of 'the whole language' but of the contents of a syllabus, or part of one. The uses of the two sorts of test are different. The attainment test provides feedback information to the teacher, it is a means of evaluating his teaching method and his teaching materials. A proficiency test provides no feedback to anyone. But it gives a measure of the learner's knowledge at a particular moment, which is used for deciding about his future, his suitability for further study in the language or of subjects requiring the use of the language, or for certain types of employment, that is, with such matters as placement and selection.

The content of the test and consequently the uses to which it is put depend upon what it samples. The form of the test, on the other hand, is to some extent independent of both these things. It is not wholly independent, since language is realized in spoken or written form, and we reveal our grammatical competence in writing or speech, or understanding writing or speech. But speaking and writing involve distinct motor-perceptual skills which we may wish to measure. Thus we must choose the written mode if we wish to test the learner's knowledge of the orthographic system, and a spoken mode if we wish to measure his knowledge of the phonology of the language. Generally speaking, it is through the written mode that we test all aspects of 'grammatical' competence except phonological knowledge, because of the administrative and technical difficulties of devising tests of spoken language. Tests, as we have seen, take the form they do because the testee is being required to make categorical judgements either of acceptability or similarity. All test questions or items involve choices. As I have said, when we speak, write or interpret utterances we are making scores of choices or judgements each second. The ideal test item is so framed that the testee is required to make only one choice. The reason for this is quite simple: if the testee has to make more than one choice in one and the same item and gets it wrong, we do not know which of his choices is responsible for his failure. A test item which succeeds in restricting the number of choices to one is called a *pure* item. An impure item is therefore one which allows the testee to make more than one choice at a time.

When we speak or write, our choices are 'internal' or hidden. A test item attempts to bring these choices to the light of day. It does so by offering the testee a *limited* range of choice by listing the permitted responses. Items of this sort are closed items or *recognition* items. If on the other hand we leave the testee to produce his own responses, we have what are called open-ended items or *productive* tests. An open-ended item is typically of the completion type:

Complete the following sentence with a suitable form of the verb 'attendre':

Jean —— ici depuis hier

The testee has at least to make decisions about tense, person, number and spelling. But apart from the impurity of such items, there is the practical difficulty of framing them so that there is one, and only one, acceptable response. In this case both *attend* and *aura attendu* are acceptable. As Ingram (1968) says:

It is difficult to find contexts which rule out all except one alternative. This happens particularly when it is a choice of a natural grammatical set which gives precise meaning to the context sentence. (p. 90)

For this reason productive or open-ended items tend towards unreliability. Objective test items are therefore generally of the recognition type. A higher degree of 'purity' is clearly attainable in such cases, since the number and nature of the choices can be controlled. Thus to make the example just given into a recognition item and as pure as possible, it would take one of these various forms:

Select the correct item to fill the space:

1. *Jean —— ici depuis hier.* (a) *attend*
(b) *attendait*
(choice of tense but not person or number)

2. *Jean —— ici depuis hier.* (a) *attends*
(b) *attend*
(choice of person but not number or tense)

3. *Jean —— ici depuis hier.* (a) *attend*
(b) *attendent*
(choice of number but not person or tense)

While each of these examples is about as 'pure' as you can get, each suffers from the obvious weakness that the testee can always get 50 per cent score by guessing! Consequently for reasons of statistical validity it is usual to include a number of further choices or *distractors*. The skill in formulating good test items is largely one of selecting good distractors. The characteristics of a good distractor is that it should genuinely distract some testees, that is, that it should serve to *discriminate* between testees, by tempting some more than others. In other words, the distractor should not be such a serious contender for the good testee's attention that he need do more than glance at it only to dismiss it. For the middling testee it must at least be a near-equal candidate for the correct answer, whilst the poor testee must fall for it.

But in what way should the distractor compete with the correct response? To answer this question we have to look at the context-sentence. A good testee is one who will more or less immediately recognize from the context given him what sort of choice is being asked of him, orthographic, semantic or syntactic, and if the latter, in which category, e.g. tense, number, person, etc. He must therefore be able to dismiss out of hand the distractors, because they are of the wrong category. Let us take our previous example again:

Complete the following sentence with the correct word:

(a) *attend*
(b) *attendait*
Jean —— ici depuis hier. (c) *entend*
(d) *attendu*
(e) *atend*

In this case the good candidate will realize from the context-sentence that he must find a *finite* verb form, therefore he will rule out *attendu*; that *entend*, whilst finite is not semantically acceptable; that *atend* is a mispelling of *attend*; that *attend* and *attendait* are both third person singular, *ergo*, the test is about *tense*.

We can now ask: is this a pure item? The answer must be that purity is in the mind of the test constructor, since we do not know what goes on in the testee's head. The effective degree of purity depends on the sort of knowledge which is presupposed in the testees. For a beginner in French the distractors for different reasons may pose *real* alternatives. For them the item is not pure. To the more advanced learner only the choice of tense is a *real* one. For him the item is pure. This is why the devising of distractors is such a skilful business; it crucially depends upon assessing what knowledge can be taken for granted in the testee. For this reason, a test, to be efficient, must be related to the level of knowledge of the learners for whom it is intended. There is no such thing as a test which measures equally efficiently the knowledge of learners at all levels of attainment.

Distractors must compete *in some way* with the correct answer or they do not distract. This means they must have some linguistic features in common with the correct response. These may be semantic, syntactic or orthographic. The ideal distractor is one which competes with the correct answer at all levels at once. Needless to say, it is virtually impossible to find more than a pair of responses which can do this. This is why in most test items we find just a pair of answers which are in maximum competition (in the example: *attend–attendait*), and a number of other items which differ in more than one respect from the correct response.

We can now summarize in Figure 54 the task of making test items in the form of a set of decisions by the test constructor:

1 Recognition or production test?

Recognition	Production

2 In written or spoken mode?

Recognition		Production	
written	spoken	written	spoken

3 Primary or secondary articulation?

		Recognition		Production	
		written	spoken	written	spoken
Primary articulation	semantics				
	syntax	▓▓▓			
Secondary articulation	orthography				
	phonology				

Figure 54 Decision making in test construction

The example we have been working with falls into the shaded box in Figure 54: recognition, written, syntactic. It is not difficult to work out what form the test would take which belonged in another box. For example, a production, spoken, semantic test would be simple; the tester might ask the testee, in speech, a question like: *What would you call a person who designs houses?* A recognition, written, orthographic test would be to ask a testee to underline the correctly spelled word: *recomend, reccomend, recommend, reccommend.* If we now ask where a dictation test fits in, we should see that it involves both the whole of the recognition, spoken column and the production, written column. In other words, it is a highly impure test. When a learner makes a mistake in dictation we simply do not know for sure why he has done so, in what area of his grammatical competence he has failed. If we ask a testee to write an essay on some subject, it involves the whole of the production, written column in addition, as we saw, to all sorts of other components of a non-linguistic sort, knowledge of the world, intelligence and belief systems. It is the most impure test of all.

Our ability to measure the learner's knowledge of a language is dependent upon our understanding of what is meant by 'a knowledge of a language'. If the task of teaching is to extend the learner's knowledge of a language, then our ability to teach effectively also depends upon our understanding of what is meant by 'a knowledge of a language'. It is the goal of the linguistic sciences to enlarge this understanding. On page 143 I quoted what has become one of Chomsky's most quoted opinions in connection with language teaching: that linguistics and psychology had not yet achieved a level of understanding that would enable them to 'support a technology of language teaching'. By this he meant that these disciplines cannot yet provide a complete set of principles for solving all the problems which arise in the course of the planning and execution of a language-teaching programme. They cannot supply a blueprint for a total language-teaching operation. He went on to say, however, that it was possible, indeed likely, that the 'principles of psychology and linguistics, and research into these disciplines might supply insights useful to the language teacher'. It has been the object of this book to look for such insights in the linguistic sciences and to consider how they might be applied in language teaching.

References

Abercrombie, D. (1963), 'Conversation and spoken prose', *English Language Teaching*, vol. 18, no. 1, pp. 10–16; reprinted in D. Abercrombie, *Studies in Phonetics and Linguistics*, OUP, 1965.

Abercrombie, D. (1967), *Elements of General Phonetics*, Edinburgh University Press.

Adams, P. (1972), *Language in Thinking*, Penguin.

Allen, W. S. (1966), 'The linguistic study of languages', in P. D. Strevens (ed.), *Five Inaugural Lectures*, OUP.

Anderson, J. M. (1971), *A Grammar of Case: Towards a Localistic Theory*, Cambridge University Press.

Austin, J. L. (1955), *How to Do Things With Words*, OUP.

Bloomfield, L. (1935), *Language*, Allen & Unwin.

Bloomfield, L. (1944), 'Secondary and tertiary responses to language', *Language*, no. 20, pp. 45–55.

Boomer, D. S., and Laver, J. (1968), 'Slips of the tongue', *Brit. J. Dis. Comm.*, no. 3, pp. 2–12.

Broadbent, D. E. (1970), 'In defence of empirical psychology', *Bull. Brit. Psychol. Soc.*, no. 23, pp. 87–96.

Brown, R., and Lenneberg, E. G. (1954), 'A study in language and cognition', *J. Abnorm. Soc. Psychol.*, no. 49, pp. 454–62.

Brown, R., and Gilman, A. (1960), 'The pronouns of power and solidarity', in T. Sebeok (ed.), *Style in Language*, MIT

Bruce, D. (1956), 'Effects of context upon intelligibility of heard speech', in C. Cherry (ed.), *Information Theory*, Butterworth; reprinted in R. C. Oldfield and J. C. Marshall (eds.), *Language*, Penguin, 1968.

Bruner, S. J., Goodnow, J. J., and Austin, G. A. (1956), *A Study of Thinking*, Wiley.

Carroll, J. B., and Casagrande, J. B. (1958), 'The function of language classifications in behaviour', in E. E. Maccoby, T. M. Newcomb, and E. L. Hartley (eds.), *Readings in Social Psychology*, Holt, Rinehart & Winston, pp. 18–31.

Chomsky, N. (1957), *Syntactic Structures*, Mouton.

Chomsky, N. (1965), *Aspects of the Theory of Syntax*, MIT.

Chomsky, N. (1966a), *Topics in the Theory of Generative Grammar*, Mouton.

Chomsky, N. (1966b), *Linguistic Theory*, North East Conference on the Teaching of Foreign Languages.

Chomsky, N. (1968a), *Language and Mind*, Harcourt, Brace & World.

Chomsky, N. (1968b), 'Noam Chomsky and Stuart Hampshire discuss the study of language', *Listener*, May, pp. 687–91.

Corder, S. P. (1971), 'Idiosyncratic dialects and error analysis', *IRAL*, vol. 9, no. 2, pp. 147–59.

Curme, G. O. (1935), *A Grammar of the English Language*, Heath, Boston.

Dakin, J. (1973), *The Language Laboratory and Language Teaching*, Longman.

de Saussure, F. (1961), *Course in General Linguistics*, W. Baskin (trans.), Peter Owen.

Dewey, G. (1923), *Relative Frequency of English Speech Sounds*, Harvard University Press.

Ervin, S. (1964), 'Imitation and structural change in children's language', in E. H. Lenneberg (ed.), *New Directions in the Study of Language*, MIT pp. 163–89.

Ferguson, C. A. (1959), 'Diglossia', *Word*, no. 15: reprinted in D. Hymes (ed.), *Language and Culture in Society*, Harper & Row, 1964, pp. 429–37.

Ferguson, C. A. (1966), *Applied Linguistics*, North East Conference on the Teaching of Foreign Languages.

Fillmore, C. J. (1968), 'A case for case', in E. Bach and R. T. Harms (eds.), *Universals in Linguistic Theory*, Holt, Rinehart & Winston.

Firth, J. R. (1957), 'The techniques of semantics', *Papers in Linguistics*, 1934–51, OUP.

Fishman, J. A. (1968), 'Introduction' to J. A. Fishman (ed.), *Readings in the Sociology of Language*, Mouton.

Fishman, J. A. (1971), *Sociolinguistics*, Newbury House.

Fodor, J., and Bever, J. G. (1965), 'The psychological reality of linguistic segments', *J. Verb. Learn. Verb. Behav.*, no. 4, pp. 414–20.

Fries, C. C. (1957), *The Structure of English*, Longman.

Fries, C. C., and Lado, R. (1957), *English Sentence Patterns*, University of Michigan Press.

Gardner, R. C., and Lambert, E. W. (1959), 'Motivational variables in second language acquisition', *Canad. J. Psych.*, no. 13, pp. 266–72.

Gardner, R. A., and Gardner, B. T. (1969), 'Teaching sign language to a chimpanzee', *Science*, no. 165, pp. 664–72.

Gimson, A. C. (1964), *An Introduction to the Pronunciation of English*, Arnold.

Goffman, E. (1959), *The Presentation of Self in Everyday Life*, Doubleday, Allen Lane, 1969.

Gougenheim, G., Michéa, R., Rivenc, P., and Sauvageot, A. (1956), *L'Elaboration, du Français Elémentaire*, Didier.

Greenberg, J. H. (1963), 'Some universals of grammar with particular reference to the order of meaningful elements', in J. H. Greenberg (ed.), *Universals of Language*, MIT.

Gregory, R. L. (1970), *The Intelligent Eye*, Weidenfeld & Nicolson.

Gumperz, J. J. (1964), 'Linguistic and social interaction in two communities', in J. J. Gumperz and D. Hymes (eds.), *The Ethnography of Communication*, *Amer. Anthrop.*, vol. 66, no. 6, pt. 2, pp. 137–53.

Gumperz, J. J. (1966), 'The ethnology of linguistic change', in V. Bright (ed.), *Sociolinguistics*, Mouton.

Halliday, M. A. K., Strevens, P. D., and McIntosh, A. (1964), *The Linguistic Sciences and Language Teaching*, Longman.

Halliday, M. A. K. (1969), 'Relevant models of language', *Educ. Rev.*, vol. 22, no. 1, pp. 26–37.

Halliday, M. A. K. (1970), 'Language structure and language function', in J. Lyons (ed.), *New Horizons in Linguistics*, Penguin.

Handscombe, R. (1969), 'Linguistics and children's interests', in H. Fraser and W. R. O'Donnell (eds.), *Applied Linguistics and the Teaching of English*, Longman.

Haugen, E. (1966), 'Dialect, language and nation', *Amer. Anthrop.*, vol. 68, no. 4, pp. 922–34.

Hjelmslev, L. (1963), *Language: An Introduction*, F. J. Whitfield (trans.), University of Wisconsin Press.

Hockett, C. F. (1967), *Language, Mathematics and Linguistics*, Mouton.

Horn, E. (1926), *A Basic Writing Vocabulary*, Monographs in Education, University of Iowa, no. 4.

Hornby, A. S. (1954), *Guide to Patterns and Usage in English*, OUP.

Hornby, A. S. (1959), *The Teaching of Structural Word and Sentence Patterns*, OUP.

Howatt, A. P. H., and Treacher, P. (1969), *Guide to the Edinburgh English Course*, (unpublished).

Huddleston, R. D. (1971), 'The sentence in written English: a syntactic study based on an analysis of scientific texts', *Cambridge Studies in Linguistics*, no. 3, Cambridge University Press.

Hymes, D. (1968), 'The ethnography of speaking', in J. Fishman (ed.), *Readings in the Sociology of Language*, Mouton.

Hymes, D. (1972), 'On communicative competence', in J. B. Pride and J. Holmes, (eds.), *Sociolinguistics*, Penguin.

Ingram, E. (1968), 'Attainment and diagnostic testing', in A. Davies (ed.), *Language Testing Symposium*, OUP.

James, W. (1890), *The Principles of Psychology*, New York.

Jespersen, O. (1921), *Modern English Grammar on Historical Principles*, Allen & Unwin.

Jespersen, O. (1933), *Essentials of English Grammar*, Allen & Unwin.

Johnson, N. F. (1965), 'The psychological reality of phrase structure rules', *J. Verb. Learn. Verb. Behav.*, no. 4, pp. 469–75.

Johnson–Laird, P. N. (1970), 'The perception and memory of sentences', in J. Lyons (ed.), *New Horizons in Linguistics*, Penguin.

Jones, Daniel, (1917), *English Pronouncing Dictionary*, revised edn, A. C. Gimson, (ed.) (1963), Dent.

Joos, M. (1962), *The Five Clocks*, IJAL, no. 28, part 5.

Kaeding, F. W. (1898), *Häufigkeitswörterbuch der Deutschen Sprache*, Berlin.

Kahn, F. (1954), *Le Système des temps de l'indicatif chez un Parisien et chez une Baloise*, Droz.

Katz, J. J., and Postal, P. M. (1964), 'An integrated theory of linguistic descriptions', *Research Monograph*, no. 26, MIT.

Kennedy, B. H. (1906), *A Shorter Latin Primer*, Longman.

Kruisinga, E., and Erades, P. A. (1947), *English Accidence and Syntax*, 7th edn, Groningen.

La Barre, W. (1972), 'The cultural basis of emotions and gestures', *J. Person.*, no. 16, pp. 49–68; reprinted in J. Laver and S. Hutcheson (eds.), *Communication in Face-to-Face Interaction*, Penguin.

Labov, W. (1966), *The Social Stratification of Language in New York City*, Centre for Applied Linguistics.

Labov, W. (1970a), *The Study of Non-Standard English*, National Association of Teachers of English and Centre for Applied Linguistics.

Labov, W. (1970b), 'The study of language in its social context', *Studium Generale*, no. 23, pp. 30–87.

Lado, R. (1957), *Language Testing: The Construction and Use of Foreign Language Tests*, Longman.

Lado, R. (1961), *Linguistics across Cultures*, University of Michigan Press.

Laver, J. (1970), 'The production of speech', in J. Lyons (ed.), *New Horizons in Linguistics*, Penguin.

Lees, R. B. (1963), *The Grammar of English Nominalisations*, Mouton.

Lenneberg, E. H. (1967), *The Biological Foundations of Language*, Wiley.

Le Page, R. B. (1964), *The National Language Question*, Institute of Race Relations and OUP.

Lyons, J. (1965), *The Scientific Study of Language*, Edinburgh University Press.

Lyons, J. (1968), *Introduction to Theoretical Linguistics*, Cambridge University Press.

Lyons, J. (1972), 'Human language', in R. A. Hinde (ed.), *Non-Verbal Communication*, The Royal Society and Cambridge University Press.

Mackin, R. (1955), *Alternative Syllabus in English* OUP, Dacca.

McNeill, D. (1966), 'Developmental psycholinguistics', in F. Smith and G. A. Miller (eds.), *The Genesis of Language*, MIT.

Marshall, J. C. (1970), 'The biology of communication in man and animals', in J. Lyons (ed.), *New Horizons in Linguistics*, Penguin.

Martinet, A. (1946), 'Phonology as functional phonetics', *Phil. Soc. Pub.*, no. 15.
Miller, G. A. (1951), *Language and Communication*, McGraw-Hill.
Miller, G. A. (1970), 'The psycholinguists', *Encounter*, no. 23, 1964, pp. 29–37, reprinted in G. A. Miller, *The Psychology of Communication*, Penguin.
Miller, G., and McKean, K. O. (1964), 'A chronometric study of some relations between sentences', *Quart. J. Exper. Psychol.*, no. 16, pp. 297–308; reprinted in R. C. Oldfield and J. C. Marshall (eds.), *Language*, Penguin, 1968.
Mittins, W. H. (1970), 'Attitudes to English usage', *Language and Language Learning*, no. 30, OUP.
Morton, F. Rand, (1965), *The Underwood Experiment*, US Department of Health, Welfare and Education.
Moulton, W. G. (1962), *The Sounds of English and German*, University of Chicago Press.

Newmark, L. (1964), *Grammatical Theory and the Teaching of English*, NAFSA Papers, no. 9, pp. 5–8.
Nickel, G. (1971), 'Problems of learners' difficulties in foreign language acquisition', *IRAL*, vol. 9, no. 3, pp. 219–27.
Nida, E. A. (1960), *A Synopsis of English Syntax*, University of Oklahoma, Summer Institute of Linguistics.

Palmer, H. E. (1924), *A Grammar of Spoken English*, Heffer.
Palmer, F. R. (1971), ' Language and the teaching of English', in N. Minnis (ed.), *Linguistics at Large*, Gollancz.
Peck, A. J. (1971), 'Talking to some purpose', in G. C. Perren and L. J. M. Trim (eds.), *Applications of Linguistics*, Cambridge University Press.
Perren, G. E. (1968), 'Testing spoken English: some unsolved problems', in A. Davies (ed.), *Language Testing Symposium*, OUP.
Piaget, J. (1926), *Language and Thought of the Child*, English edn, Routledge & Kegan Paul.
Pilliner, A. (1968), 'Subjective and objective testing', in A. Davies (ed.), *Language Testing Symposium*, OUP.
Pimsleur, Paul, (1963), 'Predicting success in High School foreign language learning', *Educ. Psychol. Meas.*, vol. 33, no. 2.
Popper, K. (1959), *The Logic of Scientific Discovery*, Hutchinson.
Poutsma, A. (1904), *Grammar of Late Modern English*, P. Noordhof, Groningen.
Prator, C. (1968), 'The British heresy in teaching English as a second language', in J. A. Fishman (ed.), *The Language Problems of Developing Nations*, Wiley.

Quirk, R., and Svartvik, J. (1966), *Investigating Linguistic Acceptability*, Mouton.
Quirk, R., Greenbaum, S., Leech, G., and Svartvik, J. (1972), *A Grammar of Contemporary English*, Longman.

Ray, D. S. (1963), *Language Standardisation*, Mouton.
Richards, J. C. (1971), 'A non-contrastive approach to error analysis', *English Language Teaching*, vol. 25, no. 3, pp. 204–19.

Rivers, W. M. (1964), *The Psychologist and the Foreign Language Teacher*, University of Chicago Press.

Roberts, P. (1964), *English Syntax*, Harcourt, Brace & World.

Rubin, J. (1962), 'Bilingualism in Paraguay', *Anthrop. Ling.*, no. 4(1), pp. 52–8.

Sapir, E. (1921), *Language*, Harcourt, Brace & World.

Saporta, S. (1966), 'Applied linguistics and generative grammar', in A. Valdman (ed.), *Trends in Language Teaching*, McGraw-Hill.

Scherer, A. C. and Wertheimer, M. (1964), *A Psycholinguistic Experiment in Foreign Language Teaching*, McGraw-Hill.

Searle, J. R. (1969), *Speech Acts*, Cambridge University Press.

Selinker, L. (1969), 'Language transfer', *Gen. Ling.*, vol. IX, no. 2, pp. 671–92.

Skinner, B. F. (1957), *Verbal Behaviour*, Appleton-Century-Crofts.

Slobin, D. I. (1966), 'Imitation and the acquisition of syntax', in F. Smith, and G. A. Miller (eds.), *The Genesis of Language*, MIT.

Smith, P. D. (1970), *A Comparison of the Cognitive and Audiolingual Approaches to Foreign Language Instruction*, Centre for Curriculum Development Inc.

Snow, C. E. (1972), 'Mothers' speech to children learning language', *Child Development*, no. 43, pp. 549–65.

Spencer, J. (1963), *Language in Africa*, Cambridge University Press.

Stockwell, R. P., Bowen, J. O., and Martin, J. W. (1965), *The Grammatical Structures of English and Spanish*, University of Chicago Press.

Strevens, P. D. (1964), 'Varieties of English', *English Studies*, vol. 45, no. 1, pp. 1–10.

Sutherland, N. S. (1966), 'Competence and performance', in J. Lyons and R. A. Wales (eds.), *Psycholinguistic Papers*, p. 161, Edinburgh University Press.

Sweet, H. (1891), *New English Grammar, Part I*, OUP.

Sweet, H. (1899), *The Practical Study of Languages*, Dent, reprinted OUP, 1964.

Thomas, O. (1965), *Transformational Grammar and the Teacher of English*, Holt, Rinehart & Winston.

Thorne, J. P. (1965), 'Stylistics and generative grammar', *J. Ling.* no. 1, pp. 49–59.

Thorne, J. P. (1966), 'On hearing sentences', in J. Lyons and R. Wales (eds.), *Psycholinguistic Papers*, Edinburgh University Press.

Thorne, J. P. (1968), 'A computer model for the perception of syntactic structure', *Proc. Royal Soc. Series B.* vol. 171, pp. 103–112.

Thorne, J. P. (1971), Interview: 'Linguistics', *Listener*, no. 68. pp. 209–44.

Thorndike, E. L., and Lorge, I. (1944), *The Teacher's Word Book of 30,000 Words*, Columbia University Press.

Vernon, M. D. (1962), *The Psychology of Perception*, Penguin.

Wales, R., and Campbell, R. (1970), 'The study of language acquisition', in J. Lyons (ed.), *New Horizons in Linguistics*, Penguin.

Weinreich, E. (1953), *Languages in Contact*, Linguistic Circle of New York.

Weinreich, E. (1966), 'Explorations in semantic theory', in T. Sebeok (ed.), *Current Trends in Linguistics*, vol. 3, Mouton.

Weir, R. (1962), *Language in the Crib*, Mouton.

Whitehall, H. (1951), *The Structural Essentials of English*, Harcourt, Brace & World.

Whorf, B. L. (1956), 'The relation of habitual thought and behaviour to language', in J. B. Carroll (ed.), *Language Thought and Reality: Selected Writings of Benjamin Lee Whorf*, MIT.

Wilkins, D. A. (1972), *The Linguistic and Situational Content of the Common Core in a Unit Credit System*, Council of Europe.

Wolff, H. (1959), 'Intelligibility and interethnic attitudes', *Anthrop. Ling.*, vol. 1, no. 3; reprinted in D. Hymes (ed.), *Language in Culture and Society*, Harper & Row, pp. 440–49.

Zandroort, R. W. (1957), *A Handbook of English Grammar*, Longman.

Index